Arthurian
Myth and Legend

AN A–Z OF PEOPLE AND PLACES

Arthurian
Myth and Legend

AN A–Z OF PEOPLE AND PLACES

Mike Dixon-Kennedy

BLANDFORD

For Gill, Christopher, Charlotte, Thomas and Rebecca.
Now you can have me back . . . for the moment.

A BLANDFORD BOOK

First published in the UK 1995 by Blandford
A Cassell Imprint
Cassell PLC, Wellington House
125 Strand, London WC2R 0BB

Distributed in the United States by Sterling Publishing Co., Inc.
387 Park Avenue South, New York, NY 10016–8810

Distributed in Australia by Capricorn Link (Australia) Pty Ltd
2/13 Carrington Road, Castle Hill, NSW 2154

A Cataloguing-in-Publication Data entry for this title is available from the British Library

ISBN 0-7137-2561-3

Celtic artwork by Chris Down
Typeset by Keystroke, Jacaranda Lodge, Wolverhampton
Printed and bound in Great Britain by Hartnolls Ltd, Bodmin, Cornwall

Contents

Preface

Over countless years, countless books about King Arthur have weighed down countless bookshelves, but none of them can rightly claim to have surveyed all the Arthurian literature and condensed the information spread throughout the numerous publications into one simple, look-it-up reference work. This book hopes to redress that situation.

When I first started to consider the sheer weight of material available concerning the legends of King Arthur and his associates, I wondered how best to present the information. I could have opted for chapters on each subject, but then I might easily have omitted certain details, details that could have been what you, the readers, were looking for in particular. The best option, therefore, seemed to be to prepare the text in dictionary format. I hope you will agree that my choice has been the right one.

In the pages of this book, which is the result of over fifteen years' research (though not solely concentrating on Arthur, for the whole subject of world mythology fascinates me), you will find many characters you might not have previously connected with the Arthurian legends. Some have very definite Celtic origins, whereas others come from still further afield. In addition, you will find all the main legends told in essence, together with geographical features connected with Arthur and his associates, and much more beside to hold your interest.

When considered against the wealth of mythology and legend that we know from all over the world, that surrounding King Arthur and his knights remains the most fascinating to study, for although many of the stories have mythological attributes (magical swords, love potions, talking animals, etc.), they all appear to have at least some foundation in history. I, for one, truly believe that King Arthur existed, though not in the heroic form we know today. No other imaginary, or mythological, character from early history has collected the number of stories that King Arthur has. To read these stories as just that, stories, is fascinating, and will bring endless enjoyment. To read between the lines and try to fathom out the historicity of these stories becomes addictive. This book is the result of my addiction.

I have tried to make this book as complete and authoritative as possible. However, I will undoubtedly have omitted something, or made some false assumption within the book – after all, to err is human. Should you want to bring anything to my attention, then please address your comments to the publisher and they will make sure your letters reach me.

No book such as this could be completed without the help of a great many people, but to list them all here would take far too much space. Suffice it to say that I offer a great big thank-you to them all: they will know who they are. There are, however, five people very close to me whom I do have to thank. They are my wife and four children. I thank them for their tolerance and patience while I have been locked away in solitary confinement, working on the research that has led to this book, and then again while preparing the text.

Mike Dixon-Kennedy,
Lincolnshire

Spelling and Pronunciation Guide

When the legends of King Arthur were being recorded, standardized spelling was not common. As a result there are a great many variations within the myriad works I have consulted during the preparation of this book. I have tried, and I must stress tried, to adopt the commonest, or most correct, form of each name. I apologize if you consider I have made mistakes in my choices. This system, however, does lead to one small problem, that of multiple entries under variant spellings.

As far as is humanly possible, I have tried to weed out these entries, but some are sure to have slipped through my net. Again I apologize. The main problem here is one of association, for how does one recognize a true variant, if the stories related under the variants differ in themselves. Here I make no apologies, for the fault is not mine but that of the romancers who first put pen to paper to preserve these stories for our enjoyment.

Although many of the names within this book may look peculiar to modern readers, they are not difficult to pronounce. A little effort and the following guide will help you to ensure that these names are pronounced correctly. Please bear in mind, however, that the same vowels can be pronounced differently depending on regional accents.

Consonants – as in English, but with a few exceptions

  c: hard, as in cat (never soft as in century)
 ch: hard, as in Scottish Loch, or Bach (never soft as in church)
 dd: th as in then (never as in thistle)
  f: v, as in of
 ff: f, as in off
  g: hard, as in girl (never as in gem)
 ll: a Welsh distinctive, sounded as 'tl' or 'hl' on the sides of the tongue
  r: trilled, lightly
 rh: as if hr, heavy on the 'h' sound
  s: always as in sir (never as in his)
 th: as in thistle (never as in then)

Vowels – as in English, but with the general lightness of short vowel sounds

  a: as in father
  e: as in met, or sometimes long, as in late

   i: as in pin, or sometimes long, as in *eat*

   o: as in n*o*t

   u: as in pin, or sometimes long, as in *eat*

   w: a 'double u', as in vac*uu*m, or t*oo*l; but becomes a consonant before vowels, such as in the name Gwen

   y: as in pin, or as in *eat*, but sometimes as 'u' in b*u*t

There is virtually no difference, for the beginner, between i, u and y.

Accent – normally on the next to last syllable

Diphthongs – each vowel is pronounced individually

how to Use This Book

Even though this book is basically arranged as a simple, straightforward dictionary, several conventions have been adopted to make cross-referencing easy and the text more accessible.

  i Where headwords have alternative spellings, these are shown under the main entry with the book. These variants are given their own, very short entry within the work to direct you to the main entry. Where these alternative spellings consist solely of the omission of, or indeed addition of, letters, then those letters affected within the headword are enclosed in brackets: e.g., **R(h)ic(c)a**, which would lead to Rica, Rhica, Ricca or Rhicca all being acceptable variants.

  ii The use of small capitals indicates that there is a separate entry for the word or words in question.

 iii The use of *italics* indicates that the reference is to a text or to words in a foreign language, such as Latin or Anglo-Saxon.

 iv Where more than one entry appears under a headword, each entry is preceded by a number. Further references to these words within the text of the book are followed by the appropriate number in superscript: e.g., Lancelot[2].

Aalardin

A knight who possessed magical knowledge. Married to GUIGENOR, the grandniece of ARTHUR; Aalardin supplied GUIGNIER, the wife of CARADOC BRIEFBRAS, whom he had once loved, with an enchanted shield boss, thus providing her with a golden breast to replace that which she had lost while helping her husband.

Abelleus

A knight who is simply described as having been slain by TOR.

Ablamor of the Marsh

By killing two of the greyhounds that belonged to GAWAIN[1] and GAHERIS, retaliation for their having killed the white hart he owned, Ablamor was challenged to do combat with Gawain. Just as Gawain was about to kill Ablamor, his lady threw herself between them, and it was she that the hapless knight killed. Gawain was so horror-stricken that he could not continue the fight, so Ablamor was spared.

Accolon

A Gallic knight with whom MORGAN[1] Le Fay had become enamoured. While out hunting in the company of URIEN and ARTHUR, the three became separated from their companions and, coming upon a vessel, they settled down for the night. To his astonishment Accolon awoke in a field where he was given the sword EXCALIBUR, being told that he would have to use it in a fight. When that time came, his opponent turned out to be none other than Arthur himself, but neither recognized the other. It seemed as if Accolon would be victorious as Arthur had been given a fake copy of Excalibur, but the LADY OF THE LAKE appeared and caused the true Excalibur to fall to the ground. Arthur immediately seized it and promptly defeated Accolon, inflicting a mortal wound upon him. However, it was then discovered that Morgan Le Fay had organized the whole affair, and Arthur assured Accolon that he would not be punished. Accolon later died from his injuries.

Acheflour

In the English romance SIR PERCEVAL OF GALLES, Acheflour is given as the sister of ARTHUR and the mother of PERCEVAL[2]. Believing her son to be dead, Acheflour went mad and took to living in the woods, where Perceval found her. With her sanity once more restored, she went to live with her son and his lover, LUFAMOUR.

Adam

The son of JOSEPH OF ARIMATHEA, according to the *Sone de Nausay*.

Addanc

A variant of AFANC.

Addanz

A character who is simply referred to as having been an ancestor of PERCEVAL[2].

Addaon

The son of TALIESIN. Noted for his wisdom, he was killed by LLONGAD GRWRM FARGOD EIDYN.

Adeluf

In Rauf de BOUN's romance PETIT BRUT several characters are given this name. Two of them were kings before the time of ARTHUR, but the third is named as a son of Arthur.

Adragain

One of the KNIGHTS OF THE ROUND TABLE who, after the death of ARTHUR, eventually became a hermit.

Adventurous Bed

A bed in Castle CARBONEK in which GALAHAD[1] slept, and where he was wounded by a fiery lance. Some dubious sources say that it was Galahad's father, LANCELOT[2], who slept in this bed, having previously lain with ELAINE[1], thereby becoming the father of Galahad.

Aédan mac Gabrain

The king of DALRIADA and father of the appropriately named ARTHUR OF DALRIADA.

Aedd

Also occurring in Celtic Irish mythology, Aedd was the father of PRYDEIN, the eponym, in Welsh tradition, of BRITAIN.

Aegidius

An historical Roman count who ruled GAUL between AD 461 and 464. The fourteenth-century writer Jacques de Guise claimed that ARTHUR flourished during this time, while the sixteenth-century Philippe de Vignelles intimated that Aegidius was actually in frequent contact with Arthur.

Aelens

The king of IRELAND and father of ESCOL, who later became one of ARTHUR's followers.

Aeleus

The king of ICELAND, according to the works of LAYAMON. As his son, by the daughter of the king of RUSSIA, is named as ESCOL, and that character is more normally associated with AELENS, the king of IRELAND, it would appear that both Aeleus and his realm of Iceland are merely transcriptive errors.

Aelle

A SAXON king of Sussex who, along with his sons CISSA, CYMEN and WLENCING, defeated the Britons at Cymenes ora in AD 477, once again fighting against them near Mearc raedesburna in AD 485, and capturing Anderida (modern Pevensey, Sussex) c. AD 491. According to BEDE, he held the title Bretwalda (Britain-Ruler), perhaps suggesting a primacy among the Saxon kings. It has also been suggested that he led the Saxons at BADON, thus seeming to indicate that he may well have been a leading adversary of the historical ARTHUR.

Aeneas

In classical Graeco-Roman mythology, Aeneas was the son of the Trojan Anchises by the Greek goddess Aphrodite (Roman: Venus). He was a member of the Trojan royal family and, following the fall of Troy, he made his way to Italy – at least according to Virgil. There he became an ancestor of the Emperor Augustus and was regarded as the founder of the Roman people.

His great-grandson, BRUTUS, brought a group of Trojans to England, where he founded the city TROYNOVANT (New Troy), later to become known as London. Through this connection Aeneas is regarded not only as the founder of the Roman people but also as the legendary founder of the British people, and the supposed forefather of King LEIR. GEOFFREY OF MONMOUTH says that Aeneas was the ancestor of the ancient British kings, while DRYDEN, quite specifically, says that he was a direct ancestor of ARTHUR.

Aesc

The traditional founder of the AESCING tribe, Aesc reigned, in KENT, between AD 488 and 512. He was possibly the son of HENGIST, and his story may be related to that of Askr, one of the first two people of Norse-Teutonic mythology, the other being Embla. This association seems to be further supported by the fact that Hengist, his father, claimed descent from WODEN, the ANGLO-SAXON version of the Norse god Odínn.

Aescing

Kentish ANGLO-SAXON tribe traditionally founded by AESC.

Aeturnus

Son of PATERNUS and father of CUNEDDA, according to the latter's traditional pedigree.

Afagddu
Also AVAGDDU

The son of TEGID VOEL and his wife, CERRIDWEN, brother of MORFRAN AB TEGID and CREIRWY. He is described as the most ill-favoured man in the world, dark and ugly, in contrast to his sister Creirwy, who was the fairest maiden in all the world, light and beautiful. Some sources, however, indicate that, rather than a personal name, Afagddu was a nickname applied to Morfran ab Tegid, and in this case Afagddu and Morfran ab Tegid would be one and the same.

Afanc
Also ADDANC

A legendary Welsh monster. In modern Welsh the word *afanc* means a beaver, and this would seem to be cognate with the watery connections usually applied to this mythical creature. The word has also been used simply to refer to a spirit that dwells in a watery location, not an actual creature.

PERCEVAL[2] overcame one example of an afanc who appears to have had manipulative skills, for it hurled spears at the knight. However, Perceval prevailed as he had been rendered invisible to the monster by means of a magical stone given to him by the EMPRESS OF CONSTANTINOPLE. ARTHUR is also said to have killed an afanc at LLYN BARFOG, while

HU GADARN is also said to have slain one. This last appearance of the afanc may well be a late concoction, as it would seem that Hu Gadarn is nothing more than the invention of Iolo MORGANNWG.

Afollonau

Welsh MYRDDIN (MERLIN) poem that names CHWIMLEIAN as a flower-maiden. She has subsequently become associated with both BLODEUWEDD and GUENDO-LOENA.

Aglovale

A brother of PERCEVAL[2] and the father of MORIAEN. He was killed on the occasion when LANCELOT[2] carried off Queen GUINEVERE.

Agned, Mount

The site of the eleventh of ARTHUR's BATTLES as listed in the writings of NENNIUS, though one tenth-century manuscript gives the name BREGUOIN. It later became known as the CASTLE OF MAIDENS, and has had High ROCHESTER suggested as its actual location.

Agravadain

The husband of the mother of ECTOR DE MARIS, the child being born after his wife's adulterous affair with King BAN.

Agravain

The son of LOT and MORGAUSE, the brother of GAWAIN[1], and one of the KNIGHTS OF THE ROUND TABLE. He married LAUREL, the niece of LIONORS and LYNETTE. Knowing of the affair between LANCELOT[2] and GUINEVERE, he, accompanied by MORDRED and twelve other knights, succeeded in trapping the lovers together in the queen's bedchamber. Though unarmed, Lancelot managed to fight his way free, killing Agravain and the other twelve knights in the process, leaving only Mordred alive to report Guinevere's infidelity to ARTHUR. Other sources say that Agravain survived Lancelot's escape, only to be killed by him when the latter rescued Guinevere after her condemnation to death for adultery.

Agrestes

During the time of JOSEPH OF ARIMATHEA, Agrestes is said to have been the ruler of CAMELOT.

Agrestizia

Otherwise known as DINDRANE, Agrestizia is the name applied to the sister of PERCEVAL[2] in the Italian romance TAVOLA RITONDA.

Agricola

Thought of as a good king by GILDAS, Agricola was the ruler of DEMETIA (DYFED), c. AD 500, well within the traditional period of the historical King ARTHUR. It seems likely that he may have been one of Arthur's commanders, and may also have liberated Demetia from the Irish dynasty that had previously ruled that region, the UÍ LIATHÁIN.

Aguisant

The son of KARADAN and an unnamed sister of ARTHUR, thus making him Arthur's nephew.

Aguysans

One of the eleven rulers who rebelled against ARTHUR at the onset of the young king's reign. He is given various names, although he is most commonly simply referred to as the KING WITH A HUNDRED KNIGHTS.

Ahes

A variant of MORGAN[1] Le Fay which is peculiar to BRITTANY, where she was held to have been responsible for the destruction of the legendary city of YS.

Aillean(n)

An OTHERWORLD woman who had a tendency to turn herself into a deer, and who appears in the Irish romance VISIT OF GREY HAM. Said to be descended from the king of ICELAND through his granddaughter RATHLEAN, she led ARTHUR and his men away to marry otherworldly women, reserving Arthur for herself. Her family tree is given in Figure 1.

Alan

The son of BRONS and ENYGEUS, though some sources make him the son of King PELLINORE. Remaining unmarried, he was made ruler over his brothers and sisters, although, in the DIDOT PERCEVAL he is said to have been the father of PERCEVAL[2], having been told by the Holy Spirit that he was destined to become the father of the GRAIL KING.

Alans

A tribe of the barbarian SARMATIAN peoples who inhabited RUSSIA in Roman times. Their blood-line still survives today in the OSSETES, who inhabit the Caucasus. These descendants tell a very similar story to that concerning the passing of ARTHUR which appears to date from when the historical Arthur is traditionally said to have lived.

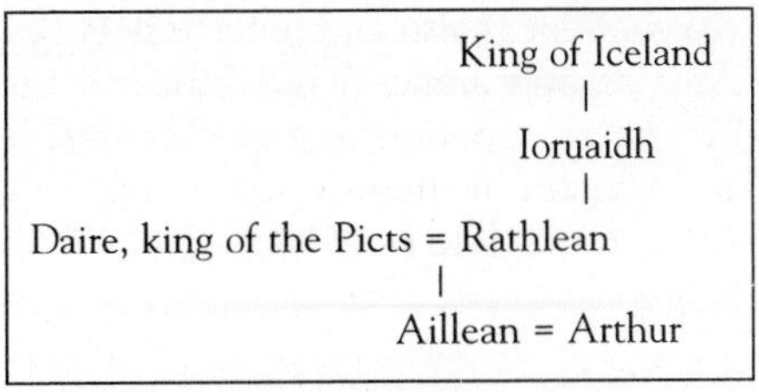

```
        King of Iceland
              |
           Ioruaidh
              |
Daire, king of the Picts = Rathlean
              |
        Aillean = Arthur
```

Figure 1   Family tree of Aillean

Albanact

The name given to the captain of ARTHUR's guard by DRYDEN in his opera KING ARTHUR. GEOFFREY OF MONMOUTH ascribes this name to a son of BRUTUS, and it seems most likely that Dryden simply borrowed it.

Albanio

The hero of a poem written by one Jegon whose works form a continuation to SPENSER'S FAERIE QUEENE. In this work Albanio was knighted by King ARTHUR.

Alba(ny)

An archaic term, traditionally Irish in origin, that is used to refer to SCOTLAND.

Albion

A legendary giant who was said to have been the first ruler of BRITAIN. His name was, according to GEOFFREY OF MONMOUTH, used to refer to the island before the arrival of BRUTUS. The career of this giant ruler was outlined in Holinshed's Chronicles of 1577, and his name is still used to refer poetically to Britain, or England.

Alcardo

The brother of ISEULT[1] and companion of TRISTAN, possibly acting as the latter's squire. Later he became known as LANTRIS, in which persona he was definitely referred to as a squire, being killed in his attempt to rescue his sister Iseult from King MARK[2].

Alchendic

A giant who ruled the ancient city of SARRAS, according to the PROPHÉCIES DE MERLIN, having gained the throne by murdering the previous ruler. Even though he became king in this manner, the people of the city were loyal to him and would not desert him, even when the city was placed under siege by Crusaders led by King Richard of Jerusalem. Successful in defeating four Crusader champions, a truce was finally negotiated. A month later the barbarian Alchendic was converted to Christianity and baptized.

Alcina

In the Italian romances of Ludovico ARIOSTO and Matteo Maria BOIARDO, Alcina appears as one of the enchantress sisters of MORGAN[1] Le Fay.

Alclud

The Roman name for DUMBARTON. It was here that ARTHUR's ally HOEL[1], King of BRITTANY, was besieged by PICTS and Scots until Arthur came to relieve him.

Aldan

An historical daughter of a South WALES nobleman and, in Welsh tradition, the mother of MERLIN.

Alderley Edge

A ridge in Cheshire, England, where, according to local legend, a farmer living at Mobberley had his horse purchased by a wizard for the use of a king and his knights who were slumbering beneath the ridge. At the time when this legend first appeared, apparently towards the end of the seventeenth century, the identity of the slumbering king was not given. However, a later rhyming version (by J. Roscoe) specifically identifies King ARTHUR.

Aldroenus
Also AUDRIEN

King of BRITTANY and the brother of CONSTANTINE[1], ARTHUR's grandfather. He sent his brother to rule the Britons at their own request.

Alemaigne

The real of NUC, which has been identified with either ALBANY (SCOTLAND) or GERMANY, the latter obviously being derived from the French for that country, a word that has its origins in the fourth-century Alemanni people of Germany.

Alemandine

The queen of a kingdom which was plagued by a wild beast until it was defeated by FLORIANT, who then refused the offer of her hand as a reward.

Alexander

1 Emperor of CONSTANTINOPLE, husband of TANTALIS and father of ALIS and ALEXANDER[2].
2 Son of ALEXANDER[1] and TANTALIS, husband of SOREDAMOR and father of CLIGÉS.
3 Son of the king of India who was changed, along with his brothers, into a variety of 'canine' creatures by his stepmother. Alexander himself was turned into a creature known as the CROP-EARED DOG.

Alexander the Great

Historical ruler of Macedonia (365–323 BC) who, at the age of nineteen, succeeded his father, Philip II, as the king of Macedon and Olympias. Alexander's historical career is of little relevance to Arthurian studies. His appearance in the Arthurian legends is totally fictitious, for in PERCEFOREST he is said to have led an invasion of BRITAIN, which he never did, making BETIS the King of England and GADDIFER the King of SCOTLAND.

Alexius

The variant of ALIS which is usually regarded as the root from which Alis is derived. Five historical emperors of CONSTANTINOPLE have had this name, the first being made emperor in 1081.

Alfasein

Following the conversion of KALAFES to Christianity, this name was given to him at his subsequent baptism.

Alice

The wife of ALISANDER THE ORPHAN, she became known as the BEAUTIFUL PILGRIM.

Alifatima

King of SPAIN and follower of the Roman emperor LUCIUS HIBERIUS. He was killed while fighting ARTHUR's forces during the latter's campaign against Rome and the Romans. It seems likely that his name has a Moorish root following their influence in SPAIN during the Middle Ages.

Alis

The son of ALEXANDER[1] and TANTALIS, and brother to ALEXANDER[2]. He became the Byzantine emperor and married FENICE[1] with whom CLIGÉS, his nephew, was also in love. Alis is a form of ALEXIUS, a name, or title, borne by a number of Byzantine emperors. Alis's family tree may be found under CONSTANTINOPLE.

Alisander the Orphan

The son of BALDWIN and ANGLIDES. Following the murder of his father by King MARK[2], his uncle, he was imprisoned by MORGAN[1] Le Fay, but was helped to regain his freedom by ALICE, the BEAUTIFUL PILGRIM. Subsequently he married Alice and was later welcomed at ARTHUR's court.

Alliterative Morte Arthure

A Middle English poem dating from c. 1400 and consisting of 4,346 lines concerning ARTHUR's war against Rome and the Romans, MORDRED's rebellion and Arthur's final battle.

Alois

The king of NORTHGALIS who went to war with AMOROLDO, the king of IRELAND. In this war, Alois was sup-ported by TRISTAN, and Amoroldo by LANCELOT[2]. In the end peace was brought about between the two warring leaders by the interventions of both ISEULT[1], Tristan's lover, and GUINEVERE, Lancelot's lover.

Alon

A grandnephew of King ARTHUR who became one of the KNIGHTS OF THE ROUND TABLE.

Alvrez

An Irish king and the father of MIROET and KAMELIN, both of whom went on to become KNIGHTS OF THE ROUND TABLE.

Amangons

The ruler of GRANLAND, according to the Old French *Le chevalier as deus espées*.

Amant

A knight who, having accused his master, King MARK[2], of treachery, was challenged to trial by combat, and duly defeated by Mark.

Amazon(s)

Medieval legend claimed that the female Amazon warriors of classical Greek mythology were, in fact, originally Goths who, under MARPESIA, formed an army of women and journeyed, by way of the Caucasus, to Africa. By simple association, the medieval writers included this wonderful mythical race in the Arthurian legends. TRISTAN THE YOUNGER was supposed to have saved their queen from the king of the IDUMEANS, and they fought with GAWAIN[1], their queen being killed by the CROP-EARED DOG.

In the ALLITERATIVE MORTE ARTHURE they were said to have been the subjects of LUCIUS HIBERIUS, ARTHUR's bitter foe, while in SPENSER's FAERIE QUEENE, their queen, RADIGUND, was killed by BRITOMART.

Ambrosius Aureli(an)us
Also AURELIUS AMBROSIUS

An undoubted historical character whose career is chronicled by GEOFFREY OF MONMOUTH. The brother of UTHER and King CONSTANS of BRITAIN, he was smuggled to BRITTANY following the murder of his brother Constans by the usurping VORTIGERN. It was from Brittany that he later returned with his brother Uther, intent on taking back the throne that was rightfully his. Landing at TOTNES in Devon, Ambrosius Aurelius was proclaimed king. He laid siege to Vortigern's tower and succeeded in burning it down, thus killing the usurper. He went on to defeat the SAXONS and had their leader, HENGIST, executed, commissioning MERLIN to build a monument on SALISBURY PLAIN to commemorate the British leaders Hengist had massacred there. Finally, PASCHENT, Vortigern's son, made war against him and succeeded in having him poisoned by a Saxon named EOPA. He was buried within the GIANTS RING he had commissioned Merlin to build.

GILDAS, who used possibly the most correct form of his name, Ambrosius Aurelianus, supports Geoffrey of Monmouth in his claim that it was he who instituted the fighting that finally put a halt to the Saxon attacks, saying that he was the 'last of the Romans'. NENNIUS, however, says that this Ambrosius was the fatherless child whom Vortigern intended to sacrifice when his tower kept falling down, but then contradicts himself by saying that Ambrosius Aurelius was the son of a Roman consul. Geoffrey of Monmouth maintains that it was Merlin whom Vortigern intended to sacrifice, and that Ambrosius Aurelius was ARTHUR's nephew. Other writers have even suggested that he is the original Arthur, while the fifteenth-century poet Rhys Goch Eryri said that, following his death at the hands of Eopa, his head was taken and buried beneath DINAS EMRYS.

Ambroy Oyselet

This knight, who appears in *Merlin* by Lovelich, owes his existence, so it would appear, to the author's misunderstanding of the French phrase *oiseau au brai*, thinking it to be a personal name.

Amene

The queen of a kingdom which had been almost entirely conquered by the evil knight ROAZ when King ARTHUR sent WIGALOIS to her aid. *En route* Wigalois was guided by LAR, the dead husband of Queen Amene, and, having routed Roaz, married her daughter LARIE as a reward.

Amesbury

Situated in a bend in the River Avon, north of Salisbury, Wiltshire, Amesbury is a small and pleasant market town. Sir Thomas MALORY asserts that Queen GUINEVERE came to Amesbury Abbey when she heard of ARTHUR's death. In AD 979 the abbey was succeeded by a nunnery that eventually became one of the richest in England, achieving fame as the retreat of Mary, daughter of King Edward I, and her grandmother, Queen Eleanor, King Henry III's widow.

Amfortas
Also ANFORTAS

The GRAIL KING or the FISHER KING, according to WOLFRAM VON ESCHENBACH. The son of FRIMUTEL, also a Grail King, he was wounded in the scrotum by a poisoned lance while jousting and, carried into the presence of the GRAIL, he awaited the coming of the questioner, PERCEVAL[2], who would ask the GRAIL QUESTION and thus restore him to health. In Wagner's PARSIVAL he is known as Anfortas, and some think that his name may be a derivation of the Latin word *infirmtas*.

Amhar

According to the MABINOGION, Amhar was a son of ARTHUR who appears to be identical with AMR.

Aminabad

According to the pedigree of JOHN OF GLASTONBURY, Aminabad was the son of JOSHUA[1], father of CASTELLORS, and an ancestor of ARTHUR.

Aminaduc

According to the LIVRE D'ARTUS, a SAXON who was the ruler or DENMARK.

Amite

In French romance, the mother of GALAHAD[1].

Amlawdd (Wledig)
Also ANLAWDD

According to Welsh sources, the husband of GWENN[2] and the father of IGRAINE[1] (EIGYR). He is also credited with being the father of GOLEUDDYDD and RIEINGULID, who were, respectively, the mothers of CULHWCH and ILLTYD, ARTHUR's cousins. Wledig is a title which, roughly translated, means chief, and would appear to indicate Amlawdd's position.

Amoroldo

Appearing in the Italian romance TAVOLA RITONDA, Amoroldo was the son of MARHAUS who was made a knight by TRISTAN. Later, he ascended to the Irish throne and became embroiled in a war against King ALOIS of NORTHGALIS, during which time he was supported by Tristan, his enemy being supported by LANCELOT[2]. ISEULT[1] and GUINEVERE, the lovers of the respective supporters, brought about the reconciliation between the warring leaders, though Amoroldo was later killed by Lancelot[2]. The name Amoroldo is Italian for Marhaus, and here the name is used for both father and son.

Amr

The son of ARTHUR, according to NENNIUS, and probably identical with AMHAR, the son of Arthur who is mentioned in the MABINOGION. Nennius states that he was buried under a mound named LICAT ANIR after he had been killed by his father at ARCHENFIELD, this burial mound giving rise to his alternative name of ANIR.

Amren

Simply mentioned as the son of BEDIVERE, though which one is not made clear. It seems most likely that he was the son of BEDIVERE[2].

Amurfine

One of the ladies who is described in various sources as having been the wife of GAWAIN[1].

Amustant

The chaplain to GUINEVERE who had previously been the chaplain to her father. Eventually he became an anchorite, or religious hermit.

Amytans

In the anonymous Scottish poem LANCELOT OF THE LAIK, which dates from the fifteenth century, Amytans appears as a wise man who scolded ARTHUR. This poem is derived from an earlier French one, but in that the wise man remains unnamed.

Andred

Originally hailing from LINCOLN, Andred was a cousin of TRISTAN who was resident at the court of King MARK[2]. He spied on his cousin and eventually betrayed the affair between Tristan and ISEULT[1] to Mark.

Andrivete

The daughter of King CADOR[2] of NORTHUMBERLAND. Following her father's death, her uncle, AYGLIN, having usurped her rightful inheritance, tried to marry Andrivete off to someone quite unsuitable, but she managed to evade his plans by escaping and marrying KAY. She prepared to overthrow her uncle with the support of King ARTHUR, but before any fighting occurred the people of Northumberland forced Ayglin to surrender, and Andrivete regained her kingdom.

Anfere

The realm of Queen LAUDAME, who married GAREL.

Anfortas

A variant of AMFORTAS which was used by Wagner in his PARSIVAL.

Angelica

The mother of TOM A'LINCOLN by ARTHUR.

Angharad Golden-hand

In the MABINOGION she appears as the lover of PERCEVAL[2] (PEREDUR), her epithet seemingly indicating her generous nature. At first she refused to become Perceval's lover, so he refused to speak to any Christian until she changed her mind, which she eventually did.

Angis

Named as a squire to Sir LANCELOT[2].

Anglides

The wife of BALDWIN and mother of ALISANDER THE ORPHAN. Following the murder of Baldwin by his brother MARK[2], she raised her son in secret.

Anglitora

The daughter of PRESTER JOHN. She eloped with TOM A'LINCOLN, ARTHUR's son by ANGELICA, and bore him the BLACK KNIGHT[1]. However, she later abandoned and then subsequently murdered Tom a'Lincoln, his death being avenged by their son, the Black Knight.

Anglo-Saxon

Collective name for the Angles and SAXONS, who, along with the Jutes, conquered much of BRITAIN between the fifth and seventh centuries. The Angles settled in East Anglia, Mercia and Northumbria; the Saxons in Essex, Sussex and Wessex; and the Jutes in KENT and southern Hampshire, most notably on the Isle of Wight. The Angles and Saxons came from the Schleswig-Holstein area, and may have united before the invasion, and the Jutes are usually said to have originated in Jutland. There was probably considerable inter-marriage with Romanized Celts, although the latter's language and civilization almost disappeared.

Following the conquest a number of kingdoms were set up, commonly referred to as the Heptarchy ('seven kingdoms'), which survived until the early ninth century, when they were united under the overlordship of Wessex.

Anglo-Saxon Chronicle, The

An history of England from the time of the Roman invasion to the eleventh century. Begun in the ninth century, during the reign of King Alfred, and written as a series of chronicles in Old English by monks, the work was still being executed in the twelfth century.

The *Chronicle*, which comprises seven different manuscripts, forms a unique record of early English history, and of the development of Old English prose up to its final stages in the year 1154, by which time it had been superseded by Middle English.

Anguisel

A variant of ANGUISH.

Anguish
Also ANGUISEL

King of IRELAND and father of ISEULT[1]. His name, a form of OENGHUS, appears to be genuinely Irish, and at the time in question a King Oenghus was believed to have reigned in southern Ireland at Cashel. The variant form of his name, Anguisel, leads to confusion with the Scottish King AUGUSELUS in GEOFFREY OF MONMOUTH.

Anir

The name applied by NENNIUS to AMR, a son of ARTHUR, who was killed by his father at ARCHENFIELD and buried under a mound known as LICAT ANIR.

Anjou

An old countship and former province in FRANCE that was conquered by VORTI-GERN and given to HENGIST. Its first count was KAY, ARTHUR's seneschal (steward), while in WOLFRAM VON ESCHENBACH its queen was HERZELOYDE. Historically, in 1154, the count of Anjou became King of England as Henry II, but the territory was lost by King John in 1204. In 1480 the countship was annexed to the French crown.

Anlawdd

A variant of AMLAWDD that is only found in the family tree for ARTHUR put forward by T. W. Rolleston. It appears to be a simple transcriptive error. Rolleston, however, also alters the normal relationships within the genealogy, and makes Anlawdd the father of YSPADDADDEN, CUSTENNIN and GOLEUDDYDD.

Anna

The sister of ARTHUR who, according to GEOFFREY OF MONMOUTH, married either LOT of LODONESIA or BUDIC, king of BRITTANY. Other sources say that she was also known as ERMINE and married Budic, while it was her sister who married Lot. It has also been suggested that she may be identified with MORGAN[1] Le Fay, and could possibly have originally derived from the Celtic goddess ANU, the earth mother.

Annales Cambriae

A set of Welsh annals dating from the tenth century that mention the battles of BADON and CAMLANN, stating that both MORDRED and ARTHUR fell in the latter.

Annales Toledanos

Spanish annals which state that the battle of CAMLANN took place in AD 580, the latest recorded date for this, the final battle fought by ARTHUR.

Annals of Tigernach

Irish annals which state that the battle of CAMLANN, ARTHUR's final battle, was fought in AD 541.

Annowre

A sorceress who wanted ARTHUR to be her lover but, even though she brought him under her spell, he still refused to comply. Tipped off by NIMUE, LANCELOT[2] rescued Arthur just as Annowre was about to have him killed, and instead it was she who was killed by Lancelot.

Annw(f)n

The name given to the Welsh OTHER-WORLD which was ruled over by ARAWN. Although usually considered as the Welsh underworld, it is described in the MABIN-OGION as a recognizable kingdom, and appears to have various regions along the same lines as Hades, the underworld of classical Greek mythology.

The early Welsh poem Preiddeu Annwfn (Spoils of Annwfn), which describes King ARTHUR's expedition to this otherworld to capture a magic cauldron, also gives a description of various features of Annwfn. The narrator of this poem is the famous

Welsh bard TALIESIN, a member of the group which took part in the expedition. Sailing overseas in the ship PRYDWEN to reach their goal the group at one point come to CAER WYDYR, a glass fort, but cannot induce its watchman to talk to them, thus suggesting a land of the silent dead, which is also referred to in NENNIUS's *Historia Britonum*. Arthur and his men also come to CAER FEDDWIDD (the Fort of CAROUSAL), which is also known as CAER SIDDI (ruled over by ARIANRHOD) or CAER RIGOR. Here the fountain runs with wine and no one ever suffers from illness or knows old age, thus suggesting an idyll. From this expedition, which would seem to have later evolved into the Quest for the Holy GRAIL, only seven returned. This final factor would seem to indicate that this story owes its origins to the story concerning the expedition of BENDIGEID VRAN to IRELAND. Taliesin is also named among the survivors of that expedition, which again numbered just seven.

Anthemius

An historical Roman emperor who ruled between AD 467 and 472, During his battle against EURIC the Visigoth, he was assisted by a large army brought across from England by King RIOTHAMUS.

Antikonie

According to WOLFRAM VON ESCHEN-BACH, the sister of King VERGULAHT of ASCALUN and the lover of GAWAIN[1].

Antony

In Continental romance Antony was an Irish bishop and secretary to MERLIN.

Antor

Appearing in French sources as the foster father of ARTHUR, Antor would seem to be a variant of ECTOR.

Anu

The earth mother of Irish mythology who is better known as Dana or Danu. In this form she would appear to be the original of ANNA, the sister of ARTHUR.

Apollo

The son of LUCIUS, according to the PROSE TRISTAN, which gives the early history of LIONES. Unwittingly he married his own mother, but later married GLORIANDE, by whom he became the father of CANDACES.

Apples, Isle of

The name given to AVALON by GEOFFREY OF MONMOUTH in his VITA MERLINI.

Aquitain(e)

According to GOTTFRIED VON STRASS-BURG, the region of south-west France in which the dwarf MELOT, who spied on TRISTAN and ISEULT[1] for MARK[2], lived. However, EILHART VON OBERGE calls the dwarf Aquitain rather than the region.

Aravia, -ius

The mountain home of the giant RIENCE (RHITTA), and better known today as Mount SNOWDON.

Arawn

The king of ANNWFN, the Welsh OTHER-WORLD, to whose kingdom ARTHUR and a band of followers travelled to capture a magic cauldron. In a Welsh version of GEOFFREY OF MONMOUTH the name Arawn is used to translate AUGUSELUS, the brother of URIEN, while the TRIADS also mention an Arawn, the son of KYNVARCH.

Archenfield

The place where AMR, son of ARTHUR, was killed by his father, and where he was buried under a mound known as LICAT ANIR.

Archier

The name taken by the cannibal King GURGURANT following his conversion to Christianity.

Arcile

A variant of ARSILE.

Ardan

An uncle of ARTHUR, according to French romance.

Ares

The father of DO and grandfather of LORETE and GRIFLET.

Ar(f)derydd

The proper Welsh name for the battle of ARTHURET.

Argan

Forced to build a castle for UTHER after the latter, who was in love with his wife, had defeated him.

Argante

An elf and the queen of AVALON, who, according to LAYAMON, received King ARTHUR after his final battle. Her name, it has been suggested, is a form of the goddess ARIANRHOD.

Argistes

According to Italian romance, MERLIN, while still a boy, foretold that Argistes would be hanged, drowned and burned. Later Argistes set fire to Merlin's house, but the flames spread to his own. Rushing to the well to fetch water to dowse the fire, the chain wrapped around his neck and he fell down the well into which people threw burning rafters. Thus Argistes was hanged, drowned and burned, fulfilling Merlin's prophecy.

Argus

In the Y Saint Graal, the Welsh version of the GRAIL story, Argus is another son of ELAINE[1], and thus a brother of GALAHAD[1].

Arguth

Simply mentioned as being an ancestor of LOT.

Ar(i)anrhod

An important Celtic goddess who appears as one of the main characters in the MABINOGION story of Math, Son of Mathonwy.

The sister of GWYDION FAB DÔN, she was put forward by her brother for the position of footholder (a court post held by a virgin) to King MATH. She failed the test to confirm her virginity when two bundles fell from her. One contained the golden-haired baby DYLAN EIL TON and the other LLEU LLAW GYFFES.

Her association with Arthurian legend is confined to the fact that she is described as the ruler of CAER SIDDI, a magical realm, to which ARTHUR and his party were said to have travelled during their expedition to the OTHER-WORLD to capture a magic cauldron. It has also been suggested that her name gave rise to ARGANTE, the elfin queen of AVALON.

Aries

According to Sir Thomas MALORY, Aries was a cowherd who raised TOR, the il-legitimate son of King PELLINORE and his wife, believing him to be his own son. However, French romance makes Aries a king and the real father of Tor.

Arimathea, Joseph of
See JOSEPH OF ARIMATHEA

Ariosto, Ludovico

Italian poet (1474–1533), born in Reggio Emilia. Originally intending to be a lawyer, he abandoned that in favour of poetry. In 1503 he entered the court of the Cardinal Ippolito D'ESTE at Ferrara, and during the next ten years produced his ORLANDO FURIOSO (1516), the ROLAND epic that forms a continuation of BOIARDO'S ORLANDO INNAMORATO. Over the next sixteen years Ariosto expanded his *Orlando Furioso* until, in 1532, it was published as a third edition in the form in which it still exists today. He died the following year and was buried in the church of San Benedetto, at Ferrara, where a magnificent monument marks his last resting place.

Arlecchino

The Italian name under which HELLEKIN appeared as the HARLEQUIN of the *Commedia dell'arte*.

Armenia

During the traditional Arthurian period this country was ruled by either Persian representatives or leaders in revolt against Persia. However, the thirteenth-century French romance FLORIANT ET FLORETE makes King TURCANS the ruler of Armenia during ARTHUR'S time.

Armes Prydein

The Prophecy of Britain, an heroic tenth-century Welsh poem that was probably written between AD 900 and 930. Unique in being the first work to refer to the magician MYRDDIN (MERLIN), this poem calls upon the British to unite against the SAXON invaders. It foretells that the last British king, CADWALLADER, son of CADWALLON, will rise to lead a great army, including the Men of Dublin, the Irish Gaels and the Men of CORNWALL and STRATHCLYDE, and drive the Saxons into the sea.

Arnive

According to WOLFRAM VON ESCHEN-BACH, the mother of ARTHUR who was rescued from KLINGSOR by GAWAIN[1].

Aron

Simply named as one of the TWENTY-FOUR KNIGHTS of King Arthur's court.

Arondiel

The horse of the ploughboy FERGUS[1], who aspired to become a knight and married GALIENE, the Lady of LOTHIAN.

Arran, Isle of

In Irish mythology, the Isle of Arran, situated in the Firth of Forth, SCOTLAND, is usually identified with the paradisaical island of EMHAIN ABHLACH (Emhain of the Apple Trees), an island associated with the Irish sea god MANANNÁN MAC LIR. In his VITA MERLINI, GEOFFREY OF MONMOUTH refers to AVALON as the Isle of APPLES, and this would seem to suggest that his naming of that idyllic land was taken from earlier Celtic tradition.

Arsile
Also ARCILE

One of the companions of MORGAN[1] Le Fay, along with MAGLORE, according to the thirteenth-century French romance li jus Aden.

Art Aoinfhear

According to the Irish romance CAITHRÉIM CONGHAIL CLÁIRINGNIGH, Art of Aoinfhear was a son of King ARTHUR. Other Irish sources make him the son of King Conn of the Hundred Battles, a legendary character who was, perhaps, originally a god, and was thought to have reigned in prehistoric times.

Artegall
Also ARTGUALCHAR

Described as an earl or count of Guarensis (Warwick), Artegall appears in GEOFFREY OF MONMOUTH as ARTGUALCHAR. Other sources make him a KNIGHT OF THE ROUND TABLE and the First Earl of Warwick, while SPENSER says that he was the son of King CADOR[1] of CORNWALL, married BRITOMART, the daughter of King RIENCE, and bore the arms of Achilles.

Artgualchar

The name under which ARTEGALL appears in GEOFFREY OF MONMOUTH.

Arthour and Merlin

An obscure fourteenth-century English poem whose author remains unknown.

Arthur

Semi-legendary, mythologized king of BRITAIN whose name is perhaps a form of Artorius, a Roman gens name, though it might also be Celtic in origin, coming from artos viros (bear man). Historically he was perhaps a fifth- or sixth-century chieftain or general, though he is not mentioned by any contemporary historian. One argument says that he is to be identified with the Celtic king RIOTHAMUS, but legend would seem to suggest that he is, rather, a composite figure, combining the attributes and achievements of more than one person.

The sixth-century monk GILDAS records a great British victory over the pagan SAXONS at Mount BADON (possibly BADBURY HILL in Devon, BADBURY RINGS in Dorset, somewhere on the north Wiltshire Downs, or a hill near BATH), a battle that later came to be associated with the name of King Arthur, and his most important victory. There are six possible sites for this battle based on place-names alone. Most people, however, think of Arthur as the idealized, chivalrous king described by Sir Thomas MALORY in LE MORTE D'ARTHUR (1470). By the ninth century the inflation of

Arthur into a superhuman being was well under way, for a description by NENNIUS says of the battle of Mount BADON that '960 of the enemy fell in a single attack by Arthur', whom he calls *dux bellorum* (leader of troops). Records kept in a Welsh monastery from about the same period refer to the victory at Mount Badon (now thought to have been fought *c*. AD 490, though the Easter Annals, a fifth-century religious tract, record it as having occurred *c*. AD 516), and to Arthur's death along with MORDRED at the battle of CAMLANN. These would seem to establish Arthur as an historic personage – though not a king. Nennius refers to Arthur as the 'leader of battles' for the British kings, a statement that is likely to have been factual. Early records serve to tell us very little extra, except that many of these sources are now considered suspect, and a more contemporary view is that Arthur was a professional soldier in service to the British kings after the Roman occupation had come to an end.

Where he actually functioned is also subject to much controversy. Different opinions place him as a leader in the south-west, the north, in WALES, or throughout Britain. The truth of the matter is that, as the evidence stands, we cannot be certain. Even the battles attributed to him do not help in deciding this matter, for many of those are suspect as well.

His family tree is just as dubious as both his role and his area of operation. Early Celtic writings make him the cousin of CULHWCH, whom he helped to win the hand of OLWEN, the daughter of the chief giant, YSPADDADEN. However, the first complete, coherent narrative of the life of King Arthur appears in the fanciful eleventh-century *Historia Regum Britanniae* (*History of the Kings of Britain*) by GEOFFREY OF MONMOUTH. This work combined the works of Nennius and Welsh folklore to give the Arthurian legends known today, along with many of the major characters and events.

Arthur's story is basically as follows. King UTHER PENDRAGON became infatuated with IGRAINE[1], the wife of Duke GORLOIS of CORNWALL, who had been waging a long war against the king. While Gorlois was besieged by Uther in Castle TERRABIL, Igraine was in the castle at TINTAGEL, but Uther could take no part in the fighting because he was sick with love for Igraine. One of his men sought out the renowned wizard MERLIN, who said he would help if the king would reward him with whatever he desired. Merlin required that any child born from their magical union be delivered to him to raise, though Sir Thomas Malory, in the fifteenth century, says the requirement was that the child should be delivered to ECTOR. Most commentators agree that Ector fostered the child.

Merlin rode to Uther's pavilion, where the king agreed to his terms, and with the aid of his magic Merlin so altered the king's appearance that, when Uther came to her in her castle at Tintagel, Igraine believed him to be her husband. That very night, while the disguised king lay with Igraine, Gorlois was killed in battle with Uther's troops. When she heard of her husband's death, Igraine wondered who the knight who had lain with her might have been. Even when she assented to marriage with Uther, to unite their two houses, he did not tell her. Their son, conceived on that night, was Arthur, brother to MORGAN[1] Le Fay, and, as Uther had agreed, Merlin came to take the baby away, reassuring the father he would be well cared for.

Uther was unable to spend a long and happy life with Igraine, for within two years he had fallen sick and died, to the great sorrow of Igraine, who had learned to love him. The rule of the kingdom fell into jeopardy, for there was no known heir. Many lords laid claim to the throne, and fought bitterly for the right to reign, but none could take the kingdom by just cause.

When Arthur was fifteen he was chosen as king. The more romantic legends say the choice was made by his drawing the magical sword EXCALIBUR from a stone, something that no other had been able to achieve, and on this sword were engraved the words 'Whosoever shall draw this sword from the stone is the true-born king of all England'. Many maintain that this sword had been placed in the stone by Merlin, who 'arranged' that Arthur should be the only person capable of drawing it out, and that the sword was not Excalibur, but a sword which received no special name. Others say Merlin or Ector brought him to London, where he won the kingship in a tournament. Still others combine both events, saying that Arthur drew the sword *en route* to the tournament.

The crowning of Arthur resulted in a rebellion by eleven rulers which Arthur successfully put down. He then led an army against the Saxons, defeating their leader COLGRIN and a mixed force of Saxons, Scots and PICTS at the River DOUGLAS. Colgrin took refuge in YORK and Arthur laid siege, but was obliged to abandon that siege and return to London. Now he sought the aid of HOEL[1], king of BRITTANY, his cousin (or possibly his nephew), who landed at SOUTHAMPTON with a great army. Together they defeated the Saxons at LINCOLN, at CELIDON WOOD, and at Bath. They put down the Scots, Picts and Irish in Moray, and toured Loch Lomond. Next they raised the siege of York, and Arthur restored that city to its former glory, returning their lands to the three dis-

possessed Yorkist princes, LOT, URIAN and AUGUSELUS.

Having now restored the entire kingdom, Arthur took as his wife the most beautiful woman in all Britain, GUINEVERE, the daughter of King LEODEGRANCE or the ward of Duke CADOR[1], and a lady of noble Roman descent. Having married, Arthur sailed to IRELAND, defeated its king, GILMAURIUS, and conquered the whole island. Hearing of his great might and prowess in battle, DOLDAVIUS and GUNPHAR, the kings of Gotland and the ORKNEYS respectively, came to pay him homage. Now Arthur began to invite the most distinguished men of other lands to join his court and the fame of his knights spread to the ends of the earth.

The romances placed his court at CAMELOT, which has been variously identified, but the name is simply the invention of twelfth-century poets. Since at least 1540, Camelot has been identified with CADBURY CASTLE in Somerset. Archaeological excavation, however, shows that Cadbury Castle might instead have been the strong post or fortified rallying point that the historical Arthur needed to defend Britain against the Saxons. The hillfort had been first built c. 500 BC, but was refortified with a stone and timber rampart and gates that can be dated to between AD 460 and 540, the years during which Arthur is now thought to have flourished. Foundations of a large hall have been discovered, and the site, some eighteen acres in area, would have been large enough to accommodate an army of over 1,000 men. Early Welsh traditions named Arthur's court as CELLIWIG, and this is probably to be identified with KILLIBURY, or with CAERLEON-ON-USK. Another tradition associated Arthur with CASTLE-AN-DINAS near St Columb, the largest Celtic hillfort in Cornwall, which was also known as the seat of Cornish kings after Arthur's time.

His next expedition was to conquer Europe, beginning with NORWAY which he duly vanquished and then gave to Lot. Sailing then to GAUL, he defeated and killed the Tribune FROLLO and took Paris. Within nine years and with the aid of HOEL, Arthur had conquered all of Gaul and, holding court in Paris, he established the government of that kingdom on a legal footing.

Returning to Britain, Arthur decided to hold a plenary court at Whitsun at the CITY OF THE LEGIONS (Caerleon-on-Usk or CHESTER), and to this court came representatives from all of Europe.

Now Arthur was summoned to Rome by LUCIUS HIBERIUS to answer the charge of having attacked the empire, and with 183,000 men Arthur crossed to FRANCE and marched southwards. *En route* he had a vision of a dragon fighting and conquering a bear, and decided that this represented his coming conflict with the emperor, though some of his company interpreted it as meaning he would fight and overcome a giant. Indeed, at the Mont SAINT MICHEL, Arthur did defeat and kill a giant. He also routed the imperial Roman troops at Saussy, and was about to march on Rome when he received news that his nephew Mordred, son of Lot, whom he had left as his regent in Britain, had usurped the throne and taken Queen Guinevere as his mistress. Some accounts, however, say that Arthur successfully defeated Lucius Hiberius and became emperor himself.

The later romances treat this period in a different manner, and include the most romantic knight of them all, Sir LANCELOT[2], his adultery with QUEEN GUINEVERE, and the quest for the HOLY GRAIL.

Having achieved the quest for the Holy GRAIL, those knights who survived returned to Arthur's court and to the company of the ROUND TABLE. For a while it seemed as if the kingdom would be restored to its former glory, but Lancelot soon forgot the repentance and vows made on the holy quest, and began to resort to Queen Guinevere again. Arthur was told of the affair, but refused to believe it unless Lancelot and his queen could be caught together.

AGRAVAIN and Mordred laid in wait with twelve other knights and succeeded in trapping Lancelot in the queen's chamber. Even though Lancelot was unarmed, he managed to fight his way free, killing all who had sought to trap him, except Mordred, who fled to the king. Guinevere was sentenced to be burnt at the stake, but Lancelot rescued her and the pair left LOGRIS for Lancelot's home in France. There is now some inconsistency in the romances, for even though Guinevere was now supposed to be in France, the next part of the romances puts her back in Logris, or England. In these cases, Guinevere was said to have been taken to JOYOUS GARD, Lancelot's castle, which has been identified with BAMBURGH Castle in NORTHUMBERLAND.

Arthur, who had earlier loved Lancelot, wished to go to France and compel him to return in peace, but upon taking the counsel of GAWAIN[1], who desired revenge, for Lancelot had slain his brethren in his escape, was persuaded that this would be folly, and so Arthur left for France, taking a vast army with him.

Leaving Sir Mordred as his regent, to rule in his absence, for Mordred was his son (the result of an unwitting incestuous affair between Arthur and his sister MORGAUSE, thus making Mordred his nephew as well), and placing Queen Guinevere under Mordred's governance, Arthur set sail for France. While waging war there, Mordred made mischief by forging letters which he said had been sent from France. They told of Arthur's death in battle, and as a result he had himself crowned king at CANTERBURY.

Next Mordred announced that he was to marry Guinevere, and though the queen still mourned Arthur, she consented. Trusting her, Mordred gave Guinevere permission to travel to London to buy what she would need for their wedding. Arriving in London, she went straight to the Tower of London, which she stocked for a long siege. News of these events reached Arthur, and he recalled his troops.

Hurrying back, Arthur landed at RICHBOROUGH, where he fought and defeated Mordred. At the battle of WINCHESTER he defeated him again (the romances make this the site of GAWAIN's death), and then pursued him to the River Camlann in Cornwall, though the romances make this SALISBURY PLAIN, the final battle to be fought on the day after the Trinity Sunday. Cornish legend associates the battle of Camlann with SLAUGHTERBRIDGE, where the river ran crimson with the blood of slain warriors.

In a dream, the spirit of Gawain appeared to Arthur and told him that, if he were to fight the following day, both he and Mordred would be slain. However, if he waited, Sir Lancelot and all his noble knights would come to his aid within the month. Waking, Arthur called his two most trusted knights, Sir BEDIVERE[2] and Sir LUCAN, and charged them with making a truce with Mordred. All was agreed, and each side, with just fourteen knights each present, met on the field of combat to sign the treaty.

Just then an adder slithered from a bush and bit one of the knights on the foot. As he drew his sword to kill the snake, the opposing armies saw the sword glinting in the sunlight and, amidst shouts of treachery, the battle began.

Mordred was slain by Arthur, but the king was also mortally wounded before the battle came to an end. Calling Sir Bedivere, he told that knight to take his enchanted sword, Excalibur, and throw it into a nearby lake. Bedivere took the sword, but hid it behind a tree before returning to Arthur to tell him that his command had been carried out. However, when Arthur asked Bedivere what he had seen, Bedivere answered that he had seen nothing but waves and wind on the water. Immediately Arthur knew he was lying, and charged Bedivere to return to the lake and carry out his command. This time Bedivere hurled the sword out over the lake, and as it fell towards the water a hand rose and caught the sword. Returning to the king, he told him what he had seen. Cornish legend says that Sir Bedivere was sent to DOZMARY POOL on Dartmoor, some six miles from Slaughterbridge, the traditional Cornish location for Camlann, but this is just one of the many locations associated with the returning of Excalibur to the LADY OF THE LAKE.

Arthur, finally satisfied that his orders had been carried out, told Bedivere to take him down to the lake, where a barge drew alongside. In the barge were a number of fair ladies, all with black hoods, who wept as they saw Arthur. Bedivere laid the weak king in the barge, which then sailed away from the site of the battle to the Isle of AVALON, AVALLACH or the vale of AVILION, so that his wounds might heal. In the imagination of Alfred, Lord Tennyson, the dying Arthur was carried down to the narrow harbour of BOSCASTLE to be borne away on the funeral barge to Avalon. Before leaving, the king gave the crown to his cousin CONSTANTINE[2], son of Cador. Duke of Cornwall. This was reputed to be in the year AD 542.

According to Geoffrey of Monmouth, Guinevere, following Arthur's death, fled to the abbey at AMESBURY, where she took the veil and finally became the abbess. After the death, her body was taken to GLASTONBURY by Sir Lancelot to be buried beside that of her husband.

The belief that Arthur would return in the hour of Britain's greatest need and inaugurate a golden age was well established in both England and France by the early part of the twelfth century, and persisted until the latter part of the nineteenth century, although accounts of how and where the king would reappear varied considerably. In his VITA MERLINI, Geoffrey of Monmouth had called Avalon the Isle of APPLES, thus suggesting an otherworldly realm, but some fifty years later, in 1190 or 1191, Avalon had become identified with Glastonbury, where Arthur's body, and that of Guinevere, were said to have been exhumed, the inscription 'Hic jacet Arthurus, rex quondam, rex futurus' ('Here lies Arthur, king that was, king that shall be') summing up the flavour of his legendary life and death. All trace of the tombs mysteriously disappeared straight afterwards, but the claim attracted widespread interest at the time when the stories of King Arthur were beginning to spread beyond purely Welsh legend. Elsewhere he is said to lie sleeping at Cadbury Castle in Somerset, in a cave on CRAIG-Y-DINAS near SNOWDON in WALES, or even in another cave on Mount ETNA, this last one probably deriving from the Norman occupation of Sicily.

So tenacious were the Cornish in their belief that Arthur would one day come again to rescue them from bondage that in 1177 there was a riot in Bodmin church between local men and some visiting French monks, one of whom had scoffed at such an article of faith. His spirit was believed to fly over the Cornish cliffs in the form of the Cornish CHOUGH – a bird now extinct in the county except for one or two pairs held in captivity.

The stories of King Arthur and his gallant knights have become some of the most potent of all European myths and legends, forming the basis of innumerable stories, poems, plays and operas, not only in Britain and France but also particularly in GERMANY, as well as occurring in most other Western European countries. The early development of these tales resulted from the cross-fertilization of Celtic and Christian material in which the king's company of knights becomes the Christian order of the Round Table, which is dedicated to chivalry and the quest for the Holy Grail.

The famous Round Table is first referred to in the ROMAN DE BRUT by the early twelfth-century writer WACE. This work was written in French, but was quickly translated and expanded by LAYAMON in his BRUT, written between 1189 and 1199.

According to Wace, the barons quarrelled over precedence, so King Arthur made the Round Table. Layamon develops this theme by saying that the quarrel arose during a Christmas feast, and resulted in the death of several men. He goes on to tell that Arthur visited Cornwall a short while afterwards, and there met a foreign carpenter who had heard of the disagreement, and offered to make Arthur a portable table at which 1,600 could sit without any one having precedence over another. Arthur immediately commissioned the piece, which was finished in just six weeks.

Later versions of the story credit Merlin with the invention and building of the Round Table, while some Anglo-French romances make the table, which now seats just 150, the gift of Arthur's father-in-law, King Leodegrance. One seat at this table, the SIEGE PERILOUS, or Seat of Danger, was reserved for the knight who was to seek and achieve the Holy Grail, the dish from which Jesus was said to have eaten lamb at the Last Supper, and which had then been used to catch drops of Christ's blood as he hung, dying, on the Cross.

The legend held that the Holy Grail had been brought to England by Jesus's uncle, JOSEPH OF ARIMATHEA, who had established a church at Glastonbury. His descendants, the FISHER KINGS, guarded the Holy Grail within the confines of their Castle CARBONEK, where it was hidden away from prying eyes. Associated with the Holy Grail was a bleeding lance that was sometimes identified with the Lance of LONGINUS. This was the lance said to have been used by the centurion to pierce Jesus's side as he hung on the cross (St John: 19.xxxiv).

Later versions of the story of the Holy Grail make it the cup from which Jesus and his disciples drank at the Last Supper (St Matthew: 26.xxvii–xxviii), though the association of the bleeding lance remains unaltered. This cup brought about many miracles when it was carried to Britain by Joseph of Arimathea, and was said to have fed the saint and his followers when they were imprisoned. Subsequently the Holy Grail disappeared, thenceforth to be seen only by those few who were 'pure in heart' – a condition medieval Christian writers define as 'celibate'. Thus the magical dish of Celtic tradition becomes the symbolic cup of the Eucharist, and paganism becomes Christianity.

In CHRÉTIEN DE TROYES's early version of the myth of the Holy Grail, the mysterious holy vessel is housed in the GRAIL CASTLE, where it is guarded by a GRAIL KEEPER. The wounded Fisher King of the castle has been maimed by a wound through his thighs (sic), and is sustained only by a magical dish. As a result the land has become infertile and will revive only if the king can be healed, but this will happen only if there is a knight brave enough to face and conquer all the dangers of the perilous journey to the Grail Castle, and then still be wise enough to ask a certain question which will immediately break the spell under which the Fisher King and the land are held. Some commentators omit the Fisher King and rather connect the story with Arthur himself. In these instances it is the king who has lost the will to survive, following the discovery of Guinevere's adultery with Lancelot and, as the king and the land are inexorably connected, the land becomes infertile. Only the discovery of the Holy Grail can restore health and prosperity to both king and country.

This curious tale appears to derive from an ancient fertility rite, and although one early writer derives the Fisher King's name from the fish symbol of Christ, it also has connections with the god of the sea, who in Celtic myth is a king of the mysterious OTHERWORLD to which selected heroes journey. The Welsh PREIDDEU ANNWFN describes one such journey, in which King Arthur travels to this mysterious land in search of a magical cauldron.

In the later, medieval legends of King Arthur, the quest for the Holy Grail is undertaken by Sir Lancelot of the Lake, Sir GALAHAD[1], Sir PERCEVAL[2] and Sir BORS[2].

Possibly the most mysterious aspect of Arthur's reign is his relationship with Morgan Le Fay. In Malory she is made his sister, but Geoffrey of Monmouth seems to know nothing of their kinship, nor does he, interestingly, mention any enmity between them. This would therefore appear to be a later development of the romances. One possible explanation is that Morgan Le Fay was originally

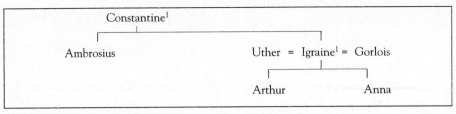

Figure 2 *Genealogy of Arthur according to Geoffrey of Monmouth*

Figure 3 *Genealogy of Arthur according to Sir Thomas Malory*

Arthur's lover, later being represented as his sister. It is, however, generally accepted that her enmity towards Arthur springs from the fact that he killed her father, Gorlois, which would of course make it impossible for her to have been his sister. Arthur was also said, by the different sources, to have had many children, including the sons LOHOLT, LLACHEU, BORRE, ARTHUR THE LITTLE, MORDRED, ROWLAND, GWYDRE, AMR, ADELUF, MORGAN THE RED, ILLINOT AND PATRICK THE RED, and the daughters MELORA, ELLEN and GYNETH.

Places linked with both the historical and the legendary Arthur are widespread throughout Britain, though most of the names connected with Arthur, King MARK[2] and TRISTAN have no genuine historical significance. All they do is show a popular habit of naming ancient ruins after long-dead heroes. However, Cadbury Castle and MOTE OF MARK have both produced pottery that dates from the correct period, *c.* AD 500, thus indicating that they may have some connection with the historical chieftain who became the most potent of all British, and indeed European, legendary figures, better remembered and more widely known than the Serbian Prince Marco, or the Russian Ilya Muromyets, for example, an enigmatic figure whose story is shrouded in such a tangle of history, myth and folklore that the truth will probably never be known.

Arthur's genealogy (Figures 2 to 4) is particularly fascinating, simply for the pure scope and diversity of lineage, especially with regard to his parentage. Geoffrey of Monmouth gives the family tree shown in Figure 2, whereas Sir Thomas Malory's version is as shown in Figure 3.

Arthur's full family tree, allowing for inconsistencies, might resemble that shown in Figure 4.

Arthur and Gorlagon

A thirteenth-century Latin work which notably features a werewolf.

Arthur of Brittany

A descendant of LANCELOT[2] and the hero of a romance in which he seeks the hand of FLORENCE, the daughter of the king of SORLOIS, a place now to be found in what is modern Iraq.

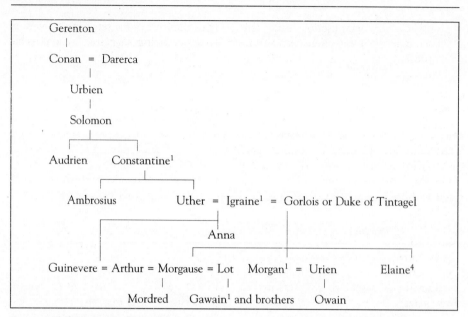

Figure 4 *Full family tree for Arthur*

Arthur of Dalriada

The son of AEDÁN MAC GABRAIN, the king of DALRIADA. Although he lived some-what later than the traditional dates ascribed to ARTHUR, it has been argued that he is the historical character around whom the myths and romances have been woven.

Arthur the Little

According to the PROSE TRISTAN, the il-legitimate son of ARTHUR following the rape of his mother by Arthur. He was said to have been a supporter of Arthur against both his SAXON and his Cornish foes, and to have been a quester in the search for the Holy GRAIL.

Arthur's battles

NENNIUS presents us with a list of twelve battles in which ARTHUR was said to have led the British forces against the SAXONS. There is no certainty that any of the

battles was actually associated with Arthur, but Nennius lists them as follows.

1 At the mouth of the River GLEIN. There are two English rivers having this name and either might be con-sidered as the site.

2–5 The River DOUGLAS in LINNIUS.

6 On the River BASSUS.

7 At CAT COIT CELIDON, or CELYDDON, in the north, the region being known in Latin as *Silva Caledonia* (Wood of Scotland). Some sources, however, locate this particular battle at CELIDON WOOD, which, though sometimes still located in SCOTLAND, is usually ident-ified with a wood to the north of LINCOLN.

8 At GUINNION.

9 At the CITY OF THE LEGIONS, ident-ified as either CHESTER (called *Urbs Legionis* in Latin) or CAERLEON-ON-USK.

10 At the River Tribuit.

11 At Mount AGNED for which High ROCHESTER has been suggested. One

tenth-century manuscript calls this place BREGUOIN, but there seems to be confusion here with a victory elsewhere ascribed to URIEN of RHEGED.

12 BADON.

Arthur's Cave

There are a number of caves associated with King ARTHUR. One is located on the Isle of Anglesey, where Arthur was said to have sheltered during his battles with the Irish. His treasure was believed to have been hidden in a cromlech, surrounded by stones, that once stood there, and was supposedly guarded by supernatural creatures. Another is located at CRAIG-Y-DINAS and yet another at ALDERLEY EDGE.

Arthur's insignia

NENNIUS says that ARTHUR carried an image of the Virgin Mary on his shoulders during the battle of GUINNION. The Church of St Mary at Wedale at Stow in SCOTLAND once held what were believed to have been fragments of the image of St Mary that Arthur wore. The ANNALS OF CAMBRIAE claim that Arthur instead carried the cross on his shoulders at BADON.

Arthur's O'on

A Roman temple near FALKIRK, SCOTLAND, that dated from the second century AD. It was destroyed in 1743, but the dovecote at nearby Penicuick House was built as a replica of it. It has been argued that the temple was used by ARTHUR and was the original of the ROUND TABLE.

Arthur's Oven

Although its location cannot be identified with certainty, this feature undoubtedly lay to the west of Exeter, King's Oven on Dartmoor being suggested as a possible site. In 1113 some French priests were reported to have been shown it.

Arthur's Quoit

ARTHUR was alleged to have thrown a great number of quoits in different parts of the country. Two notable examples are CARREG COETAN ARTHUR, a cromlech near Newport, GWENT, and the LLIGWY CROMLECH near Moelfre on the east side of Anglesey, GWYNEDD.

Arthur's Seat

A volcanic plug 823 feet high, in east EDINBURGH, SCOTLAND, that was, according to legend, the place where ARTHUR watched his army defeat the PICTS. Another such rock exists in WALES.

Arthur's Stone

There are six features known throughout BRITAIN and WALES as Arthur's Stone. The two best known are given below. The others have been omitted as there seems to be little legend attached to them, and they would appear to have been named Arthur's Stone for no reason relevant to King ARTHUR.

1 A stone at CEFN-Y-BRYN, Gower, WALES. On the way to his final battle at CAMLANN, Arthur felt a pebble in his boot. Taking it out he flung it into the distance, and it landed seven miles away at Cefn-y-Bryn. In fact this relic is an ancient burial chamber with four stones supporting a millstone-grit capstone, making it a prominent feature on the ridge. The huge capstone is thought to weigh about 25 tons, and has been partly split, either by King Arthur with EXCALIBUR or by Saint

DAVID, who wished to prove that it was not a sacred stone.

At midnight on nights of the full moon, maidens from the Swansea area used to place cakes made of barley meal and honey, wetted with milk and well kneaded, on the stone. Then, on hands and knees, the maidens would crawl three times around the stone, this ritual being carried out to test the fidelity of their lovers. If the young men were faithful, they would come to the stone. If they did not arrive, the girls regarded this as a sign of their fickleness, or their intention never to marry.

Below the stone lies a spring called FYFNNON FAWR that is supposed to run according to the ebb and flow of the tide. The water used to be drunk from the palm of one hand while a wish was made. On nights with a full moon a ghostly figure wearing shining armour emerges from under the stone and proceeds to Llanrhidian. Those who have seen this mysterious spectral figure claim that it is King Arthur.

2 A stone at Dorstone, Herefordshire, from which Arthur was alleged to have drawn Excalibur. The flaw in this legend is that it was not Excalibur that Arthur drew from the stone, but some other unnamed sword. The stone is also said to cover the burial place of king Arthur, or to mark the burial place of a king defeated by Arthur.

Arthur's Table

The name given to two prominent features in Clwyd, WALES. One is a circle of twenty-four identations in a rock which is said to represent ARTHUR's knights at a table (cf. TWENTY-FOUR KNIGHTS), and the other is a barrow at Llanfair Dyffryn Ceiriog.

Arthur's Tor

An earthwork in County Durham that is said to contain treasures that are guarded by the ghosts of ARTHUR's warriors.

Arthuret, Battle of

A battle fought c. AD 575 for a 'lark's nest' between the British prince GWENDDOLEU and his cousins GWRGI and PEREDUR. GWENDDOLEU was killed by RHYDDERCH HAEL, and MYRDDIN, having fought in the battle, winning a golden torc (a necklace or armband made of twisted metal), lost his reason and become a hermit in the Scottish forest of CELYDDON (SILVA CALEDONIAE or CAT COIT CELIDON). Fighting a battle for a 'lark's nest' seems to indicate that the combat was over ownership of the important harbour of CAERLAVERLOCK, Fort Lark.

Arthurs, Succession of

In the book *Men among Mankind* by B. Le Poer Trench (1962), an argument is put forward that there was a series of Arthurs, hereditary priests of the GREAT GODDESS, and that the last of these was identical with the ARTHUR of legend, accepting the identification of Arthur with ARVIRAGUS as proposed by J. Whitehead.

Arviragus

According to GEOFFREY OF MONMOUTH, Arviragus was a king of BRITAIN, succeeding his brother GUIDERIUS, who had been killed in CLAUDIUS's invasion of Britain in AD 43. Peace was established between Claudius and Arviragus when the latter married GENVISSA, Claudius's daughter. Later Arviragus revolted, but peace was once more restored through the offices of Genvissa.

Other sources name Arviragus as having given JOSEPH OF ARIMATHEA the twelve hides of land at GLASTONBURY on which he founded the abbey, while others argue that Arviragus may have been a local Somerset prince who maintained his independence after the invasion of Claudius. Still others identify Arviragus with CARATACUS, while others further argue that Arviragus, Caratacus and ARTHUR were different names for the same person.

Ascalun

According to WOLFRAM VON ESCHENBACH, VERGULAHT was the king of this domain.

Aschil

The king of DENMARK, according to GEOFFREY OF MONMOUTH, who makes him an ally of ARTHUR at the battle of CAMLANN.

Asclut

An intermediate form of ALCLUD, the old name for DUMBARTON, that is thought by some to have given rise to ASTOLAT.

Assurne

A river which marked the boundary between the kingdoms of SURLUSE and LOGRES.

Assysla

According to the BRETA SOGUR, a Scandinavian version of the works of GEOFFREY OF MONMOUTH, Assysla was the name of the island on which ARTHUR died, thus making it cognate with AVALON.

Astlabor

A variant of ESCLABOR.

Astolat
Also SHALLOT

The home of ELAINE[2] the White, who died for the love of LANCELOT[2]. It is thought that the name may come from ALCLUD, the old name for DUMBARTON, through the intermediate form of ASCLUT, though Sir Thomas MALORY places Astolat at Guildford in Surrey.

Athrwys

The son of MEURIG, king of GLENVISSIG, he may have been the king of GWENT, although, dealing in the shady areas of early Welsh history, this cannot be said for certain. He has been identified with ARTHUR, but as he probably lived in the seventh century he comes 200 years too late.

Atlantis

The legendary lost continent of classical Greek mythology that was, according to some occultists, the original home of both MERLIN and IGRAINE[1].

Audrien
Also ALDROENUS

The king of BRITTANY and brother of CONSTANTINE[2], ARTHUR's chosen successor.

Auguselus

Designated as the king of SCOTLAND in the writings of GEOFFREY OF MONMOUTH. The brother of URIEN, and sometimes also of LOT, he is possibly identifiable with ARAWN, the ruler of ANNWFN. An ally of King ARTHUR, he supported the latter in his campaign against the ROMAN EMPIRE, but on his return he was killed at RICHBOROUGH by MORDRED.

Aurelius Ambrosius

A variant of AMBROSIUS AURELIUS.

Aurelius Caninus

The name given by GILDAS to AURELIUS CONAN.

Aurelius Conan

According to GEOFFREY OF MONMOUTH, the second successor to ARTHUR following CONSTANTINE[2], though GILDAS, a contemporary, makes both Constantine and Aurelius Conan local kings, and calls him AURELIUS CANINUS, saying that he enjoyed making war and plundering the spoils.

Avagddu

A variant of AFAGDDU.

Avallach

A variant of AVALON, though this spelling is sometimes also used to refer to AVALLOC, son of BELI MAWR and father of MODRON.

Avallo

A variant of AVALON used by GEOFFREY OF MONMOUTH in his HISTORIA REGUM BRITANNIAE.

Avalloc(h)
Also AVALLACH

Evidently originally a god of obscure origins and attributes, William of MALMESBURY maintained that he lived on the island of AVALON with his daughters. His origin is to be found in Welsh legend, where he is named as the son of BELI MAWR and father of the goddess MODRON, while in the Arthurian romances he appears under the name of EVELAKE.

Avalon

The Fortunate Island, that magical realm to which the mortally wounded ARTHUR was taken by MERLIN and TALIESIN after his final battle with MORDRED so that his wounds might be healed by the goddess MORGAN[1] Le Fay, the shape-changing mistress of therapy, music and the arts, co-ruling the realm with her NINE SISTERS. Significantly, the ferryman for Arthur's final journey was BARINTHUS, a mysterious character who echoes the role of the ancient sea gods. It is from Avalon that Arthur will one day return in the time of BRITAIN's greatest need, to inaugurate a new golden age. GEOFFREY OF MONMOUTH refers to Avalon as the Isle of APPLES in his VITA MERLINI, while in his HISTORIA REGUM BRITANNIAE he gives it the name AVALLO.

William of MALMESBURY maintained that AVALLOC lived on Avalon with his daughters, and it is widely thought that this association, or the Burgundian place-name of Avallon, may have influenced the present form of the name. The name appears in Welsh legend, around which most of the Arthurian stories have been wound, where it is a kingdom of the dead (see ANNWFN), though an alternative school of thought says the word, and thus the place, is Irish in origin.

It was said to have been ruled over by

Morgan Le Fay and her Nine Sisters, or her lover GUINGAMUER, or by a mysterious king named BANGON. In PERLESVAUS, both GUINEVERE and LOHOLT died before Arthur, and were buried there. Still, the exact location of this wonderful realm remained a mystery. In the reign of King Henry II it came to be recognized as GLASTONBURY, as the tombs of King Arthur and Guinevere were reported to have been found there. Subsequently the tombs vanished, never to be seen again, thus adding more to the mystery. Some have identified Glastonbury with CAER WYDYR, the Fort of Glass, and as CAER WYDYR is traditionally located in the Welsh OTHERWORLD realm of Annwfn, Avalon has become connected with this realm, such is the confusion that clouds the Arthurian legends.

Avenable

A damsel who went to the court of JULIUS CAESAR disguised as a page, calling herself GRISANDOLE. Eventually marrying Julius Caesar, she was said to have introduced MERLIN to the court.

Avilion

A variant name for AVALON that has been used by Sir Thomas MALORY and, in more modern times, by Alfred, Lord Tennyson.

Ayglin

The uncle of ANDRIVETE. When he wanted Andrivete to marry someone of his own choosing, she flouted his wishes, escaped and married Sir KAY.

Babylon

Lying on the east bank of the River Euphrates and situated in modern Iraq, Babylon was the capital of the ancient Mesopotamian kingdom of Babylonia. In the Arthurian legends this city was the realm of THOLOMER, who was drawn into a war against EVELAKE when the latter became the king of SARRAS.

Bach Bychan

'Little small one', the page of TRISTAN in the Welsh romance TRYSTAN.

Badbury Hill

A hill in Devon that is considered one of the many possible sites for the battle of BADON.

Badbury Rings

A place in Dorset that is numbered among the possible locations for the battle of BADON.

Badon

There are six possible sites for this mount, the scene of the battle in which ARTHUR totally defeated the SAXONS. GILDAS makes the first reference to the battle in his DE EXCIDIO ET CONQUESTU BRITANNIAE, but does not mention Arthur by name. Arthur is named as the leader (though not a king) by NENNIUS, who describes the battle 'in which 960 enemy fell in a single attack by Arthur'. He is also named in the ANNALES CAMBRIAE and by GEOFFREY OF MONMOUTH, who regards Badon as identical with BATH. Described as a siege, it remains uncertain as to who was besieged by whom. The date is also unfixed, and is usually regarded as falling somewhere between AD 490 and 516. Various suggestions have been put forward for the location of the battle, including Bath, BADBURY HILL, BADBURY RINGS and LIDDINGTON CASTLE near Swindon, Wiltshire, though there is also a Badbury Castle on theMarlborough Downs, just to the south of Swindon, that might also be considered.

Bagdemagus

A cousin of ARTHUR, the king of GORE and one of the KNIGHTS OF THE ROUND TABLE. He appears to have been a benign character, but when TOR was made a Knight of the Round Table before him, he took umbrage. He was the father of MELEGAUNCE, whom he prevented from raping GUINEVERE when his son had carried her off. During the Quest for the Holy GRAIL he carried a special shield with a red cross on it that was intended for GALAHAD[1]. For this he was wounded by a white knight, and was eventually killed by GAWAIN[1].

Bagota

The giantess mother of GALEHAUT by BRUNOR.

Balan

The younger brother of BALIN. He had to assume the role of a knight he had slain, fighting all-comers in his place. In this capacity he was forced to fight his brother, though neither recognized the other, and during the combat each inflicted a mortal wound on the other.

Balar

Also BALOR

Known as 'Balar of the Dreadful Eye', Balar was a one-eyed giant who appears in Irish mythology and seems to be related to YSPADADDEN, the giant father of OLWEN in the MABINOGION story of CULHWCH AND OLWEN.

Balbhuaidh

The name under which GAWAIN[1] appears in Irish romances.

Baldulf

The brother of the SAXON leader COLGRIN. On his way to aid his brother during the siege of YORK, he was attacked and defeated by CADOR[2], but managed to sneak into York disguised as a minstrel. He was eventually killed at BADON.

Baldwin

A variation of BEDWIN who appears in SIR GAWAIN AND THE CARL OF CARLISLE.

Balin

The KNIGHT OF THE TWO SWORDS and brother of BALAN. Originating from NORTHUMBERLAND, he incurred ARTHUR's displeasure by killing a LADY OF THE LAKE, but he and his brother still became supporters of Arthur following their capture of RIENCE. He killed GARLON, the brother of PELLAM, who then tried to avenge his brother. Balin struck Pellam with the LANCE OF LONGINUS, a wound that was known as the DOLOROUS STROKE. Unwittingly he was challenged to combat by his brother, neither recognizing the other, and each received a mortal wound. Balin's name is thought to be a variant of BRULEN, who was, elsewhere, thought to have inflicted the DOLOROUS STROKE long before the traditional time ascribed to King Arthur.

Balor

A variant of BALAR.

Bamburgh

Situated on the NORTHUMBERLAND coast, this small town boasts a castle standing on a crag above the North Sea that was once the seat of the kings of Northumbria. It has been suggested that Bamburgh Castle is JOYOUS GARD, the castle of Sir LANCELOT[2] that was originally known as DOLOROUS GARD, and later reverted back to its former name. If Bamburgh Castle is Joyous Gard, then it was to this imposing structure that Lancelot brought GUINEVERE after he had rescued her from being burnt for adultery.

Ban

The King of GOMERET or BENWICK, but possibly best known simply as Ban of

BRITTANY, the father of Sir LANCELOT[2], brother of King BORS[1] of GAUL, and owner of the sword COURECHOUSE. He supported ARTHUR against the eleven rebellious leaders at the outset of the young king's reign, and in return Arthur aided him against his enemy, King CLAUDAS. When Claudas succeeded in destroying Ban's castle at TREBES, the king died of a broken heart. ELAINE[5] is usually named as Ban's wife, but the medieval French romance ROMAN DES FILS DU ROI CONSTANT names her as SABE, and gives him a daughter named LIBAN. He is most famous through his legitimate offspring, Lancelot, but he also had an illegitimate son named ECTOR DE MARIS, whose mother was the wife of AGRAVADAIN.

In origin it has been suggested that he was the god BRÂN, and that the name Ban de Benoic (Ban of Benwick) was simply a corruption of Bran le Benoit (Brân the Blessed). His name has also been connected with the Irish word for 'white', *bán*.

Bangon

A mysterious character who is named in some sources as being the ruler of AVALON.

Banin

One of the KNIGHTS OF THE ROUND TABLE and the godson of King BAN.

Baraton

In Arthurian romance Baraton is named as the king of RUSSIA.

Bardsey

Known as Ynys Enlli in Welsh, the small island of Bardsey lies just off the tip of the beautiful Lleyn Peninsula in GWYNEDD, at the northern entrance to Cardigan Bay. Now a bird sanctuary and observatory, the island was an important holy site to the Celts, who built a monastery there, now ruined, in the sixth century. The island became known as the Island of Twenty Thousand Saints. It is also one of the reputed sites where MERLIN is said to lie in an enchanted sleep, along with the golden throne of BRITAIN, awaiting the return of King ARTHUR.

Barinthus

A mysterious otherwordly sea deity. He was said to have been the ferryman for the final journey of the mortally wounded ARTHUR to AVALON, in the company of MERLIN and TALIESIN, to be cured of his deadly wound by the goddess MORGAN[1] Le Fay.

Baruc

In the LIVRE D'ARTUS, Baruc is simply named as a knight, while WOLFRAM VON ESCHENBACH, in PARZIVAL, names Baruc as the CALIPH OF BAGHDAD with whom GAHMURET took service. The title appears to come from the Hebrew personal name *Baruch*. The reference to the Caliph of Baghdad is an anachronism since the traditional Arthurian period predates Muhammad and the foundation of the Caliphate.

Bassus, River

According to the list given by NENNIUS, the unidentified site of one of ARTHUR's BATTLES.

Bataille Loquifer

Obscure medieval romance which contains a number of Arthurian references.

In this work CORBON is named as the son of RENOART and MORGAN[1] Le Fay, the latter being said to have a servant named KAPALU whose name no doubt derives from CAPALU, the Continental version of CATH PALUG.

Bath

One of the suggested sites of the decisive battle of BADON in which ARTHUR, assisted by his cousin HOEL[1], king of BRITTANY, finally defeated the pagan SAXONS. According to GEOFFREY OF MONMOUTH, the city was founded on the site of the healing waters by BLADUD, the magical son of King HUDIBRAS.

Batradz

The hero of the OSSETES, a SARMATIAN people who still inhabit the Caucasus today. The story of his death is remarkably similar to that of ARTHUR. Having received a mortal wound, Batradz instructed two of his companions to throw his sword into the water. Twice they pretended to have carried out the orders, but when they finally complied the waters turned blood-red and became very stormy. It has been suggested that this may have been the origin for the story of the returning of EXCALIBUR to the LADY OF THE LAKE. Sarmatian soldiers were known to have served in the Roman army in BRITAIN under Lucius Artorius Castus, so this is not wholly impossible.

Baudec

The realm of a king who was besieging Jerusalem, so the POPE sent RICHARD, son of the besieged king, to ARTHUR to ask for help.

Baudwin

The knight whom ARTHUR made a constable of his realm at the time of his accession. During Arthur's war with the ROMAN EMPIRE he was one of the governors of BRITAIN, later becoming a hermit and physician.

Bayeux

Town in Normandy that is famous for the Bayeux tapestry, depicting the Norman Conquest of BRITAIN. Arthurian sources name its founder as BEDIVERE[1], the father of PEDRAWD and grandfather of BEDIVERE[2], the companion of ARTHUR.

Bearosche

In WOLFRAM VON ESCHENBACH's PARZIVAL, the scene of a siege where its lord, Duke LYPPAUT, defended it against his sovereign, King MELJANZ of LIZ, who had declared war when the duke's daughter, OBIE, had rejected him. GAWAIN[1] fought on the side of Duke Lyppaut while PERCEVAL[2] fought on the side of King Meljanz. Peace was at last restored through the offices of OBILOT, the younger sister of Obie.

Beatrice

The wife of CARDUINO, who rescued her from an enchantment.

Beaumains

'Fair Hands', the impertinent nickname of GARETH, son of LOT and MORGAUSE, given to him by Sir KAY.

Beauté

The maid of GUINEVERE who fell in love with GLIGLOIS, Sir GAWAIN[1]'s squire.

Beautiful Pilgrim

The name by which ALICE, the wife of ALISANDER THE ORPHAN, became known.

Bedd Arthur

'Arthur's Grave' in the PRESELI HILLS, DYFED. Yet another of the many places where King ARTHUR is supposed to be buried, Bedd Arthur consists of twelve stones placed at regular intervals. However, there are references to an Arthur Petr who ruled Dyfed in the seventh century, so perhaps it was his grave.

The Preseli Hills can boast more Arthurian objects than any other region in BRITAIN for such a small area. Below Bedd Arthur is CARN ARTHUR, with a stone perched precariously on its top. It was allegedly thrown by Arthur from Dyffryn, a farm of that name being near the Gors Fawr circle. Alternatively, it is claimed that he threw it from Henry's Moat, about five miles away.

Bedd Taliesin

North-east of Talybont, on the slopes of Moel-y-Garn, DYFED, is a barrow that is reputed to contain the remains of the sixth-century bard TALIESIN. Many of the legends associated with this ancient poet are to be found in the MABINOGION. The barrow itself consists of a large stone slab and cairn. The other stones have been removed over the years.

In the nineteenth century an attempt was made to discover the bones of Taliesin and remove them for reburial in a more holy place. As the well-meaning diggers were at their work, a sudden terrible thunderstorm startled them. Lightning flashed and struck the ground near them with a loud crack. Fleeing for their lives, the men abandoned their tools and never returned to collect them, or to try again.

Bede, The Venerable

ANGLO-SAXON scholar, theologian and historian (c. AD 673–735). Born near Monkwearmouth, Durham, he was placed in the care of Benedict Biscop at the age of seven at the monastery of Wearmouth, and in 682 moved to the new monastery of Jarrow, NORTHUMBERLAND. He was ordained priest there in 703 and remained a monk for the rest of his life. He was a prolific writer, producing homilies, grammar and physical science, as well as commentaries on the Old and New Testaments. His greatest work was his Latin *Historia Ecclesiastica Gentis Anglorum* (*Ecclesiastical History of the English People*), which he completed in 731, and which remains the single most valuable source for early English history.

Bedegraine

A forest which was the site of a major battle between ARTHUR and the rebel forces of the eleven revolting leaders at the start of his reign. Sir Thomas MALORY identifies it with SHERWOOD FOREST, or a part of it. Within the forest lay the Castle of Bedegraine, which was loyal to ARTHUR, and to which the rebel forces had laid siege. One of the knights mentioned as having taken part in the battle was BRASTIAS.

Bedevere

A variant of BEDIVERE.

Bedivere

Also BEDEVERE, BEDWYR

1 The father of PEDRAWD, grandfather of BEDIVERE[2], and the founder of BAYEUX.

2 An important companion of ARTHUR, the grandson of BEDIVERE[1], founder of BAYEUX, and son of PEDRAWD. His son's name was AMREN and his daughter's ENEUAVC. He is mentioned in the earliest Welsh traditions as being one of Arthur's followers and, even though he is described as having only one hand, he helped Arthur to fight the giant of Mont SAINT MICHEL. GEOFFREY OF MONMOUTH makes him the Duke of NEUSTRIA, who perished during Arthur's campaign against the ROMAN EMPIRE. Sir Thomas MALORY, however, says he was present at Arthur's last battle at CAMLANN. He and Arthur alone survived the fight and he was charged with returning EXCALIBUR to the LADY OF THE LAKE.

Bedwin

Also BALDWIN

A bishop who appears under this name in the Welsh TRIADS as the chief bishop of KELLIWIG, while in SIR GAWAIN AND THE CARL OF CARLISLE he is named Baldwin, and made a companion of GAWAIN[1], also being mentioned by this name in the famous, anonymous poem SIR GAWAIN AND THE GREEN KNIGHT. Other sources name him as the father of ALISANDER THE ORPHAN by ANGLIDES, and state that he was murdered by King MARK[2].

Bedwyr

The original Welsh form of BEDIVERE[2]. Under this name he is mentioned as being among the party formed to help CULHWCH in his quest for OLWEN. The other members of this party were CEI (Sir KAY), CYNDDYLIG the Guide, GWRHYR the Interpreter, GWALCHMAI FAB GWYAR and MENW FAB TEIRGWAEDD. Each was chosen for their own specialist skills;

Bedwyr, even though he had only one hand (a characteristic that was carried over into the Arthurian legends when he became known as BEDIVERE[2]), was still faster with his sword than three others fighting together.

Beforet

According to WOLFRAM VON ESCHEN-BACH, the name of the domain over which IWERET was lord.

Bek, Anthony

It was said, according to the historian G. M. Cowling, that in 1282 Anthony Bek, at that time bishop-elect of Durham, met MERLIN while out hunting in the forest.

Bel

Also BELENOS, BELENUS

One of the most widespread Celtic gods, Bel represented the power of light, having many solar attributes. During the Roman period, in both BRITAIN and GAUL, Bel was identified with Apollo. It is thought that Bel became personified in the legendary early Briton BELI MAWR.

Bel Inconnu, Le

'The Fair Unknown', the name by which GUINGLAIN was known at ARTHUR's court, for he had arrived there ignorant of his own name. He was told of his parentage, GAWAIN[1] and RAGNELL, only when he went to the aid of BLONDE ESMERÉE.

Belagog

According to one tradition Belagog was a giant who guarded ARTHUR's castle, even though that castle was nothing more than a simple grotto (cf. GOGMAGOG).

Belaye

A princess of LIZABORYE who became LOHENGRIN's second wife.

Belcane

The queen of ZAZAMANC and mother of FEIREFIZ by GAHMURET.

Belenos, -us

A variant of BEL under which this god was known, mainly in the Alpine regions.

Beli (Mawr)

A legendary early Briton who is thought to have originated as a god, perhaps even BEL. His daughter, or maybe sister, was PENARDUN, who, by LLYR, was the mother of BRÂN, who was thought to be an ancestor of ARTHUR in both his paternal and his maternal pedigrees. According to HENRY OF HUNTINGDON, Beli was the brother of the first-century British king CUNOBELINUS or CYMBELINE. His name is also thought to have given rise to BELINANT, who features in the Arthurian legends as the father of DODINEL, as well as possibly being considered the etymological original of PELLINORE (Beli Mawr to Pellinore does not need too much imagination). Welsh legend makes him the father of AVALLOC, grandfather of MODRON, and Lord of the Celtic OTHERWORLD.

Belide

The daughter of King PHARAMOND' of FRANCE, who died of a broken heart when TRISTAN did not requite her love for him (cf. BELLICIES).

Belinant

The father of DODINEL whose name is thought to have derived from BELI.

Belinus

According to GEOFFREY OF MONMOUTH, the CITY OF THE LEGIONS, which in this case is taken to mean CAERLEON-ON-USK, was founded by a king named Belinus. His name perhaps derives from BEL or BELI.

Belisent

A sister to ARTHUR who, in the thirteenth-century English poem ARTHOUR AND MERLIN, married LOT. She may be cognate with both BLASINE and HERMESENT.

Bellangere

The son of ALISANDER THE ORPHAN. He was the earl of LAUNDES and the killer of King MARK[2] of CORNWALL.

Belleus

LANCELOT[2] made Belleus a KNIGHT OF THE ROUND TABLE following an unfortunate incident in which Lancelot came across Belleus's pavilion and went to bed there. When Belleus later entered the tent and climbed into the bed, he mistook the sleeping Lancelot for his lover and embraced him. In surprise and shock (and some would believe horror), Lancelot arose and wounded Belleus. When the circumstances had become apparent, Lancelot made Belleus a Knight of the Round Table to atone for the harm he had done.

Bellicies

The daughter of King PHARAMOND of GAUL, who, in Italian romance, fell in love with TRISTAN but, when her love went unrequited, she killed herself (cf. BELIDE).

Bendigeid Vran

Also BENDIGEIDFRAN, BRÂN THE BLESSED

The full name of the giant king, son of LLYR and brother of BRANWEN, more commonly referred to as Brân the Blessed, and whose story is told in the MABINOGION. He gave his sister Branwen to MATHOLWCH, king of IRELAND, together with a magic cauldron, but while Matholwch was in BRITAIN he was insulted by Bendigeid Vran's half-brother, EFNISIEN, so on his return to Ireland he treated Branwen badly.

Learning of his sister's suffering, Bendigeid Vran crossed from WALES to Ireland by walking on the seabed and, once there, he and his men totally exterminated the Irish population. Only seven of his men survived, and he had been mortally wounded in the foot with a poisoned dart. While away, CASWALLAWN, the son of BELI, disinherited MANAWYDDAN FAB LLYR, the brother and heir of Bendigeid Vran. The seven who survived were PRYDERI, Manawyddan fab Ilyr, GLIFIEU (GLUNEU EIL TARAN), TALIESIN, YNAWC (YNAWAG), GRUDYEN (GRUDDIEU) son of MURYEL and HEILYN son of GWYNN HEN. Bendigeid Vran ordered these seven to cut off his head and carry it to the WHITE MOUNT in London and there to bury it with the face towards FRANCE, to be a magical guardian over Britain. This they did, bringing Branwen home with them, but when she looked back towards Ireland and thought of the destruction that had been brought about for her sake, she died of a broken heart.

Bendigeidfran

A variant of BENDIGEID VRAN or BRÂN THE BLESSED.

Benwick

Literally the 'Kingdom of Ben' (BAN), the LESTOIRE DE MERLIN (a part of the mighty VULGATE VERSION) states that Benwick was to be identified with the town of Bourges. Sir Thomas MALORY states that Benwick should rather be identified with Bayonne or Beaune, while an association with Saumur has also been suggested.

Bercilak de Hautdesert

Alternative form of BERTILAK, the GREEN KNIGHT[1].

Bernard of Astolat

Father of the LADY OF SHALOTT, ELAINE[2] the White, and of LEVAINE.

Béroul

A twelfth-century French writer who was the author of an Anglo-Norman TRISTAN[2] romance. Very little can be said for certain about his life.

Berrant les Apres

One of the names suggested, along with AGUYSANS and MALEGINIS, for the KING WITH A HUNDRED KNIGHTS.

Bertholai

The champion of the False GUINEVERE and her partner in the deception that caused the real Guinevere, her half-sister, to go into hiding.

Bertilak

Also BERCILAK DE HAUTDESERT

The true name of the famous GREEN KNIGHT[1].

Bethides

The son of PERCEFOREST, who made an unfortunate marriage to the sorceress CIRCE.

Betis

According to the French romance PERCE-FOREST, ALEXANDER THE GREAT made Betis the king of England following the former's fictional conquest of BRITAIN. His brother, GADDIFER, was likewise made the king of SCOTLAND. Betis was quickly accepted by the populace, being renamed PERCE-FOREST after he had killed the magician DURMART.

Beund, Saint

A noteworthy saint in North WALES whose popularity survived the Reformation. Beund was said to be the grandson of King ARTHUR's sister ANNA through PERFERREN, her daughter.

Beuno

According to Welsh tradition, the off-spring of BUGI and PERFERREN, and thus the grandson of LOT. It would seem that this name is a simple derivation from, or a transcriptive error for, BEUND.

Biausdous

The son of GAWAIN[1] who managed to unsheath the sword HONOREE and by so doing win the hand of BIAUTEI, the daughter of the KING OF THE ISLES.

Biautei

The daughter of the KING OF THE ISLES whom BIAUSDOUS won the right to marry by drawing the sword HONOREE.

Birth of Arthur

A fourteenth-century Welsh work which gives unusual details about ARTHUR's lineage.

Bishop of the Butterfly

The name by which the historical bishop of WINCHESTER PETER DES ROCHES (1204–38) became known after he was given by ARTHUR the power of closing his hand and opening it again to reveal a butterfly. This gift was bestowed on him so people would believe that he had come across a house in which he found Arthur still alive.

Black Book of Carmarthen

A twelfth-century Welsh manuscript which contains Arthurian poems which is today housed in the National Library of WALES. Aberystwyth, along with the manuscripts · for the WHITE BOOK OF RHYDDERCH and the Book of Taliesin.

Black Knight

Common throughout Arthurian and medieval romance, the Black Knight was not always the villain of popular concep-tion. Five main Black Knights occur in the Arthurian legends, being:

1 The son of TOM A'LINCOLN and ANGLITORA, and thus ARTHUR's grandson.

2 Sir PERCARD, who was killed by GARETH.

3 A knight (true name unknown) with whose wife PERCEVAL[2] had innocently exchanged a ring. Furious, the Black Knight tied her to a tree, but Perceval overcame him and explained the situation. The Black Knight was then reconciled with his wife.

4 The son of the king of the CARLACHS and one of ARTHUR's knights, he was defeated by the KNIGHT OF THE LANTERN.

5 A warrior who guarded a wimple and a horn on an ivory lion. He was slain by FERGUS[2].

Blackbird of Cilgwri

A bird with whom GWRHYR conversed during the expedition mounted to help CULHWCH locate OLWEN. The bird directed them to the STAG OF RHEDYNFRC, who in turn passed them on to the EAGLE OF GWERNABWY, who took them to the SALMON OF LLYN LLW.

Bladud

The magical son of King HUDIBRAS who, according to GEOFFREY OF MONMOUTH, was directly descended from AENEAS and BRUTUS, an ancestor of ARTHUR, the founder of the hot springs and temple at BATH, and a great master of the Druidic arts, including necromancy and magical flight. This association possibly draws on Welsh or Breton bardic traditions. He is again mentioned in the VITA MERLINI as a guardian of therapeutic springs and wells. His story clearly derives from local Somerset folk tradition.

The story given by Geoffrey of Monmouth is that Bladud was sent by his father to Athens to study philosophy but while he was there his father died, so Bladud returned home, in AD 873, to claim the throne. He brought with him some of the learned Greeks he had met in Athens and with them founded a university at Stamford in Lincolnshire, which flourished until the coming of St Augustine, when Celtic learning was suppressed in favour of Catholic doctrines.

Skilled in magic, he conjured up the hot springs at Bath and built a temple to Minerva over them, and in this he placed devices he had invented for producing a perpetual flame. He also invented a means of flying with artificial wings, and on these he flew to London, but crashed on to the temple of Apollo (the present site of St Paul's cathedral) and was killed. He had reigned for twenty years and is credited with the founding of the city of Kaerbadus (Bath).

However, a legend that was current in the Somerset and Bath area from early times tells a slightly different version. This says that during his father's reign Bladud contracted leprosy and was banished from court. Prior to his banishment, he was given a ring by his mother, so that he would be recognizable to her again – a traditional token, found particularly in ballad literature. On his return from Greece following his father's death, he took up a lowly position tending a herd of swine, for no blemished king could rule. This job was said to have been at Swainswick ('swine's hollow') near Bath. While tending to the swine, he noticed that there was a favourite place in which they liked to wallow, and those with blemished skin were cured by the mud. He tried the same treatment and was cured, thus enabling him to ascend the throne. Over the spot where he was miraculously cured he built the city of Bath.

A lesser-known story concerning

Bladud and the therapeutic waters at Bath claims that these result from Bladud's experiments. Having acquired great scientific knowledge and skill from his time spend studying in Greece, he buried two tuns (a tun being a large cask capable of holding 252 gallons) containing burning brass, and two of glass, containing seven types of salt, brimstone and wild fire. These were placed over four springs, and by the 'fermentation of their contents' have caused 'that great heat which has continued for many years, and should last for ever'. Consequently, for a long time the waters were thought poisonous, and were not to be drunk, a habit that apparently did not form until the reign of King Charles II.

Blaes

Appearing in the TRIADS and possibly identical with BLAISE, the master of MERLIN, Blaes was the son of the Earl of LLYCHLYN and one of the TWENTY-FOUR KNIGHTS of ARTHUR's court.

Blaise

Hailing originally from Vercelli in Italy, Blaise was a hermit to whom MERLIN's mother was sent while she was pregnant. When the infant Merlin was just two years old he dedicated the story of the GRAIL to Blaise, who also wrote an account of ARTHUR's battles. It appears that he may be identical with the Welsh BLAES.

Blamore de Ganis

The son of LANCELOT[2], brother of BLEOBERIS and a KNIGHT OF THE ROUND TABLE, who on one occasion accused King ANGUISH of murder, only to be defeated in trial by combat by TRISTAN, after which they became firm friends.

When Lancelot quarrelled with ARTHUR, he and his brother supported their father, Blamore de Ganis being made the Duke of LIMOUSIN. Following Arthur's death he became a hermit.

Blanchard

The fairy horse that was given to LANVAL by his lover, TRYAMOUR.

Blanchefleur

1 The mistress of PERCEVAL[2] who was besieged by King CLAMADEUS, who desired her for himself. She would have killed herself had not Perceval defeated Clamadeus in single combat.
2 According to GOTTFRIED VON STRASSBURG, the sister of King MARK[2]. She eloped with RIVALIN[1] of PARMENIE, and their son was TRISTAN. Hearing of her husband's death, she died of a broken heart.

Blasine

A sister to ARTHUR who married NENTRES of GARLOT and became the mother, by him, of GALESCHIN, Duke of CLARENCE. It appears that she may be cognate with both BELISENT and HERMESENT.

Bleeding Lance

Another way of referring to the LANCE OF LONGINUS.

Blenzibly

In the Icelandic SAGA OF TRISTAN AND ISODD, Blenzibly is named as the mother of TRISTAN. Her lover, PLEGRUS, was killed while jousting with KALEGRAS, who afterwards became her paramour and the father of Tristan.

Bleoberis

The son of LANCELOT[2] (though some sources simply say that Lancelot was a relation), brother to BLAMORE DE GANIS, and a KNIGHT OF THE ROUND TABLE. When Lancelot quarrelled with ARTHUR, he and his brother supported their father. Bleoberis was made Duke of POITIERS and went on to join the Holy Crusades.

Bliocadran

The father of PERCEVAL[2], according to French romance.

Blodeu(w)edd

The flower-maiden (her name means 'Flower Face') of Welsh tradition who was created by MATH FAB MATHONWY and GWYDION FAB DÔN as a wife for LLEU LLAW GYFFES to circumvent the third curse by his mother, ARIANRHOD, that he would never have a wife. She was unfaithful to him with the hunter GRONW BEBYR, who contrived to kill her husband, though he only wounded him. Afterwards Lleu Llaw Gyffes killed Gronw Bebyr, and Blodeuwedd was changed into an owl by Gwydion fab Dôn. It is thought that she may have been the original of GUENDOLOENA, who in turn is considered by some to be the forerunner of GUINEVERE.

Bloie

The true name of the Lady of MALE-HAUT.

Blonde Esmerée

The daughter of the king of WALES. She was turned into a serpent by the magicians MABON[2] and EVRAIN, being freed from the enchantment only when GUINGLAIN kissed her.

Blunderboar

A giant who once managed to capture JACK THE GIANT-KILLER, but was killed, along with his brothers, when Jack managed to escape.

Boece, Hector

Scottish historian (c. 1465–1536), born in Dundee. He studied at Montaigu College, Paris, where c. 1492–98 he was regent, or professor of philosophy. Invited to preside over the new university of Aberdeen, Boece accepted the office and was at the same time made a canon of the cathedral. In 1522 he published, in Latin, his lives of the bishops of Mortlach and Aberdeen. His Latin SCOTORUM HISTORIA (History of Scotland) contains Arthurian information written from an anti-ARTHUR viewpoint. Published in 1527, it was deemed distinctly scholarly at the time, though it proved to contain a large amount of fiction.

Boiardo, Matteo Maria

Italian poet (1434–94), born in Scandiano, a village at the foot of the Lombard Apennines. He studied at Ferrara, and in 1462 married the daughter of the Count of Norellara. He lived at the court of Ferrara and was appointed governor of Modena in 1481, and of Reggio in 1487. His fame rests on his unfinished ORLANDO INNAMORATO (1486), a long narrative poem in which the Charlemagne romances are recast into ottava rima (Italian stanza of eight eleven-syllabled lines, ten-syllabled in English, the first six lines rhyming alternately, the last two forming a couplet). This poem was to inspire Ludovico ARIOSTO's

ORLANDO FURIOSO, the ROLAND epic that forms a continuation to Boiardo's unfinished work.

Bonedd yr Arwr

A Welsh manuscript that contains fascinating Arthurian genealogical material, making BRÂN an ancestor of ARTHUR in both the paternal and the maternal pedigrees. The paternal pedigrees may be found under LLYR.

Borre

The illegitimate son of ARTHUR by LIONORS who is usually identified with LOHOLT. When he came of age, he was made a KNIGHT OF THE ROUND TABLE.

Bors

1 The elder Bors, the king of GAUL or GANNES and an ally of ARTHUR in the battle against the eleven rebellious leaders at BEDEGRAINE. He married EVAINE and, by her, became the father of the younger BORS[2]. It is possible that this Bors should be identified with BAN.
2 The younger Bors, the son of EVAINE and the elder BORS[1], whom he succeeded as king of GANNES. A KNIGHT OF THE ROUND TABLE, he was chaste, but the daughter of King BRANDEGORIS fell in love with him. Her nurse, with the aid of an enchanted ring, forced Bors to make love to her. As a result he became the father of ELYAN THE WHITE, who later became emperor of CONSTANTINOPLE. During the Quest for the Holy GRAIL, Bors was one of the three knights who succeeded in their task. Unlike GALAHAD[1] and PERCEVAL[2], he returned to ARTHUR's court, eventually dying on a Crusade. In origin Bors might be cognate with the legendary Welsh character GWRI (cf. TWENTY-FOUR KNIGHTS).

Boscastle

Small Cornish village set in a glen whose narrow harbour is protected by cliffs on either side and was, in the imagination of Alfred, Lord Tennyson, the place from where the dying ARTHUR was borne away on the funeral barge to AVALON.

Bosherton Pools

Bosherton is a small village some six miles south of Pembroke in DYFED. Its beautiful freshwater lake is said to be one of the many reputed lakes from which ARTHUR obtained his sword, EXCALIBUR. Folklore also says that it was from this inlet that Arthur was carried away on his final journey to AVALON.

Boso

The ruler of Oxford and one of the vassals who accompanied ARTHUR on his campaign against the ROMAN EMPIRE.

Boudin

The brother of King MARK[2] of CORNWALL and father of ALISANDER THE ORPHAN, his son gaining his epithet after Mark had murdered him.

Boun, Rauf de

French chronicler and author of the PETIT BRUT.

Bourget, Lake

A lake in the French Alps near which ARTHUR was said to have killed a giant cat, a fact that is commemorated in local names such as MONT DU CHAT (Mountain of the Cat), DENT DU CHAT (Cat's Tooth) and COL DU CHAT (Cat's Neck). It is possible that this animal was a CAPALU, the Continental name for the CATH PALUG.

Brabant

Former duchy of Western Europe, comprising the Dutch province of North Brabant and the Belgian provinces of Brabant and Antwerp. They were divided when Belgium became independent in 1830. It was within this realm that ELSA of Brabant was besieged by Frederick de TELRAMUND and subsequently rescued by LOHENGRIN.

Bradmante

A female warrior of the Carolingian era (AD 751–987) who was told, according to ARIOSTO, that the House of ESTE would descend from her.

Brân (the Blessed)
Also BENDIGEID VRAN, BEDIGEIDFRAN

The son of LLYR and PENARDUN, a god-giant – god of fertility and patron of craftsmen – warrior, harpist and poet. A hero of both Irish and Welsh legend, his ranking among the gods was downgraded after the advent of Christianity. He appears to have lent much to the formation of the Arthurian tales. The story of his fateful expedition to IRELAND can be found under BENDIGEID VRAN.

He had a son named CARATACUS, who has been identified with the British leader of that name who opposed the Romans in AD 43 when CLAUDIUS landed his invasion forces. It has even been suggested, in direct contradiction to his own godly status, that the Brân himself introduced Christianity to BRITAIN.

He was said to own a magical cauldron that could restore to life any who were cast into it, and was once wounded in the foot by a poisoned spear. Connections here suggest that the cauldron was refined into the Holy GRAIL, and that the wound in the foot became the wound inflicted on the FISHER KING that could be cured only by asking the GRAIL QUESTION.

Traditionally, Brân, mortally wounded in the foot, requested of his seven companions, TALIESIN among them, that they cut off his head and bury it under the WHITE MOUNT in London, the face towards FRANCE, to serve as guardian to the country. ARTHUR was said to have later dug it up, for he alone wanted to be the sole guardian of Britain.

The genealogical material contained in BONEDD YR ARWR (Figure 5) makes Brân an ancestor of Arthur in both the paternal and the maternal pedigrees.

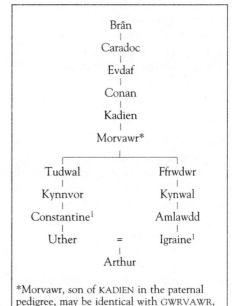

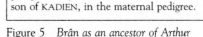

*Morvawr, son of KADIEN in the paternal pedigree, may be identical with GWRVAWR, son of KADIEN, in the maternal pedigree.

Figure 5 *Brân as an ancestor of Arthur*

Brandegoris

The king of STRANGGORE and one of the eleven kings or leaders who rebelled against the young ARTHUR at the start of his reign. His unnamed daughter became the mother of ELYAN THE WHITE by BORS[2]. Some commentators have argued that he originated from the god BRÂN, and that his name means 'Bran of Gore'.

Brandiles

The son of Sir GILBERT and a KNIGHT OF THE ROUND TABLE, he is to be found in the Second CONTINUATION to CHRÉTIEN DE TROYES's PERCEVAL and the GEST OF SIR GAUVAIN, in which he did combat with GAWAIN[1], who had defeated his father and his two brothers, as well as seducing his sister. The fight, however, was stopped, to be resumed later, but the two never crossed paths again. In the Second *Continuation*, the two did remeet, and during their second fight the ghostly image of Brandiles's sister was present, along with GUINGLAIN, her son by Gawain. It has been suggested that he is, at least in origin, identical with BRIAN DES ILES.

Brangaled

The owner of a drinking horn, CORN BRANGALED, that was numbered among the THIRTEEN TREASURES OF BRITAIN. This horn was said to be capable of providing any drink desired by its owner.

Brangien

According to GOTTFRIED VON STRASSBURG, Brangien was the exceptionally beautiful maidservant of ISEULT[1] who was given a love potion to administer to King MARK[2] and ISEULT[1]. Unfortunately, TRISTAN and Iseult drank the potion, thus expediting their famous affair. On her wedding night Iseult substituted Brangien for herself so that Mark would not guess that she had already lain with TRISTAN, and subsequently she tried to have Brangien murdered to ensure her silence. The attempt was unsuccessful, and Iseult later repented of it. Brangien had an affair with KAHEDRIN, the son of King HOEL[1] of BRITTANY.

Branwen

The unfortunate sister of BENDIGEID VRAN (BRÂN THE BLESSED) who was given to king MATHOLWCH of IRELAND. His mistreatment of her, following an insult by EFNISIEN, led to the laying waste of Ireland by Bendigeid Vran and his men, though only seven of those survived. Returning to BRITAIN with these seven, she looked back towards Ireland, and then around Britain, and died of a broken heart when she thought of the devastation that had been wreaked for her sake.

Bras-de-Fer

In his work LE TORNOIMENT DE L'ANTICHRIST, the French poet Huon de Mery tells how he went to an enchanted spring in BROCELIANDE and Bras-de-Fer, the chamberlain of the Antichrist, rode up. In his company they rode to the scene of a battle where the forces of Heaven, including ARTHUR and his knights, fought against the forces of Hell.

Brastias

Originally in the service of the duke of TINTAGEL (possibly GORLOIS), Brastias became one of ARTHUR's knights, fought against the rebellious leaders at BEDEGRAINE and was made a warden in the north of England.

Bredbeddle

In the story of KING ARTHUR AND THE KING OF CORNWALL, Bredbeddle was a knight who accompanied ARTHUR, TRISTAN and GAWAIN[1] to the king of Cornwall's residence. There, with the aid of a holy book, Bredbeddle controlled a fiend which the king of Cornwall had sent to spy on them.

Breguoin

The name given to Mount AGNED, according to one tenth-century manuscript.

Brent Knoll

A hill in Somerset, between Bridgwater and Weston-super-Mare, that was the site of a battle between YDER and three giants who lived there. Accompanying ARTHUR, Yder was sent on ahead and encountered the giants alone. By the time Arthur and his retinue arrived, Yder had dispatched the giants but had lost his own life in the fray.

Breta Sogur

A Scandinavian version of the works of GEOFFREY OF MONMOUTH that names ASSYSLA as the island on which ARTHUR died, thus making that island cognate with AVALON. This work is also unique in asserting that Arthur was buried at CANTERBURY.

Breunis Saunce Pyté

Originally knighted by ARTHUR, he seems to have had the ability to be in more than one place at a time. He turned against his original ally, and was eventually slain by GARETH.

Breunor

The brother of DINADAN, and generally known as Breunor the Black, he arrived at ARTHUR's court with such a badly tailored coat that the ever impertinent KAY gave him the nickname LA COTE MALE TAILÉE – 'the badly cut coat'. He refused to remove his coat until he had avenged his father. He helped the damsel MALEDISANT, who at first hurled abuse at him (presumably because of his coat), but eventually married him, after which he became the lord of PENDRAGON CASTLE.

Brian des Iles

Perhaps identical with BRANDILES in origin, and conceivably based on the historical Brian de Insula, the illegitimate son of Alan Fergeant (eleventh century). In PERLESVAUS, Brian des Iles, aided by KAY, who had killed ARTHUR's son LOHOLT, attacked Arthur's kingdom, laying siege to CARDUEIL but eventually being driven off by LANCELOT[2]. Subsequently he was defeated by Arthur, after which he became his seneschal (steward).

Briant of the Red Isle

The king who was the father of TRISTOUSE.

Brickus

According to WOLFRAM VON ESCHENBACH, the son of MAZADAN and thus grandfather of ARTHUR.

Brigantes

An ancient people of northern BRITAIN whose tutelary goddess was Briganti(a). CARATACUS, who was the king of the CATUVELLANI, was traditionally handed over to the Romans, with whom he was at war, by CARTIMANDUA, the queen of the Brigantes.

Brimesent

The wife of URIEN, according to the VULGATE *Merlin Continuation*.

Brisen

The maidservant of ELAINE[1] who administered an enchanted potion to LANCELOT[2] on the instructions of King PELLES. The effect of this potion, which Brisen managed to administer twice, was to cause Lancelot to think that Elaine was GUINEVERE. As a result he slept with Elaine and became the father, by her, of Sir GALAHAD[1].

Britain

The realm ruled over by ARTHUR which derives its name from the Priteni, the name the PICTS used for themselves. Even though the Roman province of Britain did not include SCOTLAND, excepting the Lowlands, Arthur, the legendary successor to the Romans, ruled the entire island.

In legend the island was first ruled over by a giant called ALBION, whose name was subsequently applied poetically to the island and whose career was outlined in Holinshed's CHRONICLES of 1577. Surprisingly, GEOFFREY OF MONMOUTH makes no mention of him, simply saying that giants predated men in Britain. He goes on to say that the island was subsequently colonized by BRUTUS, a descendant of the Graeco-Roman AENEAS, and the island maintained its independence until Roman times. The WHITE BOOK OF RHYDDERCH, which dates from the fourteenth century, contains a different version, saying that the country

was first called MERLIN'S PRECINCT, then the ISLE OF HONEY, and finally PRYDEIN (Britain) after its conquest by Prydein, the son of AEDD who may be cognate with the Irish sun god Aedh. Geoffrey of Monmouth makes no mention of this concept, but as it contradicts his own concept of Britain being derived from Brutus, this is not totally surprising. Other traditions say that Prydein came from CORNWALL and conquered Britain after the death of PORREX, the latter appearing in Geoffrey of Monmouth as one of the successors of Brutus. Irish tradition says that Britain was named after the son of NEMEDIUS, Britain, who settled on the island. Still others say that Britain simply derives from the Latin name for the island – Britannia.

There is no written history of Britain prior to the Roman occupation, archaeology perhaps being the best guide. JULIUS CAESAR made two exploratory expeditions to Britain, but it was not until the reign of CLAUDIUS that the Roman occupation began. Eventually Rome abandoned Britain and it was left to fend for itself against the PICTS from the north, the Irish from the west and the Angles, SAXONS and Jutes from the east.

Britomart

A warrior maiden, the daughter of RIENCE, who appears in SPENSER'S FAERIE QUEENE and married ARTEGALL. She takes her name from the Cretan goddess Britomartis, and was said to have killed RADIGUND, queen of the AMAZONS.

Brittany

A province of north-western FRANCE which, during the Arthurian period, was largely inhabited by an immigrant British population. According to GEOFFREY OF

MONMOUTH, the Breton royal family was very closely related to the British one, and the kingdom itself was formed when the Roman emperor MAXIMIANUS (ruled AD 383–88, and properly called MAXIMUS) bestowed the crown on CONAN MERIADOC, a nephew of Octavius, who is elsewhere called EVDAF, King of BRITAIN. When the British needed, and indeed wanted, a king, ALDROENUS, Conan Meriadoc's successor, gave them CONSTANTINE[1], his brother and ARTHUR's grandfather. In the Arthurian legends, HOEL[1] was the king of Brittany, and was Arthur's ally as well as a relation. This Hoel traditionally reigned from AD 510 to 545. Gallet names SOLOMON as the king of Brittany, and makes him the great-grandfather of Arthur.

Brobarz

According to WOLFRAM VON ESCHENBACH, the realm of Queen CONDWIRAMURS, who became the wife of PERCEVAL[2].

Broceliande

Situated in BRITTANY, and now called the Forest of Paimpont, this forest was the setting for a number of Arthurian adventures. One of the most potent stories concerning this forest is told by the French poet Huon de Mery in his work LE TORNOIMENT DE L'ANTICHRIST. In this he explains how he travelled to an enchanted spring in the forest and BRAS-DE-FER, the chamberlain of the Antichrist, rode up. In his company, Huon de Mery said, he rode to the scene of a battle where the forces of Heaven, including ARTHUR and his knights, were doing battle with the forces of Hell. The enchanted spring mentioned by Huon de Mery seems to bear close resemblance to the wondrous fountain within the forest that was said to have been guarded by ESCLADOS.

Brochmael

A legendary king who was said to have ruled the Welsh kingdom of POWYS at some stage during the traditional Arthurian period.

Bronllavyn Short Broad

The knife owned by OSLA BIG-KNIFE which was said to be capable of being used as a bridge. Its scabbard, however, proved the downfall of Osla Big-knife, for during the hunt for the boar TWRCH TRWYTH, it filled with water and dragged him under.

Bron(s)

Also HEBRON

The father of twelve sons by his wife ENYGEUS, the sister of JOSEPH OF ARIMATHEA, who gave him the Holy GRAIL. The DIDOT PERCEVAL says that Brons was the grandfather of PERCEVAL[2] and became the RICH FISHER, being carried off by angels when he had been cured of his affliction. In origin it is thought that he might have been the god BRÂN. ROBERT DE BORON specifically names Brons as the FISHER KING, and says that he gained this title as a result of supplying fish for Joseph of Arimathea.

Brulan

A variant of VARLAN, a king of GALES.

Brumart

A nephew of King CLAUDAS. He sat on the SIEGE PERILOUS but was destroyed for his boldness.

Brunissen

The wife of JAUFRÉ.

Brunor

Described as being one of the best knights of the OLD TABLE.

Brut

Usually said to have been written between 1189 and 1199, this ANGLO-SAXON alliterative-verse chronicle – a history of England which contains a great deal of Arthurian material – is a translation from French and amplification by LAYAMON of the slightly earlier ROMAN DE BRUT by the twelfth-century writer WACE. It is important in the history of English versification as the first poem written in Middle English.

Brut, Roman de

See ROMAN DE BRUT

Brut d'Angleterre

Alternative title for the work by WACE which is more commonly known as the ROMAN DE BRUT.

Bruto

Appearing as the hero of the Italian romance BRUTO DI BRETTAGNE, Bruto obtained a hawk, two small hounds or brachets and a scroll at ARTHUR's court to give to his lover.

Bruto di Brettagne

An Italian romance concerning BRUTO, who came to ARTHUR's court to obtain a hawk, two brachets and a scroll to give to his lover, who remains unnamed.

Brutus

The legendary founder of the British people, the great-grandson of the Trojan AENEAS, he traditionally conquered BRITAIN from the giants who founded London, naming it New Troy (TROYNO-VANT, TROIA NOVA or TRI-NOVANTUM).

Expelled from Italy for accidentally killing his father SILVIUS, Brutus first went to Greece, where he found a group of Trojan exiles who had been enslaved by King PANDRASUS, whom he fought and defeated. He claimed the reluctant hand of Pandrasus's daughter IGNOGE and compelled Pandrasus not only to release his Trojan prisoners but also to supply them with ships, provisions and bullion. So equipped, Brutus and the Trojans sailed west and on an island, described as being west of the Pillars of Hercules, he discovered another group of Trojans under the leadership of CORINEUS. They joined forces and, after a brief spell in Aquitaine, they landed at TOTNES, Devon, where they were attacked by the giants under the leadership of GOGMAGOG, whom Corineus defeated in single combat at Plymouth. Brutus proceeded to the banks of the Thames, where he founded his capital and was eventually buried.

His story is told by GEOFFREY OF MONMOUTH, who makes him the traditional founder of the British people, the progenitor of a line of kings and the eponym of Britain, even though it seems more likely that Britain is a corruption of Priteni, the name the PICTS used for themselves.

Bruyant

Known as 'the Faithless', he was responsible for killing ESTONNE (a minor character in PERCEFOREST), LORD OF THE SCOTTISH WILDERNESS. Estonne's son,

PASSALEON, an ancestor of MERLIN, later avenged his father's death.

Brychan

An early legendary king who is considered to have been the father of as many as sixty-three saints, Saint GWLADYS among them. He was also said to have been the grandfather of URIEN of RHEGED, by way of his daughter NEFYN.

Bryn Myrddin

A hill near CARMARTHEN, more popularly known as MERLIN'S HILL, a cave in which is said to be one of the many possible locations for the last resting place of the great wizard.

Budic(ius)

According to GEOFFREY OF MONMOUTH, the name of two early kings of BRITTANY. One was responsible for raising the exiled AMBROSIUS AURELIUS and UTHER, while the other married ANNA, ARTHUR's sister, and was the father of HOEL[1], Arthur's ally. It would seem that Budicius may be identifiable with King Budic I of Cornouaille, who traditionally reigned, in Brittany, some time prior to AD 530.

Bugi

The husband of PERFERREN, ARTHUR's niece.

Bulgaria

Though the country of Bulgaria had not come into existence during the traditional Arthurian period, tradition and romance gave this country kings named NETOR and MADAN. Many such anachronisms exist throughout the confused web woven around the Arthurian tales.

Burletta della Diserta

The abductor of MORGAN[1] Le Fay's daughter PULZELLA GAIA. She was rescued from him by LANCELOT[2].

Bury Walls

Located in Shropshire, local legends hold that this is where ARTHUR held his court.

Bwlch-y-Groes

A pass through the mountains on the highest road in North WALES, along which ARTHUR travelled on his way to visit MERLIN (MYRDDIN). *En route* he met a giant named RHITTA, who had a passion for collecting the beards from the men he had killed and had decided that Arthur's beard would make a fine collar for his cloak, which he had made from these beards. However, all did not go according to the giant's plans, and Arthur killed him, throwing his body down the hillside to where he was buried. A path leads down the hill to Tan-y-Bwlch, which is known as RHIW BARFE – 'The Way of the Bearded One'. The giant's grave consists of a long, narrow trench surrounded by large boulders. The alternative site for this battle, and for the giant's grave, is YR WYDDFA FAWR (Mount SNOWDON).

Bwlch-y-Saethu

According to Welsh legend, ARTHUR was killed by a flurry of arrows at this pass in Snowdonia, North WALES, where he had pursued his enemies following a battle at TREGALEN. When he fell, his men went to a cave called OGOF LANCIAU ERYRI to wait until he came back. A shepherd was once thought to have found the cave and seen the waiting warriors there. Over the years they seemed to have kept up with the times, for the shepherd reported they were armed with guns!

Bwrdd Arthur

ARTHUR'S TABLE, the name of two promi-nent features in Clwyd, WALES. One is a circle of twenty-four indentations in a rock (cf. TWENTY-FOUR KNIGHTS) which is said to represent ARTHUR's knights at a table. The other feature is a barrow at Llanfair Dyffryn Ceiriog.

Byanor

In the seventeenth-century unpublished poem THE FAERIE KING by Samuel Sheppard, Byanor is named as having received a sword that formerly belonged to King ARTHUR.

Byzantium

The original name of CONSTANTINOPLE.

Cabal

ARTHUR's hound. NENNIUS says that while Arthur was pursuing the boar TROYNT, Cabal's footprint was left on a stone over which Arthur erected a cairn, which has become known as CARN CABAL. Another story has Cabal participating in the hunt for the boar YSGITHYRWYN.

Cadair, neu car Morgan Mwynfawr

The chair or car of MORGAN MWYNFAWR which is numbered among the THIRTEEN TREASURES of BRITAIN, and which had the power to carry a person seated in it anywhere they desired to go.

Cadbury Castle

A site in Somerset, midway between Yeovil and Wincanton, that is considered as one of the many possible locations of ARTHUR's capital, CAMELOT. The popular tradition that Cadbury Castle was the site of Camelot seems to date from the sixteenth century, though it could quite possibly, and in all probability does, predate that time. Archaeological excavations have revealed there was a fortified leader's dwelling at Cadbury Castle during the traditional Arthurian period. Many other places have been suggested as the site of Camelot, such as WINCHESTER, COLCHESTER and CAERLEON-ON-USK, but Cadbury Castle still remains the favourite option for many people.

A lesser-known theory puts forward Cadbury Castle not as Camelot, but instead as one of the many possible locations for the last resting place of Arthur – that magical realm known as AVALON.

Cadbury Hill

A hill near Nailsea, Avon, that is the site of a cave from which, so local legend holds, King ARTHUR and his knights will one day ride forth.

Cadell

A legendary king of the Welsh kingdom of POWYS who was said to have ruled at some time during the traditional Arthurian period.

Cado

Possibly identical with CADWY, the son of GEREINT, Cado appears in the medieval LIFE OF SAINT CARANNOG, where he is said to have co-ruled in the West Country alongside King ARTHUR. It seems more likely, however, that Cado is a simple corruption of CADOR[1], who is described as being either the ruler or the duke of CORNWALL.

Cadoc, Saint

A Welsh saint who was said to be the son of King GWYNNLYM of Glamorgan and Saint GWLADYS of Brecon. In the LIFE OF SAINT CADOC, ARTHUR is said to have demanded that Cadoc hand over to him a man named LIGESSAC who had sought and found sanctuary with Cadoc for ten years, after the killing of some of Arthur's followers. To settle the matter, Arthur was offered 100 kine (cattle) as compensation, which he demanded should be red before and white behind. With the help of God, Cadoc produced the required cattle, but they turned into bundles of fern the instant Arthur's men seized them.

Cadog

A knight who numbered among the TWENTY-FOUR KNIGHTS of King ARTHUR's court.

Cador

1 Possibly to be identified with CADWY, the son of GEREINT, and identical to CADO, Cador was the ruler of CORNWALL, being variously described as a king or a duke. He was an ally of ARTHUR, whom he helped in his battles against the SAXONS, defeating BALDULF and CHELDRIC. His son CONSTANTINE[2] was handed the crown by King Arthur following the king's final battle, this event reputedly occurring in the year AD 542. A Cador, the son of the king of Cornwall, brother of GUIGNIER and friend of CARADOC BRIEFBRAS, may be the same character, or even the son of this Cador. Some sources say that this Cador was the guardian of GUINEVERE prior to her marriage to Arthur.

2 A king of NORTHUMBERLAND who later became the father-in-law of Sir KAY.

Cadwallad(e)r

Historical seventh-century Welsh hero, the son of CADWALLON, king of GWYNEDD. He defeated and killed Eadwine of Northumbria in AD 633, but, approximately one year later, was himself killed in battle. He features in the ARMES PRYDEIN, which foretells that Cadwallad will rise and lead an army to drive the SAXONS into the sea.

Cadwallon
Also CATWALLAUN

According to GEOFFREY OF MONMOUTH, Cadwallon was the father of CADWALLADER and king of the VENDOTI, who lived in North WALES.

Cadwy

The son of GEREINT who was, according to a part of the MABINOGION known as the DREAM OF RHONABWY, a contemporary of ARTHUR. It would appear that he was the original for both CADOR and CADO, though the latter is possibly a second-generation derivative.

Caelia

The fairy queen who bore the FAERIE KNIGHT to TOM A'LINCOLN, the illegitimate son of ARTHUR, and eventually drowned herself.

Caer Feddwid(d)
Also CAER RIGOR, CAER SIDDI

The Fort of CAROUSAL, which is located in the Welsh OTHERWORLD realm of ANNWFN and which contains a fountain that runs with wine. No one who resides there ever knows sickness or old age. On one occasion the fort was visited by King ARTHUR and his retinue.

Caer Gai

According to bardic tradition, Caer Gai is the place in Merioneth where ARTHUR was raised.

Caer Rigor

Also CAER FEDDWID(D), CAER SIDDI

A variant of Caer Feddwidd, which is also known as Caer Siddi, or the Fort of CAROUSAL. Though Welsh tradition states that Caer Feddwidd contains a fountain that runs with wine, and no one there knows old age, this variant would seem to suggest a realm of the dead from which there is no return.

Caer Siddi

Also CAER FEDDWID(D), CAER RIGOR

The OTHERWORLD Fort of CAROUSAL, where a fountain runs with wine and no one ever knows illness or old age. Welsh tradition makes ARIANRHOD the ruler of Caer Siddi, though Arthurian legend does not seem to mention the name of the ruler on the occasion when ARTHUR and his men visited the mysterious fort.

Caer Wydyr

A glass fort located in the Welsh OTHER-WORLD realm of ANNWFN. When it was visited by ARTHUR and his men, they were unable to make its watchman talk to them.

Caerlaverlock

'Fort Lark', the important harbour over whose ownership it is thought the battle of ARTHURET was fought.

Caerleon-on-Usk

Located on the River Usk in GWENT, the site of a Roman fort and amphitheatre, Caerleon was one of the most important cities within the realm of King ARTHUR. GEOFFREY OF MONMOUTH claims that it was called the CITY OF THE LEGION, was founded by King BELINUS (perhaps BELI), and had DUBRICIUS as the archbishop. If Caerleon is the City of the Legion, then it was here that Arthur held his plenary court at Whitsun, attended by representatives from all of Europe. Various sources name Caerleon as CAMELOT and the city where the KNIGHTS OF THE ROUND TABLE were first established.

Cai

A variant of KAY.

Caithréim Conghail Cláiringnigh

An Irish romance that names ART AOINFHEAR as a son of King ARTHUR, though other Irish sources make him the son of King Conn of the Hundred Battles.

Caladbolg

Derived from *calad* – 'hard' – and *bolg* – 'lightning' – this magical sword, borne by such Irish heroes as Cú Chulainn, has been linguistically linked with CALAD-VWLCH, the name given to EXCALIBUR in the MABINOGION story of CULHWCH AND OLWEN.

Caladvwlch

The name given to EXCALIBUR in the MABINOGION story of CULHWCH AND OLWEN. It has been linguistically linked with the Irish magical sword CALADBOLG.

Caledon Wood

The site of a battle fought against the SAXONS and won by King ARTHUR and his ally HOEL[1], being located either in the Scottish Caledonian Forest (CELYDDON or SILVA CALEDONIAE), or in CELIDON WOOD near LINCOLN.

Caliburnus

The name of one of King ARTHUR'S swords, though GEOFFREY OF MONMOUTH specifically uses this name to refer to EXCALIBUR.

Calin

According to LAYAMON, this FRISIAN king was subject to ARTHUR.

Calinan

The son of GUIRON by his lover BLOIE.

Caliph of Baghdad

WOLFRAM VON ESCHENBACH, in PARZIVAL, specifically mentions that BARUC was the Caliph of Baghdad, though the reference to the Caliphate is an anachronism, since the traditional Arthurian period predates Muhammad and the foundation of the Caliphate.

Callington

One of the places that has been connected with KELLIWIC, the Cornish stronghold of ARTHUR. Some commentators have even tried to connect Kelliwic with CAMELOT, so Callington could also be so identified by connection.

Cam

A Somerset river that flows in the vicinity of CADBURY CASTLE. A nearby field, called WESTWOODS, has revealed a large number of skeletons that bear grim witness to a battle fought on that site, leading some to suggest that this is the site of ARTHUR'S final battle of CAMLANN. Other commentators have, however, identified this as the River Cam upon which CAMBRIDGE is situated, and this has subsequently led to the identification of that city with Camlann.

Camaalis

The pagan king who, according to the Arthurian romances, was the eponym of CAMELOT.

Camal

A suitor of HERMONDINE, who was killed by MELIADOR.

Cambenet

The Duke of Cambenet, EUSTACE, is numbered among the eleven leaders who rebelled against the youthful King ARTHUR at the outset of his reign.

Camboglanna

A Roman fort on Hadrian's Wall at Birdoswald that has been put forward as a possible site for the battle of CAMLANN. Presumably it was in the north-western British kingdom of RHEGED at the time of the battle, so the siting of Camlann here would owe much to the associations between ARTHUR and URIEN.

Cambridge

A university city in the east of England which was alleged to have received its charter from ARTHUR, at least according to Prior Nicholas Cantelupe, who died in 1441. Elizabethan tradition held that the university had been founded in Anno Mundi 3588 (since the creation of the world) by the Spanish Prince Cantaber. An obscure local tradition even said that Cambridge was the site of Arthur's final battle of CAMLANN, though this would seem to stem from false etymology, and it could be said that any place-name having 'Cam' in it might be considered a worthy contender.

Camel

A Cornish river whose banks have been considered one of the many possible sites for the battle of CAMLANN. The river runs through the town of CAMELFORD, which is another possible site.

Camelford

A small town in north CORNWALL through which the River CAMEL runs, and which is given as yet another of the many possible sites for ARTHUR's final battle at CAMLANN.

Cameliard

The kingdom of LEODEGRANCE, GUINE-VERE's father. Various locations for the realm have been suggested, from SCOT-LAND to the south-west of England, possibly having some association with the north Cornish town of CAMELFORD. One of its most important cities is named as CAROLHAÏSE.

Camelot

The name given to the place where ARTHUR had his main residence and held his court. Many places have been suggested for its location, which still remains a mystery. Among these are WINCHESTER, CAERLEON-ON-USK, COLCHESTER and, most commonly and popularly, CADBURY CASTLE in Somerset.

According to the romances, Camelot was named after a pagan king CAMAALIS and, at the time when JOSEPH OF ARIMA-THEA landed in BRITAIN, when AGRESTES was its king, it is cited as being the most important city in the country. Seemingly, Agrestes embraced Christianity but, after Joseph of Arimathea had left, he persecuted the Christians until he was sent mad by God. As such, the city of Camelot is first mentioned by CHRÉTIEN DE TROYES in *Lancelot*, while Sir Thomas MALORY, who identifies it with WINCHESTER, says that the name of its chief church was St Stephen's.

Camille

A sorceress of SAXON ancestry who captured ARTHUR, who had become enamoured with her. LANCELOT[2] rescued him, after which Camille committed suicide.

Camlan(n)

The site of the third and last battle between ARTHUR and his usurping nephew MORDRED, who was killed, and Arthur was also mortally wounded. Both the date and location of the battle have caused considerable speculation. The ANNALES CAMBRIAE state quite clearly that the battle took place twenty-one years after BADON, but, as the date of that battle is also a mystery, this simply serves to confuse matters even further, leading to possible dates ranging from AD 515 to 539, GEOFFREY OF MONMOUTH, however, gives a date of AD 542, while the Irish ANNALS OF TIGERNACH date it to AD 541, and the Spanish ANNALES TOLEDANOS date it as late as AD 580. As to the site, there are many locations to choose from. Sir Thomas MALORY favours SALISBURY PLAIN, while SLAUGHTERBRIDGE on the River CAMEL in CORNWALL is a much-favoured and traditional site. The DIDOT PERCEVAL places it even further afield, this time in IRELAND, and even CAMBRIDGE has been suggested. Another suggested site, much favoured in Cumbria and the surrounding regions, is the Roman fort of CAMBOGLANNA on Hadrian's Wall.

Accounts of the battle, regardless of when and where it occurred, also vary. Sir Thomas Malory states that only Arthur, BEDIVERE[2] and, for a very brief time, LUCAN survived. Welsh traditions usually speak of seven survivors, although CULHWCH AND OLWEN refers to any number of other survivors, including SANDAV, who was so beautiful that all mistook him for an angel, and MORFRAN, who was so hideous that he was mistaken for a devil. Other survivors, mentioned in other sources, include Saint DERFEL and Saint PETROC.

Canan

The grandfather of EREC and father of LAC.

Candaces

The son of King APOLLO of LIONES, who, during his lifetime, saw the unification of Liones and CORNWALL.

Cano

An historical character who died in AD 688 and whose story is, together with those of DERDRIU and GRÁINNE, thought to have been one of the major sources of the TRISTAN story.

The son of the Scottish king GARTNÁN, he was exiled to IRELAND, where he was entertained by the elderly MARCÁN (Little Mark) and his beautiful young wife, CRÉD, the daughter of King GUAIRE of Connacht. She had fallen in love with Cano even before she set eyes on him and, at a banquet, she drugged everyone and begged Cano to become her lover. He refused to do this while in exile, but pledged that once recalled from exile the two would become lovers, and gave her a stone which embodied his life as a token. In due course Cano was recalled to SCOTLAND, where he became king. Each year thereafter he and Créd attempted to meet each other at Ibner Colptha (the Boyne estuary), but their plans were always thwarted by Créd's stepson, COLCU, and a guard of 100 warriors. Finally, the lovers arranged to meet at Lough Créde in the north, but, as they drew near to each other, Colcu once again appeared and drove Cano away. In her grief, Créd killed herself by dashing her head against a rock. In falling to the ground, she dropped the stone that Cano had given her and it smashed into tiny pieces. Three days later Cano died.

Canor

A king of CORNWALL who was aided in his battle by GONOSOR, an Irish king.

Canterbury

A cathedral city in KENT which was called Durovernum by the Romans, and was the SAXON capital of Kent. In the Arthurian romances, the archbishop of Canterbury was one of ARTHUR's advisers, though this is an anachronism as the archiepiscopal see was not founded until AD 597. The archbishop was said to have been present at Arthur's final battle and to have survived it, only to be subsequently murdered by King MARK[2] of CORNWALL. The Scandinavian BRETA SOGUR states that Arthur was buried at Canterbury, though this assertion is not found in any other Arthurian work.

Canvel

The capital of PARMENIE, according to GOTTFRIED VON STRASSBURG.

Capalu

The name for the CATH PALUG in French romance.

Caradoc

The king of VANNES AND NANTES who married the niece of ARTHUR, the unfaithful YSAIVE, who, through one extramarital encounter with the wizard ELIAVRES, became the mother of CARADOC BRIEFBRAS.

Caradoc Briefbras

In Welsh tradition the son of LLYR MARINI, husband of TEGAU EUFRON, father of MEURIC, and owner of the horse LLUAGOR. The legendary ancestor of the ruling house of MORGANNWG, it is thought that he may have founded the kingdom of GWENT during the fifth century. The romances made him the son of the philandering wife of King CARADOC of VANNES AND NANTES, the result of her affair with the wizard ELIAVRES. His epithet *briefbras* (short arm) appears to be a false translation of his Welsh epithet *vreichvras* (strong armed). Caradoc Briefbras once confronted Eliavres about his parentage and, when he did, his parents caused a serpent to twine itself around his arm. It took the combined efforts of his wife,

GUIGNIER, and her brother, CADOR[1], to get rid of it. The fidelity of Guignier was proved to Caradoc Briefbras on the occasion when King MANGOUN of MORAINE sent him a horn from which to drink, such a drink being said to expose any infidelity on the part of the wife of him that drank from it.

Carados

Identified by some with the SAXON leader CERDIC, and also sometimes known as the king of Carados, which might indicate that Carados was his realm rather than his name. He was one of the eleven rulers who rebelled against ARTHUR at the start of his reign.

Carados of the Dolorous Tower

The son of a sorceress and brother of Sir TURQUINE, he took GAWAIN[1] captive and threw him into a dungeon. LANCELOT[2] cut off his head with the only sword that could kill him – though we are not told what special properties the sword possessed – and so released Gawain and the other prisoners held in the dungeons.

Carannog, Saint
Also CARANTOC

Of Welsh origin, Carannog had a remarkable altar that had been sent from heaven. Coming to Somerset from WALES, the altar fell into the sea, so Carannog came to ARTHUR to ask if it had been found. Arthur already had the altar in his possession, but would not return it until Carannog had performed a great deed for him, the capture of a violent serpent that lived on Ker Moor. Undaunted by this mammoth task, Carannog placed his stole around the serpent's neck and pacified it. Having then ordered it to do no more harm, the saint let it go again, and Arthur duly returned the altar. Carannog then built a chapel for the altar which, so John Leland (chaplain to King Henry VIII) tells us, was at Carhampton, a short distance from Blue Anchor Bay, between Minehead and Watchet, though the church there today is not dedicated to the saint.

Carantoc

A variant of CARANNOG.

Caratacus

The King of the CATUVELLANI, a tribe of Britons who lived near what is now known as St Albans at the time of the Roman invasion in AD 43. His historicity is unquestioned. Having led a hard-fought campaign against the Roman invaders, he was handed over to his enemy by CARTIMANDUA, Queen of the BRIGANTES, but was pardoned by the Emperor CLAUDIUS. It has been suggested that his story became legendary and that he should be considered as the original King ARTHUR. However, other commentators say that Caratacus should be regarded as identical with ARVIRAGUS, or with his cousin.

Carbonek
Also CORBENIC

The GRAIL CASTLE. Within its walls was the PALACE ADVENTUROUS, and within that palace was the Holy GRAIL itself.

Cardueil

Described as being one of King ARTHUR's palaces, or residences, it has been identified by some as CARLISLE.

Carduino

The son of DONDINELLO, he was raised in secret after his father had been poisoned. When grown up he travelled to ARTHUR's court, from where he embarked on a quest to aid Queen BEATRICE, who, along with all her subjects, had fallen under the enchantment of a wizard and been turned into animals. Carduino killed the wizard and, having restored Beatrice to her former shape with a kiss, married her.

Carhules

A building near Castle DORE in CORNWALL that appears to have been named after a person called GOURLES, who was perhaps the original of GORLOIS.

Cariado

Appearing in the romance TRISTAN[1], Cariado fell in love with ISEULT[1] and told her that her lover, TRISTAN, had married ISEULT[2] of the White Hands.

Carl of Carlisle

A giant because of a spell, he once welcomed and entertained GAWAIN[1], KAY and BALDWIN. At his own request, Gawain broke the spell by cutting off the giant's head, and Carl was restored to his former size. Gawain subsequently married his daughter, and King ARTHUR knighted Carl, making him a KNIGHT OF THE ROUND TABLE and the Lord of Carlisle, hence his epithet, though some say he took the name Carl only after he had become Lord of Carlisle.

Carl of Carlisle, The

Incomplete sixteenth-century English romance that is based on the earlier fourteenth-century English SIR GAWAIN

AND THE CARL OF CARLISLE, which is also unfinished. It has been suggested that this work remains incomplete since it simply echoes the state of the earlier work on which it is based.

Carlachs

The name of either a nation or a race of people. Appearing in Irish romance, the BLACK KNIGHT[4], son of the king of Carlachs, killed the KNIGHT OF THE LANTERN, having been accepted as one of ARTHUR's knights.

Carlisle

Cumbrian city situated at the western end of Hadrian's Wall on the River EDEN. Originally called Luguvalium by the Romans, during whose occupation it was a prosperous settlement, it was later raided successively by PICTS, Vikings and Scots. CHRÉTIEN DE TROYES makes Carlisle the seat of ARTHUR's court, but this connection is not made by GEOFFREY OF MONMOUTH, WACE or LAYAMON. Later writers mainly connect GAWAIN[1] with Carlisle, especially in respect of the beheading, at his own request, of the CARL OF CARLISLE.

Carmarthen

A town in DYFED that can rightly claim to be one of the oldest in WALES, it probably began life as a Celtic hillfort that was obliterated by the Romans, who built a wooden fort on its site in AD 75. This was the most westerly of their large forts, but few traces remain. However, the discovery of an amphitheatre with a seating capacity of 500 would seem to suggest that the garrison at Carmarthen was not insignificant.

Connection to the Arthurian legend comes through MERLIN, or MYRDDIN as he is known in Welsh, the town actually being known, in Welsh, as Caerfyrddin – 'the city of Merlin'. Some suggest that Merlin took his name from the town that was his birthplace, and others say that the town was named after him. Whichever is the truth, the town certainly has many connections with the wizard and his prophecies. Possibly best known is the PRIORY OAK, or MERLIN'S TREE. Legend says that Merlin prophesied that the town would fall if this particular tree fell. Its remains now stand in the foyer of St Peter's Civic Hall, as the tree was removed in 1978 by the local authority from its site in the town, as, consisting mainly of concrete and iron bars, it constituted a traffic hazard. Carmarthen, however, is still there, awaiting Merlin's prophecy.

Carn Arthur

Situated in the PRESELI HILLS, DYFED, below BEDD ARTHUR, is Carn Arthur, which has a stone perched precariously on its top. It was allegedly thrown by ARTHUR from Dyffryn, or from Henry's Moat, which lies about five miles distant.

Carn Cabal

A large heap of stones near Carngafallt, Powys, one of which is supposed to bear the impression of a hound's foot. This hound, so legend says, was owned by King ARTHUR and was called CABAL. Arthur himself is said to have gathered together this heap of stones, placing the magic stone with the paw print on the top. Anyone who takes this stone away cannot keep it, for it will always return itself to the pile.

Carned(d) Arthur

A cairn in Snowdonia which local Welsh folklore states is the burial site of ARTHUR.

Carnedd y Cawr

'The Giant's Carn'. An alternative name for YR WYDDFA FAWR or, more commonly, Mount SNOWDON.

Carnwennan

The name of King ARTHUR's dagger.

Carolhaise

One of the most important cities that lay within CAMELIARD, the realm of King LEODEGRANCE.

Carousal, Fort of

The literal translation of the OTHER-WORLD citadel of CAER FEDDWIDD.

Carras

The brother of King CLAUDAS and himself the king of RECESSE, he waged a bitter war against King ARTHUR until, finally, he was persuaded by GAWAIN[1] to stop and sue for peace.

Carreg Coetan Arthur

Near Newport, GWENT, this cromlech is also known as ARTHUR'S QUOIT, supposedly one of the many thrown by King ARTHUR. Where this quoit was thrown from, however, remains a mystery.

Car(r)idwen

A variant of CERRIDWEN.

Cartimandua

The queen of the BRIGANTES who handed CARATACUS, king of the CATUVELLANI, over to his enemies, the Romans.

Carvilia

A daughter of the sorceress MORGAN[1] Le Fay who appears in the works of the Italian poet Torquato Tasso (1544–95).

Castellors

According to the genealogies of JOHN OF GLASTONBURY, Castellors was the son of AMINABAD and an ancestor of King ARTHUR.

Castle-an-Dinas

Situated near St Columb in CORNWALL, the largest Celtic hillfort in that county and a seat of Cornish kings after ARTHUR's time, it became associated in Cornish tradition with King Arthur himself, some sources even naming it as CAMELOT.

Castle Eden

A village located in County Durham that is said to be haunted by the spirits of King ARTHUR's knights, who appear in the guise of chickens. It was also once thought that King Arthur's hall originally stood in the village.

Castle Key

According to the medieval *History of Fulk Fitzwarin*, this earthwork in Shropshire (modern Caynham Camp) was allegedly built by Sir KAY.

Castle of Maidens

GEOFFREY OF MONMOUTH says that EBRAUCUS, king of BRITAIN, founded this castle, which was originally known as the Castle of Mount AGNED. It may have been identified with EDINBURGH, which in the Middle Ages was known as Castellum (or Castra) Puellarum, though some of the tales associated with it put it in the vicinity of Gloucester. Ruled by Duke LIANOUR, it was said to contain young women, though why is not clear. Some think that they were prisoners. Seven unnamed brothers subsequently killed Lianour and took over the castle, but they were defeated by three of ARTHUR's knights, after which the daughter of Duke Lianour took charge.

Castle Rushden

A castle on the Isle of MAN beneath which, in some caves, MERLIN was said to have imprisoned a number of giants he had defeated.

Castleford

Called Legiolium by the Romans, this town in West Yorkshire has been identified by some with the CITY OF THE LEGION.

Castris

According to WOLFRAM VON ESCHENBACH, Castris was the first husband of HERZELOYDE, from whom she inherited NORTHGALIS and WALES. Following his death, Herzeloyde married GAHMURET, by whom she became the mother of PERCEVAL[2].

Caswallawn

The son of BELI who conquered BRITAIN. In doing so, he disinherited the brother and heir of BENDIGEID VRAN (BRÂN THE BLESSED), MANAWYDAN FAB LLYR.

Cat Coit Celidon

The site of one of ARTHUR's BATTLES. It is thought to be either in the southern part of SCOTLAND, in the area once known as SILVA CALEDONIAE (Wood of Scotland) or CELYDDON, or in CELIDON WOOD near LINCOLN.

Cath Palug
Also CAPALU

The Welsh poem PA GUR tells how Sir KAY travelled to Anglesey with a view to killing lions, and especially prepared himself for an encounter with Cath Palug, a monstrous member of the cat family (*palug* means 'clawing'). Regrettably this poem is incomplete, but it may have told how Kay defeated the animal. Welsh tradition says that the creature was produced by the pig HENWEN and thrown into the sea, but it was saved and raised by the sons of PALUG on Anglesey. It has been suggested that a leopard, kept as a pet by a Welsh king, may have given rise to the legend.

ARTHUR was also said to have slain a giant cat near Lake BOURGET in the French Alps, an event that is celebrated in local names such as MONT DU CHAT (Cat's Mountain), DENT DU CHAT (Cat's Tooth) and COL DU CHAT (Cat's Neck). In the medieval French romance *Romanaz de Franceis*, Arthur fought a *Capalu*, the Continental name for the Cath Palug, in a swamp, but it killed him and then invaded BRITAIN, where it became king. The character seems to have been expanded in later romances, for in the BATAILLE LOQUIFER a servant of MORGAN[1] Le Fay appears who has the name KAPALU.

Catigern

A son of VORTIGERN.

Catuvellani

A tribe of Britons who were living near what is now known as St Albans at the time of the Roman invasion in AD 43. Their king, CARATACUS, led a fierce fight against the invaders before being handed over to them by CARTIMANDUA, the queen of the BRIGANTES. He was pardoned by the Emperor CLAUDIUS.

Catwallaun Longhand

Possibly identical with CADWALLON, who ruled GWYNEDD in ARTHUR's time. According to GEOFFREY OF MONMOUTH, he was a North Welsh ruler who allegedly drove the Irish, led by Serigi, out of Anglesey some time around AD 500.

Cavershall

The existing castle at Cavershall in Staffordshire dates from the thirteenth century, but local legend says that ARTHUR held court at Cavershall Castle, and also gave aid to a lady there.

Caw

The father of GILDAS, HUEIL and CYWYLLOG, according to Welsh tradition. He was himself regarded as a saint.

Cefn-y-Bryn

A place in Gower, WALES, where there is a burial chamber known as ARTHUR'S STONE. Tradition has it that ARTHUR, on his way to his final battle at CAMLANN, felt a pebble in his boot and, after taking it out, flung it into the distance. It landed some seven miles away at Cefn-y-Bryn.

Cei

A Welsh variant of KAY. Under this variant he appears in the MABINOGION story of CULHWCH AND OLWEN, being one of the party formed to help CULHWCH locate and gain the hand of OLWEN. All the members of the expedition were chosen for their specialist skills or attributes. Cei could remain nine days and nine nights without either breathing or sleeping, could change his height at will and had a body temperature that was so high that during a storm he never got wet, and in cold weather his companions could kindle their fires from him. The other members of the party were named as BEDWYR (BEDIVERE[2]), CYNDDYLIG the Guide, GWRHYR the Interpreter, GWALCHMAI FAB GWYAR and MENW FAB TEIRGWAEDD.

Celidoine

An ancestor of GALAHAD[1], he was the son of NASCIEN[1], who came to BRITAIN and was made king of SCOTLAND. His name appears to have been derived from the Latin name for Scotland, Caledonia, though this may be false etymology.

Celidon Wood

A wood to the north of LINCOLN that is considered by some to be the location of one of ARTHUR'S BATTLES which NENNIUS lists as having been fought at CALEDON WOOD.

Cell-y-Dewiniaid

'The Grove of the Magicians'. A grove of oak trees, long since felled, near DINAS EMRYS under which VORTIGERN's counsellors were said to meet to discuss the events of their times. They were buried in an adjacent field, each grave at one time being marked by a stone. These too have long since vanished.

Celliwig

A place-name, and variant of CELLIWITH, mentioned in the early Welsh tradition of the Arthurian legends and possibly cognate with KILLIBURY. It is more likely that Celliwig was later transmuted into CAMELOT by the twelfth-century poets in their interpretations of the legends.

Celliwith

A variant of both CELLIWIG and KELLIWIC, and thus one of the many possible origins of CAMELOT.

Celyddon

Possibly cognate with CAT COIT CELIDON, or SILVA CALEDONIAE, the Caledonian forest of southern SCOTLAND, or CELIDON WOOD near LINCOLN, the site of one of ARTHUR's BATTLES.

Ceneu

The son of COEL GODEBOG, father of MOR and great-great-great-grandfather of MERLIN, according to Welsh tradition.

Cerdic

The father of CYNRIC who is traditionally regarded as a SAXON leader, though it has also been suggested that he was a Jute. Most authorities maintain that he has a true place in history, though some consider him a fabrication. He is supposedly the founder of the kingdom of Wessex, but a problem exists in that his name is Celtic and not Teutonic. This has led to various speculations: that he was a rebellious British king; that he was a one-time ally of King ARTHUR who later changed his allegiances; that he was the original of the King CARADOS of Arthurian legend; and, most surprising of all, that he was a son of Arthur who gathered a mixed Celtic and Teutonic following on the Continent.

Cernunnos

'The Horned One', the name used as a generic term for all Celtic manifestations of this ancient fertility god. The name is found only on one damaged inscription, discovered in Paris. Cernunnos appears on artefacts found throughout the Celtic realms, commonly shown seated cross-legged. He has both animal and human ears, as well as antlers from which hang a torc, or sometimes a pair of torcs. Some pictures also show a bull and a stag accompanying him. He was associated with material wealth and, like most fertility deities, has a chthonic aspect, indicated particularly by his horned-snake companion. As MERLIN has an association with stags, it has been suggested that he had some connection with the Cernunnos cult.

Cer(r)idwen
Also CAR(R)IDWEN

The Welsh crone, the goddess of dark and prophetic powers, whose totem animal is the sow, representing the fecundity of the Underworld. Like many Celtic goddesses, she had two children, representing light and dark. Her daughter, CREIRWY, was light and beautiful, whereas her son,

MORFRAN, nicknamed AFAGDDU, was dark and ugly. Some sources, however, make Morfran and Afagddu separate characters.

She keeps the Cauldron of the Underworld, in which divine knowledge and inspiration are brewed. This brew is intended for her hapless son, but, while GWION BACH is attending the cauldron, three drops fall on to his finger and he absorbs the potency of the potion. Cerridwen pursued Gwion Bach through a cycle of changing shapes, which corresponds both to the cycle of the seasons and to totemic animals. This theme is related to that of MABON[1] and MERLIN, in which a divine youth is associated with the creatures and orders of creation. The Welsh legend, however, has a very significant ending, for Cerridwen, now in the guise of a hen, swallows Gwion Bach, who was then in the shape of an ear or grain of corn. Nine months later the goddess gave birth to a radiant child, whom she tied in a leather bag and cast into the sea. Rescued by ELPHIN, that child was named TALIESIN.

The legend appears much older than the traditional dates applied to Taliesin, and would seem to be Irish in origin, possibly enshrining an early Celtic practice that involved chewing the raw flesh of the thumb, known as Imbas Forosnai, which was meant to impart wisdom.

Cerrig Marchogion

'The Stones of Arthur's Knights' – a group of standing stones in DYFED that are located on a ridge above the CERRIG MEIBION ARTHUR. They are said to represent the knights of King ARTHUR who accompanied him in the hunt for the boar TWRCH TRWYTH.

Cerrig Meibion Arthur

Two standing stones, separated by about twenty-five feet, in DYFED. They are said to be a monument to the sons of King ARTHUR who were killed by the boar TWRCH TRWYTH, which caused havoc in their encampment having swum over from IRELAND. The story is told in great detail in the MABINOGION. Located on a ridge above the stones are CERRIG MARCHOGION – 'The Stones of King Arthur's Knights'.

Chastel Marte

A castle whose master, according to PERLESVAUS, was an uncle of PERCEVAL[2]. He seized the GRAIL CASTLE but Perceval laid siege to him and he committed suicide.

Chastiefol

The name of one of the swords that belonged to King ARTHUR.

Château de la Charette

The castle of the QUEEN OF SORESTON in which she, and three other associates of MORGAN[1] Le Fay, imprisoned Sir LANCELOT[2] until he chose which of them he loved.

Château de Morgan Le Fée, Le

The French name for a mirage that appears in the Straits of Messina. Known as FATA MORGANA in Italian, this mirage distorts both horizontally and vertically, and is said to represent one of MORGAN[1] Le Fay's fairy palaces.

Cheldric

According to GEOFFREY OF MONMOUTH, Cheldric was a SAXON leader who brought reinforcements with him from GERMANY to join COLGRIN, and took part in the battles of LINCOLN, CALEDON WOOD and BADON. Following the rout of the Saxons, he fled, but was finally defeated and killed by CADOR[1].

Chelinde

The wife of SADOR, the son of BRONS.

Chester

Named Deva in classical times, Chester was, like CAERLEON-ON-USK, also known as the CITY OF THE LEGION. It has been suggested that Chester should replace Caerleon-on-Usk when considering the location of ARTHUR's principal city and the site of the battle at the City of the Legion.

Chevrefueil

Arthurian romance written by the twelfth-century poetess MARIE DE FRANCE.

Childe Rowland

A medieval Scottish ballad that tells of how ELLEN, ARTHUR's daughter, was saved from an OTHERWORLD prison by her brother, and hence Arthur's son, ROWLAND.

Chlodomer

The king of Orleans, FRANCE, who reigned between AD 511 and 524, and was killed in a battle against Burgundian invaders. One theory put forward suggests that he was killed while fighting against ARTHUR.

Chough

Although choughs are now extinct in CORNWALL, except for a few pairs in captivity, Cornish beliefs held that the spirit of ARTHUR used to fly over the cliffs in the form of this bird. This is just one bird that has become associated with the spirit of Arthur. Others include the PUFFIN and the RAVEN, the latter being related to the Chough and possibly later replacing it, due to its rarity.

Chramm

The leader of a rebellion against CLOTHAIR, the king of the Franks, who was aided by CUNOMORUS; both leaders were allegedly killed in the course of the fighting.

Chrétien de Troyes

A medieval French poet and troubadour who was born in Troyes, in the Champagne, some time during the middle of the twelfth century. The greatest of the French medieval poets, he was the author of the earliest romances dealing with King ARTHUR. He was a member of the court of the Countess Marie de Champagne, daughter of Louis VII, and to whom he dedicated his metrical romance of courtly love *Yvain et Lancelot*. He is probably best known for the number of Arthurian romances he wrote: EREC ET ENIDE (c. 1160), *Le chevalier de Charette*, which is also simply known as *Lancelot*, CLIGÉS (c. 1164), *Le chevalier au lion*, also called *Yvain*, *Le conte de graal*, also called PERCEVAL (c. 1180), which he wrote for Philip, Count of Flanders, but which remained unfinished as he died c. 1183. His works are reputed to be the first to introduce the concept of the Holy GRAIL.

Chwimleian

Mentioned in the Welsh MYRDDIN (MERLIN) poem AFOLLONAU, Chwimleian is thought to be identifiable with GUENDOLOENA.

Circe

A sorceress of classical Graeco-Roman mythology, appearing in Homer's *Odyssey* and Apollonius of Rhodes's *Argonautica*. In the Arthurian romance PERCEFOREST, she marries BETHIDES and brings the Romans to BRITAIN.

Cissa

A son of AELLE, he accompanied his father when his SAXON forces defeated the Britons.

Cist Arthur

A burial chamber, mentioned in a survey of 1737, on MOEL ARTHUR, a hill in Clwyd, WALES. This chamber has been cited as yet another of the many possible last resting places of King ARTHUR.

City of Souls

According to PERLESVAUS, an OTHERWORLD city, haunted by spirits, that was visited by LANCELOT[2].

City of the Legion(s)

According to NENNIUS, the City of the Legion was the site of one of ARTHUR's BATTLES. GEOFFREY OF MONMOUTH identifies it with CAERLEON-ON-USK, which was called ISCA LEGIONIS and ISCA LEGIONUM in early times. It has also been identified with CHESTER, called URBS LEGIONIS in Latin, and also with CASTLEFORD, which the Romans called Legiotium. If the City of the Legion is to be identified with Caerleon-on-Usk, then it was here that ARTHUR held a plenary court that was attended by representatives from all of Europe.

Claire

The sister of SAGREMOR, she was saved by GUINGLAIN from two giants.

Clamadeus

A king who was defeated in single combat and killed by PERCEVAL[2] after he had laid siege to BLANCHEFLEUR[1]'s castle.

Clarence, Duchy of

The duchy of which GALESCHIN was said to have been made duke by ARTHUR after his defeat of the SAXONS, who were besieging the city. This is an anachronism since the duchy of Clarence was not created until 1362, and the place to which it relates, the small wool town of Clare in Suffolk, can hardly be called a city.

Clarette

The maiden whose hand was won by the KNIGHT OF THE SLEEVE at a tournament at ARTHUR's court, according to the Dutch romance *Ridder metter Mouwen*.

Clarine

The wife of King PANT of GENNEWIS, Clarine is made the mother of LANCELOT[2] in a Germanic version of his story.

Clarion

The SAXON king who was, according to some sources, the owner of the horse GRINGALET, which GAWAIN[1] took from him.

Claris

The hero of the romance CLARIS ET LARIS. He rescued his companion LARIS from the king of DENMARK, TALLAS, married LIDOINE, Laris's sister, and became a KNIGHT OF THE ROUND TABLE.

Claris et Laris

A thirteenth-century French verse romance concerning the adventures of CLARIS and his companion LARIS.

Clarissant

The mother of GUIGENOR by GUIROME-LANT, she was the daughter of MORGAUSE and LOT.

Clarisse

Simply mentioned as being the sister of GAWAIN[1].

Claudas

Possibly having an origin in Clovis I, king of the Franks between AD 481 and 511, Claudas is described as King of the Desert Land, his realm being identified with Berry, since berrie in Old French signifies a desert. The opponent of King BORS[1], whose kingdom he seized after that king's death. Bors's sons fell into the hands of Claudas's lover PHARIEN, but, when Claudas had them brought to him, they escaped in the guise of greyhounds, killing his son DORIN in the process. Claudas imprisoned GUINEVERE after insulting one of her ladies-in-waiting, and war broke out between Claudas, who was supported by the Romans, and BRITAIN, the latter finally being victorious.

Claudius

The fourth Roman emperor (10 BC – AD 54), born in Lyons, the younger son of Drusus senior, brother of Emperor Tiberius. He inaugurated the conquest of BRITAIN, taking part in the opening campaign in person (AD 43). GEOFFREY OF MONMOUTH states that ARVIRAGUS became the king of Britain following the death of his brother GUIDERIUS during the Roman invasion. Peace was established between Arviragus and Claudius when the former married GENVISSA, Claudius's daughter. Arviragus later revolted, but peace was once more restored through the offices of Genvissa.

Cleriadus

A descendant of ARTHUR; he was the successor to PHILIPPON, the father of his wife, MELIADICE, as the King of England.

Cligés

The hero of the romance CLIGÉS by CHRÉTIEN DE TROYES, he was the son of ALEXANDER[2], emperor of CONSTANTI-NOPLE, and SOREDAMOR, the daughter of LOT. While his uncle ALIS was emperor, he married FENICE[1], with whom Cligés also fell in love. Unable to make his feelings known, he left the court at Constantinople and travelled to that of ARTHUR. When Alis subsequently died, Cligés returned out of his self-enforced exile and duly married Fenice.

Cligés

Romance by CHRÉTIEN DE TROYES concerning the exploits of the hero after whom the work is named. Written c. 1164, the romance is based mainly around the imperial family of CONSTAN-TINOPLE, genealogical evidence within the work illustrating a connection between CLIGÉS and LOT.

Cliton

A sister of MORGAN[1] Le Fay.

Clodion

A son of PHARAMOND who was killed in single combat by TRISTAN.

Clogwyn Carnedd yr Wydffa

'The Precipice of the Carn on Yr Wyddfa'. A name sometimes used to refer to YR WYDDFA FAWR, or, alternatively, to the cairn that used to be situated on the top of this mountain, today more commonly known as Mount SNOWDON.

Clothair

The king of SOISSONS, who later became king of all the Franks. It is claimed that CUNOMORUS died during an uprising against him in AD 560.

Clovis

Merovingian ruler of the Franks, born AD 465, the grandson of Merovich. In AD 481 he succeeded his father, Childeric I, as king of the Salian Franks, and spent his entire life expanding the Frankish kingdom. When he died in AD 511, in his capital, Paris, the kingdom was divided between his four sons, who continued the expansion begun by their father. The anonymous *Palamedes* says that Clovis was an ancestor of GUIRON.

Clydno

One of ARTHUR's warriors who was, in Welsh tradition, the father of CYNON.

Clydno Eiddyn

The owner of a cauldron that was considered one of the THIRTEEN TREASURES of BRITAIN.

Coel

Possibly an historical figure, flourishing in the north country in the early fifth century, who successfully defended his land against the PICTS and the Scots. He is almost certainly the Old King COLE of nursery rhyme, as the adjective *hen* ('old') was applied to him. A fourth-century manuscript says that Coel was king of all BRITAIN, dying in AD 267, while a sixteenth-century manuscript says that he was an ancestor of ARTHUR through his mother. Tradition names his wife as STRADWAWL and his daughter as GWAWL, who might have been the wife of CUNEDDA. He was thought to be the founder and ruler of COLCHESTER. Legend says that his city was besieged by Constantius Chlorus, the Roman emperor, for three years, and after peace had been restored the emperor married Coel's daughter, HELENA, who is better known as Saint Helena. Their son was Constantine the Great, born in AD 265.

Coel Godebog

The father of CENEU and great-great-great-great-grandfather of MYRDDIN (MERLIN), according to Welsh tradition.

Coetan Arthur

A round barrow with burial chamber and very large capstone at St David's Head in DYFED. It is one of the numerous locations where King ARTHUR is said to be buried.

Col du Chat

'Cat's Neck.' This name is found in the vicinity of Lake BOURGET in the French Alps, and celebrates the fact that near that lake ARTHUR was said to have slain a huge cat.

Colchester

Reputedly founded by COEL and called Camulodunum in Roman times, Colchester has been identified by some with CAMELOT, this association coming from the similarity of the Roman name, though this could also be said about any place-name that has 'Cam' in it, whether Roman or British.

Colcu

The stepson of CRÉD who always managed to thwart her attempts to meet with CANO. His continual interference eventually led to the deaths of Créd and, three days later, Cano.

Cole, Old King

It is almost certain that the Old King Cole of nursery rhyme had his origins in COEL, for this possibly historical character had the adjective *hen* ('old') applied to him. Whether he was actually a 'merry old soul' though is open to speculation.

Colgrevance

A native of the realm of GORE, he became a KNIGHT OF THE ROUND TABLE. Accounts of his death vary. In one he was killed by LIONEL, but in another he was among those who surprised LANCELOT[2] and GUINEVERE together and was killed by the escaping, yet unarmed, Lancelot.

Colgrin

According to GEOFFREY OF MONMOUTH, the SAXON leader after the death of UTHER. He was defeated by ARTHUR at the battle of the River DOUGLAS, after which he fled to and took refuge in YORK, where he was joined by his brother BALDULF. Arthur laid siege to the city, and Colgrin was subsequently defeated by Arthur at both LINCOLN and CALEDON WOOD (some authorities make these one battle), even though he had been joined by CHELDRIC, who had brought reinforcements with him from the Continent. Fleeing to GERMANY, they regrouped and came back, this time to be utterly routed at BADON, where Colgrin was killed.

Colombe

The lover of LANCEOR, the son of the king of IRELAND, who killed herself when Lanceor was killed by BALIN.

Conan (Meriadoc)

According to GEOFFREY OF MONMOUTH, the ruler of BRITTANY who is claimed, by some commentators, to be an ancestor of ARTHUR.

Condwiramurs

The queen of BROBARZ and wife of PERCEVAL[2], according to WOLFRAM VON ESCHENBACH.

Conon

The father of EMMELINE who was loved by ARTHUR in John DRYDEN'S KING ARTHUR.

Conrad

A bishop who unsuccessfully, and unwisely, had MERLIN charged with heresy.

Constance

In Italian romance, the wife of King BAN of BRITTANY and the mother of LANCELOT[2].

Constans

The brother of AMBROSIUS AURELIUS and UTHER, sons of King CONSTANTINE[1] of BRITAIN, thus making him ARTHUR's uncle. When his father died, he was persuaded to become the king by VORTIGERN, though this meant that he first had to leave the monastery in which he had imprisoned himself. This fact is reflected in French romance, where he is called MOINE, a name that simply signifies a monk. As king he was merely the puppet of Vortigern, who eventually had him assassinated by the PICTS.

Constantine

1 The grandfather of ARTHUR. The brother of ALDROENUS or AUDRIEN, King of BRITTANY, he was made king of BRITAIN at the Britons' own request and had three sons, AMBROSIUS AURELIUS, UTHER and CONSTANS. He was stabbed to death by a PICT and was succeeded by CONSTANS, who was no more than a puppet of VORTIGERN, until he too was killed by a Pict. In the Welsh genealogies, his father is named as KYNNVOR, but he is also thought to have been the son of SOLOMON, king of Brittany, in which case he is the grandson of URBIEN (Figure 6). His origin has been suggested as lying with the Roman emperor Constantine III, and there are many

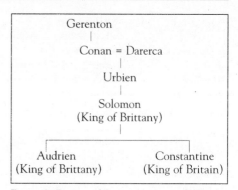

```
            Gerenton
               |
        Conan = Darerca
               |
            Urbien
               |
            Solomon
        (King of Brittany)
               |
    ┌──────────┴──────────┐
  Audrien              Constantine
(King of Brittany)   (King of Britain)
```

Figure 6 *Descent of Constantine, according to Gallet*

similarities between t

he two, not least the fact that they both had sons named CONSTANS who had immured themselves in monasteries.

2 A sixth-century king of DUMNONIA who appears in the Arthurian romances as ARTHUR's cousin, the son of Duke CADOR[1] of CORNWALL. Arthur passed the crown to this Constantine following the final battle at CAMLANN, before being borne away to AVALON, the year being recorded as AD 542. Following his ascension, the sons of MORDRED rebelled against him, but he defeated them, killing each of them separately, and each before an altar where they had sought sanctuary.

Constantinople

Formerly called BYZANTIUM, this city became, at the time when the ROMAN EMPIRE was divided into two, the capital of the Eastern or Byzantine Empire. During the traditional Arthurian period there were a number of Byzantine emperors: Marcian (AD 450–57), Leo I (AD 457–74), Leo II (AD 474), Zeno (AD 747–75 and again AD 476–91), Basiliscus (AD 475–76), Anastasius I (AD 491–518), Justus I (AD 518–27) and Justinian I (AD 527–67). The emperor considered contemporary with Arthur was simply named as Leo by

GEOFFREY OF MONMOUTH, and if Leo II ruled only in AD 474 it seems that this refers to Leo I.

Constantinople appears in a number of the Arthurian romances. In PEREDUR the empress was the lover of PEREDUR (PERCEVAL[2]), with whom she was said to have lived for fourteen years, and had previously given him an enchanted stone that made him invisible to the AFANC. In FLORIANT ET FLORETE, the emperor is named as FILIMENIS. However, most interesting of all is CLIGÉS, which gives the genealogy of the imperial family, showing its relationship to LOT. This relationship is illustrated in Figure 7.

Conte de graal, Le

An unfinished, pre-thirteenth-century work by the French poet CHRÉTIEN DE TROYES, the 484-line-long prologue to the work being known as the ELUCIDATION. It is considered the earliest work that enhances the legends of King ARTHUR and introduces the concept of the Holy GRAIL. Its unfinished state gave rise to a series of CONTINUATIONS, the first appearing c. 1200.

Continuation(s)

Since CHRÉTIEN DE TROYES left his LE CONTE DE GRAAL unfinished, it inspired various other writers to continue where Chrétien left off. These works are referred to as 'Continuations'. The first 'Continuation' appeared c. 1200, the second some time during the thirteenth century. GERBERT and Manessier also produced Continuations during the same century.

Corbenic Castle

A variant of CARBONEK Castle, the castle where the FISHER KINGS, descendants of JOSEPH OF ARIMATHEA, guarded the Holy GRAIL.

Corbon

In the obscure medieval romance BATAILLE LOQUIFER, which contains a few Arthurian references, Corbon appears as the son of RENOART and MORGAN[1] Le Fay, thus making him ARTHUR's nephew.

Cordelia

The youngest daughter of the mythical King LEIR, to whose throne she ascended. It has been suggested that she has her origins in CREIDDYLED.

Corineus

A renowned Trojan soldier and giant-killer, he landed in BRITAIN with BRUTUS, after which he received the land of CORNWALL, naming it after himself. GEOFFREY OF MONMOUTH makes Corineus a giant and says that when he landed in Britain his party found the country inhabited by a tribe of giants with whom they engaged in battle. Eventually the quarrel was decided by single combat

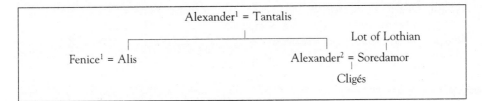

Figure 7 *Genealogy of Constantinople's imperial family*

between Corineus and GOGMAGOG. Gogmagog broke three of Corineus's ribs but, maddened with pain, the Trojan seized his opponent and hurled him into the sea off Plymouth Hoe. Two huge figures commemorating the giants were carved in white limestone overlooking Plymouth harbour. These were destroyed, having survived for many centuries, in 1671.

Cormilan

A variant of CORMORAN.

Cormoran

Also CORMILAN, GOURMAILLON

The most famous of all English giants, being the one who was disposed of by JACK THE GIANT-KILLER – or maybe by King ARTHUR, who, in Sir Thomas MALORY's MORTE D'ARTHUR and earlier, in GEOFFREY OF MONMOUTH's HISTORIA REGUM BRITANNIAE, fought the prototype of this giant, whose home was the castle on St Michael's Mount, off Penzance, CORNWALL. Jack, who was English rather than Cornish, remains the only European hero to have triumphed over a giant by natural wit and dexterity, rather than by force of arms. The giant, who was also known as CORMILAN, was said to have rejoiced in the well-known cry:

> Fee, fi, fo, fum,
> I smell the blood of an Englishman!

Identification has also been made between this giant and Gogmagog through the variant Gourmaillon, which has been applied to both. If this is the case, then Jack the Giant-killer would seem to be a commemoration of CORINEUS, the giant Trojan ally of BRUTUS, who was said to have flung GOGMAGOG into the sea at Plymouth, which is not too far distant from St Michael's Mount.

Corn Brangaled

A drinking horn that is numbered among the THIRTEEN TREASURES of BRITAIN. Owned by BRANGALED, it was capable of providing any drink its holder desired.

Cornubas

A Welsh earl whose daughter married ARTHUR's son, the KNIGHT OF THE FAIR COUNTRY.

Cornwall

Supposedly named after CORINEUS, to whom the land was given by BRUTUS, Cornwall was the realm of King MARK² in the Arthurian legends. In Arthurian times the county of Cornwall was part of the realm of DUMNONIA, though it is not impossible that someone named Mark ruled some territory within that kingdom.

Coudel

The ESTOIRE DEL SAINTE GRAAL described Coudel as an early king of NORTHGALIS who was killed fighting against the Christians.

Courechouse

The sword owned by King BAN.

Cradelment

A king of NORTHGALIS and one of the eleven leaders who rebelled against King ARTHUR at the start of his reign.

Craig-y-Dinas

A mount near SNOWDON, North WALES, that is one of the many locations regarded as the last resting place of King ARTHUR, who, in a story told by Iolo MORGANNWG (the bardic name of Edward Williams, 1747–1826), rests there, along with his knights and his treasure. He was found, according to the story, by a Welshman who was led there by a magician, though a variant account makes the visitor a Monmouthsire farmer. As Iolo Morgannwg was a bard, his material is not regarded as a reliable source, for he had doubtless simply enhanced an earlier tale, feeling that his version would be the better. Similar tales of the sleeping Arthur are found in England, notably at ALDERLEY EDGE (see also THOMPSON). A cave near to Llandebie with the similar-sounding name of OGO'R DINAS has also been mooted as one of the last resting places of Arthur.

Crearwy
Also CREIRWY

The daughter of TEGID VOEL and CERRID-WEN, she is described as the fairest maiden in all the world, being light and beautiful, in direct contrast to her brother, MORFRAN or AFAGDDU, who was described as dark and ugly.

Créd

The beautiful young wife of MARCÁN. She fell in love with CANO and, following the death of her husband, attempted to meet with her lover on numerous occasions, each time being thwarted in her endeavour by her stepson, COLCU. Eventually, due to Colcu's continual intervention, she dashed her head on a rock. Three days later Cano died. This is thought to have been one of the sources for the TRISTAN story.

Creiddylad

A variant of CREIDDYLED.

Creiddyled
Also CREIDDYLAD

The daughter of LLUD LLAW EREINT, over whom GWYNN, the son of NUDD, and his followers fought GWYTHR, the son of GREIDAWL, and his followers each May Day, being destined to do so until the end of time. Although taken from Celtic mythology, it is thought that Creiddyled is the prototype of CORDELIA, the youngest daughter of King LEIR.

Creirwy

A variant of CREARWY.

Crop-eared Dog

One of the main characters of the Irish EACHTRA AN MHADRA MHAOIL, this earless and tailless creature, while obviously canine, also had the power of human speech. Originally the Crop-eared Dog had been the prince ALEXANDER[3], the son of the king of India. However, his stepmother had changed him and his brothers into various 'canine' creatures in order to ensure that her own son, the KNIGHT OF THE LANTERN, received a handsome inheritance. The knight of the Lantern was admitted to ARTHUR's court, but while there he insulted the king and the court. GAWAIN[1] and the Crop-eared Dog went to track him down and, having at length captured him, the Knight of the Lantern removed his mother's spell, and restored ALEXANDER[3] to his original shape. He eventually went on to become the ruler of India.

Culhwch
Also KULHWCH, KILHWCH

The son of KILYDD and GOLEUDDYDD, the sister of IGRAINE[1], and by this association the cousin of ARTHUR (Figure 8). During

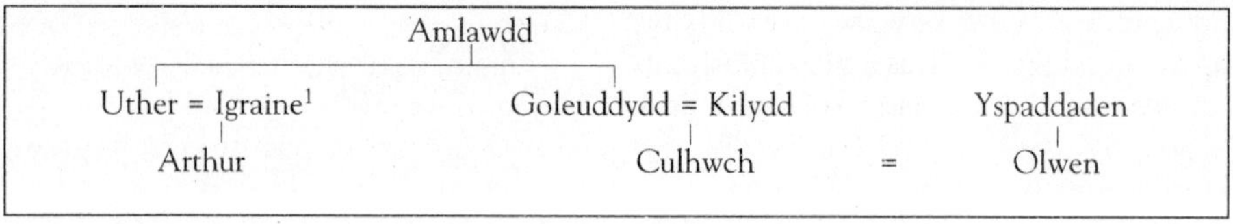

```
                            Amlawdd
        ┌──────────────────────┴──────────────────────┐
  Uther = Igraine¹        Goleuddydd = Kilydd            Yspaddaden
        │                            │                        │
     Arthur                      Culhwch        =           Olwen
```

Figure 8 *Family tree of Culhwch, Arthur's cousin*

her pregnancy Goleuddydd lost her sanity and wandered through the countryside. As her time drew close, her sanity returned to her in the middle of a herd of swine. So frightened was Goleuddydd that she immediately went into labour and her child, being born in the midst of a pig run, was named Culhwch (*hwch* = 'pig').

After Goleuddydd had died, Culhwch's father remarried, though the name of Culhwch's stepmother remains unknown. She put Culhwch under an obligation to marry none other than OLWEN, the daughter of the chief giant YSPADDADEN. Realizing the enormity of his task, Culhwch went to the court of his cousin, King Arthur, to ask for his help in winning the hand of Olwen. When Culhwch arrived at Arthur's court he was met by GLEWLWYD, the gatekeeper, who declared that Culhwch was the most handsome youth he had ever laid eyes on.

Arthur agreed to help his cousin, though he confessed that he had never heard of Olwen or her father. He sent messengers to seek them out, but, after a year, they all returned unsuccessful. A new party was formed to help Culhwch in his quest, this party being made up of CEI (KAY), BEDWYR (BEDIVERE²), CYNDDYLIG the Guide, GWRHYR the Interpreter, GWALCHMAI FAB GWYAR and MENW FAB TEIRGWAEDD. Each was chosen for his own particular skill.

Cei could stay for nine days without either sleeping or breathing. He could alter his height at will and had a body temperature that was so high that during a storm he never got wet, and in cold weather his

companions could kindle their fires from him. Bedwyr, though he had only one arm, was faster with his sword than three other fighting together. Gwalchmai fab Gwyar never gave up on any quest he had started, and Menw fab Teirgwaedd was a master of spells which would preserve the company in heathen lands. The final two, Cynddylig and Gwrhyr, were chosen for the talents their titles infer.

After some time the party came across a shepherd whose wife turned out to be an aunt of Culhwch. Even though she had already lost twenty-three of her twenty-four sons to the giant Yspaddaden, she agreed to help Culhwch meet Olwen, who came to the woman's cottage every Saturday to wash her hair.

When they met, Olwen asked Culhwch to come to their castle and request her hand. However, she warned him not to flinch from any conditions her father might set. For three days Culhwch and his companions went to Yspaddaden's castle. On each occasion the giant told them to return the following morning and then, as they turned their backs, threw a poisoned stone at them. The party, however, were always too quick and, catching it, they threw it back, which greatly concerned the giant. On the fourth day he agreed to Culhwch's suit, but imposed on him three monumental tasks. The first of these involved felling and burning a thicket, ploughing its ashes into a field and sowing it with flax. The second was to obtain a variety of items for the wedding feast, and the third was to obtain various items and preparations necessary to barber the giant, among which was a razor and comb from between the ears of the great boar TWRCH TRWYTH.

Innumerable other conditions were imposed, each of which Yspaddaden told Culhwch was impossible to fulfil. Each time Culhwch simply replied that he could complete the task with ease. Finally, with the help of King Arthur, who was most notably present in the hunt for Twrch Trwyth, he completed all the tasks set him and returned to the giant's castle in the company of all the giant's enemies. There the giant was killed and Olwen became Culhwch's wife, the couple remaining faithful for the rest of their lives.

This story forms a part of the MABINO-GION known, not surprisingly, as CUL-HWCH AND OLWEN. Study of this story seems to suggest that not all the tasks set Culhwch were completed, and various suggestions have been put forward for this. Either it was simply due to the carelessness of the author of the romance, or part of the story has been lost.

Culhwch and Olwen

The complex and possibly incomplete pre-eleventh-century romance, part of the MABINOGION, that tells the story of CULHWCH, ARTHUR's cousin, and OLWEN, the daughter of the chief giant YSPAD-DADEN. This section of the *Mabinogion* is perhaps the most important for the Arthurian student. Within its complex structure many of the characters who were later developed into the leading lights of the Arthurian legends can be found in possibly their original form.

Cundrie

This name only appears in the works of WOLFRAM VON ESCHENBACH, where it is used for two women.

1 The daughter of ARTHUR's sister SAN-GIVE and LOT, she married LISCHOIS.
2 A GRAIL maiden who told PERCEVAL[2] that his wife and sons had been summoned to the GRAIL CASTLE. There she told him the GRAIL QUESTION should be asked to free both AMFORTAS, the GRAIL KING, and his own family.

Cunedda

With a pedigree suggesting that he orig-inated from a Roman family (Figure 9), Cunedda was a ruler of the Votadini of north BRITAIN who emigrated to WALES, and rid a large part of that country of Irish settlers, some time around AD 430. According to the medieval Welsh history *Brut y Brenhinedd*, he was the father of GWEN[1], the mother of EIGYR (IGRAINE[1]), who was in turn ARTHUR's mother, thus making him Arthur's great-grandfather. It has been suggested that his wife may have been GWAWL, the daughter of COEL.

Tacitus
|
Paternus
|
Aeternus
|
Cunedda = Gwawl
|
Gwen[1]
|
Eigyr
|
Arthur

Figure 9 *Pedigree of Cunedda, Arthur's great-grandfather*

Cunobelinus

In Welsh tradition a relation of ARTHUR, and called CYMBELINE by SHAKESPEARE, Cunobelinus was a ruler of the CATUVEL-LANI who, some time in the first century AD, made himself the king of a consider-able part of southern Britain.

Cunomorus

An historical ancient ruler of CORNWALL and BRITTANY. Warned that one of his sons would kill him, Cunomorus murdered each of his wives as soon as they announced that they were pregnant. However, one wife, TREPHINA, the daughter of WAROK, chief of the VENETII, managed to avoid him until after she had given birth to JUDWAL or TREMEUR. Cunomorus then had her decapitated, and her son exposed and left to die. GILDAS restored Trephina to life and sent her back to the castle with her head neatly tucked under her arm. The battlements promptly fell on Cunomorus and killed him.

It has been suggested by several commentators that Cunomorus is the historical origin of King MARK[2] of Cornwall, or that Cunomorus at least contributed to the tyrannical aspect of Mark[2]. A family tree is given in Figure 10.

```
                    Warok
                      |
Cunomorus   =   Trephina   =   Jonas
        |                  |
    Tremeur*          Judwal*
    or Gildasor       or Tremeur
      junior

* These two are apparently identical.
```

Figure 10 *Family tree of Cunomorus, ruler of Cornwall and Brittany*

Curetana

The name of the sword that had been owned by TRISTAN and which was presented to OGIER by Charlemagne.

Custennin

A simple variant of KUSTENNIN as found in the genealogy of ARTHUR prepared by T. W. Rolleston.

Cyledyr the Wild

In the MABINOGION romance CULHWCH AND OLWEN, one of the followers of ARTHUR. He managed to obtain the shears required to barber YSPADDADEN from between the ears of the boar TWRCH TRWYTH.

Cyllel Llawfrodedd

A Druid sacrificial knife said to be one of the THIRTEEN TREASURES of BRITAIN which MERLIN took with him when he sailed away, never to be seen again, in his glass boat.

Cymbeline

The name used by SHAKESPEARE for CUNOBELINUS.

Cymen

A son of the SAXON leader AELLE who accompanied his father when his forces defeated the Britons.

Cynddylig

'The Guide'. He was one of the members of the party formed by ARTHUR to help CULHWCH in his quest to locate OLWEN. The other members were CEI, BEDWYR, GWRHYR the Interpreter, GWALCHMAI FAB GWYAR and MENW FAB TEIRGWAEDD.

Cynfarch

Also CYNVARCH, KYNFARCH, KYNVARCH

The father of URIEN.

Cyngen

A legendary king of the Welsh kingdom of POWYS who was said to have ruled at some time during the traditional Arthurian period.

Cynon

In Welsh tradition, the lover of OWAIN's twin sister, MORFUDD.

Cynric

A son of CERDIC.

Cynvarch

A variant of CYNFARCH.

Cyon

A knight who is named as being one of the TWENTY-FOUR KNIGHTS of King ARTHUR's court.

Cywyllog

Welsh tradition makes Cywyllog the daughter of CAW and wife of MORDRED who, after her husband's death, became a nun and founded the church of Llangwyllog on Anglesey.

Daghdha

The greatest Irish god of Celtic mythology who was said to have owned a magic cauldron that provided a perpetual supply of food, and could restore the dead to life. He also owned a fantastic club, one end of which brought life, the other death. These two primal and pagan magical implements were later to resurface in the Arthurian legends, having been much refined, as the Holy GRAIL and the LANCE OF LONGINUS.

Dagonet

ARTHUR's fool, but none the less knighted by ARTHUR himself.

Dahut
Also AHES

A MORGAN (a Breton class of water fairy) who was held responsible for the destruction of the legendary city of YS. It is thought by some that her class of fairy, also known as MARI-MORGANS, was the origin of MORGAN[1] Le Fay.

Daire

A Pictish king who is shown in the genealogies as being the father of the OTHERWORLD women AILLEANN.

Dal Riata

A variant on DALRIADA.

Dalriada
Also DAL RIATA

Ancient Celtic Hiberno-Scottish kindom founded on the west coast of SCOTLAND by a group of Irish emigrants, the major part of the kingdom occupying what is now known as Argyllshire, though it also included a small area of northern IRELAND. The kingdom was ruled by AEDÁN MAC GABRAIN, whose son, known as ARTHUR OF DALRIADA, has been suggested as the historical origin of King ARTHUR.

Damart

A magician who was killed by BETIS who thereafter became known as PERCEFOREST.

Damas

The brother of Sir ONTZLAKE, whom he used to make fight other knights he had trapped, a practice that was stopped by ARTHUR.

Damosel del Grant Pui de Mont Dolerous, La

According to some sources, the daughter of MERLIN.

Danain the Red

The name of the Lord of MALEHAUT.

Daniel

According to the TAVOLA RITONDA, the brother of DINADAN and the leader of the company of knights who trapped GUINEVERE and LANCELOT[2] together in the queen's bedchamber. A knight of this name also appears in a thirteenth-century German poem written by Der Stricker. As BREUNOR is also named as the brother of DINADAN, it seems that Daniel and BREUNOR were also brothers. Alternatively, it has been suggested that they were simply different names for the same character.

Darerca

According to Jocelyn's *Life of Saint Patrick*, Darerca was Saint Patrick's youngest sister and had no fewer than seventeen sons. Her sister, TIGRIDIA, was said to have married GRALLO, the grandson of CONAN, thus also connecting her with ARTHUR, for Darerca was said to have married Conan himself (Figure 11).

Darerca = Conan
|
Urbien
|
Solomon
|
Constantine[1]
|
Uther
|
Arthur

Figure 11 *Family tree of Darerca*

Datis

The king of Tuscany who was killed by GARETH during ARTHUR's campaign against the ROMAN EMPIRE.

Daughter of the King of Logres

According to *Tyolet*, this maiden challenged a knight to cut the foot off a white stag which TYOLET, the hero of the romance, succeeded in doing, afterwards becoming her husband. Her name remains a mystery as she is not named in the romance.

David, Saint
Also DEWI, SAINT

The patron saint of WALES who, unsurprisingly, is linked with ARTHUR in a number of Welsh sources. GEOFFREY OF MONMOUTH makes him Arthur's uncle; the medieval Welsh history BRUT Y BRENHINEDD makes him Arthur's second cousin; another Welsh manuscript of uncertain date makes him Arthur's grand-nephew. As the date of David's death remains unknown, it is certainly not impossible that there was some tangible link between him and Arthur.

David's Sword

Though some commentators make this sword the one-time property of Saint DAVID, it is more widely accepted as having belonged to the biblical David. It appears in the Arthurian tales as the sword used by VARLAN to kill King LAMBOR in one account of the DOLOROUS STROKE.

De Excidio (et Conquestu Britanniae)

Famous treatise, probably written between AD 516 and 547, by the British writer GILDAS, and thus making it

83

contemporary with the traditional Arthurian period. This work, which is the only extant history of the Celts, and the only contemporary version of events from the Roman invasion to his own time, mentions the battle of BADON, but does not mention ARTHUR by name.

De Ortu Waluuanii

A Latin romance of undetermined date that concerns the adventures of the young GAWAIN[1].

de Troyes, Chrétien

See CHRÉTIEN DE TROYES

Demetia

The Welsh kingdom of DYFED in southern WALES. According to GEOFFREY OF MON-MOUTH, the kingdom was ruled by STATER during ARTHUR's time, but history of the region knows nothing of him.

Demetrus

The maternal grandfather of MERLIN whose name appears to have been a simple corruption of DEMETIA, the kingdom where MERLIN's mother came from.

Demogorgon

The primeval being of classical mythology who appears in *La Caccia* by Erasmo de Valvasone when ARTHUR enters his cave *en route* through a mountain to reach the palace of MORGAN[1] Le Fay.

Denmark

Denmark and its rulers appear in several places in the Arthurian tales, but historically speaking very little is known about the Danish kings during the tra-

ditional Arthurian period. GEOFFREY OF MONMOUTH states that ASCHIL, the king of Denmark, was an ally of ARTHUR at CAMLANN, but the MORTE ARTHURE makes the Danish the allies of MORDRED. The kings themselves are also variously named. The twelfth-century Welsh writer Geoffrey Gaimar says that, in Arthurian times, the king was called GUNTER, while elsewhere he is called TRYFFIN. In DURMART LE GALLOIS he is JOZEFANT, while in the LIVRE D'ARTUS he is called AMINADUC, and is described as a SAXON. CLARIS ET LARIS gives us still further variation, stating that is was first ruled by HELDINS, who was succeeded by TALLAS. He was defeated by ARTHUR and subsequently LARIS ascended to the throne.

Dent du Chat

'Cat's Tooth'. A place-name in the vicinity of Lake BOURGET in the French Alps which commemorates the fact that ARTHUR was said to have slain a huge cat, possibly a CATH PALUG or CAPALU, near there.

Denw

The daughter of ANNA, ARTHUR's sister, and LOT, who, according to Welsh tradition, became the wife of OWAIN.

Derdriu

Tragic Celtic heroine whose story is thought to have been one of the sources for the story of TRISTAN and ISEULT[1]. She determined to meet a man who matched a set of criteria she had herself imposed, but they were forced to go into exile. When they returned her lover was killed and she was forced to spend a year with the man she most despised. At the end of that year she was sent to spend a second year with a man she hated as much. *En route* she threw herself from the chariot and dashed her brains out against a rock.

Derfel, Saint

The founder of Llanderfel in GWYNEDD, who, according to Welsh tradition, participated in, and survived, the battle of CAMLANN.

Deruvian

Named as one of the missionaries who were sent in *c.* AD 166 from Rome by Pope ELUTHERIUS at the request of the then British king LUCIUS, and founded the abbey at GLASTONBURY. The name of the other missionary is given as PHAGAN.

Destructive One

The name of the servant of MERLIN who was employed in the imprisonment of ORLANDO at the request of MADOR, who was jealous because MELORA, whom he loved, showed her preference for the hapless Orlando.

Detors

Simply mentioned as being a king of NORTHUMBERLAND.

Dewi, Saint

Saint DAVID, the patron saint of WALES.

Diana

The classical Roman goddess who, in the mighty VULGATE VERSION, is the goddess of the wood, the mother of DYONAS (DIONES) and hence grandmother of VIVIENNE.

Didot Perceval

A French prose romance that dates from *c.* 1200 and tells of PERCEVAL[2]'s quest for the holy GRAIL. Although the author of this work remains unknown, it has been suggested that he is ROBERT DE BORON.

Dillus

Appearing in the MABINOGION story of CULHWCH AND OLWEN, Dillus is described as an enemy of ARTHUR, though why is unknown. YSPADDADEN set CULHWCH the task of obtaining Dillus's beard in order to make a leash, a task that was completed by CEI (KAY), who cast Dillus into a pit and pulled out the hairs of his beard with a pair of tweezers.

Dinabutius

The name of a boy who teased the youthful MERLIN for not knowing his father's name. This taunting drew Merlin to the attention of VORTIGERN's counsellors, for Vortigern was seeking a fatherless child to sacrifice in an attempt to cure the problem he was experiencing with a tower which, every time he built it, fell down again.

Dinadan

The brother of BREUNOR the Black and a KNIGHT OF THE ROUND TABLE. He is recorded as having seen no purpose in fighting for fighting's sake, and was finally killed by MORDRED and AGRAVAIN.

Dinas

The seneschal (steward) of King MARK[2] who was a KNIGHT OF THE ROUND TABLE but none the less felt sorry for TRISTAN, whom he thought had been ill-treated, and became the latter's companion. Dinas accompanied LANCELOT[2] when that knight ran off with Queen GUINEVERE and duly became Duke of ANJOU. After the death of King Mark, Dinas, according to the TAVOLA RITONDA, became king of CORNWALL.

Dinas Emrys

Situated two miles north-east of Beddgelert, GWYNEDD, lies a wooded hill known as Dinas Emrys, just below Llyn Dinas. It was here that VORTIGERN had repeatedly attempted to build his tower, but every night the stones fell down again. His counsellors advised him that he needed to sacrifice a fatherless child, for which MERLIN was considered ideal, for he was supposed to have been born without a father, the offspring of an incubus. However, Merlin advised Vortigern that the real problem lay in the fact that there were two dragons – one white and one red – confined beneath the site in a subterranean lake. Merlin subsequently dealt with the dragons and built his own fortress on the hill-top.

Details of how the dragons came to be below the hill are to be found in the MABINOGION story of LLUD AND LLEFELYS. During LLUD's reign a scream, whose origin could not be found, was heard every year on the eve of May Day. LLEFELYS, the king of FRANCE, told Llud that it was caused by fighting dragons, which were subsequently captured and buried at Dinas Emrys.

There are still some earthworks of the ancient fort to be seen on this site, which has its main entrance on the northern side of the hill. Traces of a ruined tower some thirty-six feet by twenty-four feet have been found on the summit, though whether these are the ruins of Vortigern's tower or Merlin's fort remains open to speculation. Nearby lies a circle of tumbled stones roughly thirty feet in diameter which is said to be a mystic ring in which the battling dragons were contained. At one time the fort was known as DINAS FFORAN – 'the Fort with High Powers'.

Merlin's treasure is apparently hidden in a cave at Dinas Emrys, having been placed in a golden vessel in the cave, along with his golden chair. Merlin then rolled a huge stone over the entrance of the cave and covered it with earth and grass. Tradition states that the discoverer of the treasure will be 'golden-haired and blue-eyed'. When that person comes near to Dinas Emrys a bell will be heard, inviting him, or her, into the cave, which will open of its own accord the instant that person's foot touches the stone covering the entrance.

A youth living near Beddgelert once searched for the treasure, obviously wanting to give himself a head start in life. Taking a pickaxe with him, he climbed to the top of the hill and started to dig on the site of the tower. As soon as he did, unearthly noises began to rumble beneath his feet and the whole of Dinas Emrys began to rock like a cradle. The sun clouded over and day became as night. Thunder roared over his head and lightning flashed all around him. Dropping his pickaxe, he ran for home and, when he arrived, everything was calm, but he never returned to retrieve the pickaxe.

Not far from Dinas Emrys is CELL-Y-DEWINIAID – 'the Grove of the Magicians'. There was once a grove of oak trees at the northern end of a field here under which Vortigern's counsellors were said to meet to discuss the events of their times. They were buried in an adjacent field, at one time each grave being marked by a stone, a white thorn tree annually decorating each with falling white blossoms.

Dinas Fforan

'The Fort with High Powers', the name by which the fort atop DINAS EMRYS was once known.

Dindrane

The sister of PERCEVAL[2] who was known as AGRESTIZIA in Italian romance. She accompanied her brother on the quest for the Holy GRAIL and, when the questers came to a castle where it was the custom to demand the blood of passing women to cure the leprous mistress, Dindrane voluntarily gave her blood and died by so doing.

Diones

Possibly cognate with DYONAS, Diones was the father of NIMUE, whose godmother was said to be none other than the goddess DIANA.

Dioneta

The name of two maidens in the BIRTH OF ARTHUR, a fourteenth-century Welsh work.
1 A daughter of LLEU (LOT) and GWYAR, the sister of GWALCHMAI and MORDRED.
2 A daughter of GORLOIS and IGRAINE[1], thus a half-sister to ARTHUR.

Dionise

The enchanted mistress of a castle whom GAWAIN[1] freed but refused to marry.

Dirac

The brother of LAC and hence the uncle of EREC.

Ditas

The king of HUNGARY, who was said to have been numbered among the followers of the Roman emperor THEREUS when the latter attacked ARTHUR.

Diu Crône

Thirteenth-century GRAIL romance by HENRICH VON DEM TÜRTIN in which GAWAIN[1] features as the hero, and which names King GARLIN of GALORE as the father of GUINEVERE and GOTEGRIM.

Diwrnach

The Irish owner of a wondrous cauldron who refused to hand it over to ARTHUR during the expedition to help CULHWCH. An expedition was mounted to IRELAND, Diwrnach slain and the cauldron seized. Subsequently this cauldron became one of the THIRTEEN TREASURES OF BRITAIN. The appearance of a wondrous Irish cauldron in this tale leads to a possible identification between Diwrnach and the DAGHDHA of early Irish mythology, and latterly with the holy GRAIL.

Do

The son of ARES and father of GRIFLET and LORETE, he was employed as a forester by UTHER.

Dodinel

The son of BELINANT and EGLANTE, though one story makes his mother the LADY OF MALEHAUT. A KNIGHT OF THE ROUND TABLE, he was known as 'The Savage', as he liked to hunt wild game in the forests. He is perhaps originally identical with PERCEVAL[2].

Dogsheads

In the poem PA GUR, the Dogsheads are the opponents of ARTHUR who were fought by either Arthur himself or KAY. It has been suggested that they might, in origin, be a recollection of a legendary Irish people, the Conchind – Dog-heads. Identifications with the Cunesioi, or Concani, both said to inhabit the Iberian peninsula, have also been made. They are not fully described in *Pa gur*, and this has led to some speculation about what exactly the Dogsheads were – man or beast.

Doldavius

The king of Gotland who, along with GUNPHAR, the king of the ORKNEYS, came to pay homage to ARTHUR; having heard of his prowess and fearing his might.

Dollallolla

The ridiculous name of ARTHUR's queen in Henry Fielding's parody *Tragedy of Tragedies* (1730).

Dolorous Gard

The name by which LANCELOT's castle, JOYOUS GARD, was originally known, and to which it later reverted. It has been identified with BAMBURGH castle in NORTHUMBERLAND.

Dolorous Stroke

The name given to the blow which rendered the WASTE LAND barren and which made the quest for the Holy GRAIL necessary. The ESTOIRE DEL SAINTE GRAAL makes this the occasion when VARLAN, or BRULEN, killed LAMBOR with DAVID's SWORD. However, Sir Thomas MALORY places the event later in the Arthurian chronology, and states it was the occasion when BALIN stabbed PELLAM with the LANCE OF LONGINUS, destroying three entire countries as a result.

Dôn

The Welsh equivalent of the Irish goddess ANU, Dana or Danu. Her children, which included gods of the sky, sea and poetry, were locked in battle with the powers of darkness, known as the Children of LLYR. Welsh tradition made Dôn the mother of GILFAETHWY, ARIANRHOD and GWYDION FAB DÔN. It has been suggested that Dôn was the original or DO, even though this would mean a change of gender.

Dondinello

The father of CARDUINO who was killed by poison.

Dor(e) Castle

Cornish castle where there is an ancient, and partially unintelligible, inscription thought to link CUNOMORUS with King MARK[2]. This is said to read '*Drustans hic iacit cunomori filius*' – 'Here lies Tristan, son of Cunomorus.' If this is indeed the true meaning of the inscription, it would seem to imply that the relationship between King Mark and TRISTAN was far closer than later writers were prepared to allow.

Dorin

The son of CLAUDAS, he was killed in a fight with BORS[2] and LIONEL.

Dornar

A son of King PELLINORE, the brother of DRIANT. He and his brother were both KNIGHTS OF THE ROUND TABLE.

Douglas, River

The river in LINNIUS which was the site of four of ARTHUR'S BATTLES, when the new king, aged just fifteen and having newly ascended the throne, defeated the SAXON leader COLGRIN and a mixed force of SAXONS, Scots and PICTS. Colgrin took refuge after the fourth battle in YORK, and ARTHUR then laid siege to him there.

Dozmary Pool

A body of water lying on Bodmin Moor, just to the east of Colliford Lake, about six miles from SLAUGHTERBRIDGE, the traditional Cornish location for CAMLANN. Dozmary Pool is just one of many possible locations for the episode where EXCALIBUR was returned to the LADY OF THE LAKE.

Dream of Rhonabwy, The

A Welsh romance that forms an important part of the MABINOGION, and concerns the adventures dreamt of by the hero of the story, RHONABWY.

Driant

A son of King PELLINORE and the brother of DORNAR. Both he and his brother were KNIGHTS OF THE ROUND TABLE. He died after receiving a mortal wound in combat against GAWAIN[1].

Drudwas

The son of King TRYFFIN of DENMARK, who, while supposedly one of ARTHUR'S followers and one of the TWENTY-FOUR KNIGHTS of Arthur's court, was once to meet the king in single combat. A cunning knight, he told his three pet griffins to go ahead of him and kill the first man who came on to the field of combat, fully expecting it to be Arthur. Drudwas, however, was the first to arrive, as his sister, Arthur's mistress, delayed the king. The griffins, not recognizing their master, killed him.

Druidan

When YDAIN tried to leave her lover GAWAIN[1], the latter bestowed his mistress on this dwarf.

Drumelzier

A place in SCOTLAND that numbers among the possible locations for the burial site of MERLIN.

Dryden, John

An English poet (1631–1700). His opera *King Arthur* (1691), with music by Henry Purcell, has little actual Arthurian content. In this version ARTHUR is in love with a blind girl called EMMELINE, but she is also loved by OSWALD, the SAXON enemy of the king.

Drynog

The owner of a cauldron, known as PAIR DRYNOG, that is numbered among the THIRTEEN TREASURES OF BRITAIN and was said to boil no meat save that of a brave man.

Dubric(ius), Saint
Also DYFRIG

An important Celtic saint who died c. AD 550. He was the bishop, and possibly also the abbot, of Caldey and, according to GEOFFREY OF MONMOUTH, was also the archbishop of CAERLEON-ON-USK who crowned the young King ARTHUR. Modern thinking has sought to identify him with MERLIN.

Due Tristani

An Italian romance dating from 1551 that gives details about the son and daughter of TRISTAN and ISEULT[1].

Dumbarton

A Scottish town whose Roman name was Alclud, and in which HOEL[1] was besieged by an army of PICTS and Scots until he was relieved by his ally King ARTHUR. According to Gaelic tradition, Dumbarton was also the birthplace of MOROIE MOR, the son of Arthur.

Dumnonia

Covering Devon, CORNWALL, and other regions of the south-west of England, Dumnonia was a considerable British kingdom. ARTHUR's successor, CONSTANTINE[2], was said to be the king of this realm. It would appear that the kingdom derived its name from the Dumnonii, a British tribe who were possibly related to the Irish Fir Dhomhnann.

Dun Stallion

One of ARTHUR's horses. Its spirit is said to haunt the village of CASTLE EDEN in County Durham.

Durmart

The hero of the French romance DURMART LE GALLOIS, he fell in love with the queen of IRELAND, FENISE (FENICE[2]).

Durmart le Gallois

A thirteenth-century French romance concerning the love of the hero, DURMART, for the queen of IRELAND.

Dyfed

The modern name for DEMETIA, a kingdom in the south of WALES which GEOFFREY OF MONMOUTH says was ruled by STATER during the Arthurian period.

Dyfrig

The Welsh name for Saint DUBRICIUS.

Dylan Eil Ton

'Dylan Son of the Wave', the first of the babies born in mysterious circumstances to ARIANRHOD as she performed a rite to attest to her virginity. Described as a golden-haired baby, he was simply christened Dylan. He immediately set off for the sea, whose nature he assumed, thereafter being known as Dylan Eil Ton.

Dynevor Castle

A castle in the vicinity of Llandeilo, DYFED. A cave in the park surrounding the castle is said to be one of the many possible sites for the confinement of MERLIN.

Dyonas

Possibly cognate with DIONES, Dyonas was the father of VIVIENNE, according to the VULGATE VERSION.

Dyrnwyn

The sword of RHYDDERCH HAEL which would burst into flame from the point to the cross if any man, save himself, drew it. It is numbered among the THIRTEEN TREASURES OF BRITAIN.

Dysgyfdawd

The father of GALL.

Dysgyl a gren Rhydderch

The platter of RHYDDERCH HAEL upon which any meat desired would appear, it is numbered among the THIRTEEN TREASURES OF BRITAIN.

Dywel

The brother of GEREINT.

Eachtra an Mhadra Mhaoil

An Irish prose romance regarding a hapless Indian prince, ALEXANDER[3], who was enchanted and transformed into a doglike creature known as the CROP-EARED DOG.

Eachtra Mhelóra agus Orlando

A sixteenth-century Irish romance regarding ARTHUR's daughter MELORA that was perhaps inspired by the Italian school of chivalrous romances, particularly those of ARIOSTO.

Eagle of Gwernabwy

The oldest creature in all the world which assisted CULHWCH and his compatriots to locate MABON[2] by introducing them to the SALMON OF LLYN LLW.

Ebissa

One of the sons of HENGIST, brother to AESEC, OCTA, HARTWAKER, RONWEN and SARDOINE.

Ebraucus

The founder of the CASTLE OF MAIDENS, which was originally known as the Castle of Mount AGNED.

Ector

The father of KAY and foster father to ARTHUR, his name is the Welsh form of HECTOR. The baby Arthur was delivered to him by MERLIN and was raised by Ector until, at the age of fifteen, Ector took Arthur and his son Kay to London for a tournament at which Kay was to be knighted, with Arthur acting as his squire. When, having found that he had forgotten Kay's sword, Arthur returned with the enchanted sword that had been placed in a stone to test who should become king of all England, Kay tried to claim that it was he who had drawn it. Ector, however, made Kay tell the truth, and so Arthur became king.

Ector de Maris

The son of King BAN of BENWICK (more commonly known as Ban of BRITTANY), whom he succeeded, and brother of Sir LANCELOT[2]. He was in love with PERSE and rescued her from ZELOTES, to whom she had been promised by her father.

Ecunaver

The king of KANEDIC, who was conquered by GAREL after he had declared that he intended to attack ARTHUR.

Eda Elyn Mawr

The name of ARTHUR's killer is not usually given. However, the Harleian MS 4181 in the British Library (entry 42) gives the name of Eda Elym Mawr as the man who inflicted Arthur's mortal wound at CAMLANN.

Eden

The name of an unidentified river. It would seem to be the river of that name to be found in Cumbria, for local legend says that UTHER, a giant in this instance, founded the kingdom of MALLERSTANG and tried to form a moat around his castle by diverting a river of this name.

Edinburgh

During the Middle Ages this city was known as Castellum Puellarum, which has led to its being identified with the CASTLE OF MAIDENS. It is also the site of ARTHUR's SEAT, a volcanic plug where ARTHUR was alleged to have watched his forces defeat the PICTS and Scots.

Edor

An ancestor of LOT.

Efflam, Saint

An Irish saint who is mentioned by the hagiologist Le Grand. However, Le Grand is not considered wholly reliable, as it appears that he may have altered some of his source material. He says that Efflam travelled to BRITTANY, where he found himself face to face with a decidedly unfriendly dragon. ARTHUR, badly equipped with just a club and a lionskin shield, came to his assistance, but to no effect. Efflam blessed Arthur for his help, and then put the monster to flight.

Efnisien

The half-brother of BENDIGEID VRAN who insulted MATHOLWCH while the latter, the king of IRELAND, was in BRITAIN wooing BRANWEN, the daughter of LLYR and sister to Bendigeid Vran. Returning home to Ireland, Matholwch had his revenge by treating Branwen badly. Bendigeid Vran mounted an expedition to Ireland to rescue his sister and, after at first suffering setbacks, succeeded in utterly obliterating the Irish people, save for five pregnant women hiding in a cave.

Efrawg

In the MABINOGION story of PEREDUR, the father of PERCEVAL[2]. As the name means 'York', it would seem that this was not his true name, but simply a title indicating the city he ruled.

Efrddf

The twin sister of URIEN of RHEGED.

Eglante

The mother of DODINEL the Savage.

Ehangwen

Built by GWLYDDYN the carpenter, this was the name of ARTHUR's hall, though its precise location remains a mystery. Some authorities say that it was situated at CAMELOT (wherever that might be), while others place it in various locations around the country, including CARLISLE and CASTLE EDEN in County Durham.

Eian

The son of NASCIEN[1], father of JON-AANS, and great-great-great-grandfather of GALAHAD[1].

Eiddilig

Named in the Welsh PEDWAR MARCHOG AR HUGAN LLYS ARTHUR as one of the TWENTY-FOUR KNIGHTS of King ARTHUR's court.

Eigyr

The Welsh form of IGRAINE[1].

Eilhart von Oberge

The twelfth-century author of *Tristant*, which gives just one of the many variations on the story of TRISTAN and ISEULT[1].

Einion

The hero of the Welsh folktale EINION AND OLWEN, in which he travels to the OTHERWORLD to marry OLWEN, the daughter of the chief giant YSPADDADEN. They had a child whom they named TALIESIN. Einion would appear to be a localized direct replacement for CULHWCH, the hero of the MABINOGION story of CULHWCH AND OLWEN, who is usually connected with the quest to marry Olwen.

Einion and Olwen

Welsh folktale in which the hero, EINION, undertakes to travel to the OTHERWORLD to marry OLWEN, the daughter of YSPADDADEN. It seems without doubt that Einion was a local hero who was a direct replacement in the area of WALES where the tale originated for CULHWCH, the hero normally associated with the quest to locate and marry Olwen.

Elaine

A form of Helen, this name is borne by at least six ladies in the Arthurian tales.

1 The daughter of King PELLES, who, with the aid of an enchanted potion administered by BRISEN, tricked LANCELOT[2] into sleeping with his daughter, their night of enchanted passion leading to the conception and subsequent birth of Sir GALAHAD[1]. Lancelot was said to have lain with her on a second occasion when he thought she was his beloved GUINEVERE, again under an enchantment, but this time at CAMELOT.

2 Elaine the White, the daughter of BERNARD of ASTOLAT, she is better known as the LADY OF SHALOTT. She fell in love with LANCELOT[2], who carried her sleeve during a joust, but when her love went unrequited she died for love of him. She was brought up the Thames in a boat to ARTHUR's court, bearing with her a letter explaining the circumstances of her death.

3 The daughter of PELLINORE who took her own life after the death of her lover, Sir MILES of the Laundes.

4 The wife of King NENTRES of GARLOT, she was the daughter of IGRAINE[1], sister to MORGAN[1] Le Fay and MORGAUSE, and half-sister to ARTHUR.

5 The wife of BAN of BENWICK (Ban of BRITTANY) and mother of Sir LANCELOT[2].

6 Variously described as either the daughter of LOT or NENTRES, she was a niece of ARTHUR and fell in love with Sir PERCEVAL[2].

Elergia

A witch who imprisoned ARTHUR and from whom the king was rescued by TRISTAN, according to the Italian romance TAVOLA RITONDA.

Elf

The offspring of Prometheus, the classical Greek hero who stole fire from the gods, and a fairy from the gardens of Adonis. The inhabitants of FAIRYLAND, or FAERIE, claimed their descent from him. His son, ELFIN, ruled over both England and America.

Elfant

A ruler of FAIRYLAND.

Elfar

A ruler of FAIRYLAND who was said to have killed two giants, one of which had two heads, the other three.

Elferon

A ruler of FAIRYLAND.

Elficleos

A ruler of FAIRYLAND.

Elfiline

A ruler of FAIRYLAND who built a golden wall around the city of Cleopolis, which had been founded by his predecessor ELFINAN.

Elfin

The son of ELF, whom he succeeded as the ruler of FAIRYLAND, as well as ruling over both England and America.

Elfinan

A ruler of FAIRYLAND who founded the city of Cleopolis.

Elfinell

A ruler of FAIRYLAND who was said to have defeated the goblins in battle.

Elfinor

A ruler of FAIRYLAND who built a brazen bridge upon the sea.

Elfland

An OTHERWORLD realm with whose king ROWLAND did battle and, by defeating him, so secured the release of his sister and brothers.

Eliabel
Also ELIABELLA

Presumably identical with the ELIZABETH of Sir Thomas MALORY's works, she was the mother of TRISTAN in Italian romance.

Eliabella
Also ELIABEL

A cousin of ARTHUR who was, according to Italian romance, the mother of TRISTAN, and presumably identical with ELIZABETH, the sister of King MARK². She married King MELIODAS¹ of LIONES to bring about peace between her new husband and Arthur, who had been at war.

Eliavres

A knight with magical powers or, more simply, a wizard. He fell in love with ARTHUR's niece YSAIVE, who was the wife of King CARADOC of VANNES AND NANTES. While Eliavres slept with Ysaive, resulting in the birth of CARADOC BRIEFBRAS, the wizard enchanted Caradoc and made him sleep with a bitch, a sow and a mare. When Caradoc Briefbras discovered the truth regarding his parentage, he told Caradoc, who, in wild fury, made Eliavres firstly lie with a bitch, by which he became the father of GUINALOT, then a sow, by which he became the father of TORTAIN, and finally, in full reflection of the same partners forced on him by the wizard, Caradoc made Eliavres lie with a mare, by which he became the father of LORIGAL.

Eliazar

A son of PELLES, brother to ELAINE[2] the White, and hence an uncle of GALAHAD[1].

Elidus

A king of IRELAND.

Eliezer

A son of EVELAKE.

Elis

The son of a duke who, due to a misprint in Caxton's original edition of Sir Thomas MALORY'S LE MORTE D'ARTHUR, has also been regarded as having this name. The duke is in fact unnamed, and simply referred to as an uncle of ARTHUR.

Elivri

The head groom in ARTHUR's stables.

Eliwlod

The son of MADOG, who was, in turn, the son of UTHER, thus making Eliwlod ARTHUR's nephew. Suggested as the original of Sir LANCELOT[2], he was named as one of the TWENTY-FOUR KNIGHTS of Arthur's court and, after his death, he appeared to Arthur in the guise of an eagle, according to the early Welsh poem *Ymddiddan Arthur a'r Eryr*.

Elizabeth

Probably to be identified with ELIABEL or ELIABELLA from Italian romance, Elizabeth was the sister of King MARK[2] of CORNWALL, wife of King MELIODAS[1] of LIONES (LYONESSE[2]) and mother of TRISTAN. While heavily pregnant, she entered the woods to search for her husband, went into labour and delivered Tristan, but died in so doing.

Ellen

Referred to as Burd Ellen, *burd* meaning 'lady', in the Scottish ballad CHILDE ROWLAND, she was, according to that ballad, the daughter of ARTHUR.

Elmet

An ancient Celtic kingdom, centred on Leeds, that existed during the traditional Arthurian period, but whose exact extent remains undetermined.

Elphin

The son of GWYDDNO GARANHIR. Having rescued the child from the leather bag which CERRIDWEN had thrown into the sea, naming the radiant child TALIESIN, he was in return rescued by the bard when he was a prisoner of MAELGWYN.

Elsa (of Brabant)

The daughter of the duke of BRABANT. When she was besieged by Frederick de TELRAMUND, LOHENGRIN came to her aid and defeated her attacker. Lohengrin then married Elsa, but cautioned her that she was never to ask his name. Having borne him two children, she at length asked the forbidden question, upon which Lohengrin immediately departed.

Elucidation

A 484-line-long prologue, in French, to LE CONTE DE GRAAL by CHRÉTIEN DE TROYES.

Eluned

The owner of a ring which is numbered among the THIRTEEN TREASURES OF BRITAIN and which made the wearer invisible.

Elutherius

The POPE who, at the request of king LUCIUS, sent the two emissaries DERUVIAN and PHAGAN to invigorate the work on the abbey at GLASTONBURY. This was said to have been in c. AD 166.

Elves

Although these Teutonic creatures do not figure elsewhere in Celtic mythology, they do appear in LAYAMON's works, in which they were said to have bestowed gifts upon ARTHUR at his birth, arranging for him to be long-lived, valiant and rich.

Elyadus

The king of Sicily and father of FLORIANT, who was raised by MORGAN[1] Le Fay.

Elyan (the White)

The son of Sir BORS[2] and the unnamed daughter of King BRANDEGORIS, who later became the emperor of CONSTANTINOPLE.

Elyas Anais

The proper name of the HERMIT KING, though that title was also applied to King PELLES. He was either a maternal or a paternal uncle of PERCEVAL[2], though the sources cannot agree on the actual lineage.

Elyzabel

A cousin of GUINEVERE who was imprisoned by CLAUDAS on a charge of espionage. ARTHUR, at the behest of his queen, requested Elyzabel's release, and when this was refused he waged war on Claudas. It is possible that she is the original of ELIZABETH and ELIABEL, for etymologically the names are similar.

Emhain Abhlach

The paradisaical home of the Irish sea god. It means 'Emhain of the Apple Trees', and this may have led to its association with the Isle of APPLES, the name given by GEOFFREY OF MONMOUTH to AVALON.

Emmeline

A blind girl, the daughter of Duke CONON of CORNWALL, who in DRYDEN's opera KING ARTHUR was betrothed to the king but was carried off by Oswald, the SAXON king of KENT. Her sight was restored to her by MERLIN while she was still Oswald's prisoner. Arthur eventually defeated Oswald, thus rescuing her.

Empress of Constantinople

Unnamed, this member of the imperial family of CONSTANTINOPLE gave a magical stone to PERCEVAL[2] which rendered him invisible, and thus helped him in his fight against the AFANC.

Endelienta, Saint

The god-daughter of ARTHUR who owned a cow which was, by tradition, killed by the Lord of TRENTENY. Arthur either had him killed, or performed this deed himself, but whatever the means of his death, Endelienta restored him to life.

Eneuavc

The daughter of Sir BEDIVERE[2].

Enfaces Gauvain

A French Arthurian poem that dates from the thirteenth century concerning the life of GAWAIN[1]. This work is unusual in that it makes LOT, Gawain's father by MORGAUSE, a page at ARTHUR's court.

Engres

A king, the brother of ISEULT[1], according to the Icelandic SAGA OF TRISTRAM, who offered his sister's hand to whomsoever managed to kill a dragon.

Enid(e)

The heroine of EREC ET ENIDE by CHRÉTIEN DE TROYES and the Welsh variant GEREINT AND ENID. In both versions she is the wife of the hero, either EREC or GEREINT. Erec et Enide says that she was the daughter of LICONAUS and TARSENESYDE, while Gereint and Enid gives her father as YNWYL, her mother remaining unnamed.

Enygeus

The sister of JOSEPH OF ARIMATHEA who married BRONS and became the mother of ALAN.

Eopa

The SAXON who, at the instigation of VORTIGERN's son PASCHENT, poisoned AMBROSIUS AURELIUS and later fell in battle against UTHER.

Erbin

The father of GEREINT, although according to the Life of Saint Cyby this role is reversed and Gereint is given as the father of Erbin.

Erec

Usually given as the son of LAC, King of NANTES, whom he succeeded, although the Norse version of his story, EREX SAGA, names his father as ILAX. The hero of EREC ET ENIDE by CHRÉTIEN DE TROYES, he first encountered his future wife, ENIDE, when he gave chase to someone who had insulted queen GUINEVERE. He gave up his knightly adventures when he married Enide, but when she later scolded him for doing so, he undertook some more.

Erec

Late twelfth- or early thirteenth-century Middle High German romance by HARTMANN VON AUE concerning the exploits of EREC which closely follows the earlier work of CHRÉTIEN DE TROYES.

Erec et Enide

French romance, written c. 1160, by CHRÉTIEN DE TROYES. Introducing the characters of EREC and ENIDE, the work was followed very closely by HARTMANN VON AUE in his work EREC which was probably written within forty years of the original. Welsh romancers substituted their own hero for Erec in their version of the story, GEREINT AND ENID.

Erex Saga

Norse saga concerning EREC that is undoubtedly based on EREC ET ENIDE by CHRÉTIEN DE TROYES.

Erfddf

The daughter of CYNFARCH by NEFYN and twin sister of URIEN, according to the Welsh TRIADS.

Eries

A son of LOT, perhaps originally identical with GAHERIS, he became one of King ARTHUR's knights.

Erlan

An ancestor of LOT of LOTHIAN.

Ermaleus

The son of the king of ORKNEY and GAWAIN[1]'s cousin, he was defeated by BIAUSDOUS and sent as a captive to ARTHUR. He appears in the romance Beaudous.

Ermid

A brother of GEREINT.

Ermine

A sister of ARTHUR who is identifiable with ANNA. Some sources say that she married BUDIC while her sister married LOT, but it is more normal to equate Anna/Ermine with the wife of Lot.

Erminia

The realm of ROULAND, the father of TRISTAN by BLANCHEFLEUR[2], according to one medieval romance.

Eryri

The name by which GEOFFREY OF MONMOUTH refers to YR WYDDFA FAWR or, more usually nowadays, Mount SNOWDON. He states that it was on this mountain that ARTHUR slew the giant RITHO.

Escanor

The name of at least three knights from the Arthurian tales.
1 A knight whose strength grew to its peak at noon, and then lessened. Appearing in L'Atre Perileux, he absconded with ARTHUR's female cupbearer, but was pursued and eventually killed by GAWAIN[1].
2 Escanor Le Beau. Appearing in the obscure French romance Escanor, this knight fought a duel with GAWAIN[1], after which the two became firm friends.
3 Escanor Le Grand. The son of a giant and a witch, and the uncle of ESCANOR[2] Le Beau, he also appears in Escanor, and held GRIFLET prisoner.

Escavalon

The king of this realm is named as the father of FLORIE[2], who married GAWAIN[1] and became the mother of WIGALOIS by him.

Esclabor

Also ASTLABOR

A nobleman from BABYLON and the father of PALAMEDES. Sent to Rome as part of a tribute, he saved the Roman emperor's life. In due course he arrived in LOGRES, saved the life of King PELLINORE, and then hurried on to CAMELOT.

Esclados

The defender of a wondrous fountain in the forest of BROCELIANDE, he was killed by OWAIN, who married his widow, LAUDINE. This marriage of the victor to the widow of the vanquished is thought to encapsulate a pagan custom whereby the victor was ritually married to the territory of whomsoever he defeated.

Esclarimonde

A fairy who was the lover of both ESCANOR[2] Le Beau and BRIAN DES ILES.

Esclarmonde

The wife of HUON. She was taken by MORGAN[1] Le Fay to the TERRESTRIAL PARADISE, bathed there in the FOUNTAIN OF YOUTH and was changed by Jesus into a fairy. This story appears in *Le Chanson d'Esclarmonde*, a sequel to HUON DE BORDEAUX, which gives, as a reason for this episode, the fact that HUON's right to the throne of the kingdom of FAERIE was disputed by ARTHUR, who had resided there since his earthly days had come to an end. The fairy folk refused to obey Huon because he had not married one of their people and so, by changing Esclarmonde into a fairy, the problem was resolved, and Huon could ascend the throne.

Escol

The son of King AELENS of IRELAND, he is simply described as a follower of ARTHUR.

Escorducarla

The Lady of VALLONE, who became enamoured of MERLIN and planned to make him her prisoner. The plan, however, backfired, and Escorducarla ended up as Merlin's prisoner instead.

Este, House of

Italian family who were rulers of Ferrara between 1000 and 1875. According to ARIOSTO, BRADMANTE, a female warrior of the Carolingian era (AD 751–987), was told that the family would descend from here.

Estoire del Sainte Graal

A thirteenth-century French romance that forms a part of the VULGATE VERSION. It is unusual in identifying the WASTE LAND of the GRAIL legends with WALES, an association that is found in no other source.

Estonne

The father of PASSALEON and LORD OF THE SCOTTISH WILDERNESS, he was killed by BRUYANT the Faithless.

Estorause

The pagan king of SARRAS who, when dying, asked forgiveness of BORS[2], PERCEVAL[2] and GALAHAD[1] for imprisoning them, forgiveness which was forthcoming.

Estrangot

A variant name applied to ILLE ESTRANGE, the kingdom of VAGOR.

Estregales

The kingdom of LAC, who was also the ruler of the Black Isles and the father of EREC, BRANDILES and JESCHUTÉ.

Etna, Mount

More normally associated with classical mythology, this active volcano on Sicily is considered by some to be one of the possible last resting places of ARTHUR. It seems likely that the Arthurian tales were carried to Sicily during the Norman occupation of that island.

Ettard

The beloved of PELLEAS, she did not reciprocate his feelings. NIMUE cast an enchantment over her and she fell in love with Pelleas, but, under another enchantment cast by Nimue, Pelleas no longer loved her, his feelings having been transferred to Nimue herself. Ettard died of her then unrequited love for Pelleas.

Eudaf

A variant of EVDAF.

Eugenius

A king of SCOTLAND and an ally of MORDRED, according to the SCOTORUM HISTORIAE of BOECE, he captured GUINE-VERE, who remained a prisoner of the PICTS.

Euric

An historic king of the Visigoths between AD 466 and 484. He was opposed by the emperor ANTHEMIUS, who counted RIOTHAMUS among his supporters.

Eustace

The Duke of CAMBENET, he was one of the eleven leaders who rebelled against the youthful ARTHUR at the outset of his reign.

Evadeam

A man who fell under an enchantment and was transformed into a dwarf. GAWAIN[1], who had been told that he would assume the shape of the next person he met, came across Evadeam and, while Evadeam regained his original form, Gawain became a dwarf. Eventually Gawain was restored to his former self and Evadeam was made a KNIGHT OF THE ROUND TABLE.

Evaine

The sister of ELAINE[5], wife of BAN. She became the wife of BORS[1] and mother of LIONEL and the younger BORS[2]. Following the death of her husband, she became a nun, having left her children in the care of PHARIEN.

Evander

One of the various kings that were said to have ruled SYRIA during the traditional Arthurian period.

Evdaf
Also EUDAF

According to the paternal pedigree of ARTHUR in BONEDD YR ARWR, Evdaf was the son of KRADOC and the father of KYNAN. GEOFFREY OF MONMOUTH makes him OCTAVIUS, Duke of GWENT. The uncle of CONAN MERIADOC, he subsequently became king of BRITAIN.

Evelake

A king who was born in FRANCE. Sent to Rome as part of a tribute, he afterwards travelled to SYRIA, but there he slew the governor's son and had to flee to BABYLON, where he helped the king, THOLOMER, and as a reward was given land. He became the king of SARRAS and was baptized by JOSEPH OF ARIMATHEA, at which time he took the name MORDRAIN. He had two sons, ELIEZER and GRIMAL. He is associated with the stories of the Holy GRAIL, for it was said that he lived with unhealing wounds, sustained only by the Sacred Host, and would remain that way until the knight who would achieve his quest for the Holy Grail should release him. Evelake might, in origin, have been the father of MODRON, who is named as AVALLOC in the Welsh TRIADS. This further leads him to an association with AVALON, as Avalloc is thought to have been a god associated with apples, and Avalon is sometimes referred to as the Isle of APPLES.

Evgen

According to the sixteenth-century maternal pedigree for ARTHUR of Grufudd Hiraethog, Evgen is said to have been among his ancestors.

Evrain

One of the wizards who was responsible for changing BLONDE ESMERÉE into a serpent.

Evrawg

According to Welsh tradition, the father of PEREDUER (PERCEVAL[2]).

Excalibur

The romanticized magical sword of ARTHUR which was given to him by the LADY OF THE LAKE. The story goes that MERLIN was often afraid that Arthur would fall in battle, and so decided that he should have his own special sword. Therefore, Merlin took Arthur on a journey to the shores of a wide and still lake. There, in the middle, Arthur saw an arm, clothed in rich samite (silk), rise from the calm waters, the hand clasping a fair sword.

Merlin advised Arthur that he must speak kindly to the Lady of the Lake in order to obtain the sword. Sure enough, she invited Arthur to row out to the centre of the lake to take the sword and its scabbard. Returning to the shore, Merlin asked which he preferred, sword or scabbard? Arthur considered the question, and then replied that he preferred the sword, to which Merlin added that the scabbard was worth ten of the sword, for while Arthur carried the scabbard he would never lose blood, no matter now sorely wounded he might be.

Some sources say that, knowing he was dying, Arthur passed Excalibur on to GAWAIN[1]. However, the most popular end to the life of Excalibur is that it was returned to the Lady of the Lake by Sir BEDIVERE[2] after Arthur's last battle at CAMLANN. On the first occasion that Bedivere returned from the lake, having hidden Excalibur, meaning to keep the sword for himself, Arthur asked him what he had seen. Bedivere's answer, that he had seen nought but wind and waves, told Arthur that his instructions had not been carried out. The second time Bedivere carried out Arthur's orders and hurled the sword out over the lake. As it fell towards the water, an arm appeared and, having caught the sword, drew it back under the waters. Returning once again to Arthur, Bedivere recounted what he had seen and this time Arthur knew all was well.

Some sources incorrectly state that Excalibur was the SWORD IN THE STONE, but, even though this is not the accepted state of affairs, they do make partial amends by saying that it was placed in the stone by the Lady of the Lake.

Sir Thomas MALORY does not name the sword in his LE MORTE D'ARTHUR. In the early Welsh story of CULHWCH AND OLWEN, the sword is called CALADVWICH, which can be linguistically linked with the magical sword CALADBOLG (derived from *calad* – 'hard' – and *bolg* – 'lightning'), a sword borne by Irish heroes, and in particular Cú Chulainn. GEOFFREY OF MONMOUTH calls the sword CALIBURNUS, and so derives the Excalibur of the romances.

Faerie

Alternative name for FAIRYLAND, the allegorical realm that is SPENSER's vision of England.

Faerie King, The

An unpublished seventeenth-century poem by Samuel Sheppard which tells how BYANOR received a sword that had once belonged to king ARTHUR.

Faerie Knight, The

The son of CAELIA and TOM A'LINCOLN, ARTHUR's illegitimate son, and thus the grandson of ARTHUR himself.

Faerie Queene, The

The epic, unfinished, allegorical work of Edmund SPENSER that features the uncrowned King ARTHUR, and remains the poet's most famous work. In the poem, England is represented as FAIRYLAND, where Arthur had adventures before being crowned and where he became enamoured with GLORIANA (representing Queen Elizabeth I), the daughter of OBERON[1] and TITANIA.

Fairyland

Also FAERIE

The allegorical vision of the England of SPENSER's day as used in his poem THE FAERIE QUEENE, and a realm in which ARTHUR had adventures before becoming king. The inhabitants of this land claimed their descent from ELF, a creation of Prometheus, the classical Greek hero who stole fire from the gods, and a fairy from the gardens of Adonis. Elf's son was called ELFIN and ruled both England and America. Other rulers of Fairyland were called ELFINAN, who founded the city of Cleopolis; ELFILINE, who built a golden wall around Cleopolis; ELFINELL, who defeated the goblins in battle; ELFANT; ELFAR, who killed two giants, one of which had two heads, the other three; and ELFINOR, who built a brazen bridge upon the sea. Other kings mentioned are ELFICLEOS, ELFERON and OBERON[1], the latter being the husband of TITANIA and the father of GLORIANA, with whom ARTHUR became enamoured. These latter kings are illustrated in the family tree shown in Figure 12.

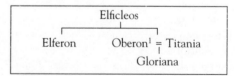

Figure 12 *Family tree of the rulers of Fairyland*

Falkirk

Town in SCOTLAND near which there used to stand a Roman temple that has become known as ARTHUR'S O'ON. The temple was destroyed in 1743, but an exact copy was built at nearby Penicuick House to serve as a dovecote. It has been suggested that ARTHUR used the original temple and that it, in turn, was the original of the ROUND TABLE.

False Guinevere, The

In French romance, the identical half-sister of GUINEVERE whom her father, King LEODEGRANCE, fathered on the same night. Championed by BERTHOLAI, this Guinevere claimed that she was the true Guinevere and enticed ARTHUR into giving up her half-sister. The true Guinevere then took refuge in SORLOIS. In the end she and her champion admitted their deception and, after two and a half years, Arthur and the real Guinevere were reunited.

Faramond

A variant of PHARAMOND.

Fata Morgana

The Italian form of MORGAN[1] Le Fay who was believed to live in Calabria, a region of southern Italy. Legends concerning Morgan Le Fay, the sister of ARTHUR, under this name are found in Sicily, possibly being introduced by the Normans, who settled on the island. The Italian term 'Fata Morgana' is still applied to a mirage, often seen in the Straits of Messina, which is traditionally ascribed to the sorcery of Morgan Le Fay. This mirage magnifies both vertically and horizontally, so that buildings appear like Morgan Le Fay's fairy palaces.

Faustus

A son of VORTIGERN.

Feimurgan

A variant of MORGAN[1] Le Fay.

Feirefiz

The son of GAHMURET and BELCANE in WOLFRAM VON ESCHENBACH'S PARZIFAL who, because his parents were of different colours, was piebald. He met his half-brother PERCEVAL[2], and the pair went to ARTHUR's court, where Feirefiz fell in love with the GRAIL damsel REPANSE DE SCHOIE. He converted to Christianity and he and Repanse de Schoie went to India, where they became the parents of PRESTER JOHN.

Felix

According to the TRISTANO RICCARDIANO, the father of MELIODAS[1] and King MARK[2], and thus the grandfather of TRISTAN. In another Italian romance, TAVOLA RITONDA, Felix was the king of CORNWALL and LIONES, while according to Sir Thomas MALORY Meliodas and King Mark were brothers-in-law.

Fenice
Also FENISE

1 According to CLIGÉS, the wife of the emperor of CONSTANTINOPLE, ALIS.
2 In DURMART LE GALLOIS, the queen of IRELAND, though here her name is spelt FENISE.

Fenise

A variant of FENICE[2] found in DURMART LE GALLOIS.

Fergus

1 Having witnessed the splendour of ARTHUR and his knights, this plough-boy aspired to become a knight. On his horse ARONDIEL, he had various adventures, finally marrying GALIENE, the Lady of LOTHIAN.

2 A KNIGHT OF THE ROUND TABLE of Cornish provenance. He was said to have slain the BLACK KNIGHT[5], who guarded a wimple and a horn on an ivory lion.

Ferragunze

A knight who, among other declarations, asserted to ARTHUR and MELIODAS[1] that he was never jealous of VERSERIA, his beautiful wife. Deciding to test him over his claim, they arranged for Verseria to be discovered in the embraces of GAWAIN[1]. True to his word, Ferragunze showed no signs of jealousy.

Ffrwdwr

According to BONEDD YR ARWR, a maternal ancestor of ARTHUR.

Ffynnon Cegin Arthur

The oily appearance of the water in this well in Caernarvon is said to have been acquired from animal fat from ARTHUR's kitchens.

Filimenis

The emperor of CONSTANTINOPLE, according to FLORIANT ET FLORETE.

Finbeus

A knight who had obtained a magical stone from his fairy mistress that made its owner beautiful, wise and invincible. He lent this stone to GUINEVERE, but, having returned it to Finbeus, she still coveted it and asked GAWAIN[1] to retrieve it for her, which he did by defeating Finbeus in combat.

Fish-knight

Closely resembling a mounted knight, this 'fishy' monster was fought by ARTHUR, who sought to release a fairy by the name of the LADY OF THE FAIR HAIR.

Fisher King(s)

The descendants of JOSEPH OF ARIMATHEA who guarded the Holy GRAIL in CARBONEK Castle. In early versions of the Grail stories, the Grail itself is said to have been the vessel in which the blood of Christ was collected after Jesus's side had been pierced with a lance by the centurion LONGINUS (St John:19.xxxiv). Later versions made the Grail the cup from which Jesus and his disciples drank at the Last Supper.

This wondrous relic is housed in the GRAIL CASTLE, where it is guarded by the GRAIL KEEPER, the wounded Fisher King. Maimed 'through the thighs' (sic), a wound said to have been caused by the DOLOROUS STROKE, he feeds only from a magical dish, his land having become infertile as a result of his wound, and will revive only if the king himself is cured. The cure will come about only if there is a knight brave enough to travel on the perilous journey through the 'land of wailing women' to the Grail Castle and, once there, wise enough to ask the GRAIL QUESTION. This would then break the enchantment under which both king and land are held captive.

The Fisher King is given various names and associations in the Arthurian tales. Sometimes, though not always, identified with the MAIMED KING, he is called PELLES in the VULGATE VERSION, which names the Maimed King as PARLAN or PELLAM. In Manessier's CONTINUATION, his wound was said to have been inflicted by fragments of the sword which killed his brother, GOON DESERT, while CHRÉTIEN DE TROYES himself says that he could not ride as a result of his infirmity, and so took to fishing as a pastime – hence his title. ROBERT DE BORON names him BRONS and says that the title Fisher King came from the fact that he supplied fish for JOSEPH OF ARIMATHEA, though another early commentator derives his name from the Christian fish symbol. WOLFRAM VON ESCHENBACH identifies him as ANFORTAS, while the *Sone de Nausay* states that the Fisher King is none other than Joseph of Arimathea himself.

It is generally agreed that the story of the Fisher King is derived from an ancient fertility myth and has associations with the sea god, the ruler of the mysterious OTHERWORLD. The PREIDDEU ANNWFN describes a journey made to this Otherworld by king ARTHUR in search of a magic cauldron, and this story is regarded as one of the sources of the Grail stories.

Floree

A variant of FLORIE.

Florence

The son of GAWAIN[1], he was among the company of knights who surprised GUINEVERE and LANCELOT[2] together in the queen's bedchamber, and was killed by the escaping yet unarmed Lancelot.

Florete

The daughter of the emperor of CONSTANTINOPLE and the wife of FLORIANT. She is the heroine of the romance FLORIANT ET FLORETE.

Floriant

The hero of FLORIANT ET FLORETE, the son of ELYADUS, king of Sicily, who was raised by MORGAN[1] Le Fay. He was said to have been brought by a WHITE STAG to his foster mother. A member of ARTHUR's court, he supported the latter in his war against the emperor of CONSTANTINOPLE, falling in love with that emperor's daughter, FLORETE, whom he married.

Floriant et Florete

A thirteenth-century French poetic romance concerning FLORIANT, the fosterling of MORGAN[1] Le Fay who, during ARTHUR's war against FILIMENIS, the emperor of CONSTANTINOPLE, fell in love with the emperor's daughter, FLORETE, and duly married her.

Florie
Also FLOREE

The name of at least two ladies from Arthurian tales.

1 The queen of KANADIC, she raised ARTHUR's son ILINOT, who fell in love with her. As a result she sent him away, and he died of a broken heart.
2 The niece of King JORAM and daughter of the king of ESCAVALON. She married GAWAIN[1] and became the mother of WIGALOIS by him.

Florisdelfa

Learning her magic arts under the tutorship of MERLIN, this enchantress sent her master a herd of magic swine and a crystal tower seated on a chariot that was drawn by fire-breathing dragons. She committed suicide when she perceived the beauty of ISEULT.

Fluratrone

A realm whose queen married GAURIEL. She deserted him, saying that she would return only when her husband had captured three of ARTHUR's knights, a task that was successfully completed.

Flurent

According to the Icelandic SAGA OF TRISTRAM, the mother of ISEULT[1].

Flying Horse

According to the French romance *The Fair Magalona and Peter, Son of the Count of Provence*, this fabulous beast was made by MERLIN.

Fool of the Forest

According to Gaelic tradition, the name by which MOROIE MOR, the son of ARTHUR who was born at DUMBARTON, was known.

Forest of Adventure

Unidentified forest, appearing in EREC ET ENIDE, where a WHITE STAG was reputedly hunted down.

Fort of Glass

CAER WYDYR, an OTHERWORLD city that has become associated with both GLASTONBURY and AVALON. Some sources have identified the Fort of Glass with CAER FEDDWIDD or CAER SIDDI, another Otherworld realm, but this mysterious fort is better, and more correctly, known as the Fort of CAROUSAL.

Fortune

A maiden whom ARTHUR dreamt he saw spinning her wheel in the MORTE ARTHURE. The king was strapped to the wheel, which was spun until he was smashed to smithereens. His dream was explained as foretelling his downfall.

Fountain of the Truth of Love

According to *Astrée*, a seventeenth-century novel started by Honoré d'Urfé (1567–1625) and finished by his secretary, Baro, this fountain was created by MERLIN and guarded by lions which would not eat people who were pure and honest. The fountain makes its appearance in the section of the novel written by Baro.

Fountain of Youth

The fountain located in the TERRESTRIAL PARADISE in which ESCLARMONDE was bathed by MORGAN[1] Le Fay.

France

This large European country is sometimes, in the Arthurian tales, referred to by its older name of GAUL. During the Arthurian period, France was a Frankish kingdom, that race having established themselves there c. AD 457. Indeed, the present name of France derives from their name. Clovis I, who came to the throne in AD 481, is possibly the original of CLAUDAS, while in some Arthurian sources PHARAMOND, who is also possibly Frankish in origin, is the king of France.

The MABINOGION story of CULHWCH AND OLWEN tells of two French kings at ARTHUR's court named IONA and PARIS.

Franchise Tristan

Formerly called SERVAGE, this country changed its name when it was conquered by TRISTAN, though some sources say that the country was given to him by its previous ruler.

Frederick

The king of the FRISIANS, according to the ALLITERATIVE MORTE ARTHURE, and an ally of MORDRED.

Frederick de Telramund

See TELRAMUND, FREDERICK DE

Frimutel

The father of AMFORTAS, the GRAIL KING, according to WOLFRAM VON ESCHENBACH.

Frisian(s)

A Germanic people who have given their name to the islands off the coast of GERMANY and the Netherlands. They were numbered among the barbarian invaders of BRITAIN by the Byzantine historian Procopius, whose writings date from the traditional Arthurian period. King CALIN of Friesland – that is, the land of the Frisians – was subject to ARTHUR, according to LAYAMON, though the ALLITERATIVE MORTE ARTHURE makes the king, FREDERICK, an ally of MORDRED.

Frocin

A dwarf whom King MARK[2] had beheaded for betraying his secret that he had horse's ears.

Frollo

The Roman tribune who ruled GAUL for the emperor Leo and who was defeated by ARTHUR when the latter first invaded Gaul at the start of his Roman campaign. Frollo took refuge in Paris, but met Arthur in single combat outside the city, and was killed. This is, at least, the conventional view of Frollo. The PROSE TRISTAN does not differ from this view, but adds that Frollo had a son named SAMALIEL, who went on to become a renowned knight. The VULGATE VERSION, *Prose Lancelot*, says he was an ally of King CLAUDAS and a claimant to the throne of FRANCE (GAUL). Elsewhere he is said to have been a German who became the Gaulish king.

Fulgentius

Listed by GEOFFREY OF MONMOUTH as an early king of BRITAIN, he was also said by the Scottish historian John of Fordun to have been an ancestor of LOT.

Fyfnnon Fawr

A spring that lies below ARTHUR'S STONE[1] at CEFN-Y-BRYN, Gower, WALES. The waters of this spring are supposed to run according to the ebb and flow of the nearby sea. The water used to be drunk from the palm of one hand while a wish was made. It is said that the spectral figure of King ARTHUR appears from beneath the stone on nights with a full moon.

Gaban

The maker of a sword, according to the *Polistoire del Eglise de Christ de Caunterbyre*, in the days when Christ was just fourteen years old. The sword was reputedly later wielded by GAWAIN[1]. This ancient metalworker may represent a survival of the ancient Celtic smith god GOFANNON or GOIBHNIU.

Gaddifer

The brother of BETIS who, when Betis was make king of England following the conquest of BRITAIN by ALEXANDER THE GREAT, was made the king of SCOTLAND.

Gaheris

The name of two KNIGHTS OF THE ROUND TABLE. Nothing else is known about one of them, but the other was a son of LOT and MORGAUSE. He surprised LAMORAK and Morgause in bed together and killed his mother, an act for which ARTHUR banished him. In the company of Agravain he hunted down and killed Lamorak. During LANCELOT[2]'s rescue of Queen GUINEVERE, Gaheris was killed by Lancelot.

Gahmuret

According to WOLFRAM VON ESCHENBACH, the father of PERCEVAL[2]. Travelling to the Orient, he entered the service of the BARUC of Baghdad, during which time he rescued BELCANE, queen of ZAZAMANC, from a Scottish army and married her. His son by Belcane was the piebald FEIREFIZ. Returning to Europe, he married again, this time HERZELOYDE, the queen of WALES and NORTHGALIS, by whom he became the father of Perceval. He left to help the Baruc of Baghdad and was killed.

Gailhom

The capital of the ancient kingdom of GORE.

Galachin

A variant of GALESCHIN.

Galagandreiz

One of the fathers-in-law of Sir LANCELOT[2].

Galahad

The name of at least three characters from the Arthurian stories.

1 The grandson of BAN and the natural son of LANCELOT[2] whose mother is variously given as ELAINE[1], AMITE or PEREVIDA. Possibly simply the creation of the author of the QUESTE DEL SAINTE GRAAL, as this is where he first appears, he may also be derived from either the Palestinian place-name Gilead or the Welsh character of GWALHAFED, who is

mentioned in the MABINOGION story of CULHWCH AND OLWEN. It has even been suggested that he derives from Saint ILLTYD.

As a child he was placed in a nunnery, where his paternal great-aunt was the abbess, later being knighted there by his father, LANCELOT. His story is almost entirely concerned with the quest of the Holy GRAIL and is, basically, as follows.

One day a sword in a marble and iron stone was spotted in a river by a company of ARTHUR's knights and taken back to CAMELOT. Galahad was brought into the presence of the king and the KNIGHTS OF THE ROUND TABLE. There he sat in the SIEGE PERILOUS, the place reserved for the purest knight, and, no calamity befalling him, he easily drew the sword from the stone which, according to an inscription, could be done only by the world's best knight. Joining the Knights of the Round Table, Galahad was present when the vision of the Grail appeared and was one of the knights chosen to go on the quest in search of this most magnificent and mysterious of relics. Before leaving, he was given a white shield which had been made by EVELAKE and which had a red cross on it that had been painted in blood by JOSEPH OF ARIMATHEA.

During the course of his quest, he met and joined up with PERCEVAL[2], BORS[2] and Perceval's sister, gaining for himself DAVID'S SWORD as they travelled aboard SOLOMON's ship. Following the death of Perceval's sister, the remaining trio parted company and, for a while, Galahad journeyed with his father. They visited Evelake, who afterwards died, and, having parted from his father, Galahad once again joined up with Perceval and Bors. These three knights came to Castle CARBONEK, where they achieved their quest by finding the Holy Grail.

When Galahad repaired the broken sword, which neither Perceval nor Bors had managed to do, Joseph of Arimathea appeared and celebrated mass with them, after which Jesus appeared to the three knights and told Galahad that he would see the Grail more openly in SARRAS. Before leaving Carbonek, Galahad anointed the MAIMED KING with blood from the GRAIL SPEAR, thus curing him of his ailment. Having left Carbonek, the three knights came to a ship on board which they once again found the Grail and in this vessel they sailed to Sarras. There the pagan king ESTORAUSE cast them into a prison, where they were sustained by the Grail. As Estorause lay dying, the three gallant knights forgave him for having imprisoned them and, following his death, Galahad became the new king of Sarras.

One year later Galahad came across Joseph of Arimathea celebrating mass and once again beheld the Holy Grail. Having done so, he asked that he should be allowed to die, which he did in peace. He was also said to have, at some stage in his life, saved the kingdom of LOGRES. Various commentators have given Galahad any number of lines of descent. However, that most widely accepted is shown in Figure 13.

2 A son of JOSEPH OF ARIMATHEA who was born in BRITAIN, ascended to the throne of WALES, when he became known as HOCELICE, and was an ancestor of URIEN.

3 The original name of the father of GALAHAD[1], better known as LANCELOT[2]. He is named as one of the TWENTY-FOUR KNIGHTS of King ARTHUR's court.

Nascien[1]
|
Celidoine
|
Narpus
|
Nascien[2]
|
Eian
|
Jonaans
|
Lancelot[1]
|
Ban
|
Lancelot[2] = Elaine[1]
|
Galahad

Figure 13   *Descent of Sir Galahad according to the most widespread version*

Galegantis

The maternal grandfather of LANCELOT[2] and also the name of one of ARTHUR's knights.

Galehaut

'The High Prince' who ruled the District Isles, SURLUSE 'and various other kingdoms. The son of BRUNOR and the giantess BAGOTA, he invaded BRITAIN. He became a firm friend of Sir LANCELOT[2] and, through that friendship, also a friend of ARTHUR, being made a KNIGHT OF THE ROUND TABLE. When he thought that his great friend Lancelot was dead, he fasted until the sickness, caused by doing so, killed him.

Galentivet

The brother of GRIFLET who once participated in a treacherous attack on ESCANOR[3] which was blamed on GAWAIN[1].

Galeron

A Scottish knight of Galloway who became a KNIGHT OF THE ROUND TABLE, even though his lands had been confiscated by ARTHUR.

Gales

A kingdom that is usually identified with WALES.

Gales li Caus

A KNIGHT OF THE ROUND TABLE who was, according to GERBERT, the husband of PHILOSOPHINE and father of PERCEVAL[2].

Galeschin

Also GALACHIN

The son of King NENTRES of GARLOT, and BELISENT, ARTHUR's sister. A supporter of Arthur in his battle against the SAXONS, who were laying siege to the city after the Saxons had been defeated. However, this story is an anachronism, as the duchy of Clarence was not created until 1362, and the place to which it related was the small wool town of Clare in Suffolk, which can hardly be called a city by anyone's standards.

Galian

According to the *Gallians tattur*, a Faeroese ballad that was written down during the eighteenth century, Galian was a son of OWAIN.

Galiene

The Lady of LOTHIAN who married FERGUS[1].

Galihodin

A KNIGHT OF THE ROUND TABLE, a cousin of GALEHAUT and sub-king of SURLUSE, one of the kingdoms ruled by GALEHAUT. When LANCELOT[2] fled ARTHUR's court, Galihodin joined him and was made the Duke of SENTOGE.

Gall

The son of DYSGYFDAWD who was said to have killed the birds of GWENDDOLAU.

Gallafer

The grandson of GADDIFER who, having been converted to Christianity, went to preach to his ancestors who still inhabited the ISLE OF LIFE.

Galore

The kingdom of King GARLIN, whom the German DIU CRÔNE makes the father of GUINEVERE.

Galvariun

Depicted on the MODENA archivolt, the underside of an arch in Modena Cathedral, this knight of ARTHUR appears nowhere else, either in literature or art.

Gandin

The grandfather of PERCEVAL[2], according to WOLFRAM VON ESCHENBACH.

Ganieda

The twin sister of MERLIN, she appears in Welsh poetry as GWENDYDD, and under this name in the VITA MERLINI, which says she was the adulterous wife of RHYDDERCH, whose philandering was spotted by her brother, Merlin. The Welsh poems do not say for definite that she was married to Rhydderch. In origin, Ganieda would appear to be LANGUORETH, the wife of Rhydderch in Jocelyn's LIFE OF SAINT KENTIGERN, who became enamoured with a soldier.

Gannes

The kingdom ruled over by King BORS[1].

Garadigan

The domain from which LORE, called the Lady of Garadigan, hailed.

Garanwyn

In Welsh tradition, a son of Sir KAY.

Garcelos

According to the sixteenth-century Welsh writer Gruffudd Hiraethog, Garcelos was a maternal ancestor of ARTHUR. It would seem that Garcelos is a simple corruption of CASTELLORS, who appears in the pedigree of JOHN OF GLASTONBURY.

Garel

The hero of the romance GAREL VON DEM BLÜHENDEN TAL by Der Pleier, Garel was a Arthurian knight who conquered KANEDIC after its king, ECUNAVER, had announced his intention to attack ARTHUR. He married Queen LAUDAME of ANFERE.

Garel von dem blühenden Tal

A thirteenth-century German poetic romance recounting the exploits of GAREL. It was written by an obscure author, simply known as Der Pleier, who may have been Austrian.

Gareth

A son of LOT and MORGAUSE. Coming to ARTHUR's court in disguise, he was put to work in the kitchens and, attracting the attention of the impertinent KAY, he was given the nickname 'Beaumains' – 'Fair Hands', indicating that his hands were unsullied and unused to hard work. When LYNETTE came to Arthur's court looking for someone to help her sister LYONESSE[1], who was being besieged by the RED KNIGHT[3] of the Red Lands, Gareth went with her, accompanied by a dwarf who knew his real identity. Throughout their journey Gareth had to endure the caustic tongue of Lynette, who had no wish to have her cause championed by a mere kitchen worker. However, Gareth prevailed against Black, Green and Red Knights before finally defeating the Red Knight of the Red Lands and subsequently marrying Lyonesse.

During Arthur's war against the Roman emperor THEREUS, Gareth killed King DATIS of Tuscany, but was himself killed by the fleeing yet unarmed LANCELOT[2], on the occasion when the latter was discovered in Queen GUINEVERE's bed-chamber. His story, recounted by Sir Thomas MALORY, seems French in origin, and it is quite possible that it was based on a now lost French romance.

Gargamelle

A giantess who was created by MERLIN from the unlikely ingredients of the bones of a cow whale and ten pounds of GUINEVERE's nail clippings. Her mate was called GRANDGOUSIER, also created by Merlin, and their offspring named GARGANTUA.

Gargantua

The giant son of GRANDGOUSIER, who MERLIN had made from a bull whale's bone and a phial of LANCELOT[2]'s blood, and GARGAMELLE, likewise created by Merlin from the bones of a cow whale and ten pounds of GUINEVERE's nail clippings. This impossible being, born of impossible parents, was obviously a simple derivation of the word 'gargantuan', but was said to have saved ARTHUR; who furnished him with a sixty-foot-long club. Gargantua also once had an encounter with the minuscule TOM THUMB, the latter managing to place him under an enchantment.

Garlin

The king of GALORE who was, according to the German DIU CRÔNE, the father of GUINEVERE and GOTEGRIM.

Garlon

The brother of King PELLAM, this evil and invisible knight was killed by BALIN.

Garlot

The realm of King NENTRES, who was married to one of ARTHUR's sisters. It was also said to have been the kingdom of URIEN, and is possibly identifiable with Galloway.

Gartnán

The king of SCOTLAND and father CANO, who later succeeded him. He certainly existed prior to AD 688, as this is the recorded date for the death of his son, Cano.

Garwen

According to the Welsh TRIADS, the daughter of HENIN THE OLD and one of ARTHUR's three mistresses.

Garwy

Given the epithet 'the Tall', Garwy was the father of INDEG, who was, according to the Welsh TRIADS, one of the three mistresses of ARTHUR.

Gascony

A region of south-west FRANCE. In CLARIS ET LARIS, it was ruled by King LADON, while in Welsh tradition the king is the elder BORS[1]. The Irish romance THE VISIT OF GREY HAM makes the HUNTING KNIGHT the son of the king of this region.

Gasozein

Appearing in DIU CRÔNE, this character claimed that GUINEVERE was his wife prior to her marrying ARTHUR, and that she should leave the king and return with him to his home. Even though the choice was left with Guinevere, and she chose to stay with Arthur, her brother GOTEGRIM considered she was wrong. In anger Gotegrim carried her off and intended to kill her. Gasozein rescued her and then fought GAWAIN[1] over her. He eventually admitted that his claim had been fictitious.

Gaste Forest

The realm of king PELLINORE, it was probably identical with the WASTE LAND.

Gaul

A Roman province in western Europe that stretched from what is now northern Italy to the southern part of the Netherlands. The name is most commonly used nowadays to refer to FRANCE, but that is not strictly true. The Gauls themselves were divided into several distinct groups, but united under a common religion that was controlled by the Druidic priesthood. One group of Gauls invaded Italy around 400 BC, sacked Rome and settled between the Alps and the Apennines. This region, known as Cisalpine Gaul, was conquered by Rome in about 225 BC. The Romans conquered southern Gaul between the Mediterranean and the Cevennes about 125 BC, and the remaining Gauls up to the Rhine were conquered by JULIUS CAESAR between 58 and 51 BC.

Gauriel

A warrior who had a pet ram which he had taught to fight and who features in a German romance written by Konrad von Stoffeln. He married the ruler of FLURA-TRONE, but she abandoned him, saying that she would return only after he had captured three of ARTHUR's knights for her, a task Gauriel accomplished. Having done so he spent a year with Arthur.

Gauvain

A variant of GAWAIN[1].

Gauwain

A variant of GAWAIN[1].

Gawain

Also GAUVAIN, GAUWAIN, GAYAIN, WALGA(I)NUS, WALEWEIN, BALBHUAIDH, GWALCHMAI

1 One of the most prominent of ARTHUR's knights, Gawain was the eldest son of LOT and MORGAUSE, though in Welsh tradition there appears to be some confusion over his parentage. Sometimes GWYAR is given as his father, sometimes as his mother. In French romances his name is variously given as Gauvain, Gauwain, Gayain, etc.; in Latin he is Walganus (GEOFFREY OF MONMOUTH calls him Walgainus); in Dutch Walewein and in Irish Balbhuaidh. Welsh tradition calls him Gwalchmai – 'hawk of May' or 'hawk of the plain', but is has been argued, some think successfully, that Gwalchmai and Gawain were originally different characters, the Welsh simply identifying their Gwalchmai with the Continental Gawain. Others have, with almost equal success, argued that the two have always been identical. In origin, if Gwalchmai and Gawain were always the same character, he appears to be the MABINOGION character GWRVAN GWALLT-AVWY, which in turn seems to have been derived from the Welsh *gwallt-avwyn* ('hair like rain') or *gwallt-advwyn* ('fair hair'). He is also possibly to be identified with UALLABH, the hero of a Scottish tale.

His story is variously given, but aside from minor differences it is as follows.

The son of King Lot of LOTHIAN, who was, in his early days, a page to Arthur's sister Morgause, and on whom he fathered Gawain. The DE ORTU WALU-UANII makes his mother ANNA rather than Morgause. Having been baptized, he was set adrift in a cask, eventually rescued by fishermen, made his way to Rome and was knighted by Pope SULPI-CIUS. Arriving at Arthur's court, he became one of that king's most prominent knights, depicted in early romance as a great champion but less likeable in later works that were influenced by the writing of Sir Thomas MALORY, who seems to have taken a particular dislike to him. French romances, on the whole, portray Gawain as promiscuous in the extreme.

Various tales give him different wives, including AMURFINE, RAGNELL, the daughter of the king of SORCHA and the daughter of the CARL OF CARLISLE. Italian romance made him the lover of PULZELLA GAIA, the daughter of MORGAN[1] Le Fay, while he was the husband or lover of YSABELE in WALEWEIN. His sons are named as FLORENCE, GUINGLAIN and LOVEL.

Following Arthur's argument with LANCELOT[2], and the latter's departure from the court, Gawain became violently opposed to Lancelot, and accompanied Arthur on his Continental expedition against the ROMAN EMPIRE. Landing back in BRITAIN, he was killed with a club, though according to Breton tradition he survived the last battle of CAMLANN and actually succeeded Arthur, who abdicated in his favour. His death did not mark his last appearance, for his ghost was reputed to have advised Arthur in the run-up to Camlann.

The owner of a horse named GRINGALET, Gawain had the strange power of becoming stronger towards noon, while his strength diminished again during the afternoon. This same trait has also been attributed to ESCANOR[1], one of Gawain's enemies. This peculiar gift appears to be Welsh in origin, as this is the special skill attributed to GWALCHMAI, who was one of the party picked to help CULHWCH in his quest to locate OLWEN. He may, therefore, have a solar origin, possibly being a memory of some ancient solar deity. Connection has also been made between Gawain and Cú Chulainn, the archetypal Irish warrior who, like

Gawain, owned an enchanted belt that rendered the wearer invulnerable.

WILLIAM OF MALMESBURY reports that his grave was discovered during the reign of King William II (1087–1100) at Ros, though this location cannot be determined with any certainty. His skull was supposed to have been held in Dover Castle.

Gawain participated in a beheading contest with a giant, the story appearing in the tales of SIR GAWAIN AND THE GREEN KNIGHT, SIR GAWAIN AND THE CARL OF CARLISLE and TURK AND GAWAIN. This story, which is paralleled in the Irish story of Cú Chulainn, possibly represents a memory of some earlier pagan hero who was the prototype of Gawain. Some have maintained that Gawain is identical with Cú Chulainn, this association being drawn not just from the similarity of the stories but also from the fact that the tales seems to come from the north of England, and in ancient times a tribe known as the Setantii lived in this region, and the original name of Cú Chulainn was Setanta. It is not very hard to see how this association was made. The anonymous but famous *Sir Gawain and the Green Knight* gives possibly the best-known account of this episode.

During Arthur's Christmas Feast the festivities were interrupted by the arrival of a GREEN KNIGHT[1], who challenged the knights present to cut off his head, setting as the only condition that he be allowed to retaliate in the same manner the following year. Only Gawain dared accept the challenge.

Another story concerning Gawain comes from the vicinity of CARLISLE during the days when Arthur was alleged to have held his court there, and is related in a traditional Border ballad. Outside the city walls Arthur was overpowered by a local knight who spared his life on the condition that within a year he would return with the answer to the question 'What is it that women most desire?' No one at his court could supply the answer, so Arthur was honour-bound to return to the knight when the year had elapsed and forfeit his life. On his way to the meeting, Arthur was approached by a hideous woman who told him that she would give him the answer, provided the king found a husband for her. Arthur agreed, and the hag told him that the one thing women desire most is to have their own way. The answer was related to the knight and, proving correct, Arthur's life was spared. Re-turning to his court, he appointed Sir Gawain to be the ugly woman's husband, thus fulfilling his promise.

Though she was hideous beyond comprehension, Gawain always treated her with knightly courtesy, and in return the woman offered Gawain a reward. She would become beautiful either by day or by night, the choice was his. Remembering the answer she had given Arthur, Gawain told her that she might have her own way and bade her choose for herself. His chivalrous answer broke the enchantment under which she had been held, and she immediately became beautiful by both day and night.

Commentators seeking the origins of the Arthurian characters have suggested that Gawain was originally Arthur's son, as the story of Gawain's birth and his subsequently being set adrift mirrors that of MORDRED. This version of events suggests that Gawain was the incestuous son of Arthur and his sister, who was MORGAN[1] Le Fay in the original story. Again Morgan Le

Fay to Morgause does not take much imagination. It has also been suggested that Gawain was originally one of the GRAIL questers, but was later replaced by GALAHAD[1] due to the former's pagan origins and continuing associations. Similarly, PERCEVAL[2] has been mooted as the replacement character.

2 'The Brown', a knight who had the baby GAWAIN[1] baptized.

Gawayne

Variant spelling of GAWAIN[1] that appears in the original title of the famous fourteenth-century SIR GAWAYNE AND THE GREENE KNIGHT.

Gayain

A variant of GAWAIN[1].

Gendawd

The father of GWYL who was, according to the Welsh TRIADS, one of ARTHUR's three mistresses.

Generon

Thomas HEYWOOD's *Life of Merlin* makes this a castle belonging to VORTIGERN, replacing the tower that refused to stand in other versions of the story.

Gennewis

The realm of King PANT, who married CLARINE, the mother of LANCELOT[2] in a Germanic version of the latter's story.

Genvissa

The daughter of the Roman emperor CLAUDIUS, according to GEOFFREY OF MONMOUTH. She married ARVIRAGUS and, when her husband revolted against her father, she restored the peace between them.

Geoffrey of Monmouth

Twelfth-century Welsh author (c. 1100 – c. 1154) of two very important Arthurian works in Latin. Thought to be the son of Breton parents, he studied at Oxford and was archdeacon of Llandarff or Monmouth (c. 1140), being appointed bishop of St Asaph in 1152. His totally fictitious HISTORIA REGUM BRITANNIAE (*History of the Kings of Britain*) deals with a pseudo-mythical history of BRITAIN, based, according to the author, on an earlier British or Welsh work that he alone had seen. Although worthless as history, it features a substantial Arthurian section, and was the first work to give a coherent narrative of the ARTHUR known today. His second work, the VITA MERLINI (*Life of Merlin*), is a poetic description of MERLIN's adventures, and his madness.

Geraint

A variant of GEREINT.

Gerbert

The thirteenth-century author of a CONTINUATION to PERCEVAL by CHRÉTIEN DE TROYES.

Gereint

Also GERAINT

The king of DUMNONIA, he married ENID, their adventures being told in the Welsh romance GEREINT AND ENID, a version of EREC ET ENIDE, the hero of the earlier French version being substituted with Gereint, a local Welsh hero. Listed as a contemporary of ARTHUR, even being made a cousin, Gereint may be older, for the MABINOGION story of THE DREAM OF RHONABWY calls his son CADWY, and makes that son the contemporary of Arthur. Another *Mabinogion* story, CULHWCH AND OLWEN, names two of his brothers as ERMID and DYWEL. His father's name is usually given as ERBIN, but the *Life of Saint Cyby* makes this character his son.

Gereint and Enid

A Welsh romance, possibly dating from the twelfth century that features in the MABINOGION. It is based on the French romance EREC ET ENIDE by CHRÉTIEN DE TROYES, but substitutes a local Welsh hero for EREC.

Gerenton

Mentioned in one of the numerous pedigrees of ARTHUR as one of his ancestors, the father of CONAN.

Germany

During the traditional Arthurian period this country was the domain of various tribes. However, the romance CLARIS ET LARIS makes its ruler the emperor HENRY[2], father of LARIS.

Gerontius

A Roman leader, he overthrew the rule of the historical Roman emperor Constantine III in BRITAIN.

Gest of Sir Gauvain

A thirteenth-century English verse romance that survives only in a fragmentary condition, and includes details of the combat between GAWAIN[1] and BRANDILES.

Giant of Mont Saint Michel

A giant, living on the Mont SAINT MICHEL off the coast of BRITTANY, who seized HELENA, the niece of HOEL[1], king of Brittany. ARTHUR, KAY and BEDIVERE[2] set off after him, but found Helena was already dead. They slew the giant none the less.

Giants' Ring, The

Name given to STONEHENGE, Wiltshire, which, according to legend, was built by MERLIN. With the help of UTHER PENDRAGON and 15,000 men, Merlin transported the ring from Mount KILLARAUS, in IRELAND, to SALISBURY PLAIN as a memorial to the British warriors slain by the SAXON leader HENGIST. The monument was allegedly commissioned by AMBROSIUS AURELIUS.

Gilan

Duke of SWALES and the original owner of the dog PETITCRIEU, which he gave to TRISTAN.

Gilaneier

The name given to ARTHUR's queen in the romance *Jaufré*.

Gilbert

A knight and the father of BRANDILES.

Gildas Junior

An alternative name for TREMEUR, the son of TREPHINA and CUNOMORUS.

Gildas, Saint

A Romano-British historian and monk working in the traditional Arthurian period. Born in STRATHCLYDE, he fled the strife that raged in his neighbourhood and went to WALES, where he married. He became a monk only after his wife had died. His famous work, DE EXCIDIO ET CONQUESTU BRITANNIAE, probably written between AD 516 and 547, and most likely written while Gildas was still quite a young man, does not mention ARTHUR by name, but it does mention the battle of BADON. It is the only extant contemporary history of the Celts, and the only contemporary British version of events from the invasion of the Romans to his own time. The MABINOGION story of THE DREAM OF RHONABWY makes him Arthur's counsellor. Other stories make him the son of CAW, brother of HUEIL and friend of Arthur. While in IRELAND he learned that Arthur had killed his brother, but he appears to have remained on friendly terms with him.

Gilfaethwy

The brother of GWYDION and ARIANRHOD, the son of the goddess DÔN, according to the MABINOGION story of MATH, SON OF MATHONWY. He is the Celtic origin of GRIFLET.

Gilierchins

One of the various names given to the father-in-law of TRISTAN. Called HAVELIN by EILHART and JOVELIN by GOTTFRIED VON STRASSBURG, this variation appears in the Italian TAVOLA RITONDA.

Gillomanius

A king of IRELAND who sided with, and aided, PASCHENT when the latter invaded BRITAIN.

Gilmaurius

Although no such king of IRELAND is known by this name, GEOFFREY OF MONMOUTH asserts that he was the king of Ireland whom ARTHUR defeated when he invaded that country.

Giomar

The nephew of ARTHUR who became the subject of MORGAN[1] Le Fay's attentions while she was a lady-in-waiting to GUINEVERE. The queen separated them, and as a result Morgan Le Fay was said by some sources to have sown the first seeds of doubt in Arthur's mind regarding the fidelity of his wife.

Giraldus Cambrensis

Norman-Welsh chronicler and ecclesiastic (c. 1146– c. 1223) of noble birth, born in Manorbier Castle, DYFED. He was educated at the abbey of St Peter, Gloucester, and later studied in Paris. He became archdeacon of St David's, but when his uncle, the bishop, died (1176), he was overlooked for the position as he was a Welshman. He was again overlooked for the same vacancy in 1198, and after that concentrated on his studies and writing. Though not usually referred to as a major Arthurian source, he did, however, comment on MERLIN, stating the reason for his period of madness, but also saying that there were two Merlins, one a wizard, the other a wild man.

Girflet

A variant of GRIFLET that would appear to be a simple spelling error.

Gismirante

A little-known knight who appears in a fourteenth-century cantare by the Italian poet Antonio Pucci. In this he is one of ARTHUR's knights who heard of a land where, every year, the king's daughter went naked to church, anyone seeing her being beheaded. Gismirante travelled to that land and abducted the girl, though later he had to rescue her from a savage man who ran off with her.

Glain

A magic snake egg which MERLIN sought. It appears only in an early Cornish poem.

Glastonbury

A small town in Somerset, England, around which many legends have arisen, particularly its famous tor (hill) and ruined abbey. According to tradition, the abbey was founded by missionaries from Rome c. AD 166, named by some as DERU-VIAN and PHAGAN, to the then British king, LUCIUS. Others say it was founded by St Patrick prior to his mission to the Irish, or, most popularly, by JOSEPH OF ARIMATHEA. However, there is no real evidence to suggest that there was an abbey on this site prior to the seventh century, although there is evidence of a much smaller and older church on the site, and it is perhaps this that has become elevated to the status of abbey prior to the true date for the foundation of the abbey church itself.

According to medieval traditions, Glastonbury was visited by Jesus as a boy, in the company of his uncle, Joseph of Arimathea, a tin trader, who came to the West Country for Mendip lead and Cornish tin. This particular trip is said to have been the inspiration for William Blake's poem 'Jerusalem', which begins:

And did those feet in ancient time
Walk upon England's mountains green?

Joseph of Arimathea, who took Jesus's body down from the Cross and placed it in his sepulchre, is said to have returned to BRITAIN some years later – AD 37 or 63 – bringing the Christian message with him. With eleven followers, he made his way to Glastonbury, wishing to be among the friendly and influential Druids he had met during his earlier visits. On arrival, he stuck his wooden staff into the ground, and it immediately took root and blossomed as a young tree. He took this as a divine sign that he had reached his journey's end. This tree is now immortalized as the HOLY THORN, which has the special attribute of blossoming twice a year, in the spring and at Christmas.

Joseph of Arimathea was alleged to have brought the Chalice Cup of the Last Supper with him, as well as two cruets containing the blood and sweat of Christ. Although the latter two were said to have been later buried with him in his Glastonbury grave, the whereabouts of the Chalice Cup was, and still remains, unknown, though some commentators have said that it too was buried with Joseph of Arimathea. It has become entangled in myth, and is identified with the Holy GRAIL of Arthurian fame.

The local king, ARVIRAGUS, gave Joseph of Arimathea and his disciples twelve hides of land – a hide being a medieval measure of land equal to the area that could be tilled with one plough in a year. On this land they built their wattle-and-daub church, dedicated to the Virgin Mary, which has its traditional site as the location of the Lady Chapel within the abbey. It had the name *Vetusta Ecclesia*, or Old Church, and, though dilapidated in later years, did not disappear until a tragic fire swept through the abbey on the night of 25 May 1184.

The legends continued in the century following Joseph of Arimathea's arrival. Pope ELUTHERIUS, at the request of King Lucius, Arviragus's grandson, sent two emissaries, Deruvian and Phagan, to invigorate the work of Glastonbury. These two are credited with the foundation of the abbey, though other accounts say that it was founded in the fifth century by Saint Patrick, who was the abbot at Glastonbury before leaving to convert the Irish people to Christianity. The patron saint of WALES, Saint DAVID, is said to have travelled to Glastonbury at a later date, accompanied by seven bishops to dedicate the Old Church, but was warned in a dream that the Lord had already done so. Instead, David added another church and dedicated that.

The legends regarding King ARTHUR and Glastonbury really start with his death. If CAMELOT is indeed to be identified with CADBURY CASTLE, across the moors, it seems perfectly reasonable to equate Glastonbury with AVALON, which is how many people saw the association. In 1911 the monks at Glastonbury claimed to have uncovered the bodies of both Arthur and GUINEVERE just south of the Lady Chapel. Their relics were said to have been sixteen feet down in the hollowed-out trunk of an oak tree. With them was a leaden cross with the Latin inscription 'Hic jacet sepultus inclitus Rex Arturius in insula avalonia' ('Here lies Arthur, the famous king of the Isle of Avalon'); or, alternatively, the inscription 'Hic jacet Arthurus, rex quondam, rex futurus' ('Here lies Arthur, king that was, king that shall be'). When the political and domestic background of the times is considered, this 'finding' of Arthur seems extremely convenient. King Henry II was having immense problems with the Welsh, who believed that Arthur was sleeping and would return to lead them to victory. To prove that Arthur was dead

by exposing his grave made sound and prudent political sense. Excavations at the same spot have revealed a break in the charred earth resulting from the fire, and the base of a pyramid that was said to have been next to the graves. These at least confirm a part of the monks' story.

Also, as the abbey had experienced its terrible fire in 1184, the additional kudos brought to the abbey through this 'discovery' ensured many more pilgrimages would be undertaken, thus bringing in the huge sums of money needed for the rebuilding work. After 600 years Arthur was becoming a cult figure, and the monks obviously saw no harm in attaching his cult status to the abbey. Some eighty-seven years after the remains of Arthur and Guinevere were 'uncovered' they were reburied in front of the abbey's high altar in 1278. Obviously they had lost none of their romantic or political importance, for this reinterment was attended by King Edward I and Queen Eleanor. The tomb into which Arthur and Guinevere were supposedly placed was made of black marble and survived until the Dissolution in 1539. Its siting was rediscovered during the excavation in 1934 and is now clearly marked within the ruins. The inscription at Glastonbury today reads:

The site of King Arthur's Tomb

In the year 1191 the bodies of King Arthur and his queen were said to have been found on the south side of the Lady Chapel.

On 19 April 1278 their remains were removed in the presence of King Edward I and Queen Eleanor to a black marble tomb on this site. This tomb survived until the dissolution of the Abbey in 1539.

Legend also says that Glastonbury is connected with the returning of EXCAL-

IBUR to the LADY OF THE LAKE, though in this instance it is a river and not a lake into which Excalibur is said to have been thrown. On the main road between Street and Glastonbury lies the POMPAR-LES BRIDGE (Pons Perilis) over the River Brue. It is from this bridge that Excalibur was said to have been thrown and, as it tumbled towards the waters of the River Brue, a hand reached out and caught it, drawing it into safekeeping beneath the water.

Another story links Arthur with the little chapel on the island of Beckery (now unfortunately located adjacent to the town sewage works). Told to go to the chapel by an angel, Arthur saw Mary and the infant Jesus there.

The quest for the Holy Grail would have involved Arthur at Glastonbury. One supposed hiding place of the Grail was at the bottom of a well which is known as the Chalice Well. This is an unlikely story, for the name was a medieval transplant and did not come into local use until after 1306. Its alternative name, 'blood spring', which some say equates it with the blood of Christ which was supposedly caught in the chalice, comes from the high concentration of iron in the water which leaves a blood-red deposit on the stones it passes over. Arthur has also been associated with the GLASTONBURY ZODIAC, being identified as Sagittarius, while the zodiac itself has been regarded as the ROUND TABLE.

Glastonbury Cross

The leaden cross that was unearthed when the grave of ARTHUR and GUINE-VERE was supposedly uncovered by the monks at GLASTONBURY in 1911. It was the inscription on this cross that led to the identification of the bodies, for it read, in Latin, 'Hic jacet sepultus inclitus Rex Arturius in insula avalonia' ('Here lies

Arthur, the famous King of the isle of Avalon'). Alternatively, the inscription was said to read: 'Hic jacet Arthurus, rex quondam, rex futurus' ('Here lies Arthur, king that was, king that shall be'). The cross was subsequently lost, but in recent times a pattern-maker named Derek Mahoney claimed to have found it and reburied it.

Glastonbury Thorn

A thorn tree situated within the grounds of GLASTONBURY Abbey that was said to have grown from the staff of JOSEPH OF ARIMATHEA. The thorn had the special attribute of flowering twice a year, in the spring and at Christmas. The tree is first mentioned in the Lyfe of Joseph of Arimathea, which dates from c. 1500, but only its descendants remain alive today, for the original thorn was cut down by a Puritan zealot. The best-known surviving tree is that in front of the Church of Saint John the Baptist in Glastonbury.

Various other legends exist about this Holy Tree. Some accounts say that the original tree, from which Joseph of Ari-mathea's staff had been cut, grew from a thorn from the Crown of Thorns worn by Christ. Local Somerset legends also tell of those who wished the tree harm. Usually the Puritans were blamed in these stories, but the tree always seemed to get the better of them. One particular assailant attacked the thorn with an axe, but the axe slipped from the trunk and embedded itself in the man's leg, while wood chips flew into his eyes.

An alternative legend says that the Glastonbury Thorn was not a thorn tree at all but rather a walnut tree. Early writers described this tree, again said to have sprung into life from the staff of Joseph of Arimathea, saying that it budded on St Barnabas's Day (11 June), and never before. It seems that, until this tree was cut down, it was held with the same degree of reverence as the Glastonbury Thorn, for both trees, walnut and thorn, were thought by some to have once existed in the town.

Glastonbury Tor

A hill at GLASTONBURY, Somerset, around which various legends have arisen, though these are only indirectly connected with King ARTHUR. The tor is said to be the home of GWYNN AP NUDD, the Lord of the Dead and of the Underworld, the tor itself sometimes being regarded as a portal to the OTHERWORLD.

Glastonbury Zodiac

According to the theory postulated by Kathryn Maltwood in her 1930s book *A Guide to Glastonbury's Temple of the Stars*, the zodiac consists of giant figures in the landscape surrounding GLASTONBURY, their outlines being delineated by such things as field edges, roads, streams, etc. These figures supposedly correspond to the heavenly signs above them, and each figure has been equated with episodes in the quest for the Holy GRAIL, ARTHUR himself said to be represented by Sagittarius. While the theory has attracted some following, many people consider the zodiac's existence to be pure fantasy.

Glein, River

Located at the mouth of either of the English rivers having this name was the site of one of ARTHUR's BATTLES.

Glenthorne

Place on the Devon coast where, in stormy weather, JOSEPH OF ARIMATHEA, with the young Christ on board, was said to have run his ship ashore. In need of fresh water, Joseph of Arimathea and Jesus went on a fruitless search. As a result Jesus caused a spring to rise and it has never failed since.

Glenvissig

The realm of ATHRWYS, which has been identified by some with GWENT.

Glewlwyd
Also GLWELWYD

Featuring in Welsh tradition, Glewlwyd appears in the MABINOGION story of CULHWCH AND OLWEN as ARTHUR's porter, and has the epithet *gafaelfawr* ('great grasp') applied to him, though he is also referred to as one of the TWENTY-FOUR KNIGHTS of King Arthur's court. In the poem PA GUR, he appears as the gatekeeper to Arthur's court who refuses to admit CULHWCH and his companions until they have identified themselves, though he declared that never in all his long and varied career had he seen so handsome a man as the youthful Culhwch.

Glifieu
Also GLUNEU EIL TARAN

One of the only seven Britons to survive the battles between BENDIGEID VRAN and MATHOLWCH and return to BRITAIN with the head of Bendigeid Vran, which had been cut off at the king's own bequest, to be carried to the WHITE MOUNT in London, there to be buried as the guardian of Britain, the face towards FRANCE. The others that returned with him were PRYDERI, MANAWYDAN, TALIESIN, YNAWC (YNAWAG), GRUDYEN (GRUDDIEU) and HEILYN, along with BRANWEN, the reason for the battles.

Gliglois

The son of a German noble who served as Sir GAWAIN[1]'s squire. Both he and his master fell in love with GUINEVERE's maid, BEAUTÉ. She chose Gliglois.

Gliten

A sister of MORGAN[1] Le Fay.

Glitonea

A sister of MORGAN[1] Le Fay. She is possibly the same character as GLITEN.

Gloier

The king of SORELOIS.

Gloriana

In SPENSER's allegorical FAERIE QUEENE, Gloriana is the allegorical representation of Queen Elizabeth I of England. ARTHUR saw her in a dream and fell in love with her. Her immediate family tree may be found in the entry for FAIRYLAND.

Gloriande

The wife of King APOLLO of LIONES.

Gluneu eil Taran

Named in some sources as one of the seven survivors of the expedition to IRELAND mounted by BENDIGEID VRAN. He is more usually referred to as GLIFIEU.

Glwelwyd

Also GLEWLWYD

The gatekeeper at King ARTHUR's court who was the first to meet CULHWCH as he came to the court to ask for help in locating OLWEN. He declared that Culhwch was the most handsome youth he had ever laid eyes on.

Glwyd(d)yn

Also GWLYDDYN

The carpenter who built ARTHUR's feasting hall, EHANGWEN. His name may be a remembrance of GWYDION, a Celtic god, the son of NODENS.

Godfrey

A Danish duke and the father of OGIER, he appears in the Carolingian romance OGIER LE DANOIS.

Gododdin, The

Traditionally composed by Aneurin, a Welsh court poet who flourished in the late sixth and early seventh centuries, this poem can claim to contain the first literary allusion to ARTHUR, unless, of course, the relevant line is a later addition. A contemporary of TALIESIN, and similarly supposed to have courtly connections with URIEN of RHEGED, Aneurin celebrated the British heroes from Gododdin, which stretched from the Forth to the Tees, who were annihilated by the SAXONS in the bloody battle of Cattraith (Catterick in Yorkshire) c. AD 600.

In the poem the prowess of a British warrior is compared to that of Arthur:

> He stabbed over three hundred of the finest,
> He glutted black ravens on the ramparts of the fort,
> Although he was no Arthur.

This reference, if in fact included in the original poem, indicates that Arthur was already widely known in the north by that time.

Gofannon

The Welsh smith god who may be cognate with the Irish GOIBHNIU. An Old Welsh law ruled that in a chieftain's court the smith should have the first drink at any feast. Gofannon may have his origins in the Welsh father god GWYDION.

Gog and Magog

During the Middle Ages these two characters were thought to be nations that were confined behind mountains, having been imprisoned there by ALEXANDER THE GREAT, who had used 6,000 iron and bronze workers to build a huge gate to hold them back. In the Arthurian tales it seems that they escaped their confinement and attacked ARTHUR, but the latter was helped by the giant GARGANTUA, and Gog and Magog were overcome. They were then said to have been chained to a palace on the site of London's Guildhall.

Not all tales make Gog and Magog separate giants, referring instead to a single gigantic character known as GOGM-AGOG. It is said that he led twenty others against BRUTUS at TOTNES, Devon, but was engaged in single combat by CORINEUS, Brutus's ally, who threw him over the cliffs to his death, though some accounts place this battle at Plymouth. This legendary giant is still remembered in Cambridgeshire, where his name is given to a range of low-lying hills outside Cambridge.

Gogmagog

See GOG AND MAGOG

Gogvran

One of the name applied to the father of GUINEVERE in Welsh tradition, along with OCVRAN.

Go(i)b(h)niu

The divine smith god of Irish mythology, he is known in WALES as GOFANNON.

Golden Island

The realm of PUCELLE AUX BLANCHE MAINS, the fairy lover of GUINGLAIN.

Goleuddydd

In Welsh tradition the wife of KILYDD, sister of IGRAINE[1], mother of CULHWCH, and as such an aunt of ARTHUR. During the latter stages of her pregnancy, she lost all reason and took to wandering in the woods. As the time for her confinement approached, her sanity returned, in the midst of a herd of swine. So frightened was Goleuddydd that she immediately delivered her baby, who, being born in a pig run, was named CULHWCH (hwch = 'pig'). Though normally given as the sister of Igraine, one genealogy for Arthur unusually makes her the sister of CUSTEN-NIN and YSPADDADDEN, and the aunt of Igraine.

Golistant

A son of MARHAUS, the daughter of King ANGUISH of IRELAND and the brother of AMOROLDO.

Golwg Hafddydd

In the Welsh version of the TRISTAN legend, Ystoria Trystan, this character is the maid of ISEULT[1].

Gomeret

The kingdom of BAN which is alternatively known as BENWICK. Most commonly, though, Ban is called the king of BRITTANY, leading to the assumption that Gomeret and Benwick were either alternative names for Brittany or sub-kingdoms within the realm of Ban.

Gonosor

A king of IRELAND who was converted to Christianity by JOSEPH OF ARIMATHEA. In respect of the help he had given King CANOR of CORNWALL, a tribute was paid by Cornwall to Ireland until TRISTAN killed MARHAUS.

Goon Desert

The brother of the FISHER KING, he was killed by PARTINAL. The sword used to kill him broke in the process, and its rejoining became one of the feats involved in achieving the Holy GRAIL.

Gore

Variously described as the kingdom of URIEN, and thus possibly preserving a memory of RHEGED, or BAGDEMAGUS. It lay on the borders of SCOTLAND, from which it was separated by the River TEMPER, crossable only by one of two bridges, one like the edge of a sword, the other under water. If one of ARTHUR's knights entered the realm, only LANCE-LOT[2] could rescue them.

Goreu

The son of CONSTANTINE[2] by an unnamed daughter of AMLAWDD WLEDIG, his name, meaning 'best', was earned for managing to gain entrance to WRNACH's stronghold with his followers. He was a cousin of ARTHUR, whom he is said to have rescued on three occasions from imprisonment. One curious family tree for Arthur, that prepared by T. W. Rolleston, makes Goreu the brother of ERBIN and IGRAINE[1], and thus the uncle of Arthur.

Furthermore, this peculiar genealogy names Goreu's father as CUSTENNIN.

Gorlagon

Featuring as the hero of the thirteenth-century Latin romance ARTHUR AND GOR-LAGON, Gorlagon was the husband of a faithless wife who, with the aid of a magic wand, turned him into a wolf, that wolf subsequently becoming ARTHUR's pet. ARTHUR obtained the wand and restored Gorlagon to his former shape.

Gorlois

The first husband of IGRAINE[1] and Duke of CORNWALL, whose castle was at TINTAGEL. While Gorlois was away fighting the forces of UTHER, that king assumed Gorlois's form with the aid of MERLIN and lay with his wife, thus precipitating the birth of ARTHUR. Gorlois was killed that very night, much to the subsequent amazement of his widow, who later married Uther. A building named CARHULES near Castle DORE in Cornwall appears to have been named after a person named GOURLES, who was, perhaps the original of Gorlois.

Gormant

According to the MABINOGION story of CULHWCH AND OLWEN, a brother of ARTHUR on his mother's side, his father being named as RICA, the chief elder of CORNWALL. In Welsh tradition it seems as if Rica occupies the position normally associated with GORLOIS.

Gormund

An African king who conquered IRELAND and established his realm there, according to GEOFFREY OF MONMOUTH. It would seem that his name has given rise to GUR-MUN, who, according to GOTTFRIED VON

STRASSBURG, was the son of an African king who became the king of Ireland and the father of ISEULT[1].

Gornemant de Goort

A KNIGHT OF THE ROUND TABLE and prince of GRAHERZ. He trained PERCEVAL[2] in all the knightly skills in the hope that he would marry LIAZE, his daughter, but that did not come about. His three sons, GURZGI, LASCOYT and SCHENTEFLEURS, all met violent deaths.

Gorvenal

Born in GAUL, Gorvenal started out as the tutor and later servant of TRISTAN. He married BRANGIEN, ISEULT[1]'s maidservant, and ascended to the throne of LIONES when Tristan left. He and Tristan were said to have been given refuge by PHARAMOND following the death of MELIODAS[1].

Goswhit

Meaning 'goose white', this was the name given to ARTHUR's helmet in the works of LAYAMON.

Gotegrim

The brother of GUINEVERE, according to the German DIU CRÔNE, whom he abducted when she refused to leave ARTHUR in favour of GASOZEIN, who claimed already to be her husband.

Gottfried von Strassburg

The thirteenth-century author (*fl.* 1200) of the masterly German romance TRISTAN AND ISOLDE, based on the Anglo-Norman poem by THOMAS. Very little is known about his life, but he was famous as an early exponent of literary criticism,

having left appraisals of the poets of the period.

Gourles

Cornish person after whom it is thought that CARHULES, a building near Castle DORE, CORNWALL, is named and who, it has been suggested, was the original of Gorlois.

Gourmaillon

An alternative name which has been applied to both CORMILAN and GOGMAGOG. This has led to a possible identification between these gigantic figures, making the giant disposed of by CORINEUS, Gogmagog, the same as the one disposed of by JACK THE GIANT-KILLER and commonly known through the nursery rhyme, Cormilan or, more correctly, CORMORAN. Furthermore, the application of this variant to both giants leads to the supposition that Jack the Giant-killer is a memory of the gigantic Trojan CORINEUS.

Gracia

One of ARTHUR's nieces, according to the fourteenth-century *Birth of Arthur* (cf. GRAERIA).

Graeria

One of ARTHUR's nieces, according to the fourteenth-century BIRTH OF ARTHUR (cf. GRACIA).

Graherz

GORNEMANT DE GOORT was described as being a prince of this domain.

Grail

Possibly the most widely known of all the Arthurian legends is the Quest for the Holy Grail. The Grail itself was thought to be the Chalice used by Christ at the Last Supper, or, according to some sources, the cup used to catch the blood of Christ from the wound inflicted upon him by the centurion LONGINUS while Christ hung upon the Cross.

When JOSEPH OF ARIMATHEA came to GLASTONBURY in either AD 37 or 63, he was said to have brought with him two cruets containing the blood and sweat of Christ, as well as the Chalice. It is this Chalice that has become embroiled in the legends concerning the Holy Grail. In essence the legend is as follows.

Each year the KNIGHTS OF THE ROUND TABLE gathered at CAMELOT for the feast of the Pentecost, to relate their deeds and the marvels they had behold. Each year, however, their company remained incomplete, for the last place, the SIEGE PERILOUS, remained empty. According to custom, they had, each year, found their names were written in gold around the ROUND TABLE, but one year they found new words written above the Siege Perilous. These read: 'Four hundred winters and four and fifty accomplished after the passion of our Lord Jesu Christ ought this siege be fulfilled.'

LANCELOT[2] stated that he had accounted for the time since the Crucifixion, and said that the siege ought to be fulfilled that very day. All the other knights agreed, and they covered the Siege Perilous with a silk cloth so that the words could not be seen until the rightful knight came to them. They did not have long to wait. As they seated themselves at their own respective places at the Round Table, an old man entered the hall at Camelot accompanied by a fresh-faced young knight who was unarmed, save for an empty scabbard at his waist.

As the entire company watched, the old man led the boy up to the Round Table, and then to the Siege Perilous beside Lancelot. Lifting the silk cloth off the siege, the gathered knights saw that the lettering had changed, and now read: 'This is the siege of Galahad the haut prince.'

Sitting the young knight on the Siege Perilous, the old man departed, leaving the boy as the centre of attention. Many marvelled that one so young should dare sit in the siege, but Lancelot recognized him as his son, and knew that all that had been prophesied had been fulfilled.

The following day Arthur led GALAHAD[1] to a lake near Camelot where his knights had found a sword set in a stone, Here accounts vary, for some say the stone, complete with sword, was taken to Camelot, though others say it was left where found. This sword was inscribed with lettering that pronounced that only the best knight in all the world would pull it clear. Many thought that this surely meant Sir Lancelot, but he declined even to try, for he remembered his sin of loving his queen. Sir GAWAIN[1] and Sir PERCEVAL[2] both tried, and failed. Arthur, sure that Galahad was the rightful owner, bade him attempt, and he easily and cleanly lifted the sword from the stone. Placing it in his empty scabbard, Galahad found it a perfect fit.

At a great jousting tournament arranged so that Galahad might test his skills against the other knights, he acquitted himself superbly, managing to unhorse a good many of the Knights of the Round Table, save two whom he did not fight, Lancelot and Perceval. That evening the knights once again gathered in the hall at Camelot and scarcely had they sat down when there was a monstrous roar of thunder that shook the very walls. Amidst this clamour, the hall was flooded with a brilliant light that was described as being 'seven times' clearer than daylight, and all the knights present felt themselves filled with the grace of the Holy Ghost. They all appeared fairer than they ever were before, and they were all struck dumb by the presence they felt.

Then a golden centre appeared to this light, and, when the knights became accustomed to the brilliance of this new light, they perceived a dish, covered in white samite cloth, so that they could not see the dish itself. This was the Holy Grail, and with it came all manner of meat and drink that the knights loved best. Slowly the Grail crossed over the length of the hall, and then vanished as suddenly as it had appeared. In the sudden emptiness of the hall the entire company burst into one voice.

Sir Gawain was the first to his feet, pledging that he would go out in quest of the Holy Grail, promising to labour 'for a year and a day or longer if needs be', not resting until he had seen the Grail more openly than it had been seen that night. Each of the other knights made similar promises, but Arthur remained silent. He remembered the prophecies and teachings of MERLIN and knew that many of his knights would never return, and the Round Table would never again be complete.

The quest continued for many years, and all the knights who set out to seek this holiest of vessels had many wondrous adventures, but none more than Lancelot, who was to see the Grail at Castle CARBONEK, or Galahad, whose destiny it was to fulfil the quest.

Lancelot rode hard for several days until he came to an old chapel where he thought he might rest. He tried to enter, but found he could reach only the altar, richly covered in silk and set with six great candles in a silver candlestick. He found no way into the chapel and at last, tired and dismayed, laid himself on his shield at a stony cross outside.

Later he was half wakened when two white palfreys (saddle horses) rode up to the cross, bearing a sick knight who moaned in pain for the Grail to come to heal him. Still half asleep, for it seemed that he could not fully awaken, Lancelot stirred and witnessed the candlestick from the altar float to the cross. It was followed by a silver table and the shining holy vessel of the Grail, though Lancelot could not see anyone bearing it aloft. He heard the sick knight sit up and welcome the Grail, and he saw him kneel on the ground to touch and kiss the vessel. Having done so, the knight rose up again, healed. The Grail remained at the cross for some time, with Lancelot looking upon it, then it glided back into the chapel. Yet Lancelot found he had no power to follow it, and drifted back off to sleep.

When, some hours later, Lancelot properly awoke, he recalled all that he had seen and heard, but it seemed as if a dream. As he pondered on his recollections, a voice spoke to him and told him to remove himself from that holy place, for he was unworthy of being there. Lancelot was greatly troubled by these words, but knew the reason behind them, for, on a holy quest, his earthly sins, his lust for his queen, had made him unworthy. He was even more troubled when he found that the knight, whom he had witnessed being so miraculously cured, had taken his horse, helm (helmet) and sword.

Removing himself from the chapel, his heart leaden with sorrow, Lancelot went to a hermitage, where the hermit heard his confession and absolved him of his sins. With the hermit's blessing, Lancelot renewed his quest and, after many months, came to the water of MORTAISE, where he laid down to sleep. In his sleep Lancelot received a vision that told him to enter the first ship he came to. Arising, he went to the strand, where he found a ship that had neither sail nor oar and he entered. Upon doing so, he was overwhelmed by a great peace and joy. He remained with the ship for more than a month.

Growing somewhat weary of the small ship, Lancelot was seated on the shore one day when he heard the thundering of a horse's hoofs and saw a fair knight ride up and dismount. Taking his saddle and bridle with him, this knight went straight to the ship. Curious about this self-assured young knight, Lancelot followed and made himself known. The young knight was none other than Galahad, Lancelot's own son. The two embraced and told each other of their various adventures.

Upon leaving Camelot, Galahad had ridden into strange lands unknown to him. Many adventures had befallen him, but he was always successful in his endeavours and gained much in knightly experience. He had defeated many knights in fair combat, had given support to the defenders in a great siege and, with their comrades BORS[2] and Perceval, had been set adrift in a boat which had beached them in the marshes of SCOTLAND, there to be challenged and do battle with many knights.

Lancelot revelled in hearing of these adventures and felt proud of his son. For a full six months, father and son voyaged together in that boat and encountered many perilous adventures, but they never came near to the Holy Grail. Finally Galahad left his father to seek the Grail, as he was ordained.

Sorry to see his son depart, Lancelot placed his trust in the boat and, after a month at sea, it beached at midnight beside a fine castle. A door opened out towards the sea and a voice bade Lancelot enter. Arming himself for the adventure he knew lay ahead, Lancelot approached the gate. As he did, he saw two lions on guard and immediately drew his sword in readiness. As he did so, it was struck from his hand by some unseen force, and a voice chided his evil faith that he put more trust in his weapons than his Maker.

Without further challenge, Lancelot entered the castle, but once inside he could find no door that would open. Behind one door he heard sweet and reverent singing and he knew full well that the Grail was within. Dropping to his knees, he prayed to God that he should be shown at least some part of the Grail. Looking up from his prayers, he watched as the chamber door swung slowly open. A green light shone out from the room, a light that was the cleanest and purest Lancelot had ever seen. Within the light coming from that room was a silver table, the Holy Grail covered in red samite cloth and all the ornaments of the altar, along with a priest who seemed to celebrate mass. Lancelot could no longer bear to remain outside the room and, taking a deep breath, he strode into the room.

Reaching out to touch the Holy vessel, Lancelot was thrown to the ground by a scorching wind. Unable to move, he felt hands all around him that carried him out of the room, leaving him in the passageway. The following morning the people of the castle found Lancelot's inert body and carried him to a bedchamber, where he lay without stirring. On the twenty-fifth day, he woke and, realizing that he had achieved as much of the Grail as he was to be allowed, gave thanks to the Lord.

Elsewhere, Galahad, since leaving his father, had had many adventures, before meeting up with Bors and Perceval again. The three knights rode together until they came to Castle Carbonek, which they entered, to be received courteously by King PELLES, who knew that the quest for the Holy Grail would now be achieved.

King Pelles, his son ELIAZAR and the three knights sat down to dine, but before they could eat a voice came to them, saying: 'There are two among you that are not in the quest for the Holy Grail, and therefore you both should depart.' Pelles and his son stood up and, with a single glance at Galahad, they slipped away. Scarce had they gone when a man and four angels appeared before the knights. The angels set the man down before a table of silver, and on that table the Holy Grail appeared. The man, who was dressed in the robes of a bishop, started to celebrate mass. He kissed Galahad and directed Galahad to kiss his fellow knights, which he did. The man then disappeared.

Looking up, the three knights saw a man come out of the Grail, a man with open wounds that bled freely, as did those of Jesus Christ. He offered the Holy Grail to Galahad, who knelt and received his Saviour, who told him that he must depart with Bors and Perceval the following morning and put to sea in a boat they would find ready and waiting for them.

The following day the three knights set out and, after three days, they came to a ship, on board which they found a table of silver and the Holy Grail covered in red samite. They fell to their knees and prayed. The ship put to sea and took them to the pagan city of SARRAS. There they disembarked, taking the table of silver with them. They remained in that city for twelve months (some accounts make this year follow a period of imprisonment during which the Holy Grail sustained them). On that day, at the year's end, a man in the likeness of a bishop came to them, carrying the Holy Grail. They celebrated mass, and the man revealed himself to the knights as JOSEPHE, son of JOSEPH OF ARIMATHEA, and Galahad realized that his time on earth was near an end.

Galahad knelt before the table which held the Holy Grail and prayed. As he did so, his soul departed his body, and Galahad, having achieved his destiny, passed away. The watching Bors and Perceval beheld a host of angels take Galahad's soul to heaven, while a great hand came down and took the vessel and bore that up to heaven as well. That was the last that any earthly man saw of the Holy Grail.

The basis of the quest appears to come from Celtic traditions and, although the story given here forms possibly the best-known version of the tale, there are innumerable variations. The word Grail is derived from the Old French *graal*, meaning a type of dish. The Grail is first mentioned in the works of CHRÉTIEN DE TROYES, in which Perceval is the hero, and the Grail itself is simply referred to as 'a grail', a common noun. It was not until later that it became '*the* Grail'.

At first Perceval fails to achieve the Grail, thanks to his not asking the GRAIL QUESTION – What is the Grail? Whom does it serve? – thereby restoring the MAIMED KING to health and the land to fertility. Even though in its final form the Grail has become the Chalice Cup of the Last Supper, its origins are not so simple to determine. Connection has been sought between the Grail of Arthurian legend and the Chalice supposedly brought to BRITAIN by Joseph of Arimathea, but the magical qualities of the Grail stories suggest a much older, OTHERWORLD connection.

Arthur's expedition to the otherworld to obtain a magical cauldron, as recorded in the PREIDDEU ANNWFN, seems to reflect the ability of the Grail to provide unending sustenance. This story has a direct parallel in the MABINOGION story of CUL-HWCH AND OLWEN. Both have aspects that directly relate to the Grail quest as we know it today, so either or both may have been used as the originals; thus the magical cauldron of Celtic tradition becomes transformed into the symbolic cup of the Eucharist. The romanticized events surrounding the quest itself are, however, without doubt purely the inventions of the various authors who have related the tale.

The FISHER KINGS, not mentioned as such in the above rendition of the Grail story, were said to be the descendants of Joseph of Arimathea who guarded the Grail in Castle Carbonek. Also associated with the Grail was a bleeding lance, usually identified with the LANCE OF LONGINUS, said to be that with which Jesus's side was pierced by the centurion [St John: 19.xxxiv]. In the instances where this connection is made, the Grail is also mentioned as having been used to catch Christ's blood as it flowed from this wound. It seems that this alone is the earlier use for the Grail, the association with the Last Supper [St Matthew: 26. xxvii–xxviii] coming later.

In the early version of the Grail myth by Chrétien de Troyes, the mysterious and wondrous vessel is housed in the GRAIL CASTLE, where it is guarded by the GRAIL KEEPER. This guard, the wounded Fisher King, has been maimed 'through his thighs' (sic) and feeds only from a magical dish – the Grail. As a result of the injury, caused by the DOLOROUS STROKE, the land around the castle has become infertile and will revive only if the king himself is healed. This, however, can happen only if there is a knight brave enough to face all the perils on the dangerous journey through the 'land of wailing women' to the Grail Castle, and then be wise enough to ask the Grail Question. This will then break the enchantment under which the king and his land are held.

This curious tale is generally agreed to have derived from an ancient fertility myth, and it is interesting that the Christian symbol of a fish (Christ) appears to have been the origin of the Fisher King. The 'land of wailing women' is obviously a reference to the otherworld, so again associations with the Celtic otherworld of ANNWFN are not hard to make.

Even though Galahad is usually portrayed as being the sole knight to achieve the Grail, other sources beg to differ. The CONTINUATIONS, WOLFRAM VON ESCHENBACH and PERLESVAUS name the successful knight as Perceval. The DIU CRÔNE names GAWAIN[1]; and Sir Thomas MALORY names Galahad, Bors and Perceval as having all been successful. The QUESTE DEL SAINTE GRAAL, and its derivatives, name Galahad, and it is this work that is alone in saying that the Grail was, after Galahad had completed his quest, carried up to heaven by a hand.

The Grail episode remains one of the most fascinating and enigmatic of all the Arthurian legends, and has found almost universal appeal, its underlying theme of seeking mystical union with God being appropriate to many religious beliefs, not solely Christianity.

Grail Castle

The castle, known as CARBONEK or COR-BENIC, in which the Holy GRAIL was housed and where it was guarded by the FISHER KINGS.

Grail Keeper

The MAIMED KING, GRAIL KING or injured FISHER KING who guards the Holy GRAIL in the GRAIL CASTLE. The Holy Grail sustains him while he waits for the purest knight to ask the GRAIL QUESTION, thus releasing him from his enchantment and achieving the goal of the quest.

Grail King

Another name for the GRAIL KEEPER, MAIMED KING or FISHER KING, who is the custodian and guardian of the Holy GRAIL.

Grail Procession

According to several versions of the GRAIL story, this procession was witnessed by PERCEVAL[2] at the GRAIL CASTLE. According to CHRÉTIEN DE TROYES, the Grail was carried in a procession led by a squire with the bleeding LANCE. He was followed by two squires carrying ten-branched candlesticks, a damsel carrying the Grail itself and a final damsel carrying a plate. The DIDOT PERCEVAL describes the order of the procession as a squire with a lance, a damsel with two silver plates and cloths, and finally a squire with a vessel (the Grail) containing the blood of Christ. The Welsh PEREDUR says that the procession consisted of two youths carrying a large spear from which blood freely flowed, followed by a damsel carrying a salver on which there was a head swimming in blood. It is worth noting that the Grail Procession only ever appears in works where it is Perceval who achieves the Grail.

Grail Question

The question to be asked of the wounded FISHER KING in order to break the enchantment under which he and his lands are held. The question is really two-fold: 'What is the Grail? Whom does it serve?' At first PERCEVAL[2] did not achieve the GRAIL simply because he forgot to ask this question. He did not make the same mistake twice.

Grail Spear

An alternative way of referring to the LANCE OF LONGINUS, or the Bleeding LANCE.

Grail Sword

Made by TREBUCHET, this sword shattered when it was used to strike down GOON DESERT, the brother of the FISHER KING. Making it whole again featured in some sources as a condition of the quest for the Holy GRAIL.

Gráinne

As with the stories of CANO and DERDRIU, the Irish story of Gráinne is thought to be one of the origins of the TRISTAN story.

A beautiful maiden, Gráinne was betrothed to the elderly Fionn mac Cumhaill, but she already loved Diarmaid ua Duibhne. On her wedding night she drugged Fionn mac Cumhaill and all his company and, casting a spell, eloped with Diarmaid ua Duibhne to a wood in Connacht. Besieged by the jilted husband and his followers, the two were helped by Diarmaid ua Duibhne's foster father, the god OENGHUS, who rescued Gráinne, while Diarmaid ua Duibhne, in a single tremendous leap, jumped straight over the heads of the attackers and so escaped. Even so, Diarmaid ua Duibhne still had not betrayed his former friend, Fionn mac Cumhaill, but finally lay with Gráinne as a result of her contemptuous mockery.

Later, having been reconciled with Fionn mac Cumhaill, Diarmaid ua Duibhne received a mortal wound that could be healed only by Fionn mac Cumhaill. Remembering Diarmaid ua Duibhne's treachery, Fionn mac Cumhaill twice went to fetch the life-giving waters, but on each occasion let the water trickle through his fingers. When he returned on the third occasion, Diarmaid ua Duibhne was already dead.

Grallo

The grandson of CONAN, he was said to have married TIGRIDIA, sister of DARERCA.

Gramoflanz

The brother-in-law of GAWAIN[1] following his marriage to the latter's sister, ITONJE.

Grandgousier

The father of GARGANTUA, this giant had been created by MERLIN from a bull whale's bones and a phial of LANCELOT[2]'s blood. His mate, GARGAMELLE, was also created by the wizard, this time from the bones of a cow whale and ten pounds of GUINE-VERE's nail clippings.

Granland

The territory ruled by the AMANGONS in the Old French *Le chevalier as deus espées* which is thought by some to have either been the original of Greenland or derived from that country's name.

Gratille

One of the two possible mothers of GRIMAL by EVELAKE, the other suggested mother being FLORIE[1].

Great Fool

An unnamed nephew of ARTHUR and the hero of the Irish romance *Eachtra an Amadán Mor*. He was raised in obscurity in the woods following his brother's unsuccessful plot against Arthur. Having grown up, he proved to be a mighty champion, defeating many knights including GAWAIN[1], the RED KNIGHT[5], the

PURPLE KNIGHT and the SPECKLED KNIGHT.

Great Goddess

Common to many cultures and beliefs was the concept of a Great Goddess, at once benevolent and malevolent. It has been suggested that ARTHUR was the last of a long line of hereditary priests of the Great Goddess, though this concept has not acquired a great following.

Great Spirits Spring

Located at Windfall Run, USA, a spring to which, according to an unlikely American legend, ARTHUR went to drink of its healing waters.

Green Chapel

The chapel to which GAWAIN[1] went in order to fulfil his promise to meet the GREEN KNIGHT[1] one year after he had been challenged in ARTHUR's court to trade blows and had struck off the Green Knight's head.

Green Knight

At least two knights in the Arthurian legends were simply known by this title.
1 The most famous Green Knight features in one of the best known of all Arthurian poems, the anonymous fourteenth-century SIR GAWAIN AND THE GREEN KNIGHT, and its derivative THE GREEN KNIGHT (c. 1500). This knight, whose name was BERTILAK and who lived at Castle HUTTON, came to ARTHUR's court and challenged any of the knights there present to trade blows. GAWAIN[1] accepted and, being allowed to strike first, cut off the Green Knight's head. Calmly, that knight picked up his severed head and told

Gawain to meet him on New Year's morn for his turn.

On his way to keep his appointment, Gawain lodged with a lord, and they agreed to give to each other what they had obtained every day during Gawain's stay. On the first day, while his host was out hunting, Gawain received a kiss from his host's wife, which was duly passed on. The second day Gawain received two kisses, and again he duly passed these on. The third day saw Gawain receiving three kisses and some green lace which would magically protect him. Only the kisses were passed on.

Having left his host's home, Gawain made his way to the GREEN CHAPEL, where he was to meet the Green Knight. He knelt to receive the blow. Three times the Green Knight aimed his sword at Gawain. The first two failed to make contact, while the third but lightly cut Gawain on the neck. Revealing himself, the Green Knight turned out to be none other than his host of previous days, who told him that he would not have cut Gawain at all had he been told about the lace.

This tale obviously has its origins in Celtic mythology, as it accurately reflects the legend of Cú Chullain and Cú Roí, where the former becomes translated into Gawain and the latter into the Green Knight.

2 The epithet of Sir PERTELOPE, who was defeated in combat by GARETH.

Green Knight, The

Based on the anonymous, fourteenth-century SIR GAWAIN AND THE GREEN KNIGHT, this work dates from c. 1500, but it is a much inferior telling of the famous incident between GAWAIN[1] and the GREEN KNIGHT[1].

Greenan Castle

Built on the site of an Iron Age fort and situated about three miles from Ayr, SCOTLAND, this has been suggested as the original CAMELOT, or even BADON.

Greenland

Called KALAALLIT NUNAAT in the native Greenlandic tongue, this island was allegedly conquered by ARTHUR, according to William Lambard in his *Archaionomia* (1568). The famous sixteenth- and seventeenth-century travel writer Hakluyt was of the opinion that Greenland was GROCLAND, while it also seems possible that Greenland may in fact be a derivation of GRANLAND, the territory ruled by the AMANGONS in the Old French *Le chevalier as deus espées*.

Gregory

A POPE who once brought MERLIN's orthodoxy into question. During his pontificate a bishop named CONRAD was reported to have charged Merlin with heresy, possibly at the instigation of Gregory, but the wizard was acquitted. If this was indeed the correct name of the Pope it is possible that Pope Gregory I (pope from AD 590 to 604) is meant, but his pontificate falls too late to have been contemporary with the traditional Arthurian period.

Greidawl

The father of GWYTHR.

Greloguevaus

In the First CONTINUATION to CHRÉTIEN DE TROYES's PERCEVAL, Greloguevaus is named as PERCEVAL[2]'s father.

Grey Lady

A ghost said to haunt MOEL ARTHUR in Llanwist, Clwyd, who, it has been suggested, is guarding the treasure of ARTHUR allegedly buried there.

Griffith

Having obtained the throne of WALES by murdering the true king, Griffith was later ousted by the rightful heir, MERIADOC.

Griflet
Also GIRFLET

The son of DO, his name is also sometimes rendered as GIRFLET, and may be cognate with JAUFRÉ, the hero of a Provençal romance. In one version of the battle of CAMLANN it was he, and not BEDIVERE[2], who was charged by the dying ARTHUR with returning EXCALIBUR to the LADY OF THE LAKE. Having seen Arthur's tomb, Griflet became a hermit, but died shortly afterwards. In origin Griflet is Celtic, a derivation of GILFAETHWY, who was described as the brother of GWYDION and son of the goddess DÔN in the MABINOGION story of Math, Son of Mathonwy. Griflet's father, Do, appears to have come from Dôn, even though this would mean a change of gender, for Dôn was Gilfaethwy's goddess mother in British tradition.

Grimal

The illegitimate son of EVELAKE, his mother being either GRATILLE or FLOREE.

Gringalet
Also KINCALED

The name given to GAWAIN[1]'s horse, which is called Kincaled in Welsh tradi-

tion. The account of how he came to own Gringalet varies. One story says that he took it from the SAXON king CLARION, while another says he won it in a duel from ESCANOR[3] Le Grand, even though at that time Gringalet was owned by Escanor's nephew, to whom it had been given by the fairy ESCLARIMONDE.

Grisandole

The name used by the maiden AVENABLE when she went to the court of JULIUS CAESAR disguised as a page. She introduced MERLIN to the imperial court and eventually married JULIUS CAESAR.

Grocland

According to the Itinerary of Jacob Cnoyen, Grocland was an island in the polar regions, possibly cognate with GREENLAND, that was colonized by ARTHUR c. AD 530. The inhabitants of this land were alleged to have been twenty-three feet in height. Surrounding the Pole was a range of mountains through which four channels passed, forming four INDRAWING SEAS. Four thousand of Arthur's men were said to have gone to the Pole via these channels, but none returned. In 1364, it was alleged that seven of the men, plus one of Flemish descent, presented themselves to King Magnus of NORWAY. If true, then the date is wrong, for at that time Norway was ruled by King Haakon VI, and it would appear that the Magnus referred to was his predecessor, Magnus VII, who ruled between 1319 and 1355.

Gromer

A knight who, under an enchantment, was made to resemble a Turk, his story being told in the poem TURK AND GAWAIN, which dates from about c. 1500.

He and GAWAIN[1] travelled to the Isle of MAN, where, after various adventures, they killed the king and Gromer took his place, having been decapitated at his own request in order to break the spell.

Gromer (Somer Joure)

Better known simply as Gromer, this knight once captured ARTHUR and kept him prisoner.

Gronois

A son of Sir KAY.

Gronw Bebyr

Hunter with whom BLODEUWEDD had an affair, and with whom she plotted to kill her husband, LLEW LLAW GYFFES. The attempt was unsuccessful, Llew Llaw Gyffes only being wounded. Gronw Bebyr was killed by Llew Llaw Gyffes, while Blodeuwedd was turned into an owl by GWYDION FAB DÔN.

Gruddieu

Also GRUDYEN

One of only seven Britons to survive the battles between BENDIGEID VRAN and MATHOLWCH and return to BRITAIN carrying the head of Bendigeid Vran, which the king himself had commanded be cut off and buried at the WHITE MOUNT in London, there to serve as guardian of the country, his face forever facing FRANCE. The others that returned with him were PRYDERI, MANAWYDAN, TALIESIN, YNAWC (YNAWAG), GLIFIEU (GLUNEU EIL TARAN) and HEILYN, along with Branwen, the reason for the battles.

Grudyen

A variant of GRUDDIEU.

Guaire

The king of Connacht who was the father of the beautiful CRÉD, wife of the elderly MARCÁN.

Guendoloena

Possibly associated with the flower-maiden BLODEUWEDD, this similar woman appears in the VITA MERLINI, where she becomes the wife of MERLIN, only to be later divorced by him. It is thought that she may be the forerunner of the unfortunate GUINEVERE, found in the Arthurian legends that were soon to follow. It is also thought that she might be identical with CHWIMLEIAN, who is mentioned in the Welsh MYRDDIN (MERLIN) poem AFOLLONAU.

Guenever(e)

A little-used variant of GUINEVERE.

Guengasoain

He was guarded by a bear, for he knew that he could be slain only by a pair of knights. This came to pass when, to avenge RAGUIDEL, GAWAIN[1] and YDER slew him, the latter then marrying his daughter.

Guenloie

The wife of YDER. It is possible that she was the unnamed daughter of GUENGASOAIN whom YDER married after he and GAWAIN[1] had slain Guengasoain to avenge RAGUIDEL.

Guiderius

According to GEOFFREY OF MONMOUTH, this king of BRITAIN was killed during the Roman invasion led by CLAUDIUS. He was succeeded by his brother ARVIRAGUS.

Guigenor

A grandniece of ARTHUR, daughter of CLARISSANT and granddaughter of LOT and MORGAUSE, she married AALARDIN. Her family tree is given in Figure 14.

```
        Gorlois = Igraine¹ = Uther
          |
     Lot = Morgause      Arthur
          |
       Clarissant
          |
     Guigenor = Aalardin
```

Figure 14 *Family tree of Guignor, Arthur's grandniece*

Guignier

The pure wife of King CARADOC BRIEF-BRAS whose fidelity was tested and proved by a mantle which a boy had brought to ARTHUR's court, stating that it would fit only faithful wives. Various ladies tried it on, but it fitted only Guignier. She lost one of her breasts while dealing with a magical serpent that had entwined itself around her husband's arm. This was replaced by a magical golden shield boss, made for her by AALARDIN, who had once been in love with her. Guignier is identifiable with the Welsh TEGAU EUFRON.

Guinalot

The offspring of ELIAVRES and a bitch with which the wizard had been forced to copulate.

Guinebaut

The brother of BAN and the elder BORS¹. He was an accomplished wizard who made a magic chessboard and caused a dance to continue perpetually.

Guinevere

Also GUENEVER(E), GWENHWYFAR, GWEN-HWYVAR

The wife of King ARTHUR and, according to Sir Thomas MALORY, the daughter of King LEODEGRANCE of CAMELIARD. Welsh tradition calls her Gwenhwyfar (Guinevere is simply a straight translation into English), and calls her father GOGVRAN or OCVRAN. She has a sister named GWENHWYFACH in the Welsh MABINOGION and she may have been preceded by GUENDOLOENA, who was said to have been married to, and subsequently divorced by, MERLIN. The German DIU CRÔNE makes her father King GARLIN of GALORE, and gives her a brother named GOTEGRIM. In French romance she had an identical half-sister who, for a while, took her place (see FALSE GUINEVERE). WACE says she was MORDRED's sister, while GEOFFREY OF MONMOUTH says she was of noble Roman descent and the ward of Duke CADOR¹.

Early versions of the Arthurian legends make no mention of the famous love affair between her and LANCELOT², and instead give the reason for Arthur's absence, leaving Mordred the chance to seize the throne and Guinevere, as Arthur's campaign against the ROMAN EMPIRE. It is the later version of the legends that most are familiar with, and in these she is the mistress of Lancelot. This version of her story is basically as follows.

Arthur wished to marry the daughter of King Leodegrance of Cameliard the very first time he saw her, thinking her the fairest and most valiant lady in all the land. However, as ever in these early years of his reign, he asked for the counsel of Merlin, for he was still guided by this wise wizard's words.

Merlin agreed that she was above all women in beauty and fairness, but warned Arthur that she would fall in love with Lancelot, and that this love would ultimately bring about the king's downfall. Arthur's heart was set and nothing Merlin said would make him change his mind. Finally Merlin went to King Leodegrance to tell him that Arthur wanted his daughter for his wife.

Naturally, King Leodegrance was overjoyed and immediately gave his consent, adding that he would sent a gift to Arthur that would be far more pleasing than any land, for Arthur already had land enough. Instead he sent the ROUND TABLE, given to him by UTHER, which was capable of seating 150 knights, along with a company of 100 of the most noble knights in his realm. Arthur was rightly delighted with this gift and, while he made preparations for the coming wedding, he dispatched Merlin to find another fifty knights to complete the company that would become known as the KNIGHTS OF THE ROUND TABLE. When Merlin returned from his mission, there was but one remaining place to be filled, the SIEGE PERILOUS.

As the knights assembled in CAMELOT for the wedding of Arthur to Guinevere, the Knights of the Round Table had their duties set out for them by Arthur. He charged them never to commit murder or treason, never to be cruel, never to enter into battle for a wrongful reason whatever the reward, but ever to grant mercy when it was asked for, and ever to help ladies, whether gentlewomen or damsels, whenever help was needed. Every knight was sworn to this oath, and every year at Pentecost they returned to Camelot to reaffirm it.

Lancelot was a latecomer to the Knights of the Round Table and, almost immediately after his arrival, it became clear that he was attracted to Guinevere, and she likewise. In clandestine meetings they affirmed their love, but, even though other members of his court knew of the affair, Arthur would hear nothing against his queen unless proof could be given to him. This played straight into the hands of the scheming Mordred, who wanted the throne as his own. In the company of twelve other knights, he trapped Lancelot and Guinevere in the queen's bedchamber, but Lancelot, even though unarmed, managed to fight his way to freedom, killing all but one of the knights who sought to capture him.

Reluctantly Arthur tried his queen and sentenced her to be burnt. Lancelot snatched her from the pyre and championed her cause in combat, thus earning her pardon. Lancelot then exiled himself. Arthur was fully prepared to travel to FRANCE to make his peace with Lancelot, but he took the advice of Mordred, and instead went to war against his old friend. In his absence Mordred was made regent.

While Arthur was away, Mordred faked reports of the king's death and had himself proclaimed king, announcing that he was to marry Guinevere. She consented to the forthcoming marriage and, with Mordred's approval, travelled to London to buy all manner of things for the wedding. When there, she laid in supplies for a long siege and locked herself away within the Tower of London.

News of Mordred's treachery reached Arthur and he returned home, landing at RICHBOROUGH, where he defeated Mordred. Giving chase, he fought and again defeated Mordred at WINCHESTER, before the forces gathered at CAMLANN for the fatal last encounter. Mordred was killed, and Arthur received a mortal wound. When news of Arthur's death reached Guinevere, she quietly stole away to the abbey at AMESBURY, and took the veil, spending the rest of her days in penance for her sins.

Lancelot landed within the month at Dover and, though too late to save Arthur, he was determined to see Guinevere once more. For seven days he was on the road and on the eighth he came to a nunnery. As he entered the cloisters, a nun dressed in black and white saw him and swooned, for it was Guinevere. When she had recovered, they talked for a while and once Lancelot saw that she had taken to a life of penance, he too decided that this should be his destiny. Taking his leave of Guinevere, he rode to GLASTONBURY, and there took the monk's habit. Many years later a vision charged Lancelot to ride as fast as he could to Amesbury. This he did, but he was too late, for Guinevere had died not half an hour earlier. Without Guinevere, Lancelot could neither eat nor drink. Within six weeks he too was dead. Guinevere's body was taken from the nunnery and laid to rest beside that of Arthur.

In 1911, during restoration work at Glastonbury, the monks of the abbey reported that they had uncovered the grave of Arthur and Guinevere. Their bodies were subsequently reinterred in front of the high altar within the abbey. This find, politically astute for the time, led to the association of Glastonbury with AVALON, but whether or not the bones uncovered were actually those of Arthur and his queen remains in doubt.

There are obviously many variations on this story. Guinevere's death is just one point of contention. In PERLESVAUS she was said to have died during Arthur's lifetime, while BOECE stated that she ended her days as a prisoner of the PICTS. She was said to have had a son by Arthur,

LOHOLT, though that same character was also said to have been the son of Arthur and LIONORS, and the ALLITERATIVE MORTE ARTHURE averred that she and Mordred were the parents of two sons. GAWAIN[1] and KAY were also said to have numbered among her lovers, and Welsh tradition states that she is not just one character but rather three, all having the same name and all, at one stage or another, married to Arthur.

Guinevere is very definitely Celtic in origin, but the main problem lies in determining from whom she originated. She may simply have been a local Welsh maiden who married a local king, their story becoming expanded and enlarged over the years into the Arthurian legends known and loved today.

Guingamuer

Identified by some as the ruler of AVALON, and the lover of MORGAN[1] Le Fay.

Guinganbresil

The husband of ARTHUR's niece TANCREE.

Guinglain

The son of GAWAIN[1] and RAGNELL who became known as Le BEL INCONNU ('The Fair Unknown'), for he turned up at ARTHUR's court ignorant of his own name. He was sent by Arthur to the aid of a princess, with 'the daring kiss', after her maid had arrived at court, accompanied by a dwarf, to ask for assistance. After a while, and following some adventures, Guinglain, the maid and the dwarf came to the GOLDEN ISLAND, where PUCELLE AUX BLANCHE MAINS, a fairy, offered him her love. He turned her down, and the party continued on to the palace of the princess. Once there, Guinglain defeated a knight riding a horned and fire-breathing horse and, having done so, the land was plunged into darkness. A snake appeared which kissed him, and he heard his name spoken, and was told of his parentage. When he later awoke he found a princess, BLONDE ESMERÉE, at his side, who explained that she had been the snake and that he had broken the enchantment that held her when they had kissed. After a brief interlude on the Golden Island with Pucelle aux Blanche Mains, Guinglain returned and married the princess.

Guinnion

The unidentified site of one of ARTHUR'S BATTLES.

Guiomar

The cousin of GUINEVERE and nephew of ARTHUR. He fell in love with MORGAN[1] Le Fay while she was a lady-in-waiting to the queen, but Guinevere found out about this and parted them. Some commentators have sought to suggest that this was the reason behind Morgan Le Fay's enmity towards Arthur, though the idea has not been widely accepted.

Guiromelant

The lover of CLARISSANT, GAWAIN[1]'s sister, even though he was an enemy of that knight. Much to Gawain's annoyance, ARTHUR arranged the marriage between Clarissant and Guiromelant, bestowing the city of Nottingham on him after the wedding

Guiron

Known as 'The Courteous', he was the essence of a gentleman. Appearing in the anonymous *Palamedes*, Guiron was the lover of BLOIE, by whom he had a son named CALINAN. He refused the advances of his friend DANAIN's wife and, when Danain had carried off Bloie, he spared him when he caught up with them. *Palamedes* says that Guiron was a descendant of the Frankish king CLOVIS and that he eventually retired to a cave, where he died.

Gundebald

The ruler of a mysterious realm known as the LAND FROM WHICH NO ONE RETURNS, from which MERIADOC did return, having rescued the daughter of the German emperor from Gundebald.

Gunphar

The king of the ORKNEYS who, along with DOLDAVIUS, King of Gotland, voluntarily submitted to ARTHUR following the latter's defeat of GILMAURIUS and his conquest of IRELAND.

Gunter

The king of DENMARK who was killed by ARTHUR for refusing to pay homage to him.

Gurgurant

A cannibal king whose son was slain by a giant, who was in turn killed by GAWAIN[1]. His son's corpse was then cooked and eaten by the king's followers. Following his conversion to Christianity, he took the name of ARCHIER and lived as a hermit in the vicinity of the GRAIL CASTLE.

Gurmun

According to GOTTFRIED VON STRASS-BURG, the son of an African king who was the king of IRELAND and father of

ISEULT[1]. His name is probably derived from GORMUND, who, according to GEOFFREY OF MONMOUTH, was an African king who conquered Ireland and established his realm there.

Gurzgi

One of the three sons of GORNEMANT DE GOORT, all of whom met with violent deaths.

Gwalchafed
Also GWALCHAVED

'Falcon of Summer'. Suggested by some sources as originally being identical with GWALCHMAI, this character is thought by a few to have been the original of GALAHAD[1].

Gwalchaved

Variant of GWALCHAFED.

Gwalchmai (fab Gwyar)

One of the party formed to help CULHWCH locate OLWEN, the other members being CEI, BEDWYR, CYNDDYLIG the Guide, GWRHYR the Interpreter and MANAWYDAN FAB TEIRGWAEDD. His epithet 'fab Gwyar' simply means 'son of GWYAR'. It is thought that he was the original of GAWAIN[1].

Gwales

Place mentioned in the MABINOGION where the seven returning from IRELAND remained for four score years with the head of BENDIGEID VRAN while *en route* to bury that head in London. They lived in a spacious hall for the allotted time, forgetting all the bad that had passed. When they opened a door and looked towards CORNWALL at the end of their time there, all their past miseries returned to them and they continued towards London.

Gwalhafed

Possibly the original of GALAHAD[1], this character appears in the MABINOGION as the son of GWYAR and brother of GWALCHMAI. It would appear that this name is a simple spelling mistake for GWALCHAFED.

Gwarthegydd

The son of CAW and a counsellor to ARTHUR.

Gwawl

The daughter of COEL, who, possibly, married CUNEDDA.

Gweir

Variously described as an adviser of ARTHUR and a knight, he was the son of GWESTYL.

Gweir Gwrhyd Ennwir

According to the MABINOGION story of CULHWCH AND OLWEN, a maternal uncle of ARTHUR.

Gweit Paladyr Hir

According to the MABINOGION story of CULHWCH AND OLWEN, a maternal uncle of ARTHUR.

Gwenddolau
Also GWENDDOLEU

MERLIN's lord at the battle of ARTHURET, according to the Welsh MYRDDIN (MERLIN) poems. His retainers were described as being one of the six faithful companies of BRITAIN who continued to fight for six weeks after Merlin's death. One of the Welsh TRIADS says that he had birds which had a golden yoke, and required two corpses for their dinner and supper. They were killed by GALL, the son of DYSGYFDAWD. In direct contrast to this, the VITA MERLINI says that Gwenddolau was a British prince who fought on the opposing side to Merlin at Arthuret. Fighting against his cousins GWRGI and PEREDUR, he was killed in the fracas. Gwenddolau was said to have owned a GWYDDBWYLL board that was one of the THIRTEEN TREASURES OF BRITAIN.

Gwenddoleu

Variant of GWENDDOLAU.

Gwendolen

According to Sir Walter Scott's *Bridal of Triermain* (1813), Gwendolen was the half-fairy mother of GYNETH by ARTHUR.

Gwendydd

The name under which GANIEDA appears in Welsh poetry, as well as in the VITA MERLINI by GEOFFREY OF MONMOUTH, where she appears as the philandering wife of RHYDDERCH HAEL whose infidelities were spotted and reported to her husband by her twin brother, MERLIN.

Gwenhwyfach
Also GWENHWYVACH

In Welsh tradition, the sister of GUINEVERE, whom she struck, thus leading to the battle of CAMLANN. A more modern story, Thomas Love Peacock's *Misfortunes of Elphin* (1829), makes her the wife of MORDRED.

Gwenhwyfar

Welsh for GUINEVERE.

Gwenhwyvach

Variant of GWENHWYFACH.

Gwenhwyvar

Variant of GWENHWYFAR, the Welsh for GUINEVERE.

Gwen(n)

1 In the MABINOGION story of the DREAM OF RHONABWY, Gwenn is the name given to a mantle that belonged to ARTHUR which made its wearer invisible. In other sources it is simply referred to as MANTELL, or as the MANTLE OF INVISIBILITY, and was said to be numbered among the THIRTEEN TREASURES OF BRITAIN.

2 In Welsh tradition, the daughter of CUNEDDA and maternal grandmother of ARTHUR.

Gwent

Kingdom of southern WALES that is thought to be identifiable with GLENVISSIG, the realm of MEURIG, the father of ATHRWYS.

Gwenwynwyn

ARTHUR's chief fighter in the MABINOGION story of CULHWCH AND OLWEN.

Gwestyl

The father of ARTHUR's adviser GWEIR.

Gwinam Goddwf Hir

The horse of Sir KAY.

Gwion (Bach)

The son of GWREANG who was guarding the cauldron of CERRIDWEN, in which she was brewing the essence of knowledge for her son when three drops landed on his finger. He absorbed the potency of the brew, either through the skin or by sucking his finger, and immediately gained divine knowledge and inspiration, understanding all that had happened and all that would happen. He fled but was chased by the goddess through a cycle of shape changes which correspond both to totem animals and to the cycle of the seasons. Cerridwen, in the guise of a hen, finally caught Gwion Bach when he was an ear of corn, and swallowed him. Nine months later the goddess gave birth to a radiant child who was named TALIESIN by ELPHIN.

This story seems to have its roots in Irish tradition, as it parallels the story of Fionn mac Cumhaill (Finn mac Cool), who sucked his thumb when some of the essence of the Salmon of Knowledge was on it. It has been suggested that the stories of Fionn mac Cumhaill and Gwion Bach preserve the memory of a pagan practice of divination involving chewing the skin of the thumb.

Gwladys, Saint

In Welsh tradition, the daughter of BRYCHAN who was abducted by GWYNLLYM FILWK, King of GWYNLLYWG. ARTHUR saw Brychan giving chase, but gave his help to Gwynllym Filwk, as they had reached his realm. Gwladys and Gwynllym Filwk, according to Welsh tradition, became the parents of Saint CADOC.

Gwlyddyn

Variant of GLWYD(D)YN.

Gwreang

The father of GWION BACH.

Gwrfoddhu Hen

According to the MABINOGION story of CULHWCH AND OLWEN, a maternal uncle of ARTHUR.

Gwrgi

One of the cousins of the British prince GWENDDOLAU, the other being PEREDUR, who fought against the prince at the battle of ARTHURET.

Gwrhyr

Known as 'The Interpreter', he was among the party that aided CULHWCH in his quest to locate OLWEN, the other members of the company being CEI, BEDWYR, CYNDDYLIG the Guide, GWALCHMAI FAB GWYAR and MENW FAB TEIRGWAEDD. He acted as an interpreter at ARTHUR's court and, when searching YSPADDADEN in the quest to locate his daughter, Olwen, he asked the BLACKBIRD OF CILGWRI for directions, being able to converse in animal languages. This bird sent them to the STAG OF RHEDYNFRC, who in turn passed them on to the EAGLE OF GWERNABWY, who took them to the SALMON OF LLYN LLW.

Gwri

The name given to the foundling infant who later became known as PRYDERI. It is thought that this legendary Welsh character is the origin of BORS[2].

Gwrvan Gwallt-avwy

A character who appears in the MABINOGION, and is thought by some to be the origin of GAWAIN[1].

Gwrvawr

According to the pedigree contained in BONEDD YR ARWR, a maternal ancestor of ARTHUR.

Gwyar

One of the parents of GAWAIN[1]. In the Welsh tradition from which Gawain is derived, Gwyar appears to have been the father of GWALCHMAI and his sister DIONETA[1]. However, when the Welsh came into contact with the Continental tales that made LOT the father of Gawain, it seems that they simply changed Gwyar's gender, and made this character Gawain's mother instead. This is certainly the case in later Welsh stories. However, since Lot is not really a name, rather a title that means 'Lothian-ruler', it is not impossible that his real name was Gwyar.

Gwyddawg

In Welsh tradition, the slayer of KAY, who was in turn slain by ARTHUR.

Gwyddbwyll

An early Celtic board game, the same as the Irish *fidchell*, meaning 'wood sense', the board representing the world in miniature. On one occasion ARTHUR played OWAIN in what was possibly a ritual match, but the outcome remains unclear. The Gwyddbwyll board of GWENDDOLAU is numbered among the THIRTEEN TREASURES OF BRITAIN.

Gwyddno Garanhir

The father of ELPHIN who owned a prolific weir yielding many salmon. He also owned a *mwys*, or basket, which could feed 100 persons at a time, which seems to recall the earlier memories of the magic cauldron common in Celtic mythology. This basket, or hamper, was said to have been one of the THIRTEEN TREASURES of BRITAIN.

Gwydion (fab Dôn)

All-powerful British father god, magician and poet. The brother of ARIANRHOD, son of DÔN, he fostered LLEU LLAW GYFFES and helped him to overcome the three magical restrictions or bindings placed on him by his mother, concerning his name, his bearing of arms and his marriage. Appearing in the MABINOGION as a shapeshifter (meaning he had the ability to change his shape at will), it would appear, at least according to one tradition, that he was responsible for the magical creation of TALIESIN.

Gwydre

According to the MABINOGION story of CULHWCH AND OLWEN, a son of ARTHUR who was killed by the boar TWRCH TRWYTH.

Gwyl

The daughter of GENDAWD who, according to the Welsh TRIADS, was one of ARTHUR's three mistresses.

Gwynedd

A medieval kingdom of North WALES, and still the name of a county or region within that country. In Latin it was known as VENDOTIA, the home of the VENDOTII. While early kings are legendary, the names of the rulers around the traditional Arthurian period were thought to have been Einion (*c.* AD 443), CADWALLON I (AD 443–517) and MAELGWYN (AD 517–47). GEOFFREY OF MONMOUTH makes Cadwallon the contemporary of ARTHUR.

Gwynllym (Filwk)

The king of GWYNLLYWG and abductor of Saint GWLADYS. Her father, BRYCHAN, gave chase, but GWYNLLYM was helped to escape by ARTHUR. In Welsh tradition, he and Gwladys are the parents of Saint CADOC.

Gwynllywg

The realm of GWYNLLYM FILWK.

Gwyn(n) (ap Nudd)

The son of NODENS (NUDD), a Welsh Lord of the Dead, Lord of the Underworld and Master of the WILD HUNT. He is said to dwell in GLASTONBURY TOR, Somerset, which was regarded, so it has been suggested, as a portal to the OTHERWORLD. Later belief made him a warrior who led his followers into battle against the followers of GWYTHR, son of GREIDAWL, the reason for their fight being the maiden CREIDDYLED. To put a halt to the senseless bloodshed, ARTHUR arranged that each leader, Gwynn and Gwythr, should fight each other every May Day until Doomsday, the winner obtaining the hand of Creiddyled. His earlier connection with the otherworld was retained in the legend that says Arthur made him the ruler over the demons of ANNWFN in order to stop them escaping and destroying all humanity. A further connection between Gwynn and Glastonbury Tor is made in the story that say it was there that Gwynn suffered defeat at the hands of Saint TOLLEN.

Gwynn (Hen)

The father of HEILYN.

Gwyrangon

During the reign of VORTIGERN, Gwyrangon ruled KENT, though Vortigern subsequently gave Kent to HENGIST.

Gwythr

The son of GREIDAWL who, with his followers, entered into a battle against GWYNN AP NUDD and his followers over the maiden CREIDDYLED. To end the senseless bloodshed, ARTHUR arranged that each leader should fight every May Day until Doomsday, the winner gaining the hand of Creiddyled.

Gyneth

In a fairly modern work, Sir Walter Scott's *Bridal of Triermain* (1813), Gyneth is the daughter of ARTHUR by GWENDOLEN, who is half-fairy. MERLIN caused her to fall into an enchanted sleep on account of her cruelty, from which she was awakened by Sir Roland de VAUX.

Hags of Gloucester

Collective term for nine witches who lived in Gloucester with their father and mother. They killed PERCEVAL[2]'s cousin, whose head was subsequently seen by Perceval on a platter, but one of their number trained Perceval in the use of arms. Perceval, with the help of ARTHUR's men, destroyed all nine of them.

Harlequin
Also ARLECCHINO

The name by which HELLEKIN became known in the Italian *commedia dell'arte*, and under which guise he appeared in the Arthurian pantomime *Merlin* (1734) by Lewis Theobald.

Hart Fell

A mountain in SCOTLAND which has been proposed by N. Tolstoy as the dwelling place of MERLIN.

Hartmann von Aue

A German poet (*c.* 1170–1215) of the Middle High German period and a participant in the crusade of 1197. He is the author of two Arthurian romances, *Erec* and *Iwain*, both of which closely follow the works of CHRÉTIEN DE TROYES.

Hartwaker

The son of HENGIST, whom he may have succeeded as the ruler of German Saxony, reigning between AD 448 and 480. His brothers are named as AESC, OCTA and EBISSA, his sisters as RONWEN and SARDOINE.

Havelin

A variant for HOEL[1].

Hebron

An alternative name given to BRONS which is thought to have been the invention of ROBERT DE BORON, who wanted to make Brons sound more Hebrew. Hebron is a well-known name from the Holy Bible, being a place-name in Palestine.

Hector

According to the Old French romance *Roman de Troie*, this famous classical Trojan hero, the son of Priam and defender of Troy during the Trojan War, who was slain by Achilles, was loved by MORGAN[1] Le Fay. Spurned by him, she turned against him.

Heilyn

The son of GWYNN HEN and one of the seven Britons to survive the battles between BENDIGEID VRAN and MATHOL-WCH and return to BRITAIN, carrying the head of Bendigeid Vran which had been cut off at the King's own bequest to be buried at the WHITE MOUNT in London, the face towards FRANCE, forever acting as a guardian over the country. The others that returned with him were PRYDERI, MANAWYDAN, TALIESIN, YNAWC (YNAWAG), GRUDYEN (GRUDDIEU) and GLUNEU EIL TARAN (GLIFIEU), along with BRANWEN, the unfortunate maiden who was the cause of the battles.

Heinrich von dem Türtin

The thirteenth-century German poet and author of DIU CRÔNE, a GRAIL romance which makes GAWAIN[1] the hero.

Hel Tor

On top of this peak, near Moreton-hampstead, Devon, is a circular stone, said to be a quoit thrown by the Devil in the course of a fight with King ARTHUR. The Devil lost and crept, sulking, back to Northlew, where he died of cold.

Helain the White

The son of the daughter of King BRANDE-GORIS and BORS[2] who eventually became the emperor of CONSTANTINOPLE.

Helaius

According to the pedigree of JOHN OF GLASTONBURY, the nephew of JOSEPH OF ARIMATHEA and a maternal ancestor of ARTHUR.

Heldins

The first ruler of DENMARK, according to CLARIS ET LARIS, he was succeeded by TALLAS.

Helena

1 The daughter of COEL who, legend says, married the Roman emperor Constantius Chlorus after peace had been restored between her father and the emperor, who had been besieging his city of COLCHESTER for three years. Their son, born in AD 265, was Constantine the Great. Helena is better known as Saint Helena, her dates being given as c. AD 255–330. Tradition makes her the daughter of an innkeeper in Bithynia. She was divorced, for political reasons, in AD 292, but when Constantius Chlorus was declared emperor by his army in YORK, he made her the Empress Dowager. In AD 312, when toleration was extended to Christianity, she was baptized and in AD 326, according to tradition, she visited Jerusalem and founded basilicas on the Mount of Olives and at Bethlehem. Her feast day is 18 August.
2 The niece of HOEL[1], King of BRITTANY, who was seized by the GIANT OF MONT SAINT MICHEL. ARTHUR, KAY and BEDIVERE[2] came to her aid but, finding her already dead, they killed the giant.

Heliades

An ally of MORDRED to whom the latter awarded the kingdom of SCOTLAND.

Helie

The name of the damsel who brought GUINGLAIN to the aid of her mistress, BLONDE ESMERÉE. At first she despised

Guinglain, thinking him unworthy to champion her mistress, but as time passed her contempt turned into respect for his prowess.

Helis

The son of ARDAN, an uncle of ARTHUR and hence his cousin.

Hellekin

In the thirteenth-century LI JUS ADEN, Hellekin appears as a fairy king who became the lover of MORGAN[1] Le Fay. An established figure in Teutonic lore, he is first mentioned in the eleventh- or twelfth-century *Ecclesiastical History* by Ordericus Vitalis. In this he is described as a giant with a club who leads the WILD HUNT. Later, in Italy, Hellekin became the HARLEQUIN (ARLECCHINO) of the *commedia dell'arte*, and in this guise appears in the Arthurian pantomime *Merlin* (1734) by Lewis Theobald.

Helm Wind

A miniature hurricane that occurs in the Lake District and which, in Cumbrian tradition, is associated with ARTHUR.

Hemison

A knight who was the lover of MORGAN[1] Le Fay but was killed by TRISTAN. In Italian romance he was said to have been the father of PULZELLA GAIA by Morgan Le Fay.

Hengist

A semi-legendary SAXON leader who, with his brother HORSA, settled in KENT c. AD 449, the first ANGLO-SAXON settlers/ invaders in BRITAIN. Hengist was originally a leader of the Jutes, and thus he and his brother are said to have come from Jutland.

According to legend, the brothers became allies of VORTIGERN, and Hengist's daughter RONWEN became Vortigern's queen, Hengist receiving Kent as the bride price. Defeated in battle by VORTIMER, he fled to GERMANY, but Vortigern recalled him and he returned with 300,000 men and persuaded Vortigern to summon all the British leaders to a meeting at Salisbury. There he had the entire company massacred. Hengist was eventually defeated by AMBROSIUS AURELIUS, his actual death being attributed to Count ELDOL. The ANGLO-SAXON CHRONICLE places his death in AD 448, but neglects to say how he died. His story is told by BEDE and GEOFFREY OF MONMOUTH.

Hengist, who is nowadays generally regarded as an historical figure, is usually credited with sons named HARTWAKER (who may have succeeded him as the ruler of German Saxony and reigned between AD 448 and 480), AESC, OCTA and EBISSA. His daughters are given as SARDOINE and RONWEN. However, the latter appears to be a Latinization of her true name, for, in various sources that appear to adhere to accepted Anglo-Saxon spellings, the name of Hengist's daughter who became Vortigern's queen is given as HROTHWINA.

Henin the Old

The father of GARWEN, according to the Welsh TRIADS, his daughter being named as one of the three mistresses of ARTHUR.

Henry

1 Referred to as 'The Courtly', he appears in the PROPHÉCIES DE MERLIN, where he was the leader of a force sent to give aid to Jerusalem.

2 The emperor of Germany and father of LARIS and LIDOINE, according to the romance CLARIS ET LARIS.

Henry of Huntingdon

English chronicler (c. 1084–1155) and archdeacon of Huntingdon from 1109. In 1139 he visited Rome and compiled his *Historia Anglorum* down to 1154.

Henwen

In Welsh tradition, a pig which, while gravid, was chased by ARTHUR and gave birth to a variety of progeny, each of which was meant to be capable of causing havoc. She was eventually chased to the cliff-tops and dived into the sea at Penryn Awstin. It is suggested by some sources that Henwen was the mother of the CATH PALUG.

Heri

In the Icelandic SAGA OF TRISTRAM, the informer who told King MARK[2] about the affair between TRISTAN and ISEULT[1].

Hermesent

The daughter of IGRAINE[1] and HOEL[2], a sister to ARTHUR. It is thought that she may be identifiable with BELISENT, who appears in ARTHOUR AND MERLIN, or BLASINE.

Hermit King

Proper name ELYAS ANAIS, though the title was also applied to King PELLES, this character was either a maternal or a paternal uncle of PERCEVAL[2], whom the latter visited. The sources remain divided as to the correct lineage he belongs in.

Hermondine

The daughter of the king of SCOTLAND. She became the wife of MELIADOR after he had slain her other suitor, CAMAL.

Hern(e) the Hunter

The leader of the WILD HUNT, an antlered giant said to be still living in Windsor Great Park. He is probably a survival of the CERNUNNOS cult and has even been linked with that other great British legendary character, Robin Hood.

Herowdes

Having gone blind, this emperor of Rome consulted MERLIN. His advice was that the emperor should kill the Seven Sages, who were the imperial counsellors. When he did this his sight was restored to him.

Herzeloyde

According to WOLFRAM VON ESCHENBACH, the mother of PERCEVAL[2]. Her first husband was CASTRIS, from whom she inherited NORTHGALIS and WALES. Following his death, she married GAHMURET, Perceval's father.

Hesperides

The daughters of Atlas in classical Graeco-Roman mythology who had fabulous gardens, located either on the slopes of Mount Atlas or on islands, where trees with golden apples grew. In Irish romance they became the domain of MADOR's father.

Heywood, Thomas

The seventeenth-century (c. 1574–1641) author of *Life of Merlin*. Born in Lincolnshire, the son of a clergyman, he was educated at Cambridge and was writing plays by 1596. Up to 1633 he had a large share in the composition of 220 plays. Twenty-four of them have survived.

Hind of the Fairies

In the Arthurian romance *La Caccia* by Erasmo de Valvasone, this deer-like animal led ARTHUR through a mountain to MORGAN[1] Le Fay's palace, where the king was shown the heavens and the earth in order to guide his future destiny.

Historia Britonum

This clumsily put-together Latin work is ascribed to NENNIUS and dates from, perhaps, the ninth century. This work purports to give an account of British history from the time of JULIUS CAESAR to towards the end of the seventh century. It gives a mythical account of the origins of the British people and recounts the Roman occupation, the settlement of the SAXONS and King ARTHUR's twelve victories. Although it contains fanciful material of doubtful historical significance, its real value lies in its preservation of material needed for the study of early Celtic literature in general, and the Arthurian legends in particular.

Historia Meriadoci

A Latin romance that tells of the adventures of MERIADOC, the foster son of KAY.

Historia Regum Britanniae

'*History of the Kings of Britain*', the eleventh-century Latin work by GEOFFREY OF MONMOUTH that gives the first coherent narrative of the legends surrounding King ARTHUR as we know them today.

Hocelice

The name by which GALAHAD[2], a son of JOSEPH OF ARIMATHEA, became known after he had ascended to the throne of WALES.

Hoel

1 The king of BRITTANY, a cousin (or possibly nephew) of ARTHUR who landed at SOUTHAMPTON with a large army in response to Arthur's request for help. Together they defeated the SAXONS at LINCOLN, at CALEDON WOOD and at BADON. They put down the Scots, PICTS and Irish in Moray, and toured Loch Lomond. Next they raised the siege of YORK, where COLGRIN, the defeated Saxon leader, had taken refuge, and, having defeated him, Arthur restored that city to its former glory, and returned their lands to the three dispossessed Yorkist princes, LOTH, URIAN and AUGUSELUS. Hoel also helped Arthur to defeat the whole of GAUL within nine years, and to establish his court and a proper government in Paris.

GEOFFREY OF MONMOUTH says that he was the son of BUDICIUS, but does not name his mother. Some commentators have suggested that she was the sister of AMBROSIUS rather than Arthur, thus leading to the ambiguity of his relationship to Arthur. Traditional Breton dating places his rule between AD 510 and 545. He is possibly best known as the father of ISEULT[2] of the White Hands and her brother KAHEDRIN, but the PROSE TRISTAN makes him the father of RUNALEN. The fourteenth-century Welsh BIRTH OF ARTHUR makes him the son of Arthur's sister GWYAR by YMER LLYDAW.

2 An alternative name for IGRAINE[1]'s first husband, more normally given as GORLOIS, according to ARTHOUR AND

MERLIN. Their daughters are named in this work as BLASINE, BELISENT and HERMESENT. This Hoel is also mentioned in the VULGATE *Merlin Continuation*, where he is given the title Duke of TINTAGEL. He is also named as being among the TWENTY-FOUR KNIGHTS of King Arthur's court.

Hogalen Tudno

The whetstone of TUDNO that is numbered among the THIRTEEN TREASURES OF BRITAIN, being said to sharpen none but the weapons of brave men.

Holger

A Danish hero whom the Danes hold is to be identified with OGIER.

Holy Grail

See GRAIL

Holy Thorn

Another way of referring to the GLASTONBURY THORN that reputedly rooted when JOSEPH OF ARIMATHEA stuck his staff into the ground.

Honoree

BIAUSDOUS, the son of GAWAIN[1], unsheathed this sword and by so doing gained the right to marry BIAUTEI.

Honorius

The fifth-century Roman emperor of the Western Empire. The second son of Theodosius I, at whose death the empire was divided between his sons Arcadius and Honorius, the latter, then only ten years old, receiving the western division.

Horn of Brangaled

Also CORN BRANGALED

One of the THIRTEEN TREASURES OF BRITAIN. MERLIN had to acquire it before he could be given any of the others. Originally it had belonged to a centaur that was slain by Hercules, its particular property being that it was capable of containing any drink one wished it to.

Horsa

The brother of HENGIST who accompanied him to BRITAIN and was killed by a cousin of VORTIGERN. His memorial is thought to have been a flint pile near Horsted in KENT (his brother's realm).

Hrothwina

Alternative spelling for RONWEN, the daughter of HENGIST who married VORTIGERN. This appears to be the original ANGLO-SAXON form of her name, Ronwen simply being the Latinized version.

Hu Gadarn

Hero of a story by Iolo MORGANNWG who was said to have killed an AFANC. It would appear that Hu Gadarn was simply the invention of the bard, for his name appears nowhere else.

Huail

Variant of HUEIL.

Hudibras

According to GEOFFREY OF MONMOUTH, an early king of BRITAIN and the father of the magical BLADUD. He sent his son to Athens to study philosophy, but while there his father died and he returned to claim the throne.

Hueil

Also HUAIL

A son of CAW and the brother of GILDAS. An opponent of ARTHUR, their feud beginning when Arthur stabbed GWYDRE, Hueil's nephew. They fought and Arthur was wounded in the knee, but said he would not kill Hueil on the condition that the wound was never mentioned. Some time later Hueil forgot his promise and Arthur had him executed. Another version of this story says that Arthur and Hueil, son of KAW of Brydyn, fought over the favours of a lady. They were both wounded and went their own separate ways, but Arthur always limped after this incident. Some years later they met again and, even though Arthur was in disguise, Hueil recognized him by the limp. They fought again over the same lady. Arthur managed to throw his opponent against a large stone and, drawing his sword, cut off Hueil's head.

Hueil's Stone

The stone in Ruthin, Clwyd, on which ARTHUR was said to have beheaded HUEIL.

Humber

It has been suggested by Scottish writers that ARTHUR fought his last battle, CAMLANN, on the shores of this east of England river that empties into the North Sea.

Hunbaut

When ARTHUR sent GAWAIN[1] on a mission to the KING OF THE ISLES, Hunbaut went as his companion, and tended to proceed with much greater caution than Gawain in the course of the adventures the pair had together.

Hunbaut

A thirteenth-century French verse romance that deals with the adventures of HUNBAUT and, more particularly, his companion GAWAIN[1].

Huncamunca

The name of ARTHUR's daughter in Henry Fielding's *Tom Thumb* (1730).

Hungary

Though the inclusion of Hungary in the Arthurian romances is an anachronism – it did not exist as a single country until about the ninth century, much later than the traditional Arthurian period – several kings are assigned to it. CLARIS ET LARIS names the king as SARIS, saying he captured Cologne, but was subsequently killed by LARIS. Elsewhere a king named JEREMIAH is mentioned, the father-in-law of GAWAIN[1], while SAGREMOR is called the son of the king of Hungary. King DITAS of Hungary was said to have been among the followers of the Roman emperor THEREUS when the latter attacked ARTHUR.

Hunting Causeway

Route between CADBURY CASTLE and GLASTONBURY that local Somerset legend says King ARTHUR rides along each Christmas Eve in the company of his knights. Usually he remains invisible except for the glint of his silver horseshoes, but the sounds made have reputedly been heard by many people.

A local variant of this story says that, rather than Christmas Eve, the spectral ride occurs on 24 June, St John the Baptist's Day, when Arthur and his knights ride to Glastonbury to do homage to the abbot there (cf. WILD HUNT).

Hunting Knight

This son of the king of GASCONY came to ARTHUR's court to learn valour and chivalry.

Huon

The hero of the thirteenth-century romance HUON DE BORDEAUX, which is set in Carolingian (AD 751–987) times. This tale, which SHAKESPEARE obviously drew a great deal of material from, names OBERON[1] as the king of the fairies who assigned his kingdom to Huon. ARTHUR, who had lived in FAIRYLAND since the end of his earthly reign, had come to think that the realm would be passed to him and was greatly troubled. However, Oberon threatened Arthur and thus ensured that there would be peace between him and Huon.

Huon de Bordeaux

Thirteenth-century French romance concerning the ascension of HUON to the throne of FAIRYLAND, called MOMUR in this work, in preference to ARTHUR.

Huth-Merlin

An alternative name for the SUITE DU MERLIN.

Hutton, Castle

The home of BERTILAK, the GREEN KNIGHT[1] of the famous poem SIR GAWAIN AND THE GREEN KNIGHT.

Hygwydd

When ARTHUR captured the cauldron of DIWRNACH, this servant of his carried it on his back.

Ibert

According to WOLFRAM VON ESCHEN-BACH, a character, possibly cognate with IWERET, who had a wife named IBLIS and who castrated KLINGSOR.

Iblis

The wife of IBERT, according to WOLFRAM VON ESCHENBACH, though that author also names LANCELOT[2] as her husband. It would appear that he simply invented the name, using *Sibile* (a Sibyl) as the root.

Iceland

Part of ARTHUR's kingdom, whose king AELEUS, at least according to LAYAMON, voluntarily submitted to Arthur and sent his son ESCOL by the king of RUSSIA's daughter to Arthur's court. GEOFFREY OF MONMOUTH names the king of Iceland as MALVASIUS (cf. AELENS).

Iddawc

In the MABINOGION story of the DREAM OF RHONABWY, Iddawc was the companion of RHONABWY when they encountered KAY.

Iddawg

A messenger sent by ARTHUR to MORDRED before the final battle at CAMLANN. Iddawg, however, delivered the message in such a way that it enraged Mordred, and as a result Iddawg became known as the 'Embroiler of Britain'.

Idres

A king of CORNWALL who was among the eleven leaders who rebelled against the youthful ARTHUR at the start of his reign.

Idumean(s)

An alternative name for the Edomites, an ancient people inhabiting a region south of the Dead Sea. Traditionally descended from the biblical Esau, they appear in the Arthurian legends of later writers, who said that the queen of the AMAZONS was rescued from their king by TRISTAN THE YOUNGER. They were also said to have done battle with GAWAIN[1], their own queen being killed by the CROP-EARED DOG.

Igerna, -e

Variant of IGRAINE.

Ignoge

The daughter of the Greek king PANDRA-SUS, whom BRUTUS fought and defeated, thus claiming the hand of the reluctant Ignoge, compelling the king to release his Trojan captives and to supply them with ships, provisions and bullion to enable them to leave Greece.

Igraine

Also EIGYR, IGERNA, IGERNE, YGERNA

1 The mother of ARTHUR. The daughter of AMLAWDD, she married GORLOIS (sometimes called HOEL[2]) and had a number of daughters by him. UTHER became infatuated with her and, while at war with her husband, had MERLIN make him resemble her absent husband by magic. On the very night that Gorlois was killed in a battle against Uther's troops, the latter lay with her, the resulting child of their union being Arthur. Uther later married her but, even though she had grown to love him, their happiness was short-lived, for Uther died within two years.

Various ancestries have been given for Igraine. That of JOHN OF GLASTONBURY is given in Figure 15, whereas the sixteenth-century Welsh historian Grufudd Hiraethog gives the pedigree shown in Figure 16. An even more interesting pedigree is given in BONEDD YR ARWR (Figure 17).

2 The sister of ARTHUR with whom he had an incestuous relationship, according to the VULGATE *Merlin Continuation*.

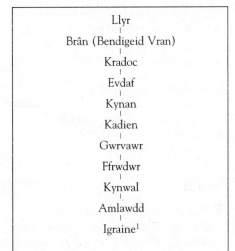

Evgen
|
Joshua[3]
|
Garcelos
|
Manael
|
Lambor
|
Amlawdd
|
Igraine[1]

Figure 16 *Ancestry of Igraine according to Grufudd Hiraethog*

Llyr
|
Brân (Bendigeid Vran)
|
Kradoc
|
Evdaf
|
Kynan
|
Kadien
|
Gwrvawr
|
Ffrwdwr
|
Kynwal
|
Amlawdd
|
Igraine[1]

Figure 17 *Ancestry of Igraine as given in* Bonedd yr Arwr

Helaius
|
Joshua[2]
|
Aminabad
|
Castellors
|
Manael
|
Lambord
|
a son
|
Igraine[1]

Figure 15 *Ancestry of Igraine, Arthur's mother, according to John of Glastonbury*

Ilax

The father of EREC, according to the Norse version of the story of Erec, the EREX SAGA.

Ilinot

According to WOLFRAM VON ESCHENBACH, this son of ARTHUR ran away as a child and was raised by Queen FLORIE of KANADIC. He fell in love with her, but she expelled him from her realm and he died of a broken heart.

Illan

A traditional king of Leinster, IRELAND, who was thought to have led raids into BRITAIN and who traditionally reigned between AD 495 and 511. The history of Leinster at this time is obscure, and Illan may have reigned to either side of these dates, or not at all. It has been argued that he was an historical enemy of ARTHUR.

Ille Estrange

Otherwise known as ESTRANGOT, this kingdom was ruled by VAGOR, who kept LIONEL a prisoner. Lionel was due to fight MARABRON, Vagor's son, but, being injured, was unable to do so and LANCELOT[2] acted as his substitute, successfully defeating Marabron and so earning Lionel's release.

Illtyd, Saint

The daughter of RIEINGULID, according to Welsh tradition, Illtyd was said to have been related to ARTHUR and to have served as a warrior under him. She founded the monastery of Llanilltud Fawr (now Llantwit Major) in WALES.

Indeg

The daughter of GARWY the Tall, she was, according to the Welsh TRIADS, one of the three mistresses of ARTHUR.

Indrawing Seas

The name given to four channels that passed through the mountains that surrounded the North Pole on the island of GROCLAND. Four thousand of ARTHUR's men were supposed to have gone to the Pole via these channels, but none returned. In 1364, it was alleged that seven of the men, plus one of Flemish descent, presented themselves to King Magnus of NORWAY.

Ineen

A kingdom that appears in the Scottish Gaelic folktale of UALLABH. It is said that the son of the king of Ineen, who was also the brother of the queen (which, if taken literally, would mean that he had married his daughter, or stepdaughter), imprisoned Uallabh, but he was rescued by the queen's younger sister.

Inogen

In Richard Hole's ARTHUR (1789), she was a daughter of MERLIN with whom ARTHUR fell in love.

Iona

The name of a king of FRANCE who, according to the MABINOGION story of CULHWCH AND OLWEN, came to ARTHUR's court.

Ioruaidh

The son of the king of ICELAND, father of RATHLEAN and, through her, according to the Irish romance VISIT OF GREY HAM, the grandfather of AILLEAN.

Ireland

Traditionally a part of ARTHUR's kingdom. His conquest of the island and defeat of its king, GILMAURIUS, is described by GEOFFREY OF MONMOUTH. Other sources name the king as ANGUISH, ELIDUS, MARHALT and GURMUN, while DURMURT LE GALLOIS names a queen of Ireland as FENISE (FENICE[2]), and says that the royal standard-bearer of Ireland was PROCIDES, governor of Limerick.

The country features most prominently in ancient myths that later became embroidered and sewn into the Arthurian sagas, such as the battles between BENDIGEID VRAN and MATHOLWCH, and CUL-HWCH and OLWEN. It seems possible that, due to the OTHERWORLD themes of the Irish stories incorporated into Arthurian legend, the inclusion of Ireland in Arthur's domain was intended to signify his rule over not just the land of the living but also the land of the dead.

Irion

A king who was the father of MARTHA and father-in-law of YSAIE THE SAD, TRISTAN's son.

Ironside

A KNIGHT OF THE ROUND TABLE. This was the more common name of the RED KNIGHT[3] of the Red Lands. He was the father of Sir RAYNBROWN and was defeated by GARETH.

Isaiah

Son of EIAN and father of JONAANS, according to the traditional lineage of GALAHAD[1].

Isca Legionis, -um

The name by which CAERLEON-ON-USK was known in early times, which has led to its identification with the CITY OF THE LEGION.

Iseo

The daughter of TRISTAN who married King JUAN of Castile in Spanish Arthurian romance. The romances also say that TRISTAN THE YOUNGER, Iseo's brother, married MARIA, the sister of King Juan, though some sources make Maria the king's daughter.

Iseult
Also ISODD, ISOLDE

The name of at least four ladies from the Arthurian legends.

1 The fated daughter of King ANGUISH of IRELAND. She cured the poisoned wounds of TRISTAN which he had sustained fighting the Irish king MORAUNT and his ally, the giant Sir MORHOLT. He told his uncle, King MARK[2], of her beauty, and was sent to woo her on Mark's behalf. She consented to the marriage and returned with Tristan, but, as the result of drinking a love potion, became hopelessly enamoured of Tristan. So began their famous and unfortunate love affair. Having already lain with Tristan, she substituted her maid for herself on her wedding night so that King Mark would not learn the truth. Subsequently, their affair uncovered, Tristan fled to BRITTANY, where he married ISEULT[2] of the White Hands. When Tristan died, Iseult's heart broke and she died as well. Although she is said to be the daughter of the king of IRELAND, her name derives from the ancient British *Adsiltia* – 'She who is gazed on'.

2 Iseult of the White Hands, who married TRISTAN after he had left ISEULT[1]. She is variously described as the daughter of HOEL[1] or JOVELIN, Duke of Arundel. Even though married, the union was never consummated, for Tristan still loved Iseult, something she very naturally resented. When Tristan was fatally wounded he sent for Iseult, believing that she could heal him, making the captain of the ship that was to fetch her agree to hoist black sails if she had refused to return with him and white

sails if she was on board. When the ship returned, it was showing white sails, but Iseult of the White Hands lied to her husband, saying the sails were black, and he died before Iseult arrived. Some sources say Iseult did refuse to come, and so Tristan died, while others say that the jealous King Mark killed Tristan. Classical influences obviously play a very important part here, particularly the story concerning Aegeus and his son Theseus with regard to the white and black sails. An Icelandic version of the Tristan story says that this Iseult was Spanish, being given to Tristan when he defeated the king of SPAIN.

3 Queen of IRELAND, wife of ANGUISH and mother of ISEULT[1].

4 TRISTAN's god-daughter.

Isle of Honey

An early name for BRITAIN, according to the WHITE BOOK OF RHYDDERCH.

Isle of Life

Possibly to be identified with the Isle of Wight and where the ancient British kings GADDIFER and PERCEFOREST were said to have enjoyed a lengthy existence. This life-prolonging island seems to have connections with the Isle of APPLES, which GEOFFREY OF MONMOUTH makes AVALON, and, by association with Irish mythology, might possibly be identified with the Isle of MAN.

Isodd

Norse and Icelandic variant of ISEULT.

Isolde

Variant of ISEULT used in the thirteenth century by GOTTFRIED VON STRASSBURG,

and in the nineteenth century by Richard Wagner.

Ither

The son of UTHER's sister and therefore a cousin of ARTHUR. He was raised by his uncle and became the king of KUKU-MARLANT, but later claimed Arthur's throne and stole a golden goblet from him. He was slain by PERCEVAL[2].

Itonje

Sister of GAWAIN[1] who married King GRAMOFLANZ.

Iubhar

The Irish name for the father of ARTHUR. However, one Irish romancer misunderstood this name and made Iubhar Arthur's grandfather, calling Arthur's father UR.

Ivoine

In French romance, the original name of MOINE or CONSTANS.

Ivoire

The sister of BAN who was married to King CONSTANTINE[1] of BRITAIN and had three sons: UTHER, IVOINE (MOINE or CONSTANS) and PANDRAGON (AMBROSIUS).

Ivor

The huntsman who raised MERIADOC.

Iwain

Middle High German romance by the late twelfth- and early thirteenth-century poet HARTMANN VON AUE that clearly follows the earlier works of CHRÉTIEN DE TROYES.

The hero of this work is usually known as OWAIN.

Iweret

According to WOLFRAM VON ESCHEN-BACH, the father of IBLIS and hence father-in-law of LANCELOT[2]. The Lord of BEFORET, he raided the territories of Lancelot's foster brother MABUZ, as a result of which Lancelot killed him. He appears to be of Celtic origin, possibly coming from YWERIT, the father of BRÂN, though he may also be identified with IBERT.

Jack the Giant-killer

The famous giant-killer from nursery stories who is perhaps best known for his exploits with a beanstalk and a goose that laid a golden egg. Thought to have flourished during the traditional Arthurian period, Jack started out on his career by killing a giant whom he trapped in a large pit. He was then himself captured, by the giant BLUNDERBOAR, but managed to escape and killed Blunderboar and his brothers. He was also said to have tricked a Welsh giant into killing himself. His first appearance in the Arthurian saga says that he became the servant of ARTHUR's son and, in the course of this service, obtained a wonderful sword, shoes of swiftness, and caps of knowledge and invisibility. He continued to rid the land of giants, married a duke's daughter and was given a noble residence by Arthur himself. There is no evidence that Jack was a hero of early tales and he is possibly a composite of several, being invented some time around the end of the eighteenth or beginning of the nineteenth century. Classical influences may have played some part in his creation, for there are marked similarities between his character and that of Perseus who killed the Gorgon Medusa and married Andromeda. Even his attributes are similar.

Jaufré

Possibly cognate with GRIFLET, Jaufré appears in a romance that carries his name and tells how TAULAT came to ARTHUR's court, killed a knight in front of the queen and promised to return each year to do exactly the same again. Jaufré was dispatched after him and, following a variety of adventures, killed him, marrying BRUNISSEN, whom Taulat had made suffer.

Jeremiah

An alleged king of HUNGARY during the Arthurian period.

Jeschuté

A character appearing in the story of PERCEVAL[2]. Named by WOLFRAM VON ESCHENBACH only as the daughter of King LAC, and thus the sister of EREC, she was the wife of ORILUS, Duke of LALANDER. Perceval's mother had told her son to demand a jewel or a kiss from any lady he met. He came upon a girl in a tent and demanded both, this story appearing in works by both Wolfram von Eschenbach and CHRÉTIEN DE TROYES.

Joan go-to-'t

In the play *The Birth of Merlin*, published in 1662 but written at an earlier date, Joan go-to-'t is the mother of MERLIN.

Although anonymous, the play may have been written by W. Rowley (d. 1626), though the style indicates that Shakespeare may have had a hand in it.

Johfrit de Liez

During LANCELOT[2]'s stay in MAIDENLAND, this character was responsible for training the knight as a mighty warrior.

John of Glastonbury

The fourteenth-century author of a Latin history of GLASTONBURY which includes some Arthurian material, most notably genealogical information.

Jonaans

A virtuous ancestor of LANCELOT[2] who emigrated from BRITAIN to GAUL, where he married the daughter of King MARONEX, from whom he inherited his kingdom.

Jonas

The first husband of TREPHINA, daughter of WAROK, and father by her of JUDWAL or TREMEUR. It is possible that the couple remained childless, for Tremeur is also named as the son of CUNOMORUS, whowas also, at some stage, married to Trephina.

Joram

In the medieval *Wigalois* by WIRNT VON GRAFENBERG, Joram was a king who left GUINEVERE a magic girdle, saying either she could regard it as a gift or he would come and fight for the right to present it to her. She asked him to do the latter, which he did, successfully defeating several champions, but to one, GAWAIN[1], he presented the girdle. Gawain subsequently married FLORIE[2], the niece of King Joram.

Josa, Saint

According to Coptic tradition, the daughter of JOSEPH OF ARIMATHEA.

Joseph d'Arimathia

Important work by the twelfth-century Burgundian ROBERT DE BORON that deals with the GRAIL legends, particularly those surrounding the biblical associations of JOSEPH OF ARIMATHEA.

Joseph of Arimathea

A biblical character who was either the uncle of Jesus and a tin trader who regularly visited the West Country for Mendip lead and Cornish tin, on one occasion allegedly accompanied by Jesus, or a soldier of Pilate, who gave him the Chalice Cup used at the Last Supper. The former version is possibly the better known of the two.

The tradition that he was the uncle of Jesus also says that, following the Crucifixion, he travelled to BRITAIN in either AD 37 or 63, bringing the Christian Gospel with him and accompanied by eleven or twelve disciples. Arriving at GLASTONBURY, he pushed his staff into the ground and it immediately rooted, a divine sign that his journey had come to an end. The local king gave him and his followers twelve hides of land, and on that land they founded the Old Church, later to be incorporated into Glastonbury Abbey. The sprouting staff grew into a thorn tree, the GLASTONBURY THORN, that had the special distinction of flowering twice a year, once in the spring and again at Christmas. Tradition also says that Joseph brought three holy relics with him, the first two being cruets containing the blood and sweat of Jesus, while the third, and the most famous, was the Chalice Cup used by Christ at the Last

Supper, and also, according to some sources, used to catch the blood of Christ while on the Cross from the wound in his side made by the LANCE OF LONGINUS. This vessel has become known as the Holy GRAIL, the subject of the quest by ARTHUR's knights.

According to the alternative tradition that makes Joseph a soldier of Pontius Pilate, following the Resurrection, and having been thrown into a dungeon, Joseph was visited by Jesus, who returned to him the Chalice Cup of the Last Supper, which Pilate had originally given Joseph but which had become lost. Joseph was set free when Jerusalem fell to the armies of Vespasian and, with his sister ENYGEUS and her husband, BRONS or HEBRON, went into exile with a group of companions. When suffering from famine, those among them who had not sinned were sustained by the Chalice Cup – the Grail. Brons and Enygeus had twelve sons, eleven of whom married, but the twelfth, ALAN, did not. Placed in charge of his brothers, he sent them out to preach Christianity. His father, Brons, was told to become a fisherman, thus becoming known as the RICH FISHER. Joseph himself meanwhile travelled to Britain, most sources saying that he brought the Grail with him, though ROBERT DE BORON says that Brons was entrusted with the holy vessel. His journey to Britain is variously described, and in one version he crosses the sea on a miraculous shirt (sic), the property of his son JOSEPHE.

Joseph and his followers were also said to have converted the pagan city of SARRAS to Christianity, though this does not correspond to the later Grail legends which still make Sarras a pagan city. Its king, EVELAKE, having adopted the Christian faith, was then able, with divine help, to defeat his enemy, King THOLOMER. Sarras, from which the SARACENS are sometimes said to have derived

their name, but which is not known outside romance, is variously located either in the East, meaning Asia, or in Britain itself.

Other legends exist concerning Joseph of Arimathea. The romance Sone de Nausay relates how he drove the Saracens out of NORWAY, married the daughter of the pagan king and became king himself. God then made him powerless and the land became infertile. Fishing was his only pleasure, thus leading to his becoming known as the FISHER KING, though he was finally cured of his ailments by a knight. This is a curious version of the story of the Fisher King, who is usually described as one of Joseph's descendants, and appears to have been lifted directly from the Grail legends. He was then said to have provided for the foundation of the GRAIL CASTLE, though monastery would be a better description, for it was to have thirteen monks in charge to reflect Christ and his twelve apostles.

JOHN OF GLASTONBURY provides us with some information about Joseph's arrival in Britain. He mentions the cruets of blood and sweat, but does not mention the Grail. He also says that Joseph was dispatched to Britain by Saint Philip who was preaching in GAUL. Gallic tradition states that he was placed in an oarless boat in the company of Lazarus, Martha, Mary Magdalene and others which was then guided by the divine hand to Marseilles. Another tale, Spanish in origin, says that this party went to Aquitaine, while an Aquitainian story says that Joseph and his party landed at Limoges. All these seem to be an attempt to claim Joseph for Gaul, but most are now not seriously regarded by hagiologists.

The Sone de Nausay says that Joseph had a son named ADAM, while the ESTOIRE DEL SAINTE GRAAL says his son was called JOSEPHE. Coptic tradition claims that he had a daughter, Saint JOSA. Attempts have been made to connect Joseph with Joachim, the father of the Virgin Mary, or with Joseph the father of Jesus. These attempts have found no following, for biblical information alone is sufficient to prove their invalidity.

Josephe

The son of JOSEPH OF ARIMATHEA who is first mentioned in the ESTOIRE DEL SAINTE GRAAL. When his father and his followers crossed the sea to BRITAIN, it was said that the pure ones did so on Josephe's outstretched shirt (*sic*). He became the first GRAIL KEEPER of Arthurian legend, and consecrated ALAN as his successor before he died and was buried in SCOTLAND. However, the QUESTE DEL SAINTE GRAAL had him living long enough to administer the Communion to GALAHAD[1].

Joshua

The name of at least three characters from Arthurian legend.

1 The son of BRONS and ENYGEUS, brother of ALAN and nephew of JOSEPH OF ARIMATHEA. He married the daughter of King KALAFES of TERRE FORAINE, later inheriting that kingdom. He succeeded Alan as the GRAIL KEEPER, following the normal line of descent for the FISHER KINGS.
2 According to the pedigree of JOHN OF GLASTONBURY, the son of HELAIUS and an ancestor of ARTHUR.
3 According to the pedigree of Grufudd Hiraethog, the son of EVGEN, father of GARCELOS, and an ancestor of IGRAINE[1].

Jovelin

According to GOTTFRIED VON STRASSBURG, the Duke of Arundel (Sussex) who was the father of ISEULT[2] of the White Hands.

Joyous Gard

Originally called DOLOROUS GARD, presumably because the DOLOROUS STROKE was delivered there, this castle was captured by and became the property of LANCELOT[2], who changed its name. Located in the north of England and identified by many with BAMBURGH Castle, it was to this castle that Lancelot took GUINEVERE once he had rescued her from being burnt alive. The castle later reverted to its original name.

Jozefant

According to DURMART LE GALLOIS, the king of DENMARK.

Juan

The king of Castile in Spanish romance who married ISEO, the daughter of TRISTAN. His sister, or daughter, MARIA, married TRISTAN THE YOUNGER.

Judwal

The alternative name for TREMEUR, the son of TREPHINA and either CUNOMORUS or JONAS.

Julain

The husband of YGLAIS and mother of PERCEVAL[2], according to PERLESVAUS.

Julius Caesar

A famous Roman statesman, born 100 or 102 BC, made ruler of Rome in 49 BC, and assassinated in the Forum in 44 BC. He appears in several of the Arthurian sources. The VULGATE VERSION calls him 'emperor', though he never actually was, and makes him the contemporary of ARTHUR, though some 500 years too early for the traditional Arthurian period.

MERLIN was introduced to the imperial court and told Caesar that a dream he had had could be interpreted only by the Wild Man of the Woods. The latter was captured by Merlin and GRISANDOLE, and told Caesar that his dream was about his wife's infidelities. Even more fantastically, the romance HUON DE BORDEAUX makes Julius Caesar the father of OBERON[1] by MORGAN[1] Le Fay.

Kadien(n)

According to the Welsh BONEDD YR ARWR, both a maternal and a paternal ancestor of ARTHUR, directly descended, on both occasions, from LLYR.

Kadwr

A paternal ancestor of ARTHUR in the line of descent from LLYR as found in the Mostyn MS 117.

Kahedrin

The son of King HOEL[1] of BRITTANY and brother of ISEULT[2] of the White Hands. His good friend TRISTAN married his sister, but Kahedrin fell in love with ISEULT[1] and wrote poems and love letters to her. She replied in all innocence, but Tristan misunderstood, and Kahedrin had to jump from a window to avoid being killed by the enraged Tristan. He landed on a chess game which King MARK[2] was playing below the window, and eventually died of his love for Iseult. Some people say that this story led to the belief that King Mark killed Tristan in jealousy, believing that it was he, and not Kahedrin, who had been corresponding with his wife.

Kai

An alternative Welsh form for KAY. This variant of the name is used when the knight of ARTHUR was said to have been encountered in a dream by IDDAWC and RHONABWY, a tale that is related in the MABINOGION story of the DREAM OF RHONABWY.

Kalaallit Nunaat

The native name for GREENLAND.

Kalafes

The king of TERRE FORAINE who, following his cure from leprosy by ALAN, became a Christian and took the name ALFASEIN at his baptism. His daughter married Alan's brother JOSHUA[1], another son of BRONS. He died after having been speared through the thighs (a common wound in the GRAIL legends) for watching the GRAIL PROCESSION.

Kalegras

The name of TRISTAN's father in the Icelandic SAGA OF TRISTRAM, and also the name given to Tristan's son by ISEULT[2] of the White Hands. This younger Kalegras was eventually said to have become the king of England.

Kamelin

The son of the Irish king ALVREZ, a KNIGHT OF THE ROUND TABLE and brother of MIROET, also a Knight of the Round Table.

Kanadic

The domain over which FLORIE[1] was queen.

Kanahins

The squire of Sir LANCELOT[2].

Kanedic

The realm of ECUNAVER who was conquered after he had stated that he intended to attack ARTHUR. It is possible that Kanedic is to be identified with KANADIC, the realm of FLORIE[1].

Kapalu

A servant of MORGAN[1] Le Fay who appears in the BATAILLE LOQUIFER. It seems as if this character has his origins in CAPALU, the Continental name for the monstrous cat, the CATH PALUG.

Karadan

The husband of an unnamed sister of ARTHUR, and father by her of AGUISANT.

Karadawc

Presumed to be a variant of KARADOC and KRADOC, this name appears in a paternal pedigree found in the Mostyn MS 117 that gives the descent of ARTHUR from LLYR.

Karadoc

According to two pedigrees found in the Welsh BONEDD YR ARWR, an ancestor of ARTHUR. It is thought that he is to be identified with KRADOC and KARADAWC, names which appear in other manuscripts and pedigrees, and which are illustrated under LLYR.

Kardeiz

According to WOLFRAM VON ESCHENBACH, one of the twin sons of PERCEVAL[2].

Kaw

A variant of CAW.

Kay
Also CAI, CEI, KAI, KEI

The son of ECTOR and foster brother of ARTHUR. Though appearing in the earlier romances as a model of chivalry, later stories made him a troublesome and somewhat childish character who believed that his relationship to Arthur gave him the right to behave in any way he chose. Originally he claimed that it was he, not Arthur, who had withdrawn the SWORD IN THE STONE, but Ector compelled him to tell the truth. He married ANDRIVETE, the daughter of King CADOR[2] of NORTHUMBERLAND and is credited with a daughter named KELEMON, and two sons called GARANWYN and GRONOIS. His horse was known as GWINAM GODDWF HIR.

Many different stories are told about Kay, some obscure and some well known. In Welsh tradition he was a member of the party formed to help CULHWCH in his quest to locate OLWEN. PERLESVAUS recounts how he killed LOHOLT, Arthur's son, and joined BRIAN DES ILLES in a rebellion against the king. The accounts of his death vary. Throughout Welsh literature and tradition he was said to have been killed by GWYDDAWG, who was in turn killed by Arthur. He was also said to have been killed during Arthur's campaign against the ROMAN EMPIRE, or in the war against MORDRED. One source lists him among the knights killed by the escaping yet unarmed LANCELOT[2] when the latter had been caught in compromising circumstances in GUINEVERE's bedchamber.

Keeper of the Forest

A character who is possibly to be identified with CERNUNNOS and is referred to in the Welsh poem OWAIN.

Kehydius

A variant form of KAHEDRIN that was used by Sir Thomas MALORY.

Kei

A variant of KAY.

Kelemon

The daughter of Sir KAY, according to Welsh tradition.

Kelliwic
Also KELLIWIG

A Cornish stronghold of ARTHUR. Possibly to be identified with Castle KILLIBURY, it has also been connected with CALLINGTON, CELLIWITH and KELLY ROUNDS.

Kelliwig

A variant of KELLIWIC.

Kelly Rounds

A place in CORNWALL that, it has been suggested, is identifiable as KELLIWIC.

Kent

The kingdom of GWYRANGON during VORTIGERN's time, which the latter gave to the SAXON leader HENGIST. During the traditional Arthurian period the county seems to have been under ANGLO-SAXON rule and may have been ruled by AESC, Hengist's son, who traditionally reigned between AD 488 and 512. WILLIAM OF MALMESBURY says that Aesc had to defend the kingdom, implying that he had a formidable enemy, such as ARTHUR. BEDE says that Kent was originally settled by the Jutes, and this has led to an association between Hengist, his brother HORSA, and Jutland, the homeland of the Jutes.

Kentigern, Saint

The son of THANEY (the daughter of LOT), according to the LIFE OF SAINT KENTIGERN. Also called Mungo, Saint Kentigern was a Celtic churchman and the apostle of Cumbria. According to his own legend, he was the son of a Princess Thenew, which is not too dissimilar to THANEY, who was cast from TRAPRAIN LAW, then exposed on the Firth of Forth in a coracle. This carried her to Culross, where she bore a son (c. AD 518). Mother and child were baptized, an anachronism, by Saint Serf, who reared the boy in his monastery, where he was so loved that his name, Kentigern ('chief lord'), was often exchanged for Mungo ('dear friend'). He founded a monastery at Cathures (Glasgow) and in AD 543 was consecrated bishop of Cumbria. In AD 553 he was driven to seek refuge in WALES, where he visited Saint DAVID, and where he founded another monastery and a bishopric, which still bears the name of his disciple Saint Asaph. In AD 573 he was recalled by a new king, RHYDDERCH HAEL, and about AD 584 was visited by Columba. He died in AD 603 and was buried in Glasgow Cathedral, which is named after him as Saint Mungo's.

Kilhwch

A little-used variant of CULHWCH.

Killaraus, Mount

The mount in IRELAND from where MERLIN was said to have transported the GIANT'S RING that was re-erected on SALISBURY PLAIN as STONEHENGE.

Killibury

Place in CORNWALL that, it has been suggested, is identifiable as CELLIWIG, and thus CAMELOT.

Kil(w)ydd

The father of CULHWCH and GOLEUD-DYDD, ARTHUR's aunt.

Kincaled

The name by which GAWAIN[1]'s horse GRINGALET is known in Welsh tradition.

King Arthur

An opera written in 1691 by John DRYDEN, with music by Henry Purcell, that has little actual Arthurian content. In it, ARTHUR is in love with the blind EMMELINE, daughter of Duke CONON of CORNWALL. She is carried off by OSWALD, the SAXON king of KENT and Arthur's enemy. While held captive, her sight was restored to her by MERLIN, and she was eventually rescued when Arthur finally defeated Oswald.

King Arthur and (the) King (of) Cornwall

A sixteenth-century English ballad that featured ARTHUR and the sorcerer King Cornwall.

King of the Isles

The father of BIAUTEI, whose hand was won by GAWAIN[1] when the latter managed to unsheath the sword HONOREE.

King with a Hundred Knights

One of the eleven leaders who rebelled against the youthful ARTHUR at the start of his reign. He has been variously identified with BERRANT LES APRES, AGUYSANS and MALEGINIS, though the DUE TRISTANI implies that he originated from Piacenza and had a wife called RICCARDA.

Klingsor

The Duke of TERRE LABUR, according to WOLFRAM VON ESCHENBACH, who, after being emasculated by King IBERT of Sicily, became a wizard. It would appear that his realm was in Italy, as its capital is named as Capua. In Wagner's opera *Parsifal* he is portrayed with a black character, but this is not usually how he is seen; normally he is shown as courteous and a man whose word was his bond, one tradition making him a bishop rather than a sorcerer. He was said to have kept ARTHUR's mother (named by WOLFRAM VON ESCHENBACH as ARNIVE) and several other queens captive, but they were released by GAWAIN[1].

Knight of the Dragon

The name by which SEGURANT THE BROWN, a knight of the OLD TABLE and UTHER's mightiest warrior, was known. He was also sometimes known as the KNIGHT OF THE OLD TABLE.

Knight of the Fair County

The brother of King ARTHUR who married the daughter of Earl CORNUBAS of WALES and became the father of the GREAT FOOL.

Knight of the Lantern

The title of the son of LIBEARN, this knight was also the son of the king of the CARLACHS who slew the BLACK KNIGHT[4], thus suggesting that LIBEARN was either married to, or had an affair with, the king of the CARLACHS.

Knight of the Lion

A title given to OWAIN, who was usually accompanied by a lion.

Knight of the Old Table

A name by which SEGURANT THE BROWN, a knight of the OLD TABLE and UTHER's mightiest warrior, was known. He was also sometimes known as the KNIGHT OF THE DRAGON.

Knight of the Sleeve

Winning the hand of CLARETTE at a tournament at ARTHUR's court, this knight is the hero of the Dutch romance *Ridder metter Mouwen*.

Knight of the Two Swords

Honorific given to BALIN.

Knights of the Franc Palais

An order of knights, eventually wiped out by the Romans, that was founded by PERCEFOREST.

Knight(s) of the Round Table

The most chivalrous order of knights ever to have been formed. They obtained their name from the table at which they were seated, so that none had precedence over the other. They vowed to uphold a code of ethics laid down by ARTHUR, and reasserted this oath every year at the feast of Pentecost, meeting in the great hall at CAMELOT.

The number of knights in the order varies greatly, but those specifically mentioned in this book as being Knights of the Round Table are:

ADRAGAIN, AGRAVAIN, ALON, ARTEGALL, ARTHUR (whom most forget), BAGDEMAGUS, BANIN, BEDIVERE[2], BELLEUS, BLAMORE DE GANIS, BORRE, BORS[2], BRANDILES, CARL OF CARLISLE, CLARIS, COLGREVANCE, DINADAN, DINAS, DODINAL, DORNAR, DRIANT, EVADEAM, FERGUS[2], GAHERIS, GALAHAD[1], GALEHAUT, GALERON, GALES LI CAUS, GALIHODIN, GAWAIN[1], GORNEMANT DE GOORT, IRONSIDE, KAMELIN, LAC, LAMORAK, LANCELOT[2], LOHOLT, MADOR, MARROK, MERAUGIS, MIROET, MORDRED, NENTRES, OWAIN THE BASTARD, PELLEAS, PERCEVAL[2], POLIDAMAS, PRIAMUS, SAGREMOR, TOR, TRISTAN, TRISTAN THE YOUNGER and YDER.

Kradoc

Thought to be identifiable with KARADAWC or KARADOC, an ancestor of ARTHUR.

Kukumarlant

The realm of which ITHER became king before claiming ARTHUR's throne, though related to him, and finally being killed by PERCEVAL[2].

Kulhwch

An alternative form of CULHWCH.

Kustenhin

Also CUSTENNIN, KUSTEN(N)IN, MUS-
TENNIN

The early Welsh form of CONSTANTINE[1],
it was used to designate the Constantine
who was ARTHUR's grandfather, and is
found in this form, or its alternative
Kustenin, in the paternal descent of
Arthur from LLYR in the Mostyn MS 117
and in the Welsh BONEDD YR ARWR. The
curious variant of Mustennin appears in
one version of Arthur's paternal pedigree
found in the *Bonedd yr Arwr*. It seems
most probable that this variant is simply
a transcriptive error.

Kusten(n)in

Variant of KUSTENHIN.

Kynan

According to the paternal pedigrees contained in the Welsh BONEDD YR ARWR,
and in the Mostyn MS 117, a maternal
and paternal ancestor of ARTHUR in his
line of descent from LLYR.

Kynfarch

A variant of KYNVARCH.

Kynnvor

The father of CONSTANTINE[1] and grandfather of ARTHUR, according to the paternal
pedigree of Arthur found in the Welsh
BONEDD YR ARWR.

Kynor

Variant form of KYNUAWR that is found in
ARTHUR's line of descent from LLYR as
contained in the BONEDD YR ARWR.

Kynotus

The rector of CAMBRIDGE who was
installed by ARTHUR himself.

Kynuawr

Also KYNOR

According to the pedigree in the Mostyn
MS 117, the paternal great-grandfather
of ARTHUR in his line of descent from
LLYR.

Kynvarch

Also KYNFARCH

According to Welsh tradition, the father
of URIEN of RHEGED by NEFYN, the daughter
of BRYCHAN.

Kynwal

According to the pedigree found in the
Welsh BONEDD YR ARWR, a maternal
ancestor of ARTHUR.

Label

A king of Persia whose daughter married CELIDOINE following her conversion to Christianity. Label died either in retreat at a hermitage or in battle.

Labiane

The niece of King MARK[2] and mother of MERAUGIS following her rape by her uncle. Mark subsequently murdered her.

Lac

A KNIGHT OF THE ROUND TABLE, the son of CANAN and brother to DIRAC. He was king of ESTREGALES and ruler of the Black Isles, and father of EREC, BRANDILES and JESCHUTÉ. His family tree is as shown in Figure 18.

Canan		
	Lac	Dirac
Erec	Brandiles	Jeschuté

Figure 18 *Family tree of Sir Lac*

Ladis

The ruler of LOMBARDY in the Arthurian romances.

Ladon

The elderly king of GASCONY who was married to LIDOINE, the sister of LARIS.

Lady of Shalott

The name by which ELAINE[2], the daughter of BERNARD of ASTOLAT, is possibly best known, appearing under this title in Alfred, Lord Tennyson's famous poem *The Lady of Shalott*.

Lady of the Fair Hair

A fairy whom ARTHUR saved from the FISH-KNIGHT and subsequently became her lover.

Lady of the Lake

The mysterious lady from whom ARTHUR received EXCALIBUR, and to whom it was returned on his death. Very little is said about her in the Arthurian romances, except that she took LANCELOT[2] while still a child to raise him (hence his title Lancelot of the Lake), and later cured him when he lost his senses. She is sometimes identified with VIVIENNE, or NIMUE, though usually remains nameless. According to ULRICH VON ZARZIKHOVEN, the fairy who raised Lancelot was the mother of MABUZ and, as Mabuz is thought to be identical with the Celtic god MABON[1], this would suggest that the Lady of the Lake in this instance was none other than MORGAN[1] Le Fay, for she was, in origin, Mabon's mother, MATRONA. It seems highly likely, therefore, that the Lady of the Lake has her origins in a Celtic lake divinity, a possibility further supported by the fact that some sources say that she was one of the three queens aboard the ship that ferried the dying Arthur to AVALON.

BALIN was said to have killed a Lady of the Lake, though not necessarily the one who delivered and received Excalibur.

Lahelin

The German form of the Welsh Llewelyn. The brother of ORILUS, he stole the kingdoms of WALES and NORTHGALIS from HERZELOYDE following the death of GAHMURET.

Lailoken

Celtic tradition makes Lailoken a wild man whose career closely resembles that of MERLIN, leading some commentators to make him the original of the wizard. However, it seems likely that Lailoken was simply a nickname for Merlin, as the name closely resembles the Welsh word for a twin, and tradition states that Merlin had a twin sister. Lailoken spent some time at the court of RHYDDERCH HAEL, revealed the adulterous nature of the wife of King MELDRED to her husband, and prophesied his own death. These events should be compared with those in Merlin's life.

Lake District

Picturesque region of Cumbria that has been suggested (by S. G. Wildman) as the birthplace of ARTHUR or, failing that, the region in which he was raised. The most famous Lakeland legend concerning King Arthur is that of the HELM WIND, though local Lake District folklore almost unreservedly claims that Arthur was king in that region.

Lalander

The duchy of ORILUS, the husband of JESCHUTÉ.

Lambor

The king of either TERRE FORAINE or LOGRES, he was killed by BRULAN (VARLAN), following which both his realm and that of his slayer were diseased, thus originating the WASTE LAND of the GRAIL stories. It is possible that he may be identical with LAMBORD.

Lambord

The maternal great-grandfather of ARTHUR, according to the pedigree of JOHN OF GLASTONBURY.

Lamorak

The son of King PELLINORE, brother of PERCEVAL[2] and a KNIGHT OF THE ROUND TABLE. He was killed by GAWAIN[1] after sleeping with the latter's mother, MORGAUSE.

Lance of Longinus

The lance with which the centurion LONGINUS was said to have pierced the side of Jesus while the latter hung on the Cross following the Crucifixion [St John: 19.xxxiv]. This has led to its also being known as the BLEEDING LANCE. It has become associated with the Holy GRAIL, being carried in the GRAIL PROCESSION and being sought by MELORA, the warrior daughter of ARTHUR.

Lancelot

The name of two related characters from the Arthurian legends and, aside from ARTHUR, possibly the best known of all the Arthurian characters.

1 The grandfather of LANCELOT[2], he married the daughter of the king of IRELAND and, by her, became the father of BAN and BORS[1].

2 The most famous of all Arthur's knights, the king's champion, friend and confidant. He was a KNIGHT OF THE ROUND TABLE and a most complex character. Different commentators are still undecided on his origin. Was he Celtic or merely the invention of the Continentals? His name is generally regarded as a double diminutive o the German word *Land*, though it has been argued, some feel successfully, that LLWCH LLEMINAWC, a character who accompanies Arthur to the OTHERWORLD in PREIDDEU ANNWFN, is his original. By the same token, this journey has been identified with the expedition Arthur makes to IRELAND in the MABINOGION story of CULHWCH AND OLWEN and, if this is indeed the case, Lancelot appears to number among the accompanying party as LLENLLEAWC, though in this instance an Irishman. These identifications have been called into doubt through the appearance of the names LANSLOD and LAWNSLOT, which seem to have been used to translate Lancelot from other languages into Welsh. This is certainly possible, and may be a retranslation of Lancelot back into Welsh when those writers who came across the name Lancelot failed to recognize its origins in LLWCH LLEMINAWC or LLENLLEAWC.

Celtic origins certainly figure in the version of Lancelot's story told by ULRICH VON ZARZIKHOVEN. Here, Lancelot is the son of King PANT of GENNEWIS, and CLARINE. As his father had been killed during an uprising, Lancelot was taken away by a fairy and raised in MAIDENLAND, but she would not tell him his name until he had fought IWERET of BEFORET. He was trained as a knight and in the use of all manner of weapons by JOHFRIT DE LIEZ and married the daughter of GALAGANDRIEZ. The fairy had a son, MABUZ, whose lands were being invaded by IWERET, whom Lancelot fought and killed, thus learning his name. He married IBLIS, Iweret's daughter, and had four children by her, and eventually won back the kingdom of his father, Pant. The appearance of MABUZ, who is thought to have originated in the Celtic god MABON, certainly indicates that Lancelot had a Celtic origin. Parts of this story are common with the more normal story of Lancelot as related in French and German sources, as well as by Sir Thomas MALORY. ULRICH VON ZARZIKHOVEN determines his family tree as shown in Figure 19.

The more usual version of Lancelot's story is, in essence, as follows.

The son of King BAN and ELAINE[5] (Figure 20) was left on the shores of a lake by his mother after Ban had died. He was found by the LADY OF THE LAKE, who raised him, and because of this he became known as Lancelot of the Lake. Having grown to manhood, he joined ARTHUR's court, became a KNIGHT OF THE ROUND TABLE, and Arthur's most trusted companion. However, just as MERLIN had foretold, he fell in love with

Galagandriez	Pant = Clarine	Iweret
daughter =	Lancelot	= Iblis
		four children

Figure 19 *Family tree of Lancelot according to Ulrich von Zarzikhoven*

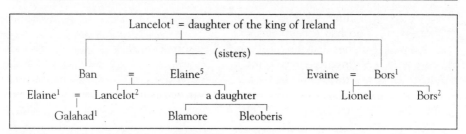

Figure 20   *Family tree of Lancelot according to French sources*

GUINEVERE, who reciprocated his feelings, and so began the famous, and
sometimes stormy, love affair between
them. Guinevere was not the only lady
to love Lancelot, for he was also loved
by ELAINE[2] of Astolat (the LADY OF
SHALOTT), who died of her love for him,
her body being brought up the Thames
on a barge along with a note saying why
she had died.

During his many adventures,
Lancelot visited Castle CARBONEK, and
there rescued ELAINE[1] from a bath of
boiling water, though some say that this
rescue happened in a brazen tower some
distance from the castle itself. However,
some further describe the tower itself as
the 'fairest Lancelot had ever seen'.
Entertained by King PELLES, Elaine's
father, the king and BRISEN, Elaine's
handmaiden (or, alternatively, an enchantress), conspired to have Lancelot
sleep with Elaine, for it had been prophesied that he should father the purest
knight on her. At a feast in Lancelot's
honour, during which, according to some
sources, Lancelot witnessed the GRAIL
PROCESSION, Brisen administered a love
potion and Lancelot, enchanted into
thinking that Elaine was Guinevere,
lay with Elaine. As a result GALAHAD[1]
was conceived. Later the two slept
together again (once more with the
help of Brisen's magic), this time at
CAMELOT, but they were discovered by
the furious Guinevere, who banished
her lover from the court. He went mad,

running wild in the forests, sometimes
tended by hermits and village folk. Only
after many years was he restored to
sanity by the GRAIL, the holy vessel he
subsequently quested for.

Having returned to Arthur's court,
the king still refused to believe that the
rumours he was hearing about Lancelot
and his wife were true. Lancelot championed the queen's cause when she was
abducted by MELEAGAUNCE, the son
of King BAGDEMAGUS. The only mode of
transport that was available to Lancelot
was a cart, in which he was most reluctant to travel but did, none the less,
crossing a 'sword bridge' to reach the
castle in which Meleagaunce had
taken refuge. The two fought, but
Bagdemagus pleaded with Guinevere to
save his son, so the fight was stopped, on
the condition it be taken up in one
year's time. Later Meleagaunce accused
Guinevere of committing adultery with
KAY, and once again Lancelot championed her cause. Again Bagdemagus
had to plead for his son's life, which was
on this occasion spared, but Lancelot
finally killed him in combat at Arthur's
court.

Lancelot's adultery with Guinevere
was now brought to Arthur's attention,
but he refused to believe it unless con-
clusive evidence was brought before
him. Finally Lancelot and Guinevere
were trapped together in the queen's
bedchamber, but Lancelot, though
unarmed, managed to fight his way

to freedom, killing all but one of the knights who had caught him and Guinevere together. Lancelot fled and Guinevere was sentenced to be burnt at the stake, being rescued in the nick of time by Lancelot, who secreted her in his castle, JOYOUS GARD. Even now Arthur, wary of Merlin's prophecies, wanted nothing more than to make peace with his old friend, but he mistakenly took the advice of his nephew MORDRED, who had designs on the throne, and Arthur went to war against Lancelot. While absent, Mordred seized the throne and Arthur cut off his fight with Lancelot to return to deal with the situation at home. Lancelot followed some time later, but arrived one month after the final battle of CAMLANN, and thus too late to help his old friend. He travelled to AMESBURY, where Guinevere had taken the veil and, realizing that she was lost to him, he went to GLASTONBURY, where he became a monk, then returning to Amesbury following a dream which told him to ride there as fast as he could. He arrived too late, for Guinevere had died not half an hour earlier. Grief-stricken, Lancelot could neither eat nor sleep and within a matter of a few short weeks he too had died.

Lancelot of the Laik

An anonymous fifteenth-century Scottish verse romance.

Lancelot of the Lake

The full title by which LANCELOT[2] was known, for he was, allegedly, raised by the LADY OF THE LAKE, who was identified, in thirteenth-century sources, as VIVIENNE.

Lanceor

The son of the king of IRELAND who was sent by ARTHUR to slay BALIN, for the latter had killed the LADY OF THE LAKE. Balin, however, killed him, and his lover, COLOMBE, took her own life. It is alleged that subsequently King MARK[2] rode by and, seeing their bodies, buried them.

Lancien

Now known as LANTYAN, CORNWALL, this was the site of King MARK[2]'s palace.

Land from Which No One Returns

A mysterious realm that was ruled over by GUNDEBALD. MERIADOC did, however, manage to escape from this realm, having rescued the daughter of the German emperor.

Land of Pastures and Giants

One of the various realms ascribed to the rule of RIENCE. The name of this domain would seem to connect RIENCE with the giant of Welsh tradition RHITTA, RICCA or RITHO, who was associated with YR WYDDFA FAWR (Mount SNOWDON).

Languoreth

The wife of RHYDDERCH in Jocelyn's LIFE OF SAINT KENTIGERN, she became enamoured of a soldier. It seems that she may be identifiable with GANIEDA, MERLIN's twin sister.

Lansdown Hill

Called Mons Badonicus in early times, this hill, near BATH, has become associated with the site of the battle of BADON. During the Middle Ages it was reported that the skeleton of King ARTHUR had been found there.

Lanslod

A name that, along with LAWNSLOT, seems to have been used to translate LANCELOT[2] into Welsh.

Lantris

The brother of ISEULT[1], though this is a later name for ALCARDO. Under the name of Lantris, Alcardo is said to have been a squire, possibly to TRISTAN, and was killed in his attempt to rescue his sister from King MARK[2].

Lantyan

Place in CORNWALL, formerly called LAN-CIEN, that is said to have been the site of King MARK[2]'s palace.

Lanval

One of ARTHUR's knights who became the lover of a mysterious woman, having solemnly promised to keep their affair secret. GUINEVERE subsequently attempted to seduce Lanval, but, when he would have nothing to do with her, she falsely accused him of making advances to her. He was put on trial and told to prove he was enamoured of someone other than the queen but, true to his promise, he refused. However, when all seemed lost the mysterious lady arrived, and together they left for AVALON. He was given the fairy horse BLANCHARD by his lover, TRYAMOUR. Lanval's story is recounted several times, first of all in the twelfth-century *Lanval* by MARIE DE FRANCE, and subsequently in English in the fourteenth-century *Sir Landeval*, and in two sixteenth-century works *Sir Lambewell* and *Sir Lambwell*.

Lapis Exillis

Meaning 'worthless stone', and probably owing its origin to the alchemists' philosopher's stone, this was the name given to the GRAIL by WOLFRAM VON ESCHENBACH, who thought it not a holy vessel but rather a stone.

Lapland

This region of Scandinavia was said to have formed the eastern border of ARTHUR's territories by Hakluyt in his sixteenth-century *Travels*.

Lar

The husband of Queen AMENE. When Amene was besieged by the evil ROAZ after Lar's death, his ghost guided WIGALOIS to help his widow.

Larie

The daughter of LAR and AMENE, she married WIGALOIS after the latter had defeated ROAZ.

Laris

The son of HENRY[2], emperor of GERMANY and one of the heroes of CLARIS ET LARIS. He loved MARINE, the daughter of URIEN, but had a rival in the form of King TALLAS of DENMARK, who laid siege to Urien. ARTHUR arrived and defeated the Danes, but Laris had been taken prisoner and had to be rescued by CLARIS and others. He became king of Denmark in place of the defeated Tallas.

Lascoyt

One of the three sons of GORNEMANT DE GOORT, he, like his brothers, met with a violent death.

Laudame

The queen of ANFERE whom GAREL married.

Laudine

The lady of the fountain, first married to ESCLADOS, she married OWAIN after the death of her first husband.

Laufrodedd

Also LLAWFRODEDD

The owner of a knife which was considered one of the THIRTEEN TREASURES OF BRITAIN.

Launcelot

A variant of LANCELOT[2].

Laundes

The Earl of Laundes was BELLANGERE, the son of ALISANDER THE ORPHAN and the killer of King MARK[2] of CORNWALL.

Laurel

The niece of LIONORS and LYNETTE, she married AGRAVAIN.

Lavaine

The son of BERNARD of ASTOLAT and brother of ELAINE[2] (the LADY OF SHALOTT). He became a follower of Sir LANCELOT[2].

Lawnslot

A name that, along with LANSLOD, seems to have been used to translate LANCELOT[2] into Welsh.

Layamon

A Worcestershire poet and priest (*fl. c.* 1200) at Ernley (now Areley Regis) on the Severn near Bewdley. In c. 1200 he wrote an alliterative-verse chronicle, the ANGLO-SAXON BRUT, a history of England which contains much Arthurian material, and which was an amplification of WACE's slightly earlier ROMAN DE BRUT or BRUT D'ANGLETERRE. It is an important work in the history of English versification, as it is the first poem written in Middle English.

Laziliez

Named as an ancestor of PERCEVAL[2].

Le Cote Male Tailée

'The badly cut coat', a nickname given to BREUNOR by the ever-impertinent KAY when Breunor arrived at ARTHUR's court in a badly tailored coat.

Le Morte d'Arthur

Completed in 1470 and published by Caxton in 1485 as one of the first books to use modern printing, this fifteenth-century work by Sir Thomas MALORY comprises a series of episodes from the legendary life of King ARTHUR. It is regarded as the first great prose work in English literature, but in actual fact only the last eight books of the series are titled *Le Morte d'Arthur*. The series omits a few of the tales, and contains many inconsistencies, particularly its multitude of women named ELAINE and wounded kings. However, it still remains the main English source on the Arthurian legends and is an undoubted literary masterpiece.

Le Tornoiment de l'Antichrist

A French poem by Huon de Mery which tells how he, the poet, went to an enchanted spring in BROCELIANDE where BRAS-DE-FER, the chamberlain of the Antichrist, rode up. Together they rode to the scene of a mighty battle where the forces of Heaven, which included ARTHUR and his knights, were fighting the forces of Hell.

Lear

The Shakespearian variant of LEIR.

Leir
Also LEAR

The son of King BLADUD who became the prototype for SHAKESPEARE's tragic hero, King LEAR. He ruled for sixty years and founded the town of Kaerleir, that is Castle Leir, or Leicester. When he died he was buried downstream from Leicester in a vault dedicated to the Roman god Janus, and there the town's craftsmen annually came to observe that god's festival.

Leodegrance

The king of CAMELIARD and father of GUINEVERE. Some sources say he presented the ROUND TABLE to ARTHUR.

Lestoire de Merlin

A part of the VULGATE VERSION that gives one version of the history of MERLIN.

Leudonus

An early form of the name LOT, both meaning 'LOTHIAN-ruler'.

Levaine

The daughter of BERNARD of ASTOLAT and sister to ELAINE[2] the White.

Levander

A servant of the king of Africa who was sent, by that king, to give assistance to MELORA, ARTHUR's daughter, on her quest.

Li jus Aden

Thirteenth-century French romance that says that HELLEKIN, already an established figure in Teutonic lore, was a fairy king who became the lover of MORGAN[1] Le Fay, whose companions are named as ARSILE and MAGLORE.

Lianour

The ruler of the CASTLE OF MAIDENS who is described as a duke.

Liaze

The daughter of GORNEMANT DE GOORT whom her father wanted PERCEVAL[2] to marry, but this did not come about. Her three brothers, GURGZI, LASCOYT and SCHENTEFLEURS, all met violent deaths.

Liban

A daughter of King BAN and the mother of illegitimate twins by PANDRAGUS.

Libearn

The stepmother of ALEXANDER[3], Prince of India, who turned him into the CROP-EARED DOG by magic.

Licat Anir

An earthen mound at ARCHENFIELD said to mark the burial place of ARTHUR's son AMR. Each time the length of the mound was measured, it allegedly gave a different reading.

Liconaus

The father of ENIDE by TARSENESYDE, according to EREC ET ENIDE.

Liddington Castle

Near Swindon, Wiltshire, Liddington Castle is one of the various locations suggested as the site of the battle of BADON.

Lidoine

The sister of LARIS and the daughter of HENRY^2, emperor of Germany, according to CLARIS ET LARIS. At first married to the ageing King LADON of GASCONY, she was captured by SAVARI, King of SPAIN, after his death. She was rescued by ARTHUR, after which she married her brother Laris's companion, CLARIS.

Life of Saint Cadoc

According to this work, which details the life of Saint CADOC, the son of GWYNNLYM and Saint GWLADYS, LIGESSAC sought and found sanctuary from ARTHUR with Saint Cadoc for ten years after he had killed some of Arthur's followers.

Life of Saint Carannog

A medieval work which states that CADO, who is possibly cognate with CADWY, co-ruled the West Country alongside King ARTHUR.

Life of Saint Kentigern

According to this work by Jocelyn, which details the life of Saint KENTIGERN, LOT was the father of THANEY, and thus Kentigern's grandfather.

Ligessac

A fugitive from King ARTHUR who sought, and found, refuge with Saint CADOC for ten years.

Lile

A mysterious lady from AVALON who brought a great sword to ARTHUR's court. Only BALIN managed to withdraw it from its scabbard, but when asked to return it he refused. Lile then foretold that the sword would bring about his own destruction and kill his dearest friend.

Limousin

Former province and modern region of central FRANCE. Arthurian legend says that, when ARTHUR quarrelled with LANCELOT^2, BLAMORE DE GANIS and BLEOBERIS both supported their father in the dispute, Blamore de Ganis being made the duke of Limousin.

Lincoln

County town of Lincolnshire, England. Known as Lindum to the Romans, Lincoln had a flourishing wool trade in medieval times. Paulinus built a church in Lincoln in the seventh century, and the eleventh- to-fifteenth-century cathedral has the earliest Gothic work in BRITAIN. The twelfth-century High Bridge in the High Street is the oldest in Britain still to have buildings on it.

As to Arthurian connections, Lincoln is cited as the birthplace of ANDRED,

TRISTAN's cousin and a resident at MARK[2]'s court. It is also used as a surname for TOM A'LINCOLN (Tom of Lincoln), the RED ROSE KNIGHT, the illegitimate son of ARTHUR and ANGELICA. However, Lincoln is possibly the best known in connection with CAT COIT CELIDON, a wood slightly to the north of the city which is cited by NENNIUS as the location of one of ARTHUR'S BATTLES.

Lincoln, Battle of

The site of a battle at which ARTHUR and HOEL[1] defeated the SAXON hordes. It is possible that this battle is cognate with the battle of CALEDON WOOD.

Linnius

The scene of four battles fought by ARTHUR in the catalogue of battles found in the works of NENNIUS. It is possibly to be identified with Lindsey (Lincolnshire), and might therefore also be considered identical with the Battle of Lincoln.

Lion

Though the lion is not native to BRITAIN, it appears in several Arthurian stories. The sixteenth-century Scottish historian BOECE claimed that lions were once native to SCOTLAND. Both GAWAIN[1] and BREUNOR were said to have killed lions, while OWAIN was said to have had a lion as a companion. KAY was also, in PA GUR, said to have killed some lions of Anglesey, but it is thought that this is rather a reference to animals of a supernatural nature.

Lion the Merciless

The name of the person from whom ARTHUR won his pet PARROT.

Lionel

The son of BORS[1] and brother of BORS[2]. A fearsome character, he was given the throne of GAUL by ARTHUR but, following the latter's death, he was killed by MORDRED's son, MELEHAN.

Liones

Thought by some commentators to be identical with LYONESSE[2], this kingdom was that ruled by MELIDOAS[1], the father of TRISTAN. The early history of the realm is supplied by the PROSE TRISTAN, which says that one of its kings, PELIAS, was succeeded by his son LUCIUS, who was in turn succeeded by APOLLO. This king unwittingly married his own mother, but later married GLORIANDE, by whom he became the father of CANDACES, later king of both Liones and CORNWALL. The VULGATE VERSION makes LOT one of the early kings of Liones, which would seem to suggest that Liones and LOTHIAN are one and the same.

Lionors

The daughter of SEVAIN and mother of LOHOLT by ARTHUR. Sir Thomas MALORY makes her the mother of BORRE, the illegitimate son of Arthur who is possibly identical with Loholt.

Lischois

The husband of CUNDRIE[1], the daughter of SANGIVE and LOT.

Listinoise

The kingdom of King PELEHAN that, following the delivery of the DOLOROUS STROKE, became the WASTE LAND of the GRAIL legends.

Lit Merveile

A marvellous bed that GAWAIN[1], having travelled to rescue the captives held in a certain castle, saw moving around on its own. He jumped on to it and it darted from wall to wall, smashing itself against them. Coming to rest, some 500 pebbles were shot at Gawain from sling-shots, following which numerous crossbow bolts were fired at the knight, but his armour proved sufficient to protect him.

Livre d'Artus

A French CONTINUATION to ROBERT DE BORON's work MERLIN.

Liz

The realm of King MELJANZ, who declared war on Duke LYPPAUT after OBIE, the duke's daughter, had refused him.

Lizaborye

A kingdom of which BELAYE, LOHENGRIN's second wife, was a princess. However, her parents, and presumably rulers of Lizaborye, sent mercenaries to kill Lohengrin, for they believed their daughter was under his spell.

Llacheu

According to Welsh tradition, a son of ARTHUR who became identified with LOHOLT, though the two were probably originally different characters.

Llallawc

A Welsh variant for the wizard MYRDDIN (MERLIN).

Llallogan Vyrdin

A Welsh variant for the wizard MYRDDIN (MERLIN).

Llamrei

The mare owned by King ARTHUR.

Llawfrodedd
Also LAUFRODEDD

According to some sources, the owner of CYLLEL LLAWFRODEDD, a Druidic sacrificial knife that is numbered among the THIRTEEN TREASURES OF BRITAIN.

Llefelys

A king of FRANCE who, in the MABINOGION story of LLUD AND LLEFELYS, told LLUD that a scream heard on the eve of every May Day, and whose source could not be found, was actually caused by fighting dragons. These were subsequently caught and interred at DINAS EMRYS.

Llen Arthur

The veil of ARTHUR which would render the wearer invisible. It is numbered among the THIRTEEN TREASURES OF BRITAIN.

Llenlleawc

An Irishman who appears as a companion of ARTHUR in the MABINOGION story of CULHWCH AND OLWEN and helped in the seizure of the cauldron of DIWRNACH. He is normally identified with LLWCH LLEMINAWC, who appears in a similar role of companion to Arthur in the PREIDDEU ANNWFN, and it is possible that both Llenlleawc and Llwch Lleminawc formed the prototype character of Sir LANCELOT[2].

Lleu

Thought by some commentators to be an early form of LOT, possibly deriving from LEUDONUS.

Lleu Llaw Gyffes

The second son of ARIANRHOD, born during the ceremony of stepping over the wand, a rite performed to attest her virginity, her first son, also born at this time, being DYLAN EIL TON.

This second child was hurriedly concealed in a chest by GWYDION FAB DÔN, Arianrhod's brother, and later adopted by him. Four years later he could not resist bringing the child to show his sister, but she, reminded of her shame, cursed the boy, saying that he should have no name until she herself first gave him one. Gwydion fab Dôn managed to circumvent this curse by disguising both himself and the boy, and tricking Arianrhod into naming him Lleu Llaw Gyffes (Bright-one-with-the-nimble-hand). Next Arianrhod swore that her son would never bear arms, but again she was tricked into providing them. Finally she swore that he would never marry, this final curse being evaded by Gwydion fab Dôn and MATH FAB MATHONWY, who made the boy a bride out of the flowers of oak, broom and meadowsweet, naming her BLODEUWEDD ('Flower Face').

However, she was unfaithful to him with GRONW BEBYR and, at her lover's suggestion, she contrived to discover how her husband might be killed. At length he told her that he was vulnerable to a spear that had been worked for a year at mass time on Sundays if he were standing with one foot on the back of a billy goat, the other on a bathtub. After trying for a year, Blodeuwedd managed to contrive that Lleu Llaw Gyffes should be in such a position and Gronw Bebyr, armed with the necessary spear, cast it at him and wounded him. Lleu Llaw Gyffes turned into an eagle and flew away.

Gwydion fab Dôn sought him, tracking him down by following a sow which was feeding on the maggots that dropped from the eagle's festering wound. He found the dying Lleu Llaw Gyffes perched in a tree and healed him. Lleu Llaw Gyffes turned Blodeuwedd into an owl and killed Gronw Bebyr.

Llevelys

The brother of LLUDD, though it appears that this is simply a variant of LLEFELYS, a king of FRANCE during Lludd's reign, and, if the two are the same character, it would seem to imply that either they were true brothers or at that time BRITAIN and France were closely allied.

Llew

A variant of LLEU LLAW GYFFES.

Lligwy Cromlech

Located near Moelfre on the east side of Anglesey, GWYNEDD, this cromlech is also known as ARTHUR'S QUOIT, though just where ARTHUR was meant to have thrown this quoit from is unknown (see also CARREG COETAN ARTHUR).

Llongad Grwrm Fargod Eidyn

The slayer of TALIESIN's son, ADDAON.

Llongborth

The site of a battle in which ARTHUR's men fought. The RED BOOK OF HERGEST says that GEREINT was killed during this battle, but the preferred BLACK BOOK OF CARMARTHEN makes no mention of this.

Lluagor

The horse belonging to King CARADOC BRIEFBRAS.

Llud and Llefelys

A part of the MABINOGION which tells how every May Day Eve a scream was heard, the source of which could not be located. LLEFELYS, the king of FRANCE, told LLUD that the scream was caused by fighting dragons. These were eventually caught and interred at DINAS EMRYS.

Llud Llaw Ereint

The father of CREIDDYLED whose name means 'Llud of the Silver Hand', perhaps betraying his generous nature. His origins are Irish, though this character is Welsh.

Llud(d)

The father of GWYNN AP NUDD and brother of LLEVELYS, he is the British and Welsh variant of the Irish Lugh. He is of great mythical importance in a Welsh legend concerning the two brothers and two dragons which battle for supremacy. The dragons are, however, imprisoned in an underground chamber in the centre of the land. Direct comparison can be made between this tale and that concerning the dragons found in an underground lake, as foretold by MERLIN, on the site where VORTIGERN was attempting, without success, to erect his tower. Perhaps they were the same dragons.

Llwch Lleminawc

A companion of ARTHUR in the PREIDDEU ANNWFN, and it is possible that both LLENLLEAWC, with whom he is normally identified, and Llwch Lleminawc formed the prototype character of Sir LANCELOT[2].

Llychlyn

The Welsh name for Scandinavia which, like the similar Irish Lochlann, may originally have signified an OTHERWORLD realm. The character of BLAES, who appears in the Welsh TRIADS and is apparently identical with MERLIN's master, BLAISE, is described as being the son of the Earl of Llychlyn.

Llygadnudd Emys

A maternal uncle of King ARTHUR.

Llyn Barfog

A lake located in GWYNEDD, where ARTHUR was alleged to have done battle with an AFANC.

Llyn Eiddwen

A lake in DYFED that, according to legend, must never be allowed to dry up, for MERLIN prophesied that, if it did, CARMARTHEN would suffer some great and catastrophic disaster.

Llyn Llech Owen

Located one mile north of Gorslas in west Glamorgan, WALES, this pool now covers the site of a magic well that never ran dry so long as the stone slab covering it was replaced after water had been drawn from it. One day, one of King ARTHUR's knights stopped to drink from the well, but dozed off to sleep and forgot to replace the slab. When he awoke he found that the well had overflowed and was flooding the surrounding countryside. He hurriedly mounted his waiting horse and quickly rode around the edge of the flood waters, which stopped encroaching over the land when they touched his horse's hoofs. The resulting lake is still there to be seen today.

Llyr

A king of BRITAIN, the father of BENDI-GEID VRAN, BRANWEN and MANAWYDDAN. In origin he was a Celtic sea deity (Welsh *llyr* = 'sea'). He is listed in two paternal pedigrees found in BONEDD YR ARWR as the direct descendant of ARTHUR, though the genealogies themselves, as shown in Figure 21, differ quite markedly. However, when studied more closely, it becomes obvious that the pedigree which appears first in the work has skipped three generations. Another interesting paternal pedigree for Arthur, which names his descent as direct from Llyr, is to be found in the Mostyn MS 117. The three lines of descent have been specifically laid out in Figure 21 to allow easy comparison.

It is not hard to see that all three are obviously based on the same source material.

Llyr Marini

According to Welsh pedigrees, an ancestor of ARTHUR on both his maternal and his paternal sides. In origin he may have been LLYR, a sea deity, and the legendary ancestor of a number of royal houses. He would also seem to have some connection with the King LEAR of SHAKESPEARE and, though this character is normally associated with LEIR, may have originated from Llyr.

Llywarch Hen

A celebrated Welsh poet who is thought to have flourished *c.* AD 600. Said to have been the cousin of URIEN of RHEGED, he is sometimes, incorrectly, identified with TALIESIN. Various traditions place him in POWYS, or among the north Briton tribesmen. He is listed as one of the TWENTY-FOUR KNIGHTS of King ARTHUR's court, but appears to have been a reasonably late addition to the Arthurian tales.

Bonedd yr Arwr: 1	*Bonedd yr Arwr: 2*	Mostyn MS 117
Llyr	Llyr	Llyr
Brân	Brân	Brân
Karadoc	Karadoc	Karadoc
	Evdaf	Kynan
	Kynan	Kadwr
	Kadienn	Eudaf
Turmwr Morvawr	Morvawr	Moruawr
Tutwal	Tudwal	Tutwal
Kynor	Kynnvor	Kynvawr
Mustennin	Kustenin	Kustenhin
Uther	Uther	Uther
Arthur	Arthur	Arthur

Figure 21 *Three versions of Arthur's descent from Llyr, king of Britain*

Lodonesia

A early name for LOTHIAN, the realm of LOT, who is sometimes referred to as LOTH of Lodonesia.

Logistilla

According to the ORLANDO FURIOSO of ARIOSTO, a sister of MORGAN[1] Le Fay.

Logres

The name given to England in Arthurian romance. It derives from Lloegr, the Welsh for England, but may have originally come from *legor*, an ANGLO-SAXON element found in the place-name of Leicester.

Lohengrin

Lohengrin appears in the works of WOLFRAM VON ESCHENBACH as the son of PERCEVAL[2] and a member of the GRAIL community. He sailed to BRABANT in a boat drawn by an angel, disguised as a swan, to help ELSA, the daughter of the Duke of Brabant, who was besieged by Frederick de TELRAMUND, who claimed that Elsa had promised to marry him. Lohengrin defeated this unworthy suitor in combat, and duly married Elsa, but made her promise never to ask his name. They had two children. Eventually, Elsa asked the forbidden question and Lohengrin immediately left her. Subsequently he married Princess BELAYE of LIZABORYE, but was murdered by mercenaries sent by her parents, who believed that their daughter was under his spell. Belaye died of grief and the country had its name changed to Lothringen (Lorraine) in his honour. The story of Lohengrin, and his adventures, are told by WOLFRAM VON ESCHENBACH and in *Rigomer*, a later, anonymous poem.

Loholt

A KNIGHT OF THE ROUND TABLE and the son of ARTHUR, though his mother is not so definitely named, being either GUINEVERE or LIONORS. In PERLESVAUS, he was murdered by KAY, but this episode, which does not appear elsewhere, seems to have been concocted by the author of this work.

Lombardy

The realm of King LADIS which had not, in reality, been conquered by the Lombard people by the traditional Arthurian period.

Longinus

The name of the Roman centurion who was said to have pierced the side of Jesus while Christ hung on the Cross following the Crucifixion (St John: 19.xxxiv).

Lord of the Scottish Wilderness

The title of ESTONNE, a minor character in PERLESVAUS. He was killed by BRUYANT, his death being avenged by his son PASSALEON.

Lore

The Lady of GARADIGAN, she brought a swordbelt with her when she arrived at ARTHUR's court and challenged anyone to unfasten it, a task that only MERIADOC was able to accomplish.

Lorete

The sister of GRIFLET.

Lorie

The mistress of GAWAIN[1] in the anonymous RIGOMER.

Lorigal

The offspring of ELIAVRES and the mare with which he had been forced to mate.

Lot(h)

The king of LOTHIAN (LODONESIA), ORKNEY and NORWAY, and brother-in-law of ARTHUR, his wife being named as ANNA by GEOFFREY OF MONMOUTH and MORGAUSE by Sir Thomas MALORY. He was the father of five sons, GAWAIN[1], GAHERIS, AGRAVAIN, GARETH and MORDRED, and two daughters, SOREDAMOR and CLARISSANT. Geoffrey of Monmouth makes Lot a supporter of Arthur, already the king of Lothian. He was one of the three dispossessed Yorkist princes, the others being URIAN and AUGUSELUS, to whom Arthur restored their lands after he and HOEL[1] raised the siege of YORK. Arthur gave Lot the kingdom of Norway after he had defeated that country. His kingship of Orkney appears to be a later development of the stories. Other sources, however, state the opposite, making Lot one of the eleven rebellious leaders who revolted against Arthur at the start of his reign. He was killed by King PELLINORE, which resulted in a continuing feud between his sons and those of his slayer. The ENFACES GAUVAIN makes Lot a page at Arthur's court, becoming the father of GAWAIN[1] following an affair with MORGAUSE. The LIFE OF SAINT KENTIGERN makes him the father of THANEY, KENTIGERN's mother – provided, of course, that it is the same Lot that is being referred to. BOECE further claimed that he was the king of the PICTS.

The name Lot appears to mean simply 'LOTHIAN-ruler' (taken from its early form of LEUDONUS). It has been suggested that his personal name may have been GWYAR, though it seems certain that here the truth will remain a mystery. It would seem that there was indeed a king in the Lothian region during the fifth century who had his headquarters near EDINBURGH at TRAPRAIN LAW.

His ancestry has also been variously described. The *Chronica Gentis Scotorum* by John of Fordun claims his descent from FULGENTIUS, an early king of Britain according to Geoffrey of Monmouth. His more accepted ancestry is that described by JOHN OF GLASTONBURY, who gives a line of descent from PETRUS, one of the companions of JOSEPH OF ARIMATHEA. Taking this line of descent, Lot's complete family tree might resemble that shown in Figure 22. Welsh tradition, on the other hand, almost always makes ANNA his wife, his descendants being as shown in Figure 23.

Lothian

The realm of LOT which is also known as LODONESIA. Historically speaking, Lothian comprised all the eastern part of the Lowlands of SCOTLAND from the Forth to the Cheviots, and between the seventh and eleventh centuries it was a part of Northumbria.

Lotta

The queen of IRELAND and mother of ISEULT[1], according to the TAVOLA RITONDA.

Lovel

One of the sons of GAWAIN[1], he was among the party that caught LANCELOT[2] and GUINEVERE together, and one of those killed by the escaping though unarmed Lancelot.

Lucan

The Duke of Gloucester, brother of BEDIVERE[2], ARTHUR's butler and one of his

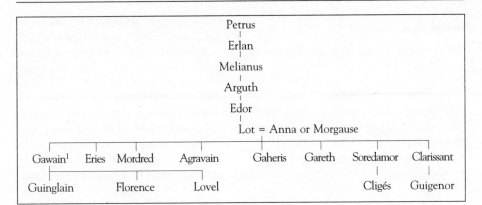

Figure 22   *Ancestry and descendants of Lot, king of Lothian, Orkney and Norway, and Arthur's brother-in-law, according to John of Glastonbury*

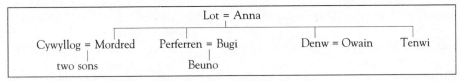

Figure 23   *Lot's wife and descendants according to Welsh tradition*

knights. After Arthur's final battle at CAMLANN, he attempted to help his brother lift the dying king but, being so badly wounded, the effort killed him. A variant of this story says that the dying king embraced him, and the strength of this embrace finished him off.

Lucius

The son of PELIAS, father of APOLLO and an early king of LIONES.

Lucius Hiberius

The name of the Roman 'emperor' whose empire ARTHUR attacked. Lucius summoned Arthur to Rome but was defeated. Both WACE and Sir Thomas MALORY emphatically refer to him as 'emperor', though GEOFFREY OF MONMOUTH calls him

the 'procurator' (governor), and implies that he was inferior to the emperor of CONSTANTINOPLE, Leo.

Lufamour

In the English verse romance SIR PERCEVAL OF GALLES, the lover of the hero of that work, PERCEVAL[2].

Luguain

The servant of YDER whose loyalty was rewarded when he was made a knight.

Lunete

The cousin of NIMUE, from whom she learned her magic arts, using them to create a fountain in the forest of BROCELIANDE to be defended by her lover.

Lybius Desconus

'The Fair Unknown One', an illegitimate son of GAWAIN[1] whose mother kept his ancestry a secret. He came to ARTHUR's court, where he was made a knight, later to be sent to rescue the Lady of SINADONE, being accompanied on the journey by the damsel ELLEN. Lybius Desconus is actually a nickname, the character being the same as GUINGLAIN.

Lybius Desconus

The fourteenth-century English poem concerning the adventures of a hero having the same name.

Lynette

The sister of LYONESSE[1] who was besieged by the RED KNIGHT[3] of the Red Lands when she came to ARTHUR's court to seek help. She was given the services of GARETH, but her manner towards him was at first derisory, improving only as their adventure progressed and Gareth proved himself to her.

Lyonesse

1 The sister of LYNETTE. Her realm was being attacked by the RED KNIGHT[3] of the Red Lands when Lynette went to ARTHUR's court to seek help. She returned with Gareth who rescued and subsequently married her.
2 A lost land said to have existed in CORNWALL, or to have lain off the coast. It is possible that it was the realm of LYONESSE[1]. Some commentators have suggested that it is to be identified with LIONES, though this may have originally been LOTHIAN (Leoneis). Later confusion identified this fabled realm with a region of BRITTANY (Leonais).

Legend states that, following the death of ARTHUR at CAMLANN, MORDRED's forces pursued the remnants of Arthur's army to Lyonesse. The ghost of MERLIN appeared and the land sank, destroying Mordred's army, but Arthur's men reached what are now the Isles of Scilly. Local legend says this fabled land sank in 1099, but the bells of its churches are still said to be heard sometimes, ringing beneath the waters.

Reference is made to Lyonesse in William Camden's *Britannia* (1586) and in George Carew's *Survey of Cornwall* (1602). Before that the medieval Arab geographer Idrisi used the word *Dns* for a place that is perhaps the Scilly Isles, *Dns* possibly being a scribal mistake for *Lns* (Lyonesse). The origin of the legend seems to stem from Roman times, when the Isles of Scilly appear to have been a single island that was partially submerged by the sea. More recently, Lyonesse was mentioned by Alfred, Lord Tennyson as the site of Arthur's final battle.

Lyppaut

The Lord of BEAROSCHE and the father of OBIE and OBILOT.

M

Mabinogion

A Welsh work whose title is taken from the word *mabinogi* – instruction for young poets – and is of prime importance to the Arthurian student. Drawn from THE WHITE BOOK OF RHYDDERCH (1300–1325) and THE RED BOOK OF HERGEST (1375–1425), the *Mabinogion* was compiled in the mid-nineteenth century and is a collection of medieval Welsh myths and folktales. Properly speaking the *Mabinogion* consists of four tales – PWYLL, BRANWEN, MANAWYDAN and MATH – three of which concern a hero named PRYDERI, but none of which are Arthurian. By extension the *Mabinogion* has come to include the Arthurian works of GEREINT AND ENID, CULHWCH AND OLWEN, OWAIN, PEREDUR and the DREAM OF RHONABWY. Possibly the most famous translation of all, that by Lady Charlotte Guest, also includes the story of TALIESIN.

Mabon

1 This Celtic god of liberation, harmony, unity and music, also known as MAPONUS, was undoubtedly the original of the Arthurian characters having the same name, as well as several others. He was possibly one of the most universally worshipped of all the Celtic deities, the centre of the Druidic cosmology, the original Being, pre-existent, the Son of the Great Mother. In mythology he is represented as both a prisoner and a liberator. Many other heroic and divine figures, and not just those in the Arthurian legends, are related to Mabon.

As Maponus, this deity was worshipped in the north of BRITAIN and GAUL, and is widely associated with therapeutic springs. In the most common Welsh tradition he is Mabon, son of MODRON ('son of the Mother'), held captive since he was stolen from his mother aged just three days. He is equated in a Romano-Celtic inscription with Apollo Citharoedus – 'the player of the lyre'. This would indicate that Mabon was a youthful god of the Apollo type, connected to therapy, music and a ritual hunt. Furthermore, his legends suggest that he was linked to the order of creation, for an increasingly complex cycle of animals lead the Arthurian warrior to rescue him.

2 The Welsh poem PA GUR names two of ARTHUR's followers as Mabon. One is the son of MODRON (the most common association for Mabon), who is described as the servant of UTHER. The other is called the son of MELLT. Some sources say that these two are one and the same, with Modron being the mother (derived from the Celtic goddess MATRONA), and Mellt the father (possibly derived from a god called MELDOS). The MABINOGION story of CULHWCH AND OLWEN says that he was stolen away from his mother when just three nights old and taken

to Caer Loyw (Gloucester), which here is used to symbolize the OTHERWORLD. It became a necessary part of CULHWCH's quest to find and rescue him. Arthur attacked his prison while KAY and BEDIVERE[2] rescued him. Subsequently he took part in the hunt for the magic boar TWRCH TRWYTH and succeeded in taking the razor that Culhwch required from between the beast's ears. Mabon appears to have had several variants within the Arthurian sagas – MABONAGRAIN in EREC ET ENIDE and MABUZ in *Lanzelet* by ULRICH VON ZARZIKHOVEN.

It has been argued that MERLIN acted as prophet to MABON[1], thus bringing a direct connection to the Arthurian tradition, and leading some to refer to Mabon himself as a sorcerer. In later tradition the story of Mabon seems to have been replaced by that of GAWAIN[1].

Mabonagrain

In French romance, Mabonagrain appears as the opponent of EREC in EREC ET ENIDE, in which he was kept as a prisoner in a castle with an 'airy' (*sic*) wall, and was the lover of the lady of that mysterious OTHERWORLD place. When Erec defeated him, he told Erec to blow a horn, and this freed him from his magical imprisonment. Identification has been made between this character and MABON[2], and through that to the Celtic deity MABON[1].

Mabuz

The son of the LADY OF THE LAKE, according to ULRICH VON ZARZIKHOVEN. In his story, *Lanzelet*, LANCELOT[2] comes to the aid of Mabuz, whose territory is under attack from IWERET, and defeats the invader. Connection has been made between Mabuz and both MABON[2] and MABON[1]. This would, in turn, identify his mother, the Lady of the Lake, with MODRON/MATRONA.

Macsen Wledig

The name by which the Roman emperor MAXIMUS was known in Welsh tradition.

Madaglan

Following the death of GUINEVERE, this king, whose story appears in PERLESVAUS, demanded that, as he was the dead queen's relation, ARTHUR should give him the ROUND TABLE. If Arthur refused, he further demanded that the king marry his sister. Arthur refused on both counts, and Madaglan was twice defeated by LANCELOT[2] – presumably once for each demand.

Madan

The king of BULGARIA in Arthurian romance.

Madoc

This name appears on several occasions in the Arthurian tales. Welsh legend makes him a legendary prince of GWYNEDD who was supposed to have discovered the Americas and been the ancestor of a group of light-skinned, Welsh-speaking Indians in the American west. French romance names a Madoc or MADUC as an opponent of ARTHUR. He also makes an appearance as the son of UTHER in the *Book of Taliesin*, though this reference seems to be a translator's error. In the Welsh poem *Ymddiddan Arthur a'r Eryr*, ELIWLOD, Arthur's nephew, appears in the guise of an eagle. This character's father is named as Madoc, thus implying that he was Arthur's brother-in-law.

Madog Morfryn

According to Welsh genealogies, the father of MERLIN, though some sources name him as MORGAN FRYCH.

Mador

One of the KNIGHTS OF THE ROUND TABLE who also partook in the Quest for the Holy GRAIL (as indeed did most of this company of knights, if the Grail legend is to be taken literally). He is given the epithet, or surname, *de la Porte* ('of the Door'). In the sixteenth-century Irish romance EACHTRA MHELÓRA AGUS ORLANDO, he is referred to as the son of the king of the HESPERIDES.

Maduc

A variant of MADOC.

Maelgwyn

A sixth-century ruler of GWYNEDD who has been, though tenuously, identified with MELKIN.

Maen Arthur

The name of a stone which allegedly had a hollow in it made by the hoof of ARTHUR's horse. This stone, which was in the vicinity of Mold, Clwyd, can no longer be identified – perhaps it has been stolen. Another stone having the same name is in Maen Arthur Wood near Llanafan, DYFED.

Maglore

According to the thirteenth-century French romance LI JUS ADEN, a companion of MORGAN[1] Le Fay.

Maid of the Narrow Wood

A maid who fell in love with GAWAIN[1] but subsequently tried to kill him when he did not return her feelings.

Maidenland

The home of the foster mother of LANCELOT[2], and where that knight was raised. As Lancelot was raised by the LADY OF THE LAKE, this would seem to draw its origin from the Irish TÍR INNA MBAN, the Land of Women, an OTHER-WORLD realm.

Maimed King

Named PARLAN, ÞELLEAM, PELLEHAN or PELLES, this character parallels the FISHER KING and was, according to the VULGATE VERSION, a being created when the Fisher King divided into two. His injury, usually described as a 'wound through the thighs' (*sic*), has been variously explained: as being inflicted by Balin, or as a punishment for his drawing the SWORD OF STRANGE HANGINGS.

Malduc

A wizard who promised to rescue GUINE-VERE from VALERIN, provided he was given GAWAIN[1] and EREC as prisoners. He duly freed Guinevere and received his captives, but they were subsequently rescued from him by LANCELOT[2].

Maledisant

The damsel helped by BREUNOR the Black. At first Maledisant was abusive to Breunor, presumably as he refused to remove his ill-fitting coat, which had earned him the nickname Le COTE MALE TAILÉE, until he had avenged his father. However, Maledisant obviously changed her opinion of him, for she subsequently married him.

Maleginis

One of the possible names of the KING WITH A HUNDRED KNIGHTS, one of the eleven rebellious leaders at the outset of ARTHUR's reign, though he has also been identified with BERRANT LES APRES and AGUYSANS.

Malehaut

A city of Arthurian BRITAIN, supposedly in the realm of the KING WITH A HUNDRED KNIGHTS, whose location remains a mystery. The lord of this city was called DANAIN THE RED, while his wife, BLOIE, was the lover of GALEHAUT and the mother of DODINEL. Elsewhere, Bloie is known as EGLANTE.

Mallerstang

A kingdom supposedly founded by UTHER, according to local Cumbrian legend, which also made Uther a giant.

Malmesbury, William of

English chronicler (c. 1090 to c. 1143), born probably near Malmesbury, Wiltshire. He became a monk in the monastery at Malmesbury, and in due time became librarian and precentor. He took part in the council at Winchester in 1141 against King Stephen. His *Gesta Regum Anglorum* provides a lively history of the kings of England from the SAXON invasion until 1126. The *Historia Novella* takes the narrative to 1142. His *Gesta Pontificum* is an ecclesiastical history of the bishops and chief monasteries of England to 1123. Other works are an account of the church of GLASTONBURY, and the lives of Saint Dunstan and Saint Wulfstan.

Malory, Sir Thomas

A fifteenth-century knight about whose life little can be said with any certainty. He is most famous as the author of the LE MORTE D'ARTHUR, printed by Caxton in 1485, and for many the classic Arthuriad. Caxton's preface to this work states that Malory was a knight, that he finished the work in the ninth year of the reign of King Edward IV (1470), and that he 'reduced' it from a French book. It is possible that he was the Sir Thomas Malory of Newbold Revel, Warwickshire, whose quarrels with a neighbouring priory and (probably) Lancastrian politics led to his imprisonment. Of Caxton's black-letter folio, only two copies now exist. An independent manuscript was discovered at Winchester in 1934. *Le Morte d'Arthur* is the best prose romance in English and was a happy attempt to give epic unity to the whole mass of French Arthurian romance.

Malvasius

The king of ICELAND, according to GEOFFREY OF MONMOUTH.

Man, Isle of

An island in the Irish Sea that was, during the traditional Arthurian period, ruled by a number of Celtic kings about whom very little is known. The enchanted knight GROMER became king with the help of GAWAIN[1]. The island also figures in a tale concerning MERLIN, who allegedly defeated a number of giants and interred them in caves beneath Castle Rushden on the island. Recent works have attempted to connect the Isle of Man with AVALON, perhaps due to the naming of Avalon as the Isle of APPLES by GEOFFREY OF MONMOUTH and the Irish connection of the island with EMHAIN

ABHLACH ('Emhain of the Apple Trees'), the home of the Irish sea god MANANNÁN MAC LIR.

Manael

According to the pedigree of JOHN OF GLASTONBURY, the son of CASTELLORS and an ancestor to ARTHUR.

Manannán mac Lir

The Irish primal god of the ocean depths who is otherwise known as BARINTHUS. In the VITA MERLINI, he is the ferryman on the barge which transports the dying ARTHUR to AVALON, accompanied by MERLIN and TALIESIN. His home was said to be the Isle of MAN, but is also associated with EMHAIN ABHLACH ('Emhain of the Apple Trees'), a paradisaical island that is usually identified with the Isle of Arran. Some commentators believe that this is why Avalon is sometimes referred to as the ISLE OF APPLES.

His connection with Arthurian legend is tenuous, to say the least. He is, however, said to have met BENDIGEID VRAN when the latter set out to journey to TÍR INNA MBAN ('Land of Women'). His main connection is through his Welsh counterpart, MANAWYDAN FAB LLYR.

Manawyd(d)an fab Llyr

'Manawydan, son of LLYR'. Probably originating as the Welsh counterpart to the Irish sea deity, MANANNÁN MAC LIR, Manawydan fab Llyr appears in the MABINOGION as the brother of BENDIGEID VRAN, and also in CULHWCH AND OLWEN as a follower of King ARTHUR. As the brother and heir to Bendigeid Vran, the *Mabinogion* says that he was among the party that accompanied his brother to IRELAND to rescue BRANWEN, and one of the seven who returned with Bendigeid

Vran's head for burial under the WHITE MOUNT in London. The others who returned with him were PRYDERI, GLUNEU EIL TARAN (GLIFIEU), TALIESIN, YNAWC (YNAWAG), GRUDYEN (GRUDDIEU), the son of MURYEL, and HEILYN, the son of GWYNN HEN, along with the unfortunate BRANWEN. When he returned he found he had been disinherited by CASWALLAWN, son of BELI. To compensate, Pryderi, about whom three of the four original *Mabinogion* stories relate, gave Manawydan fab Llyr his own mother, RHIANNON, for a wife, and with her the seven cantrefs of DYFED, so that he was no longer landless. He appears in many other stories, but has no other direct, or indirect, connections with the Arthurian sagas.

Mangoun

The king of MORAINE who sent King CARADOC a horn that was capable of exposing any infidelity on the part of his wife.

Mantell

A robe that was one of the THIRTEEN TREASURES of BRITAIN and had the ability to keep the wearer warm, no matter how severe the weather. Some sources say that this robe was owned by ARTHUR and, rather than keeping the wearer warm, would render that person invisible (cf. MANTLE OF INVISIBILITY).

Mantle of Invisibility

The loose-fitting cloak of ARTHUR that became one of the THIRTEEN TREASURES OF BRITAIN.

Maponos, -us

A variant of MABON[1], he was the son of MATRONA. An early Celtic deity, he was known as MABON[2], MABONAGRAIN and MABUZ in Arthurian legend.

Marabron

The son of King VAGOR of the ILLE ESTRANGE who was defeated in battle by Sir LANCELOT[2].

Maragoz

The steward of King ELYADUS of Sicily. He killed his master and thus caused the queen to flee, for her own safety was in doubt. In exile she gave birth to FLORIANT, who was reared as the foster son of MORGAN[1] Le Fay.

Marc

The son of YSAIE THE SAD and so the grandson of TRISTAN. He married ORIMONDE, the daughter of the Amir of Persia.

Marcán

'Little Mark'. The ageing husband of the beautiful, and young, CRED. He entertained the exiled CANO, with whom his wife had fallen in love before setting eyes on him and who attempted to conduct a love affair following Marcán's death.

March

The son of MEIRCHIAUN, king of Glamorgan, and identified by some commentators with King MARK[2].

Mardoc

Possibly to be identified with MORDRED, this character appears on the battlements of the Arthurian bas-relief in MODENA Cathedral, alongside WINLOGEE, who is thought identifiable with GUINEVERE.

Marfisa

A female knight who appears in ORLANDO FURIOSO and is thought to have been the inspiration for BRITOMART in SPENSER'S allegorical FAERIE QUEENE.

Margante

An alternative name for ARGANTE, a queen who appears in BRUT by LAYAMON, and, in this work, an alias for MORGAN[1] Le Fay.

Marhalt

According to Sir Thomas MALORY, the king of IRELAND and father of MARHAUS. However, the chronology in Malory is a little peculiar. When Marhaus fought with TRISTAN, he was the brother-in-law of the then king, ANGUISH, his father, Marhalt, only ascending the throne some time later. His family tree, drawn from a number of sources, is shown in Figure 24.

Marhaus

The son of MARHALT and brother of ISEULT[1] who was slain in combat by his sister's lover, TRISTAN. Prior to this, according to Sir Thomas MALORY Marhaus had been a supporter and follower of ARTHUR and had killed the giant TAULURD. Married to the daughter of ANGUISH, the king of Ireland before Marhalt ascended the throne, he had two sons named AMOROLDO and GOLISTANT. The works of GOTTFRIED VON STRASSBURG supply the information that Marhaus was a duke, but of where remains a mystery.

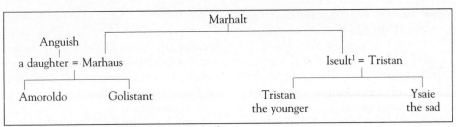

Figure 24   *Family tree of Marhalt, king of Ireland*

Mari-Morgan(s)

A class of water fairies of Breton origin. It has been suggested that they gave rise to MORGAN[1] Le Fay, as they are sometimes simply referred to as MORGANS. One in particular is of interest. Called either AHES or DAHUT, this fairy was held responsible for the destruction of the legendary city of YS.

Maria

The sister of King JUAN of Castile in Spanish romance. She was taken captive by an African potentate, but rescued by TRISTAN THE YOUNGER, whom she subsequently married.

Marie de France

A twelfth-century (*fl. c.* 1160–90) French poetess and authoress of two Arthurian romances – *Chevrefueil* and *Lanval*. Born in Normandy, she spent most of her life in England, where she wrote her *Lais* some time before 1167 and her *Fables* some time after 1170. She translated into French the *Tractatus de Purgatorio Sancti Patricii* (*c.* 1190), and her works contain many classical allusions. The *Lais*, her most important work, comprises fourteen romantic narratives in octosyllabic verse based on Celtic material.

Marinaia

MERLIN's mother, according to Pieri's fourteenth-century *Storia de Merlino*.

Marine

The daughter of URIEN who was loved by LARIS.

Marius

An early king of BRITAIN who was the son of ARVIRAGUS, according to GEOFFREY OF MONMOUTH. He soundly defeated the PICTS under SODRIC, but still bestowed Caithness on them.

Marjodoc

The steward of King MARK[2] who was at first friendly towards TRISTAN. However, when he discovered the affair between Tristan and ISEULT[1], he turned against his old friend.

Mark

1 King of Glamorgan who is possibly to be identified with MEIRCHIAUN, his son, MARCH, being identified, by some, with MARK[2], king of CORNWALL.
2 The brother to ELIZABETH/ELIABEL or BLANCHEFLEUR[2], king of CORNWALL, uncle of TRISTAN and husband of the unfortunate ISEULT[1]. Generally portrayed as something of a tyrant,

Sir Thomas MALORY referring to him as 'bad King Mark', it seems that this tyrannical aspect owes to his association with an ancient and historical ruler, CUNOMORUS, who reigned in both Cornwall and BRITTANY. Cunomorus, warned that one of his sons would kill him, murdered each of his wives as soon as they announced that they had fallen pregnant. However, one wife, TREPHINA, the daughter of WAROK, chief of the VENETII, managed to escape him until after she had given birth. Having borne JUDWAL, or TREMEUR, Cunomorus had her decapitated, and her son was left to die. GILDAS restored Trephina to life, and she went back to the castle, neatly carrying her head, whereupon the battlements fell on Cunomorus and killed him.

The Mark known from Arthurian legend is usually depicted as the injured party in the tragic love affair between Iseult, his wife, and Tristan. His name in Welsh, March, means 'horse', and BÉROUL says that he had horse's ears, a trait shared with many other legendary and mythological characters. The MABINOGION story of the DREAM OF RHONABWY makes him the cousin of ARTHUR, while his nephew, Tristan, is lowered to the status of a swineherd in the Welsh TRIADS. Not much is said of Mark during the life of his wife and her lover, the emphasis being placed firmly on that famous affair. It is generally stated that he remained ignorant of the events occurring around him for some time. One version says that on the death of the lovers Mark had them buried in a single grave, though in MALORY Mark is said to have actually killed Tristan in a blind rage when he caught him playing the harp to Iseult.

The story of Tristan and Iseult appears in the romances of many countries, and so, by association, does the character of Mark. His family tree, however, differs greatly. That most commonly referred to is the pedigree given by Sir Thomas Malory (Figure 25). The Italian romance TRISTANO RICCARDIANO gives the version shown in Figure 26. The similarity with the details given by Sir Thomas Malory is quite obvious.

There are several versions of what actually happened to Mark following Tristan's death. The Italian romance *La vendetta che fe messer Lanzelloto de la morte de miser Tristan* states that LANCELOT[2] invaded Cornwall and killed him. Other sources sat that he was defeated and killed by TRISTAN THE YOUNGER, or that he was placed in a cage which overlooked the graves of Tristan and Iseult. Another says that the son of ALISANDER THE ORPHAN, BELLANGERE, killed him, while yet one more says that when Lancelot died he invaded LOGRES and subsequently destroyed much of CAMELOT, including the ROUND TABLE. He fell at the hands of PAMLART, a direct descendant of BAN.

The origin of Mark remains somewhat obscure, the most tenable link being made with Cunomorus. The writer Wrmonoc says that Cunomorus was also called Mark, though this may be an identification with MARCH, the son of the king of Glamorgan, MEIRCHIAUN. A further link between Mark and Cunomorus may lie in an ancient, and partially unintelligible, inscription at Castle DORE in Cornwall. This may read *Drustans hic iacit cunomori filius* – 'Here lies Tristan, son of Cunomorus.' If this is indeed the true meaning of the inscription, it would seem to imply that the relationship between Mark and Tristan was far closer than later writers were prepared to allow. Even in those fairly amoral times, an affair between son and step-

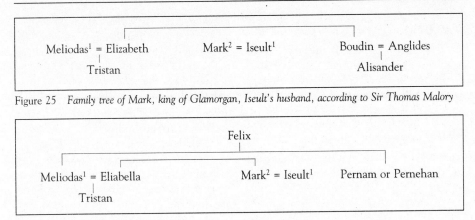

Figure 25 *Family tree of Mark, king of Glamorgan, Iseult's husband, according to Sir Thomas Malory*

Figure 26 *Family tree of Mark according to* Tristano Riccardiano

mother may have been a little too strong to stomach.

Breton tradition carries the name of King Mark to this day, for it is said that he rides a winged horse, named Mormarc'h, when the sea off Penmarc'h, Mark's Head (a headland in Brittany) is rough.

Marlborough

A town in Wiltshire whose borough arms bear the motto *Ubi nunc sapientis ossa Merlini* – 'Where are the bones of MERLIN now?' Until the fourteenth century, tradition stated that Merlin was buried under an earthen mound at the western end of the town which now lies in the grounds of Marlborough College.

Marlyn

The son of OGIER and MORGAN[1] Le Fay and hence a nephew of King ARTHUR.

Marmyadose

A sword, said to have belonged once to Hercules and to have been made by the god Vulcan. It was won by ARTHUR from RIENCE, a giant whom the king killed when that giant demanded Arthur's beard to add to his cloak, which was made from the beards of those men he had conquered and killed.

Maronex

A king of GAUL whose daughter married JONAANS, the latter inheriting Maronex's kingdom following his death.

Marpesia

Medieval legend claimed that this king of the Goths formed an army of women, among them the AMAZON warriors of classical mythology, and journeyed, by way of the Caucasus, to Africa.

Marrion

According to the romance BATAILLE LOQUIFER, one of MORGAN[1] Le Fay's sisters.

Marrok

One of the KNIGHTS OF THE ROUND TABLE, he was changed into a werewolf by his wife for a total of seven years.

Marsique

A fairy who obtained the enchanted scabbard of EXCALIBUR for GAWAIN[1] after that knight had fought the wizard MABON[2] over her.

Martha

The daughter of King IRION who married TRISTAN'S son, YSAIE THE SAD.

Math fab Mathonwy

A magician, son of MATHONWY, who features in the Arthurian sagas only as the king to whom ARIANRHOD was put forward for the post of footholder. He later helped her son, LLEU LLAW GYFFES, with the aid of GWYDION FAB DÔN, to evade the third curse placed on him by his mother, Arianrhod, that he would never have a wife until she herself gave him one. He and Gwydion fab Dôn made him the flower maiden BLODEUWEDD for a wife from the flowers of oak, broom and meadowsweet. The events are related in the MABINOGION story of Math, Son of Mathonwy.

Matholwch

The king of IRELAND to whom BENDIGEID VRAN gave his sister, BRANWEN, for a wife, together with a magic cauldron. However, while in BRITAIN he was insulted by EFNISIEN, the half-brother of Bendigeid Vran, and when he had returned to Ireland he exacted his revenge by mistreating Branwen.

News of her suffering reached her brother and he mounted an expedition to save her. At first his forces suffered badly, for those of Matholwch were sustained by the magic cauldron. Each night they placed their dead and wounded into it, and they were restored to full health.

However, Efnisien managed to destroy it and eventually Bendigeid Vran and his forces were victorious, though only seven men survived of his original party, he himself mortally wounded. Of the Irish, only five pregnant women remained hidden in a cave. The seven who survived, and carried Bendigeid Vran's severed head back for burial under the WHITE MOUNT in London were PRYDERI, MANAWYDAN, GLIFIEU (GLUNEU EIL TARAN), TALIESIN, YNAWC (YNAWAG), GRUDYEN (GRUDDIEU) and HEILYN.

Mathonwy

The father of the magician MATH and a central figure in the MABINOGION.

Matrona

The Divine Mother, an early Celtic goddess and probably the mother of MABON[1]/MAPONUS. She was worshipped in both BRITAIN and GAUL, where she was the goddess of the River Marne, near the mouth of which lies her sanctuary. Her association with Mabon has led to her being considered as the original of MORGAN[1] Le Fay.

Maxim(ian)us

A Roman emperor who was known, in Welsh tradition, as MACSEN WLEDIG. He was called Maximianus by GEOFFREY OF MONMOUTH, who said that he made CONAN MERIADOC the ruler of BRITTANY.

Mazadan

A fairy and husband of TERDELASCHOYE who was, according to Wolfram VON ESCHENBACH, the great-grand-father of ARTHUR and an ancestor of PERCEVAL[2] (Figure 27).

```
┌─────────────────────────────────┐
│   Mazadan = Terdeleschoye       │
│            │                     │
│          Brickus                 │
│            │                     │
│           Uther                  │
│            │                     │
│          Arthur                  │
└─────────────────────────────────┘
```

Figure 27 *Family tree of Mazadan, great-grandfather of Arthur, according to Wolfram von Eschenbach*

Mazoe

Named as a sister of MORGAN[1] Le Fay.

Medrawt

The name by which MORDRED is referred to in the ANNALES CAMBRIAE.

Me(i)rchiaun

An early king of Glamorgan, and the father of MARK[1] of Glamorgan. His son may have been the original for King MARK[2] of CORNWALL, or the association may simply be one of confusion.

Melchinus

A Latinized version of MELKIN.

Meldos

Originally a Celtic god and possibly the origin of MELLT. The father of MABON[2] in Welsh tradition.

Meldred

A king who had the infidelities of his wife revealed to him by LAILOKEN.

Meleagaunce
Also MELWAS

The son of King BAGDEMAGUS. A scurrilous knight, he once abducted GUINEVERE and took her back to his own territory. There he was about to rape her, but his father prevented him from doing so. She was rescued by her champion, and lover, Sir LANCELOT[2], who fought Meleagaunce and spared his life only after Bagdemagus had beseeched Guinevere to intercede. The combat was stopped, to be recommenced in a year's time. Again, Bagdemagus begged for Meleagaunce to be spared when the two met on this second occasion. As with many of the Arthurian legends, there are several different versions of what actually befell Meleagaunce. One says that he and Lancelot fought in single combat over Guinevere and Lancelot killed him. Whether this was on the first, second or a subsequent occasion when the pair met is unclear. Another says that Meleagaunce actually imprisoned Lancelot, but was slain while the latter escaped. A Welsh version of this story, which uses Meleagaunce's Welsh name, Melwas, says that he was the ruler of Somerset, and carried off Guinevere to GLASTONBURY. ARTHUR (not Lancelot in this tale) laid siege to the town, but the abbot and GILDAS beseeched Melwas to return his captive, which he did.

Melehan

A son of MORDRED who, with his brother, seized the kingdom following the death of their father. They were defeated by LANCELOT[2], Melehan later being killed by BORS[2].

Meliadice

The heroine of the fifteenth-century French romance *Cleriadus*, which was published in Paris in 1495. A descendant of ARTHUR, she was the daughter of King PHILIPPON, the king of England. She married CLERIADUS, who succeeded Philippon.

Meliador

The son of the Duke of CORNWALL and a member of King ARTHUR's court, though his capacity remains unknown. He married the daughter of the king of Scotland, HERMONDINE, after killing his rival for her hand, CAMAL.

Meliant de Lis

A knight whose hatred for LANCELOT[2] was founded in the fact that Lancelot had killed his father. He was eventually killed by Lancelot.

Melianus

An ancestor of LOT.

Meliodas

The name of two related characters from Arthurian legend.

1 The king of LIONES and father of TRISTAN. He carried off the queen of SCOTLAND while still a young man, which led to war between him and ARTHUR. She became the mother of MELIODAS[2] by him. His relationship to King MARK[2] of CORNWALL is a little confused, for Sir Thomas MALORY makes him his brother-in-law, having married ELIZABETH, while in Italian romance he is the brother of Mark, the romance TRISTANO RICCARDIANO calling their father FELIX. If Malory is to be used, Meliodas became the father of Tristan by Elizabeth. Subsequently, following Elizabeth's death, he married a daughter of HOEL[1], while another of Hoel's daughters was to marry his son, Tristan. ISEULT[2] of the White Hands would therefore be both sister-in-law and daughter-in-law to Meliodas. His death is put down to knights of the count of NORHOUT.

2 The son of MELIODAS[1] and the queen of SCOTLAND. His mother set him adrift as a baby and he was raised by the LADY OF THE LAKE, though this may be a different lady from that associated with EXCALIBUR, or even the one said to have raised LANCELOT[2].

Meljanz

The king of LIZ who went to war against Duke LYPPAUT when his advances were rejected by the latter's daughter.

Melkin

A vaticinator (prophet) mentioned by JOHN OF GLASTONBURY, who says that he lived before MERLIN and uttered prophecies about GLASTONBURY so couched in obscure Latin phraseology that they are difficult to interpret. It has been suggested that they may refer to Glastonbury as a place of pagan burial, and to the future discovery of the tomb of JOSEPH OF ARIMATHEA there. Melkin may possibly be identifiable with MAELGWYN, a sixth-century ruler of GWYNEDD, though this seems tenuous. John Leland (c. 1503–52), royal antiquary to King Henry VIII, claimed to have seen Melkin's book at Glastonbury Abbey.

Mellt

The father of one of the two Mabons (see MABON[2]) listed as being followers of ARTHUR, though it is now generally assumed that these are the same character, thought of as two previously for the simple reason that one had his mother only named, and the other his father, Mellt.

Melodian

A son of King PELLINORE.

Melora

A daughter of King ARTHUR who according to an Irish romance fell in love with ORLANDO, the son of the king of Thessaly. Jealously, MADOR bribed MERLIN to rid him of the troublesome prince, a request which Merlin complied with, employing his servant, simply named as the DESTRUCTIVE ONE, to imprison the hapless Orlando. He was surrounded by enchantments that only the LANCE OF LONGINUS, the carbuncle of VERONA, daughter of the king of NARSINGA, and the oil of the pig of TUIS could dispose of. Melora disguised herself as a knight and set out to find these items. She defeated the king of Africa on behalf of the king of BABYLON, and as a reward was given the Lance of Longinus and LEVANDER as her companion. They were imprisoned by the king of Asia, but escaped with the help of URANUS, a guard, and successfully obtained the oil of the pig of Tuis from their captor. They finally managed to lure Verona and her father, the king of Narsinga, on to a ship, but they became firm friends, and the carbuncle was given freely to Melora. Returning, Orlando was freed and the happy couple went on to Thessaly, while Levander married Verona.

Melot

An Aquitainian dwarf who spied on TRISTAN and ISEULT[1] for the jealous King MARK[2], according to GOTTFRIED VON STRASSBURG. His story is again told by EILHART, but he simply refers to the dwarf as AQUITAIN.

Melwas

The Welsh for MELEAGAUNCE.

Menw (fab Teirgwaedd)

A sorcerer who appears in the MABINOGION story of CULHWCH AND OLWEN as a member of the party formed by ARTHUR to aid CULHWCH in his quest to locate OLWEN. The other members of the party, each chosen for their special skills, were CEI (KAY), CYNDDYLIG the Guide, GWRHYR the Interpreter, GWALCHMAI FAB GWYAR and BEDWYR (BEDIVERE[2]). Menw fab Teirgwaedd was a master of spells and had the ability to make any member of the party invisible, should the need arise.

Meraugis

The offspring of the violation of LABIANE by her uncle, King MARK[2] of CORNWALL. His father, Mark, murdered Labiane and abandoned Meraugis in the woods, where he was found and raised by a forester. He became a KNIGHT OF THE ROUND TABLE, fought at the battle of CAMLANN and, following ARTHUR's death, became a hermit in the company of BORS[2] and some others.

Meriadeuc

The hero of the thirteenth-century romance that carries his name. He became known as the KNIGHT OF THE TWO SWORDS (a title also conferred on BALIN) after he proved himself the only member of ARTHUR's knights able to unfasten a swordbelt which LORE, Lady of GARADIGAN, whom he subsequently married, had brought to Arthur's court.

Meriadeuc

A thirteenth-century French verse romance concerning a hero having the same name as the title of the work.

Meriadoc

The son of King CARADOC whose inheritance was usurped by GRIFFITH when the latter took the throne by murdering CARADOC. Meriadoc and his sister were despatched to the woods to be killed, but the executioners failed in their task. Subsequently the children were raised by IVOR the Huntsman and his wife, MORWEN. ORWEN was abducted by URIEN, in this instance called king of the Scots, who married her. Meriadoc meanwhile went to King ARTHUR's court to ask for help in regaining his rightful throne and, with ARTHUR's help, succeeded in ousting GRIFFITH only to hand over the throne, once he had regained it, to URIEN. Travelling on to the Continent, Meriadoc rescued the daughter of the emperor of Germany from GUNDEBALD, the king of the LAND FROM WHICH NO ONE RETURNS, and married her.

Merlin
Also MYRDDIN

The most famous wizard of all times, ARTHUR's counsellor who guided the young king at the start of his reign, though later the king did not always follow the advice given to him. We know of Merlin by that name simply because the Latinized form of his Welsh name, Myrddin, would be Merdinus, and that would unfortunately have connected it with the Latin word *merdus* – 'dung'. Merlin is not a personal name but rather a place-name, the Welsh form of his name, Myrddin, originating in the Celtic *Maridunon* – CARMARTHEN, Welsh *Caerfyrddin*. It seems that the wizard was so called because he originated from that city. At least GEOFFREY OF MONMOUTH seems to think so. Other sources agree in principle, but rather say that the city was founded by him, and therefore named after him.

ROBERT DE BORON says he was born in BRITTANY, but this is commonly regarded as an attempt by that author to claim him for his own country of birth.

Many stories abound about the birth of Merlin, but usually he is said to have been the offspring of an incubus (evil spirit) and a nun, set on earth by the devils of Hell, who were determined to counterbalance the good introduced by Jesus Christ. However, their plans went awry when their intended evil being was promptly baptized. This is not by any means the only account of his birth, but does appear to predate any of the others. In Welsh tradition his mother was called ALDAN, but whether or not she was a nun is not made clear. French romance calls her OPTIMA, while Pieri's fourteenth-century *Storia di Merlino* names her as MARINAIA. The Elizabethan play *The Birth of Merlin* calls her JOAN GO-TO-'T. Welsh tradition further contradicts his supposed lack of a father by giving him the paternal pedigree shown in Figure 28.

His father, named as MADOG MORFRYN in Figure 28, was also said to have been MORGAN FRYCH, claimed by some to have been a prince of GWYNEDD, thus making Merlin of royal blood. Geoffrey of Monmouth made him the King of POWYS, and this idea that Merlin was of royal stock is later found in *Venetia edificia* (1624) by Strozzi.

Merlin's story, and his connection with the Athurian legends, begins long before

Coel Godebog
|
Ceneu
|
Mor
|
Morydd
|
Madog Morfryn
|
Myrddin (Merlin)

Figure 28 *Merlin's paternal pedigree according to the Welsh tradition* the birth of the king he was to advise, and whose downfall he so rightly prophesied. While still a youth, he became connected with VORTIGERN, the king of BRITAIN some time after the end of the Roman occupation. Vortigern was attempting to erect a tower on DINAS EMRYS, but with little success, for every time he built it up it promptly fell down again. His counsellors told him that it would be necessary to sacrifice a fatherless child in order to rectify the problem and, as these were hardly thick on the ground, the supposedly fatherless son of the incubus, Merlin, now a youth, was picked. When brought to the site of the tower, Merlin told Vortigern that the problem lay beneath the ground in the form of two dragons secreted in an underground lake. Excavation of the site proved this to be the case (subsequent archaeological excavation has revealed the underground pool), and two dragons, one red and one white, emerged, causing Merlin to utter a series of prophecies.

There seems to be an unrecorded gap in Merlin's life at this point, for he next appears when AMBROSIUS AURELIUS defeated Vortigern and wished to erect a monument both to his success and to commemorate the dead. Merlin advised him to go to Ireland and bring back from there certain stones that formed the GIANTS' RING. This was done and they were erected on SALISBURY PLAIN as STONEHENGE. Following the death of Ambrosius Aurelius, UTHER ascended the throne, but during a war with GORLOIS, he became infatuated with IGRAINE[1], the wife of Gorlois, so one of Uther's men suggested they consult Merlin. When they did so, Merlin consented to enable Uther to lie with Igraine on the condition that any child born of the union should be entrusted to him to raise. Uther agreed and Merlin altered his appearance so that he resembled Gorlois and, on the night Uther lay with Igraine, her true husband

was killed in battle. When the child was born, Merlin appeared and took the child away, as had been agreed, placing him with ECTOR. This child was the infant ARTHUR. Uther married Igraine, but two years later he died. The country was thrown into disarray, for there was no worthy successor to the throne, a situation that continued for thirteen years after Uther's death.

Meanwhile the young ARTHUR was raised by Ector, unaware of his parentage or destiny. When aged just fifteen, he accompanied his foster father and KAY, Ector's son, to a tournament in London, acting as Kay's squire. However, when they arrived Arthur found, to his horror, that he had forgotten Kay's sword. He remembered seeing one embedded in a rock some distance away and went to fetch it. Arthur easily removed the sword from the stone, a test devised by Merlin to find the next true king, and hurried back to the tournament. Kay recognized the sword which so many had tried to remove but none had been able to, and tried to make his father believe that he had removed it himself. However, Ector prevailed upon his son to tell the truth, fully realizing what the sword signified, and Kay owned up. Arthur once more drew out the sword, this time in public, and was duly proclaimed king.

Events after the crowning of King Arthur differ according to source, some even attributing the manufacture of the ROUND TABLE to Merlin. When Arthur wanted to marry GUINEVERE, Merlin advised him against it, saying that she would be unfaithful to him, and would ultimately bring about the destruction of his realm and lead to his death. Arthur none the less ignored the advice of his counsellor.

According to Sir Thomas MALORY, Merlin became infatuated with the LADY OF THE LAKE, called NIMUE by Malory but referred to as VIVIANE/VIVIENNE elsewhere. He taught her his magical secrets, but she turned these against him and imprisoned him in a cave or an oak tree, the spell holding him there capable of being broken only when Arthur once again rules.

Geoffrey of Monmouth, and earlier Welsh sources, say that Merlin was still in circulation following the battle CAMLANN, being one of those aboard the barge, along with TALIESIN and the ferryman BARINTHUS, who brought the dying king to AVALON to be healed of his deadly wound by the goddess MORGAN[1] Le Fay, shape-changing mistress of therapy, music and the arts, co-ruling with her NINE SISTERS. With the kingdom in disarray, Merlin went mad following the battle of ARTHURET and took to living as a wild man in the woods. One source, GIRALDUS CAMBRENSIS, gives the reason for Merlin's loss of sanity, saying that it followed his beholding some horrible sight in the sky, a bad omen, during the fighting in which he had been on the side of RHYDDERCH HAEL, king of Cumbria and husband of Merlin's sister GANIEDA. Three of Merlin's brothers were also reputed to have been killed during the battle. After a while Ganieda persuaded Merlin to give up his wild life in the woods and return to civilization, but upon his return he revealed to Ganieda's husband, Rhydderch Hael, that she had been unfaithful to him. Once again madness took hold of Merlin and he returned to the forest, urging his wife, the flower-maiden GUENDOLOENA, to marry again, apparently divorcing her to free her. She agreed, but in his madness Merlin arrived at the wedding riding a stag and leading a herd of deer (clearly a reworking of an earlier pagan tradition). In his rage, forgetting that it was he who had urged his wife to remarry, he tore the antlers off the stag and hurled them at the bridegroom, who remains unnamed, and killed him. He returned to the forest once more, and his sister Ganieda built him an observatory from which he could study the stars.

Welsh poetic sources that are considerably earlier in date than the writings of Geoffrey of Monmouth largely agree with his account (they are obviously his sources), though they state that Merlin fought against Rhydderch Hael, rather than for him. Similar tales are told in Welsh tradition regarding a character by the name of LAILOKEN, who was in the service of Rhydderch Hael, and it would appear that this caused Geoffrey of Monmouth to change the allegiance of Merlin. Lailoken is similar to the Welsh word meaning 'twin brother' and, as Merlin and Ganieda were thought to be twins, this may have simply been a nickname for Merlin himself, though, as has already been said, Merlin is not actually a personal name.

Many other legends and tales surround the character of Merlin. He was said to have saved the baby TRISTAN, to have had a daughter named La DAMOSEL DEL GRANT PUI DE MONT DOLEROUS, and that he was not imprisoned by Nimue, but instead voluntarily retired to a place of confinement to live out the remainder of his days. This last option seems to have some connection with the story of Ganieda building him an observatory in the forest, for that would have been a splendid place for the wizard to spend his final years.

Geoffrey of Monmouth appears to draw further on earlier Welsh sources when he connects Merlin with Taliesin, a character with whom he seems to be inexorably intertwined in the Welsh mind. One Welsh tradition says that Merlin was not just one but three incarnations of the same person, the first appearing in Vortigern's time, the second as Taliesin himself, while the last was as Merlin the wild man of the forests. This idea of a multiple Merlin is again found in the writings of the twelfth-century Norman-Welsh chronicler Giraldus Cambrensis, who says there were two, wizard and wild man. This theory doubtless springs from the impractically long lifespan usually attributed to Merlin. Modern thinking even had him reincarnated once more as Nostradamus (Latinized form of Michel de Notredame), the sixteenth-century prophet. This idea has not found popular following, though, and is now almost universally disregarded.

The legends of Merlin are not simply confined to British and Breton tradition. The Italian romances also add a great deal to his story, stating, in one instance, that he was unsuccessfully charged with heresy by a Papal bishop named CONRAD, and that he uttered prophecies about the House of Hohenstaufen. An Italian poet, BOIARDO, mixes Merlin into the story of TRISTAN and ISEULT[1], saying that Merlin created a fountain of forgetfulness for Tristan to drink from and thus forget Iseult. Tristan never found it. ARIOSTO says that his soul lives on in a tomb, and it informed the female warrior BRADMANTE that the House of ESTE would descend from her. Strozzi further adds that at the time when Attila the Hun invaded Italy, Merlin lived in a cave and, while there, invented the telescope (another reference to Ganieda's observatory?).

His death is as clouded in legend and fable as is his life. One Welsh tradition says that he was held captive by a scheming woman in a cave on BRYN MYRDDIN near Carmarthen, a location shown on Ordnance Survey maps as MERLIN'S HILL. This seems to echo the story of his being held captive by Nimue. Some say that if you listen in the twilight you can still hear his groans and the clanking of the iron chains which bind him, while others say that this is the noise of him still working away in his underground

prison. His place of confinement is also said to be a cave in the park of DYNEVOR CASTLE, DYFED, in the vicinity of Llandeilo. It is also claimed that he died and was buried on BARDSEY Island, while Breton tradition has him spellbound in a bush of white thorn trees in the woods of Bresilien in Brittany.

The Welsh TRIADS, however, say that he put to sea in a house of glass and was never heard of again. On this voyage he took with him the THIRTEEN TREASURES or Curiosities of BRITAIN, which were:

1 LLEN ARTHUR – the veil of ARTHUR, which made the wearer invisible. This is sometimes referred to as the MANTLE OF INVISIBILITY.

2 DYRNWYN – the sword of RHYDDERCH HAEL, which would burst into flame from the cross to the point if any man, save himself, drew it.

3 CORN BRANGALED – the horn of BRANGALED, which would provide any drink desired.

4 CADAIR, NEU CAR MORGAN MWYN-FAWR – the chair or car of MORGAN MWYNFAWR, which would carry a person seated in it anywhere he wished to go.

5 MWYS GWYDDNO – the hamper of GWYDDNO, which had the power to turn any meat placed on it into sufficient to feed 100 people.

6 HOGALEN TUDNO – the whetstone of TUDNO TUDGLYD, which would sharpen none but the weapon of a brave man.

7 PAIS PADARN – the cloak of PADARN, which would make the wearer invisible.

8 PAIR DRYNOG – the cauldron of DRYNOG, in which only the meat of a brave man would boil.

9 DYSGYL A GREN RHYDDERCH – the platter of RHYDDERCH, upon which any meat desired would appear.

10 TAWLBWRDD – a chess or rather backgammon board, having a ground of gold and men of silver who would play themselves.

11 MANTELL – a robe that would keep the wearer warm no matter how severe the weather.

12 MODRWY ELUNED – the ring of ELUNED, which conferred invisibility on the wearer.

13 CYLLEL LLAWFRODEDD – a Druid sacrificial knife.

It should be noted that these were by no means the only items considered to number among the Thirteen Treasures, but they are the most common in Welsh tradition (a list of the most common variants is included on pages 269–70).

Modern times have not entirely forgotten Merlin either. Yearly pilgrimages continued to MERLIN'S SPRING at Barenton, Brittany, until they were stopped by the Vatican in 1853. His ghost is still said to haunt MERLIN'S CAVE at TINTAGEL, while the wizard is said to be buried in almost as many locations as Arthur. These locations include DRUMELZIER in SCOTLAND, under MERLIN'S MOUNT in the grounds of MARLBOROUGH College, at MYNYDD FYRDDIN in WALES, and in MERLIN'S HILL CAVE near Carmarthen.

Merlin's historicity is now thought to be without doubt, but he was not the mythologized wizard of the Arthurian legends. There were in fact two Merlins alive during the time of Vortigern and Arthur. One was called MYRDDIN WYLLT and lived in Scotland, but it is MYRDDIN EMRYS, born and raised in Carmarthen, that has become the Arthurian Merlin. It is generally believed that he must have been a man of very high intelligence with extremely advanced knowledge for his time, when magic was simply another name for scientific expertise. He may have been, as has been suggested, a latterday Druid who took part in shamanistic rituals, but many attempts have also been made to link Merlin with earlier Celtic deities.

One theory states that Merlin represented the morning star while his sister Ganieda was the evening star. His character may indeed have been that of a deity, for the Welsh TRIADS indicate that he may have had territorial rights as a god over Britain, for this work says that the earliest name for Britain was MERLIN'S PRECINCT. However, the truth behind this is probably that the prophet became connected with an earlier deity, and took on many of his attributes, such would have been the astonishing power of this character. To the peasants of the time, his wisdom and foresight must have seemed very godly indeed. Other attempts have been made to connect him with the god MABON[1] or, through his association with stags, with CERNUNNOS. Many theories have been put forward, but the truth of the matter, as with so much of Arthurian legend, may never be known.

There are countless prophecies attributed to Merlin, some of which appear to have been strangely fulfilled and others of which may well be fulfilled in the future. In the Vale of Twy near Abergwili there stands a large stone in a field. Many years ago a young man was killed while digging under this stone for buried treasure, it being popular belief at the time that such stones marked the burial sites of riches beyond belief. Myrddin had once prophesied that one day a raven would drink the blood of a man from this stone. Whether or not a raven actually did so is not known, but the prophecy seems to have come true.

The most famous prophecies attributed to Merlin were those relating to the town of Carmarthen, which still awaits some fearful catastrophe.

Llanllwch a fu,
Caerfyrddu a sud,
Abergwili a saif.

Llanllwch has been,
Carmarthen shall sink,
Abergwili shall stand.

and

Caerfyrddin, cei oer fore,
Daerr a'th lwnc, dwr i'th le.

Carmarthen, thou shalt have a cold
morning,
Earth shall swallow thee, water into thy
place.

There are still old folk living in Carmarthen who await the catastrophe that they believe will one day befall their town. At the end of one street, there used to stand an ancient and withered old oak tree known as MERLIN'S TREE or the PRIORY OAK. Every care was taken over the centuries to protect it from falling, for Merlin had prophesied that when it did Carmarthen would fall. However, in 1978 the local authority decided to risk the prophecy and remove the tree, which had become a hazard to the town's traffic and consisted mainly of concrete and iron bars anyway.

Merlin also prophesied that Carmarthen would sink when LLYN EIDDWEN, a lake in DYFED (then Cardiganshire), dried up. He also foretold that one day a bull would go to the very top of the tower of St Peter's Church in Carmarthen. This strange prophesy was one day fulfilled by a calf.

Merlin

Important twelfth-century romance by the Burgundian author ROBERT DE BORON.

Merlin's Cave

A cave at TINTAGEL, CORNWALL, that is said to be haunted by the ghost of MERLIN.

Merlin's Entertainments

HEYWOOD, in his *Life of Merlin*, reports that VORTIGERN became melancholy and, in an attempt to cheer him, MERLIN provided various forms of entertainment, including invisible musicians and flying hounds that chased flying hares.

Merlin's Hill

A hill, three miles east of CARMARTHEN, at the summit of which there is a rock resembling a chair. Legend says that this was where MERLIN sat to deliver his various prophecies. It is also the alleged site of a cave where Merlin was buried, but this cave has yet to be found. However, there is a cave situated under an overhang behind a waterfall in the upper reaches of the Afon Pib which is sometimes locally referred to as OGOF MYRDDIN.

Merlin's Hill Cave

The so far undiscovered cave on MERLIN'S HILL in which the wizard is said to have been buried.

Merlin's Mount

A earthen mound in the grounds of MARLBOROUGH College, Wiltshire, which is one of the many locations cited as the burial place of MERLIN.

Merlin's Precinct

An early name for BRITAIN which appears in the Welsh TRIADS and has been taken by some to indicate that MERLIN was, in origin, a deity who had territorial rights.

Merlin's Spring

A spring at Barenton, BRITTANY, that was the focus of pilgrimages until they were stopped by the Vatican in 1853.

Merlin's Tree

Also called the PRIORY OAK, this tree in CAMARTHEN was believed to maintain the good fortune of Camarthen, for, it was believed, if it fell, so would the city. The tree was removed by the local authority in 1978, as it constituted a traffic hazard, and to date MERLIN's prophecy of the destruction of Carmarthen has not been fulfilled.

Merveilles de Rigomer

A thirteenth-century French verse romance, normally simply referred to as RIGOMER, by an obscure poet named Jehan. It tells the story of the adventures of GAWAIN[1] and LANCELOT[2].

Meuric

The son of CARADOC BRIEFBRAS in Welsh tradition.

Meurig

A king of GLENVISSIG whose son, ARTHRWYS, has been identified with ARTHUR. It is possible that Meurig is to be identified with Meurig ap Tewdrig, prince of Glamorgan, whose daughter, Anna, was the mother of Saint SAMSON by Amwn.

Meurvin

The son of OGIER and MORGAN[1] Le Fay, and thus ARTHUR's nephew. He became the father of ORIANT and was an ancestor of the SWAN KNIGHT.

Midsummer Night's Dream, A

Comedy by William SHAKESPEARE that was first performed in 1595 or 1596. Although not directly connected with the Arthurian legends, it is of great interest because of the inclusion of characters such as PUCK, OBERON[1] and TITANIA.

Mil the Black

Welsh tradition makes this character an opponent of ARTHUR, who killed him.

Miles

The knightly lover of ELAINE[3], the daughter of PELLINORE, who committed suicide after his death.

Miraude

The wife of TOREC. Having been sent to obtain the circlet belonging to his grandmother, Miraude promised to marry him if he successfully overcame the KNIGHTS OF THE ROUND TABLE, a feat he fulfilled.

Miroet

The son of an Irish king named ALVREZ and brother of KAMELIN. He and his brother both became KNIGHTS OF THE ROUND TABLE.

Modena

City in Emilia, Italy. The capital of the province of Modena, lying north of Bologna, its twelfth-century cathedral is of interest to Arthurian studies. Within the cathedral is an arch, the underside of which depicts Arthurian scenes that include several characters not known of anywhere else, whether in art or literature. This frieze is usually referred to as the Modena archivolt.

Modron

Ancient Welsh goddess, daughter of AVALLOC, whose name simply means 'Mother'. She is apparently a form of MATRONA, the Roman name for the Great Mother Goddess. Her divine child was known as MABON[1], which in turn simply means 'son' or 'son of the Mother'. She is thought to be the prototype of the Arthurian MORGAN[1] Le Fay, though some Welsh sources make her the mother of OWAIN, the son of URIEN of RHEGED.

Modrwy Eluned

The ring of ELUNED, one of the THIRTEEN TREASURES, which made the wearer invisible.

Moel Arthur

A hill in Clwyd, WALES, where, according to legend, ARTHUR's table was situated. A hillfort exists on the site, and it is quite possible that this was in use during the traditional period ascribed to Arthur. A survey of 1737 mentions a burial chamber named CIST ARTHUR, which has again been linked with the last resting place of Arthur.

Moine

The name of the elder brother of AMBROSIUS AURELIUS and UTHER, according to the PROSE TRISTAN. More commonly his name is given as CONSTANS. His real name was IVOINE, which is taken from IVOIRE, his mother's name, but he was given the name Moine, which means 'monk', as he was raised in a monastery.

Momur

According to the French romance HUON DE BORDEAUX, the fairy realm ruled over by OBERON[1].

Mongibel

The name given to Mount ETNA on Sicily when it is mentioned in the Arthurian romances. It is mooted as the location to which MORGAN[1] Le Fay intended to bring the wounded ARTHUR to effect his cure. The king was reported as being seen alive underneath the mountain by Gervase of Tilbury and Caesarius of Heisterbach.

Mont du Chat

Apparently the Alpine site ('Mountain of the Cat' or 'Cat Mountain') of the Continental version of the CATH PALUG legend, where ARTHUR was said to have done battle with a large cat. A Savoyard was said to have met with Arthur's men one night in the vicinity of this mountain and to have been taken by them to a palace which had vanished by the morning.

Mor

According to Welsh tradition, the great-grandfather of MERLIN.

Moraine

The realm of MANGOUN, who sent CARADOC BRIEFBRAS a horn which would indicate the fidelity of the wife of the drinker.

Moraunt

During a fight with this king of IRELAND and his ally, Sir MORHOLT, TRISTAN received poisoned wounds that were healed by ISEULT[1] prior to her affair with him and her journey back to England to marry King MARK[2].

Morchades
Also ORCADES

The name by which MORGAUSE is referred to in DIU CRÔNE. This would seem to indicate that she originated from the ORKNEYS, one of the realms of her husband, LOT. It appears to come from the Latin *Orcades* – 'Orkneys' – and it is Morchades that is thought to have been the origin of Morgause. A variant, Orcades, appears for this character in some translations of *Diu Crône*, which would seem to suggest that some translators literally translated her name, while other sought, through the use of Morchades, to bring her name into closer alignment with Morgause.

Morda

The blind man placed by CERRIDWEN to kindle the fire under the cauldron stirred by GWION BACH in which she was brewing a magical potion. When Gwion Bach ran away after imbibing the potency of the brew, Cerridwen at first blamed Morda, and beat him so hard over the head with a billet of wood that one of his eyes fell out on to his cheek. When Morda protested his innocence Cerridwen stopped and saw that he was telling the truth, and that it had been Gwion Bach who had spoiled her work.

Mordrain

The baptismal name taken by EVELAKE.

Mo(r)dred

The incest-begotten nephew of ARTHUR, son of LOT, who usurped the throne once Arthur had left him as his regent, when he undertook his Continental campaign. Faking news of Arthur's death, Mordred had himself proclaimed king, and said that he would take GUINEVERE as his wife. She went to London and barricaded herself in the Tower of London, laying in sufficient provisions for a long siege. News reached Arthur of his nephew's treachery, and Mordred was duly defeated by Arthur on his return at the battle of RICHBOROUGH. He was again defeated at WINCHESTER and pursued to CORNWALL, where the two forces met for the third, and final battle, that of CAMLANN. Mordred was slain and Arthur taken off to the Isle of AVALON so that his mortal wounds might be healed. This was reported to be in the year AD 542. *Ly Myreur des Histoires* claimed that Mordred survived the last battle, only to be subsequently defeated by LANCELOT[2]. This work also says that Lancelot executed Guinevere, believing she had complied with Mordred's plans, and incarcerated the live Mordred in the same tomb as the dead queen, Mordred cannibalizing Guinevere before dying of starvation.

The ANNALES CAMBRIAE say that both Arthur and MEDRAWT (Mordred) perished at Camlann, but do not say that they were on opposing sides. This assertion does not come until later sources. GEOFFREY OF MONMOUTH says that Mordred was Arthur's nephew, the son of the king's sister ANNA and her husband, LOT. The idea that Mordred was the offspring of an incestuous relationship appears later, the earliest occurrence being in the

MORT ARTU. Sir Thomas MALORY also carries this theme, saying that Mordred was the result of a liaison between Arthur and his sister MORGAUSE, though Arthur did not know they were related. When he discovered the truth, he attempted to kill Mordred by having all the children born on the same day as Mordred set adrift. Mordred was shipwrecked, but survived and was fostered and raised by NABUR. The MABINOGION story of the DREAM OF RHONABWY makes Mordred Arthur's foster son as well as his nephew. WACE makes Mordred the brother of Guinevere, whom Arthur had seized and made his queen. The ALLITERATIVE MORTE ARTHURE further states that Mordred and Guinevere had a child.

As an adult, Mordred came to Arthur's court, was made a knight and was, for some time, the companion of Lancelot. When the ruling family of the ORKNEYS were in conflict with PELLINORE, Mordred took their side in the battle and killed LAMORAK, Pellinore's son. Early Welsh sources tend to portray Mordred as a heroic figure, rather than a villain, and Welsh tradition says he married CYWYLLOG, daughter of CAW, by whom he had two sons.

Morfran (ab Tegid)

The ugly and hapless son of CERRIDWEN and TEGID VOEL who was nicknamed AFAGDDU. One of the TWENTY-FOUR KNIGHTS of ARTHUR's court, he was said to have survived the final battle at CAMLANN on account of his extreme ugliness. Believing him to be a devil, no one dared attack him. Some sources name Afagddu and Morfran as independent characters, and in this case it would seem to be Afagddu who survived Camlann.

Morfudd

The twin sister of OWAIN in Welsh tradition. She was the lover of CYNON, the son of one of ARTHUR's warriors, CLYDNO.

Morgan

The name of at least two characters from Arthurian legend.

1 Morgan Le Fay (Morgan the Fairy). First referred to by GEOFFREY OF MONMOUTH in his VITA MERLINI as the chief of the nine *fays*, or fairies, living in the OTHERWORLD realm of AVALON. MERLIN and TALIESIN accompanied the dying ARTHUR on the barge steered by BARINTHUS to the Isle of APPLES following the battle of CAMLANN, there to be healed by Morgan Le Fay, the chief of nine sisters who included MORONOE, MAZOE, GLITEN, GLITONEA, CLITON, TYRONOE and THITIS. No mention is made at this early date of any relationship between Morgan and the dying king, but she is described as the shape-changing mistress of therapy, music and the arts who could fly through the air on enchanted wings. She also appears in this role as Queen ARGANTE (MARGANTE) in BRUT by LAYAMON. Later romances represent her as a fearsome witch queen, most probably due to Christian hostility, though it also seems that her later character may have been influenced by memories of the ancient Irish goddess, the MÓRRÍGHAN. In medieval romance she is Arthur's illegitimate half-sister who was educated in a convent, where she perversely spent her days studying the powers of evil. The ambi-valent LADY OF THE LAKE is also said to be another aspect of the same character.

Sir Thomas MALORY makes her the daughter of IGRAINE[1] by her first marriage, and thus half-sister to Arthur, while both the *Vulgate Merlin* and the HUTH-MERLIN make her the daughter of LOT, and thus Arthur's niece. She became a lady-in-waiting to GUINEVERE and fell in love with GIOMAR, Arthur's nephew. Guinevere, however, parted them and, as a result, according to some versions of the story, Morgan spread the seeds of doubt in Arthur's mind concerning the affair between Guinevere and LANCELOT[2]. She learned much of her magic from Merlin, though this seems to contradict earlier sources which say she learned these skills while a student in a convent. She was said to have married URIEN, according to traditional sources, and was the mother of OWAIN. Her lover was ACCOLON of GAUL, whom she had attempt to murder Arthur, though unsuccessfully. She was also said to have fallen in love with Lancelot and to have imprisoned him, but he managed to escape. Sir Thomas Malory, who seems to have drawn on many of the earlier sources, echoes most of these stories about her, stating that she was one of the queens on the barge which bore the dying Arthur to Avalon, rather than the queen to whom he was taken to be healed.

Her origin almost certainly lies with the goddess MODRON, who in turn had her origin in MATRONA. Modron was thought to have married the historical figure of Urien of RHEGED, and to have borne him two children, Owain and his twin sister MORFUDD. Though usually solely associated with the Arthurian legends, many commentators have drawn on the fact that she existed in earlier times. The *Roman de Troie*, published *c.* 1160, states that she was alive during the Greek siege of Troy, while PERCEFOREST places her in early BRITAIN. Her divinity also seems to

have been apparent to the romancers, for the anonymous author of SIR GAWAIN AND THE GREEN KNIGHT refers to her as 'Morgan the goddess' (line 2,452).

While it would appear that her name has Irish or Welsh origins, there is a popular belief that the name Morgan itself may be Breton, for there a belief was held in a class of water fairies called MARI-MORGANS, or simply MORGANS. One particular MORGAN, identified as AHES or DAHUT, was thought to have caused the destruction of the legendary city of YS. Her wickedness seems to have been caused through a combination of may different characteristics, though in origin she may have been an ambivalent figure whose character did nothing to inspire the authors of the Arthurian romances.

As the romances spread throughout the Continent, so did the character of Morgan Le Fay. One of the most famous sights connected with this fairy, good or evil, is a mirage that sometimes appears in the Straits of Messina, and which is locally referred to as FATA MORGANA, or in French as Le CHATEAU DE MORGAN LE FÉE. This mirage, which distorts both vertically and horizontally, is thought to give the image of one of Morgan's fairy palaces. French and Italian romance further embroider her character. In ARIOSTO'S ORLANDO FURIOSO she is given two sisters, MORG-ANETTA and LOGISTILLA, while other Italian romances gave her a daughter named PULZELLA GAIA. The Italian poet Torquato Tasso (1544–95) gave her three daughters, Morganetta, NIVETTA and CARVILIA, while the *Vita di Merlino* (an Italian version of the VITA MERLINI) stated that she was the illegitimate daughter of the duke of TINTAGEL. The thirteenth-century French romance LI JUS ADEN associates her with companions named MAGLORE and ARSILE.

2 The illegitimate daughter of the duke of TINTAGEL. While the Italian *Vita di Merlino* makes this character the same as MORGAN[1] Le Fay, she is quite separate and married NENTRES.

Morgan(s)

A class of Breton water fairies that are more usually known as Mari-Morgans.

Morgan the Black

A son of ARTHUR, according to the PETIT BRUT of Rauf de BOUN.

Morgan Frych

The father of MERLIN, according to Welsh tradition, he was sometimes identified as MADOG MORFRYN and sometimes said to have been a prince of GWYNEDD.

Morgan Mwynfawr

The owner of a magical form of transport, described as either a chair or a car, that would carry a person seated in it to wherever they wanted to go. This magical item was known as CADAIR, NEU CAR MORGAN MWYNFAWR, and is numbered among the THIRTEEN TREASURES of BRITAIN. Some commentators have incorrectly sought to identify the ownership of this enchanted mode of travel with MORGAN[1] Le Fay.

Morgan the Red

One of the numerous sons attributed to ARTHUR.

Morgan Tud

The name of ARTHUR's physician.

Morganetta

According to the poet Torquato Tasso (1544–95), the daughter of MORGAN[1] Le Fay.

Morgan(n)a

A variant of MORGAN[1] Le Fay that has found popularity in later works, film and television.

Morgannwg

A minor kingdom of WALES of which CARADOC was alleged to have been the progenitor of the royal line.

Morgannwg, Iolo

The bardic name of Edward Williams (1747–1826). His renditions of Arthurian legends are held to be most unreliable for, being a bard, he undoubtedly felt he could improve on the material he used as his sources.

Morgause

Half-sister to ARTHUR, wife of LOT and mother of GAWAIN[1], GAHERIS, AGRAVAIN, GARETH and MORDRED. Various romances credit her with a number of affairs. The ENFACES GAUVAIN makes Lot her page, with whom she had a brief liaison, which resulted in the birth of Gawain. Sir Thomas MALORY, however, makes her Lot's queen, her usual role, but says that she had a brief affair with Arthur, who did not know they were related, and subsequently gave birth to Mordred. When her son Gaheris found her in bed with LAMORAK, the son of PELLINORE, following the death of Lot at the hands of her lover's father, her son killed her.

It appears that Morgause may not have been the original name of this character, and may simply be a territorial designation, much in the same way as her husband's name Lot means 'LOTHIAN-ruler'. This seems likely, for in DIU CRÔNE she is referred to as ORCADES or MOR-CHADES, which seems to indicate that she originally hailed from the ORKNEYS, which was one of Lot's kingdoms (the Latin for Orkneys = Orcades). The variant Morchades is thought to have given rise to Morgause. In Malory, the wife of Lot is called Anna, the sister of Arthur, while in DE ORTU WALUUANII, Morgause is replaced again by Anna, though this time in the role given in the *Enfaces Gauvain*, the mother of Gawain following an intrigue with her page, Lot.

Morgen

A variant of MORGAN[1] Le Fay.

Morghe

A variant of MORGAN[1] Le Fay used by Jean d'Outremeuse of Liège in *Ly Myreur des Histoires*, written sometime prior to 1400.

Morholt

During a fight with this giant knight, who is also known as MARHALT, and his ally MORAUNT (MORHAUS), king of IRELAND, who demanded a tribute from his uncle, King MARK[2] of Cornwall, TRISTAN received poisoned wounds that were healed by ISEULT[1]. It was this that led Tristan to report Iseult's beauty to his uncle, and ultimately led to their famous yet ill-fated affair.

Moriaen

The son of AGLOVALE by a Moorish princess, according to the Dutch romance *Moriaen*. Aglovale left the princess before the birth of his son, but the couple were eventually reunited thanks to Moriaen. It appears that this romance was based on an earlier French romance in which PERCEVAL[2] featured as the father of Moriaen.

Moroie Mor

According to Gaelic tradition, the son of ARTHUR, known as the FOOL OF THE FOREST, who was born at DUMBARTON.

Moronoe

A sister of MORGAN[1] Le Fay.

Mórríg(h)an

Known simply as the Mórríghan, this character appears in Irish legend and mythology as the red-haired goddess of battle and procreation, often in triune form, her name meaning 'Phantom Queen'. Her other aspects were Nemhain and Badhbh, meaning 'Frenzy' and 'Crow' or 'Raven' respectively. She combines the threefold energies of life and death, sexuality and conflict in one terryfying image. Though Irish in this form, she was known throughout the Celtic world and is thought by some to have been the prototype for MORGAN[1] Le Fay.

Mort Artu

A part of the French VULGATE VERSION of Arthurian romance.

Mortaise

A lake or sea beside which LANCELOT[2], during his quest for the Holy GRAIL, lay down and, in his sleep, received a vision that told him to enter the first ship he came to. He did so and was joined about a month later by his son, GALAHAD[1], and together they continued their quest.

Morte Arthure

A Middle English Arthurian poem by Thomas HEYWOOD (c. 1574–1641) that was written towards the close of the sixteenth century.

Moruawr

Variant of MORVAWR found in the descent of ARTHUR and LLYR contained in the Mostyn MS 117.

Morvawr

Also MORUAWR, TURMWR MORVAWR

This character appears in a number of Welsh pedigrees as a paternal ancestor of ARTHUR.

Morvran (ab Tegid)

A variant of MORFRAN AB TEGID.

Morwen

The wife of IVOR the Huntsman who fostered and raised MERIADOC.

Morydd

The grandfather of MERLIN, according to a traditional Welsh genealogy.

Mote of Mark

Cornish fortress that has yielded pottery dating from c. AD 500, leading some to propose it as a possible location for the encampment of a mighty chieftain who might be cognate with the historical figure who has, over the centuries, become known as King ARTHUR.

Moys

A follower of JOSEPH OF ARIMATHEA, according to ROBERT DE BORON. He wished to sit in the SIEGE PERILOUS at the ROUND TABLE, but the earth opened and swallowed him for his presumptuous behaviour.

Mu(i)rcheartach

An historical fifth-century Irish king ruling at Tara who is thought to have been the origin of the various characters named MARHAUS and MARHALT in the Arthurian tales.

Mule sans Frein

A damsel brought this bridleless mule to ARTHUR's court and requested a knight should be dispatched to find the missing tackle. KAY was sent on this quest, but failed. Subsequently GAWAIN[1] completed the task.

Mule sans Frein

A twelfth-century French poem concerning the quest of GAWAIN[1] to locate a missing bridle. The author is usually given as Paien de Maisière, but this could be a pseudonym.

Munsalvaesche

According to WOLFRAM VON ESCHENBACH, this was the name of the mountain where the GRAIL was kept. The name, meaning 'wild mountain', probably derives from Wildenberc, Wolfram von Eschenbach's home, modern Wehlenberg near Ansbach, and shows his attempt to claim the Grail for his home country.

Mureif

The realm of URIEN, according to GEOFFREY OF MONMOUTH. Some think that it may be identifiable with Monreith, but it is usually taken to refer to Moray.

Muryel

The father of GRUDYEN.

Mustennin

A curious variant of KUSTENNIN found in one version of ARTHUR's paternal line of descent from LLYR contained within the Welsh BONEDD YR ARWR. It is probably due to a simple translative error.

Mwys Gwyddno

The hamper or basket that belonged to GWYDDNO and said to be one of the THIRTEEN TREASURES of BRITAIN. It had the power to turn any meat placed in or on it into enough to feed 100 people.

Mynydd Fyrddin

A hill at Longtown, Herefordshire, which is considered to be one of the many possible sites where MERLIN is buried.

Myrddin

The original Welsh name for the wizard MERLIN. According to early Welsh poems, which seem to have had only fragmentary influence on later Arthurian writers, Myrddin fought at the battle of ARTHURET, where his lord GWENDDOLEU was killed. Grief for his fallen master sent him mad. He spent the rest of his life as a hermit living wild in the forest of CELYDDON (Caledonia), lamenting Gwenddoleu's death. In his frenzy he acquired the gift of prophecy. This story relates Myrddin to the Irish king Suibne Geilt, from whose legend the tale may be derived, although Myrddin is first referred to in the tenth-century poem *Armes Prydein*, while the *Buile Suibne*, which recounts the Irish legend, is probably two centuries older. It is hard to tell which tale influenced the other, or if both derive from independent sources. It has been suggested that Myrddin derives from a mistaken analysis of *Caerfyrddin* (CARMARTHEN). In other early Welsh poems he is called LLALLAWC and LLALLOGAN VYRDIN.

Myrddin Emrys

The full name of MYRDDIN, better known simply as MERLIN.

Myrddin Wyllt

Living in SCOTLAND at the same time as MYRDDIN EMRYS, this character has sometimes been incorrectly identified as the historical person who became better as known as MERLIN. However, the true wizard of the Arthurian legends was the Welsh Myrddin Emrys, who was born and raised in CARMARTHEN.

Nabon

The giant ruler of the Isle of SERVAGE who gave his realm to SEGWARIDES, and was killed by TRISTAN.

Nabur

The foster father of MORDRED who found the shipwrecked infant after he had been set adrift by ARTHUR in an attempt to kill him.

Nadus

According to some sources, a king of SYRIA during the Arthurian period.

Nantes

Situated in western France, on the River Loire, the seat of ARTHUR's court, according to WOLFRAM VON ESCHENBACH. Arthurian legend makes Nantes, along with VANNES, the realm of CARADOC, while Nantes alone is also made the realm of RIVALIN[2].

Narpus

An ancestor of GALAHAD[1], he was the father of NASCIEN[2].

Narsinga

A kingdom whose ruler was the father of VERONA, whose carbuncle was needed by MELORA as one of the items required to free ORLANDO from the enchantment that held him captive.

Nascien

The name of at least three characters from the Arthurian legends.

1 The son-in-law of EVELAKE (MORDRAIN) who was blinded by coming too close to the Holy GRAIL, but cured again by drops of blood from a BLEEDING LANCE (presumably the LANCE OF LONGINUS). Originally called SERAPHE, it seems that Nascien was his Christian name. When Mordrain died, he was blamed and thrown into prison, but was miraculously rescued and placed on the TURNING ISLAND, where he saw SOLOMON's ship. He attempted to take King DAVID's sword, but it broke in his unworthy hands. Eventually Nascien came to BRITAIN.

2 The son of NARPUS, a descendant of NASCIEN[1] and an ancestor of GALAHAD[1].

3 The name of a hermit who sent GALAHAD[1] to ARTHUR[1]. Some commentators make the assumption that he is the same as NASCIEN[2] but this is unfounded.

Nasiens

Named as one of the TWENTY-FOUR KNIGHTS of King ARTHUR's court, it seems likely that this is a simple variant of

NASCIEN, the most likely contender being Nascien[1].

Natalon

According to some sources, a king of SYRIA during the Arthurian period.

Nathaliodus

A person of no background whom, so BOECE relates, UTHER made a commander. As a direct result of this commission, half of BRITAIN fell into SAXON hands.

Nef de Joie

The 'Ship of Joy' which was made by MERLIN and used by MABON[2] to bring TRISTAN to him. Appearing in French romances, Merlin stipulated that the ship was to be destroyed following ARTHUR's final battle, but whether or not it actually was remains a mystery.

Nefyn

The daughter of BRYCHAN who married CYNFARCH and became the mother of URIEN.

Nemedius

Irish tradition states that the son of Nemedius was the eponym of BRITAIN, as he was apparently called 'Britain' and settled on the island. This, however, is not the accepted manner by which Britain gained its name.

Nennius

Welsh writer (*fl.* AD 769) who was reputedly the author of the clumsily put together Latin work HISTORIA BRITONUM, which purports to give a history of BRITAIN from the time of JULIUS CAESAR until towards the end of the seventh century. The book gives a mythical account of the origins of the Britons, the settlement of the SAXONS and King ARTHUR's twelve victories.

Nentres

Although one of the eleven rulers who rebelled against the youthful ARTHUR at the start of his reign, this ruler of GARLOT married ELAINE[4], Arthur's half-sister and eventually became a KNIGHT OF THE ROUND TABLE.

Nereja

The female emissary of the beleagured Queen AMENE. She was sent to ARTHUR's court to obtain help in defending her territory from the evil ROAZ, who had already almost totally overrun it.

Nero

The brother of RIENCE who fought against, but was defeated by, ARTHUR.

Nestor

1 The brother of King BAN of BRITTANY and the father of BLEOBERIS who was accidentally killed by his son.
2 The son of BLEOBERIS and thus grandson of NESTOR[1].

Netor

The king of BULGARIA in Arthurian romance.

Neustria

The duchy ascribed to BEDIVERE[2] by GEOFFREY OF MONMOUTH.

Nicodemus

The cadaver of this biblical character was first said to have been kept at CAMELOT, and subsequently at the GRAIL CASTLE. Finally it was said to have accompanied PERCEVAL[2] on board the ship on which he made his final journey.

Nimiane

An early version of NIMUE/NINIANE/VIVIANE/VIVIEN/VIVIENNE, the LADY OF THE LAKE.

Nimue

The lover of MERLIN and one of the names applied to the LADY OF THE LAKE, who is also known as NIMIANE, NINEVE, NINIANE, VIVIANE, VIVIEN and VIVIENNE. Merlin became so infatuated with her that he taught her his magic arts, but she turned against him and imprisoned him in a tower, cave, tomb or oak tree where she could visit him, but from which he could not escape. It was said that the enchantment that held Merlin prisoner could be broken only when ARTHUR once more reigned. Having imprisoned Merlin, she became the lover of PELLEAS. Her father was named as DIONES, a vavasour – holder of feudal lands but lesser in rank than a baron. Her name appears to have a mythological origin, possibly deriving from the Irish Niamh or the Welsh RHIANNON.

Nine Sisters

The collective term by which the sisters of MORGAN[1] Le Fay, joint rulers of AVALON, are referred to. It is not certain whether or not all are named, but various sources suggest that this is the correct number.

Nineve

A variant of NIMUE. Some sources, however, make her an entirely separate character, saying that she was the daughter of a Sicilian siren.

Niniane

A variant of NIMUE.

Niobe

The lover of SAGREMOR.

Nivetta

According to the Italian poet Torquato Tasso (1544–95), a daughter of MORGAN[1] Le Fay.

Nodens, -ons

The Romano-Celtic version of NUDD, he is also to be identified with the Irish Nuadha and the Welsh LLUD LLAW EREINT. Occasionally he is equated with the Roman Neptune, making him a sea deity, and also sometimes with a river god, so he is definitely connected with water and healing.

Norhout

MELIODAS[1], the father of TRISTAN, was killed by soldiers under the control of the count who ruled this region.

Northgalis

An Arthurian kingdom that appears to be identifiable with North WALES, but which might, at least at times, have been used to identify a north Briton kingdom, say STRATHCLYDE, for it was said to have been near to NORTHUMBERLAND. The ESTOIRE DEL SAINTE GRAAL names an early king of this realm as COUDEL, who fell while fighting the Christians. WOLFRAM VON ESCHENBACH makes its ruler HERZELOYDE, while it is, elsewhere, given kings named CRADELMENT and ALOIS. The kingdom may have its origin in the realm rule by a king named CADWALLON, said to have ruled the VENDOTI (according to GEOFFREY OF MONMOUTH) during the traditional Arthurian period.

Northumberland

A realm in northern England that, in the Arthurian romances, is variously ruled by the kings PELLINORE, CLARION, CADOR[2] and DETORS.

Norway

Although it is impossible to say how complete a kingdom Norway was during the Arthurian period, the country possibly being divided between many smaller kings and chieftains, the country was, according to GEOFFREY OF MONMOUTH, ruled by King SICHELM, who bequeathed the realm to LOT. ARTHUR had to enforce Lot's right to the throne, for it had been usurped by RICULF. Geoffrey of Monmouth further states that the king of Norway, ODBRICT at this time, supported Arthur at CAMLANN, but met his own death that day.

Nuc

The father of YDER who fought his son, both parties being ignorant of the other's identity. However, during the course of the fight they recognized each other and stopped. Nuc eventually married Yder's mother, suggesting that this may, in part, have been the reason for the fight. Nuc is named as the duke of ALEMAIGNE, by which either ALBANY (SCOTLAND) or GERMANY is intended.

Nudd

The popularized and shortened version of GWYNN AP NUDD, Master of the WILD HUNT and Lord of the Dead. A major Celtic deity, he was probably derived from the Irish Nuadha, which had, in turn, led to the Romano-Celtic variant of NODONS.

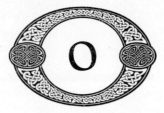

Oberon

1 The king of the fairies who, according to the thirteenth-century French romance HUON DE BORDEAUX was the illegitimate son of JULIUS CAESAR by MORGAN[1] Le Fay, ruling a kingdom called MOMUR. Other sources say that he was originally an excessively ugly dwarf by the name of TRONC, but the fairies took pity on him, removed all traces of his former ugliness and gave him a kingdom. Shortly before his death, Oberon resigned his throne to HUON of Bordeaux. This angered ARTHUR, who had retired there after his days on earth came to an end and fully expected to succeed Oberon. His protests were firmly quashed by Oberon, who threatened to turn him into a werewolf. A short time later Oberon died.

He first appeared in English literature in a prose translation of the earlier French romance c. 1534. Possibly the best-known use of this character is in A MIDSUMMER NIGHT'S DREAM by William SHAKESPEARE. In this Oberon is shown as a magical figure, married to TITANIA and accompanied by an impish servant, PUCK, Titania does not figure widely in Arthurian literature, though she does appear in two more modern works: *The Masque of Gwendolen* (1816) by Reginald Heber and *The Quest of Merlin* (1891) by Richard Hovey.

Oberon himself is also a fleeting character within the mainstream Arthurian sources. He was said in one to have been the companion of TRISTAN's son YSAIE THE SAD, and in another to have been the father of ROBIN GOODFELLOW by a human girl. SPENSER, in his famous poem THE FAERIE QUEENE, makes him the father of GLORIANA, with whom ARTHUR fell in love.

2 A non-Arthurian medieval French romance about OGIER, OGIER LE DANOIS, names Oberon as a brother of MORGAN[1] Le Fay.

Obie

A daughter of Duke LYPPAUT, sister to OBILOT. She rejected the advances of King MELJANZ of LIZ, which led to a war between her father and the king. Peace was finally restored through the efforts of her younger sister OBILOT.

Obilot

A daughter of Duke LYPPAUT, younger sister of OBIE, who, while still a child, had a pretend relationship with Sir GAWAIN[1], styling herself as his 'lady'.

Octa

A son of HENGIST who is thought to be identifiable with OSLA BIG-KNIFE.

Octavius

The Duke of GWENT, according to GEOFFREY OF MONMOUTH. He is to be identified with EVDAF.

Ocvran

The father of GUINEVERE, also called GOGVRAN, according to Welsh tradition.

Odbrict

The king of NORWAY who was said to have been a supporter of ARTHUR at the final battle of CAMLANN, but lost his life in that fight.

Odgar

The king of IRELAND during the expedition mounted by ARTHUR to locate and procure the cauldron of DIWRNACH, who was Odgar's supervisor.

Odyar Franc

The steward at King ARTHUR's court.

Oeng(h)us

Oenghus mac ind Og was the son of the supreme Irish god, the DAGHDHA, and is thought to have been the prototype of the Celtic deity MABON[1]/MAPONOS. An alternative school of thought makes him an historical king of Cashel, southern IRELAND, whose death is said to have occurred in AD 490. Both have been considered to be the original of King ANGUISH who appears in the Arthurian romances.

Oesc

A king of KENT who was said to have been the son or grandson of HENGIST and who

ruled during the traditional Arthurian period. It also seems possible that the name is a variant of AESC.

Ogier

The son of GODFREY, a Danish duke and the hero of the Carolingian (AD 751–987) romance OGIER LE DANOIS. At Ogier's birth, MORGAN[1] Le Fay said that one day she would take him away with her to AVALON. This she eventually did, and he stayed there for 200 years before returning to fight for Christendom. Afterwards he went back to Avalon, where he and Morgan Le Fay were said to have had a son, MEURVIN.

This story appears to be reflected, in part, in Ly Myreur des Histoires, written some time before 1400 by Jean d'Outremeuse of Liège. This says that, in AD 896, Ogier was shipwrecked some nine days' sail from Cyprus and, washed ashore, did battle with a CAPALU and other monsters. Having defeated them, he was attacked by ARTHUR and GAWAIN[1], but was rescued by angels. Welcomed by MORGHE (Morgan Le Fay) to her palace, he lived happily there with her, and in peace with both Arthur and Gawain.

His prototype in history may have been OTKER, the advocate of Liège in Charlemagne's time, but the Danes themselves regarded Ogier as the Danish hero HOLGER. Charlemagne features in his story, as it was said that this king presented him with TRISTAN's sword, which Ogier called CURETANA. Danish tradition, which appears to draw heavily on Arthurian themes, says that Ogier and his men are sleeping in a cave in DENMARK, or that he perpetually wanders through the Ardennes. According to Sir John Mandeville's Travels (1356–57), Ogier was an ancestor of PRESTOR JOHN.

Ogier le Danois

Important Carolingian romance that details the life of the Danish duke OGIER.

Ogof Lanciau Eryri

A cave in north WALES where ARTHUR's men are said to be asleep, awaiting their king's return. They were supposed to have been seen there by a shepherd who fled when he almost awakened them.

Ogof Myrddin

A hill near CARMARTHEN that is more popularly known as MERLIN'S HILL.

Ogo'r Dinas

A cave near Llandebie that has been mooted as one of the many possible last resting places of ARTHUR (cf. CRAIG-Y-DINAS).

Old Table

The name given to the ROUND TABLE when it was in the ownership of UTHER. He too used it to seat the knights of his company, who numbered fifty, one of the best knights of this order being Sir BRUNOR. It is thought that the Old Table found its way into many Italian romances, where it is still mentioned, but of the romances that concerned this use of the Round Table none appears to have survived.

Olwen

The daughter of the chief giant YSPADD-ADEN whose name is thought to mean 'white track', though an argument has been presented to support derivation from the word olwyn – 'wheel'. She is the heroine of the MABINOGION story of CULHWCH AND OLWEN, and also of a Welsh folktale EINION AND OLWEN in which a shepherd, EINION, travelled to the OTHERWORLD to marry OLWEN. They had a son whom they named TALIESIN. It is worth comparing this story with that of Culhwch and Olwen which is told under CULHWCH.

Olyroun

The father-in-law of LANVAL who was a fairy king living on an enchanted island.

Ontzlake

One of King ARTHUR's knights and the younger brother of the evil Sir DAMAS.

Optima

According to Welsh tradition, one of the names applied to MERLIN's mother, the other being ALDAN.

Orainglais

An Irish princess who was said to have borne a son to Sir SAGREMOR.

Orcades
Also MORCHADES

Appearing in some translations of DIU CRÔNE, this alternative for MORGAUSE appears to have been derived from Orcades, the Latin for her husband, LOT's realm of the ORKNEYS. Some commentators think that this was the first translation of her name, and that the variant Morchades came later in an attempt to bring her name more into line with Morgause. This theory is, however, open to speculation.

Orcant

The ruler of the ORKNEYS who was converted to Christianity by PETRUS, a follower or disciple of JOSEPH OF ARIMATHEA. It would appear that this name is derived from the Latin name for his realm, *Orcades*, and may simply be a title rather than a personal name.

Orguelleuse

A proud lady who appears in the works of both CHRÉTIEN DE TROYES and WOLFRAM VON ESCHENBACH, and who maintained that the only way to gain fulfilment in courtly love was through persistence of courtship and deeds of outrageous courage. WOLFRAM VON ESCHENBACH suggests that she had an intrigue with AMFORTAS which culminated in his receiving the wound which so incapacitated him. PERCEVAL[2] once spurned her attentions, and she finally gave her love to GAWAIN[1].

Oriant

The son of MEURVIN, according to OGIER LE DANOIS, the son of MORGAN[1] Le Fay and OGIER, and hence a nephew of King ARTHUR.

Orilus

The Duke of LALANDER and husband of JESCHUTÉ.

Orimonde

The daughter of the Amir of Persia who became the wife of MARC, son of YSAIE THE SAD and grandson of TRISTAN.

Orkney(s)

The Orkney Islands form part of the kingdom ruled over by LOT, according to Sir Thomas MALORY, though this seems to be a later development. GEOFFREY OF MONMOUTH, writing at an earlier date, makes Lot the king of LOTHIAN who also becomes the king of NORWAY following the voluntary submission of GUNPHAR. This association seems to be as a direct result of the numerous Norse connections with the Orkneys. The Latin for Orkneys, *Orcades*, appears to have given rise to ORCADES, an alternative name for MORGAUSE, as well as ORCANT, who was described as a king of Orkney. During the sixth century the Orkneys seem to have been organized into some form of kingdom that was subject to Pictish kings.

Orlando

The son of the king of Thessaly and lover of MELORA, ARTHUR's daughter.

Orlando Furioso

Italian Carolingian romance by Ludovico ARIOSTO that forms a sequel to the unfinished ORLANDO INNAMORATO of BOIARDO and was published in 1532. Featuring some Arthurian material, the poem describes the unrequited love of ORLANDO for ANGELICA, set against the war between the SARACENS and Christians during Charlemagne's reign. It influenced SHAKESPEARE, Byron and Milton, and is considered to be the perfect poetic expression of the Italian Renaissance.

Orlando Innamorato

Unfinished epic narrative poem, written between 1441 and 1494 by Mattheo Maria BOIARDO, in which the Charlemagne romances were recast into '*ottava rima*'. Being incomplete, this work gave rise to the ORLANDO FURIOSO of Ludovico ARIOSTO.

Orribes

A giant who, according to Spanish romance, wrought havoc in BRITAIN before he was killed by TRISTAN THE YOUNGER.

Orwen

The sister of MERIADOC, she was abducted and subsequently married by UTHER.

Osla Big-Knife

Possibly in origin OCTA, the son or grandson of the SAXON HENGIST. He features in the MABINOGION story of the DREAM OF RHONABWY as an adversary of ARTHUR at BADON. However, another source says that he was a companion of Arthur during the hunt for the boar TWRCH TRWYTH. During this episode, the scabbard for his knife, BRONLLAVYN SHORT BROAD, which could be used as a bridge, filled with water and dragged him under.

Osmond

Appearing in DRYDEN's *King Arthur* as a SAXON sorcerer, Osmond treacherously tried to force EMMELINE into his clutches, but ended up having the tables turned on him and being confined to a dungeon.

Ossetes

Descendants of the ALANS, a SARMATIAN people who still inhabit the Caucasus today. They tell a story that is very similar to the death of ARTHUR. In this their hero, BATRADZ, received a mortal wound and, knowing that his time was limited, commanded that his sword be thrown into some nearby water.

Oswald

The king of KENT who appears in DRYDEN's KING ARTHUR as an opponent of ARTHUR who, like the king, loved EMMELINE. They fought for the lady's favours, Arthur winning and subsequently expelling Oswald from BRITAIN. He is a purely fictional character, as there is no king of Kent called Oswald known to history.

Otherworld, The

Although sometimes given a single name, such as ANNWFN, or later AVALON, the Otherworld is often conceived of as comprising several realms. It is not simply or primarily the world of the dead, although it undoubtedly has connections with the realm usually referred to as the Underworld. It is more a paradisaical fairyland, whose rulers feast their guests from magical cauldrons. The story of ARTHUR travelling to the Otherworld to obtain such a magic cauldron gives various descriptions of parts of the realm. In one place it is cold and forbidding, while in another a fountain flows, and no one knows sickness or old age.

Otker

The advocate of Liège in Charlemagne's time who is thought might be the historical prototype of OGIER.

Owain
Also YVAIN

An historical character, the son of URIEN of RHEGED, whom he succeeded. He has subsequently passed into the realms of myth and legend, and has countless associations with ARTHUR. Although he certainly lived later than the traditional Arthurian period – he was said to have heavily defeated the British c. AD 593

– both he and his father have been drawn into Arthurian legend. In this role he is the son of Urien by Arthur's sister, MORGAN[1] Le Fay, who appears to have her origins in the goddess MODRON, whom some Welsh sources name as the mother of Owain. Welsh tradition made him the husband of PENARWAN and DENW, the latter being a niece of Arthur. The MABINOGION story of the DREAM OF RHONABWY has Owain and Arthur playing GWYDDBWYLL – a type of board game – during which Owain's ravens fought with Arthur's men and were almost defeated. However, Owain raised his flag and the ravens set about their opponents with renewed vigour.

French romance gives us the most details about the Arthurian Owain, particularly the French romance *Yvain* by CHRÉTIEN DE TROYES. In this Owain learns of a wondrous spring or fountain in the forest of BROCELIANDE, where he goes, defeating ESCLADOS, the knight who protected it. He chased the knight back to his castle and there the latter died of his wounds. Owain tried to follow the knight into his castle, but became entangled in the portcullis. He was rescued by LUNETE, the sister of LAUDINE who was the widow of the slain knight. Owain fell in love with Laudine, and her sister persuaded her that she should marry him. When Arthur and his followers arrived at the castle, Owain went with them, but promised that he would return to his wife within a year. However, he did not keep an eye on the time and failed to honour his promise. When he did return, Laudine rejected him and he went mad, taking to living wild in the forest. His sanity returned only when an enchanted ointment was administered, after which he went to the help of a lion that was fighting a serpent. The lion then became his constant companion and earned Owain his nickname, the KNIGHT OF THE LION. He is also named as one of the TWENTY-FOUR KNIGHTS of King Arthur's court.

Owain

A Welsh prose romance thought to date from the thirteenth century that is found in the MABINOGION and concerns OWAIN, the son of URIEN.

Owain the Bastard

The half-brother of OWAIN whom URIEN fathered on the wife of his seneschal, or steward. A KNIGHT OF THE ROUND TABLE, he was noted for his common sense, but was killed in a joust by GAWAIN[1], who had failed to recognize him.

Pa gur

A famous Welsh poem that tells how Sir KAY travelled to Anglesey with a view to killing lions, especially preparing himself for an encounter with the CATH PALUG, a monstrous feline creature.

Padarn Redcoat

The owner of a coat, known as PAIS PADARN, that was one of the THIRTEEN TREASURES of BRITAIN.

Padstow

A Cornish town that, according to Henry VIII's librarian, Leland, was the birthplace of ARTHUR.

Pair Drynog

The cauldron of DRYNOG in which only the meat of a brave man would boil. It is numbered among the THIRTEEN TREASURES of BRITAIN.

Pais Padarn

The coat or cloak of PADARN REDCOAT that rendered the wearer invisible and was one of the THIRTEEN TREASURES of BRITAIN.

Palace Adventurous

A palace within Castle CARBONEK that housed the Holy GRAIL.

Palamedes

A pagan knight, the son of King ASTLABOR (ESCLABOR), he fell hopelessly in love with ISEULT[1]. When TRISTAN came to IRELAND, he found Palamedes vying for Iseult's hand, but he defeated him in single combat. Some time later Palamedes obtained her through deception, but Tristan rescued her. Palamedes gave chase and caught up with the lovers. He would have fought Tristan again had not Iseult intervened. However, they later met again and during the course of this fight, Palamedes's sword was knocked from his hand, and in that moment, it was said, he became a Christian. The fight was stopped, never to be resumed, and Palamedes eventually became the Duke of Provence.

Palante

A cousin of TRISTAN, the husband of the Duchess of Milan, who, following Tristan's death, invaded CORNWALL but was eventually killed by Tristan's one-time rival for ISEULT[1], PALAMEDES.

Palug

The father of the sons who, according to Welsh tradition, lived on Anglesey and saved the CATH PALUG, the monstrous feline offspring of HENWEN, and raised it.

Pamlart

A descendant of BAN who is numbered among the contenders for the killer of King MARK[2] of Cornwall.

Pandragon

A name or title given to AMBROSIUS AURELIUS in the *Vulgate Merlin*. It is, without doubt, a simple variant of PENDRAGON.

Pandragus

The father of illegitimate twins by LIBAN, a daughter of King BAN.

Pandrasus

A Greek king who had enslaved a group of Trojan exiles. He was fought, and defeated, by BRUTUS, who then claimed the hand of Pandrasus's reluctant daughter, IGNOGE. Brutus also compelled Pandrasus to release his Trojan slaves, and to equip and provision them to enable them to leave Greece.

Pannenoisance

The name given to ARTHUR's capital in PERLESVAUS.

Pant

The father of LANCELOT[2], according to ULRICH VON ZARZIKHOVEN, who further states that he was the king of GENNEWIS and was killed in a rebellion.

Paris

A Frenchman and friend of ARTHUR in the French romance *Ly Myreur des Histoires*. He received the kingdom of SAYNES from Arthur, who bestowed it and the deposed king's daughter on Paris after he had conquered the kingdom. It is thought that Paris may be identical to the French King Paris mentioned in the MABINOGION story of CULHWCH AND OLWEN who, along with another French king, IONA, was said to have been at Arthur's court.

Paris, Battle of

The battle at which ARTHUR and HOEL[1] defeated the Roman tribune FROLLO. Within nine years Arthur had conquered all of GAUL and held a court in Paris, establishing the government of that kingdom on a legal footing.

Parlan

One of the various contenders for the role of the MAIMED KING. His story says that he found SOLOMON's ship and attempted to draw the sword which he found on board, but, being unworthy, he was wounded through the thighs with a lance. This, however, was not the act or the wounding which turned his realm into the WASTE LAND of the GRAIL legends.

Parmenie

The realm of TRISTAN's father with its capital at CANVEL, according to GOTTFRIED VON STRASSBURG. It is simply a variant of ARMENIE (or vice versa), the name applied to the same territory by THOMAS. Some sources name the ruler of Parmenie as RIVALIN[1].

Parrot

ARTHUR's garrulous pet which was originally owned by LION THE MERCILESS, who lost his arm while fighting Arthur. Attended by a dwarf, the parrot was said to have gone with Arthur on a couple of his quests.

Parsifal

The German version, along with PARZIVAL, of Sir PERCEVAL[2].

Parsifal

An opera by Richard Wagner that is based on the legends surrounding PERCEVAL[2] and was first performed in 1882, just one year before the sudden death of the composer.

Partinal

The killer of the brother of the FISHER KING, GOON DESERT. Probably a knight, he later fell at the hands of PERCEVAL[2].

Parzival

The German version, along with PARSIFAL, of Sir PERCEVAL[2].

Parzival

A thirteenth-century work by WOLFRAM VON ESCHENBACH recounting Arthurian tales, particularly those concerning Sir PERCEVAL[2].

Pascen

A son of URIEN of RHEGED.

Paschent

The third son of VORTIGERN who fled to GERMANY after his father had been ousted by AMBROSIUS AURELIUS, but later returned with a large army. He was soundly defeated. He then fled to IRELAND, where he obtained the help of King GILLOMANIUS for his second invasion attempt. This time he had more success, for Ambrosius Aurelius was sick and EOPA, a SAXON in the employ of Paschent, disguised as a doctor, gained entry to the ailing king and administered a poisoned potion from which he died.

Passaleon

The son of ESTONNE, LORD OF THE SCOTTISH WILDERNESS according to PERCE-FOREST, which further said he lived in pre-Roman BRITAIN. He was given to MORGAN[1] Le Fay by ZEPHYR and became the lover of her daughter, and through her an ancestor of MERLIN. He killed BRUYANT the Faithless, who had previously killed Estonne, his father. While still a child he was said to have been given a tour of Tartarus (the Underworld of classical Greek mythology), presumably by Morgan Le Fay.

Passelande

According to BÉROUL, this was the name of King ARTHUR's horse.

Paternus, Saint

An abbot and bishop said to have associations with DYFED. He passed into the Arthurian legends through a single instance when it was said that ARTHUR had tried to procure Paternus's tunic. The ground opened and swallowed the king, and he was released only after he had begged forgiveness and repented of his sin. The traditional pedigree of CUNEDDA makes Paternus the son of TACITUS and father of AETURNUS, but it appears that this character may be a separate one to Saint Paternus.

Patrick the Red

According to the PETIT BRUT of Rauf de BOUN, a son of ARTHUR.

Patrise

An Irish knight (his name possibly starting life as Patrick) who was mistakenly poisoned by Sir PINEL when the latter was in fact attempting to poison GAWAIN[1]. GUINEVERE was at first accused of his murder, but the truth was discovered by NIMUE.

Patrocles

According to the Icelandic SAGA OF TRISTRAM, the paternal grandfather of TRISTAN.

Pedivere

A knight who murdered his own wife. He was sent by LANCELOT[2] with her dead body to beg forgiveness of GUINEVERE, and eventually became a hermit.

Pedrawd

The father of BEDIVERE[2] (BEDWYR) in Welsh tradition.

Pedwar Marchog ar Hugan Llys Arthur

Important fifteenth-century, or earlier, Welsh work which gives a list of knights at ARTHUR's court. These knights, thought to represent a company formed before the KNIGHTS OF THE ROUND TABLE, are collectively known as the TWENTY-FOUR KNIGHTS.

Pela Orso

The Italian poem *Pulzella Gaia* makes this the name of the castle of MORGAN[1] Le Fay.

Peleur

According to the Welsh Y SAINT GRAAL, the name of the owner of the GRAIL CASTLE.

Pelias

Named as being an early ruler of LIONES.

Pellam

The king of LISTINOISE whose brother, the invisible knight Sir GARLON, has been killed by BALIN. Pellam, determined to exact his revenge, fought with Balin and, during the course of the fight, succeeded in breaking Balin's sword. While Pellam was chasing Balin around the castle, Balin came across the LANCE OF LONGINUS and, taking it up, he stabbed Pellam with it. This was called the DOLOROUS STROKE, which was said to have been responsible for creating the WASTE LAND of the GRAIL legends.

Pelleam

The name given to the MAIMED KING in French romance. It appears to be a simple variation of PELLAM, though other names are also given to this character in the GRAIL legends, such as PELLEHAN.

Pelleas

An unfortunate knight, one of the KNIGHTS OF THE ROUND TABLE, who became the progenitor of a one-sided love affair with ETTARD, who did not reciprocate his feelings. GAWAIN[1] said he would act on his behalf, but instead betrayed Pelleas and bedded Ettard himself. However, NIMUE, a LADY OF THE LAKE, now entered the picture and made Pelleas become enamoured of her by her magic, making Ettard fall in love with Pelleas by the same means. Finding her love now unrequited, Ettard died of a broken heart.

Pellehan

One of several names applied to the MAIMED KING. He was said, in the QUESTE DEL SAINTE GRAAL, to have received his maiming wound when he attempted to draw the SWORD OF STRANGE HANGINGS. Elsewhere, his character becoming much the same as that of PELLAM, it is stated that he received his wound when BALIN stabbed him with the LANCE OF LONGINUS.

Pelles

The son of PELLAM and king of LISTI-NOISE, though he is also called the king of TERRE FORAINE ('the Foreign Land'), while the VULGATE VERSION makes him the FISHER KING. The father of ELAINE[1], he had her handmaiden, BRISEN, administer LANCELOT[2] a love potion so that he would sleep with his daughter and father GALAHAD[1]. PERLESVAUS calls the HERMIT KING Pelles, but it is assumed that this is an entirely different character.

Pellinore

A subordinate king to ARTHUR who is variously described as the ruler of LISTINOISE, NORTHUMBERLAND or the GASTE FOREST. The LIVRE D'ARTUS makes him the RICH FISHER, saying that he was wounded in the thighs for doubting the Holy GRAIL. This would suggest that he was originally identical to PELLAM. Sir Thomas MALORY says he was the father of AGLOVALE, PERCEVAL[2], DORNAR, DRIANT, LAMORAK, ALAN, MELODIAN and ELAINE[3], though he does not mention TOR, whom he fathered on the wife of ARIES. He pursued the QUESTING BEAST and killed King LOT, eventually being slain by GAWAIN[1], Lot's son. Pellinore may have originated in BELI MAWR (Beli the Great), the Celtic ancestor god, for the pronunciation of their names is similar. If this is the case, it seems equally possible to suggest that Beli Mawr was the origin of similarly named FISHER KINGS and MAIMED KINGS.

Penardun

Daughter or sister of BELI who, by LLYR, became the mother of BRÂN and therefore an ancestor of ARTHUR.

Penarwan

The wife of OWAIN who was, according to the TRIADS, unfaithful to him.

Penbedw

The name of a farm in Clwyd whose lands contain a menhir and standing stones that have been put forward by R. Holland in *Supernatural Clwyd* (1989) as one of the possible resting places of King ARTHUR. This seems to have some local support, for local folklore says that MOEL ARTHUR, which lies nearby, was the site of Arthur's palace.

Pendragon

An amalgamation of the Brythonic (a group of Celtic languages comprising Welsh, Cornish and Breton) *pen* signifying 'head' or 'main' and the Old Welsh *dragawn* meaning 'leader', this title was taken by both UTHER and later ARTHUR, though in the case of the former it has usually been used as a surname. It simply signifies the position of the titleholder as the chief leader.

Pendragon Castle

The castle of BREUNOR following his marriage to MALEDISANT.

Percard

The proper name of the BLACK KNIGHT[2], who was killed by GARETH.

Perceforest

The hero of a romance by the same name. This says that when ALEXANDER THE GREAT conquered England (which he never actually did) he made BETIS the king, and his brother, GADDIFER, king of SCOTLAND. As the line of BRUTUS had died out, Betis was quickly accepted by the populace, being renamed Perceforest after he had killed the magician DAMART. He founded the chivalrous order of the KNIGHTS OF THE FRANC PALAIS and built a temple to the Supreme God. His son BETHIDES made an unwise marriage to the sorceress CIRCE, who brought the Romans to Britain. They defeated the Knights of the Franc Palais, wiping them out, and Gaddifer, Perceforest's brother, went to live in the ISLE OF LIFE. After ALAN, the GRAIL KEEPER, came to BRITAIN, GALLAFER, Gaddifer's grandson converted to Christianity and went to preach to his ancestors, who still inhabited the Isle of Life. They too accepted Christianity, were baptized and left the island, coming to a place where five monuments awaited them, and there they died.

Perceforest

A fourteenth-century French romance describing the early history of BRITAIN, including the fictitious invasion of the island by ALEXANDER THE GREAT.

Perceval

1 The father of PERCEVAL[2], according to the English romance SIR PERCEVAL OF GALLES. He had apparently been killed, some years before his son became aware of his identity, by the RED KNIGHT[1], whom his son killed.

2 Known among Welsh sources as PERE-DUR, Perceval appears to have been the invention of CHRÉTIEN DE TROYES, for this is the earliest reference made to a character by this name. In German sources he is called PARSIFAL or PARZIVAL.

Raised in the woods by his unnamed mother, for she wanted him to know nothing of knighthood, he saw some of ARTHUR's knights and was determined to go to Arthur's court and become one. His mother, unable to convince him otherwise, told him to demand either a kiss or a jewel from any lady he should meet. When Perceval came across a lady asleep in a tent, he kissed her and purloined her ring. On his arrival at Arthur's court he heard that the RED KNIGHT[1] had absconded with a valuable cup. He pursued him and killed the knight, afterwards staying with GORNEMANT DE GOORT, an elderly knight who taught him chivalry and knighted him. He returned to Arthur's court and became one of the KNIGHTS OF THE ROUND TABLE, leaving again to undertake the Quest for the Holy GRAIL. He arrived at the castle of BLANCHEFLEUR[1], who was being besieged by King CLAMADEUS. Perceval became Blanchefleur's lover and succeeded in defeating King Clamadeus in a single combat.

Desiring to visit his mother, Perceval was directed by a fisherman to a castle where he beheld the GRAIL PROCESSION, saw a man reclining on a couch and was given a sword. However, Perceval failed to ask the GRAIL QUESTION, and next morning, when he awoke, he found the castle deserted and only just escaped from it. The sword he had been given had fragmented and, encountering his cousin, who told him that he should have asked the Grail Question, he took the sword to TREBUCHET. *En route* Perceval was challenged by the husband of the lady he had encountered in the tent, and from whom he had stolen the kiss and jewel. He had misunderstood that Perceval had acted in innocence and was overcome by the latter. Perceval was then said to have forgotten about God for a total of five years, but his uncle, the HERMIT KING, absolved him.

This is as much as Chrétien de Troyes tells us, for his work was unfinished. However, in his *Continuation* Manessier takes up the story and tells how Perceval returned to the castle and asked the appropriate Grail Question. He discovered that the FISHER KING had been wounded by fragments from a sword that had killed GOON DESERT, the Fisher King's brother. Perceval, discovering that the wounds would not heal until the murderer had been dealt with, sought him out and killed him. The Fisher King was healed and his lands restored to fertility. Perceval's identity was then revealed to him as the nephew of the GRAIL KING who had been sustained by the Grail during his incapacitation and, when that King died, Perceval succeeded him, though, upon successfully achieving the Grail, after which GALAHAD[1] died, Perceval

was said to have lived on for at least a year.

From these origins, Perceval subsequently appeared in romances on both sides of the English Channel. The English SIR PERCEVAL OF GALLES says that his mother was ACHEFLOUR, the sister of Arthur, and his father, also called PERCEVAL[1], had been killed many years previously by the RED KNIGHT[1]. His lover was called LUFAMOUR. Perceval was said to have died while away on a Holy Crusade. The DIDOT PERCEVAL says that the RICH FISHER revealed to Perceval the secret words which Jesus had passed on to JOSEPH OF ARIMATHEA. In PEREDUR, the Welsh variation of his story, his father is named as EFRAWG. The Grail Procession is described as having included a maiden carrying a salver on which there was a head surrounded by blood. This head, Perceval later found out, was that of his cousin, whose death he had to avenge. It was in this version of Perceval's story that he was said to have done battle with an AFANC.

In the later QUESTE DEL SAINTE GRAAL, and in the works of Sir Thomas MALORY, Perceval has to some degree become supplanted by Galahad, though it was he who was at first thought to have achieved the Grail. Malory calls Perceval's father PELLINORE. WOLFRAM VON ESCHENBACH makes his father GAHMURET, his mother HERZELOYDE, his sister DINDRANE and his sons KARDEIZ and LOHENGRIN (Figure 29). PERLESVAUS again differs, making his father JULIAN and his mother YGLAIS. GERBERT makes them GALES LI CAUS and PHILOSOPHINE. *Bliocadran* makes his father, BLIOCADRAN, the hero of that work, while the TAVOLA RITONDA makes his sister AGRESTIZIA.

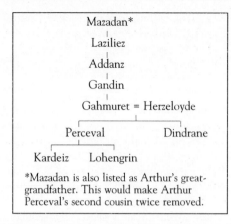

```
        Mazadan*
           |
        Laziliez
           |
         Addanz
           |
         Gandin
           |
   Gahmuret = Herzeloyde
   ┌─────────────┴──────┐
 Perceval           Dindrane
 ┌───┴─────┐
Kardeiz  Lohengrin
```

*Mazadan is also listed as Arthur's great-grandfather. This would make Arthur Perceval's second cousin twice removed.

Figure 29   *Descent of Perceval according to Wolfram von Eschenbach*

Perceval

Unfinished work by CHRÉTIEN DE TROYES, probably better known as LE CONTE DE GRAAL. Written for Philip, Count of Flanders, and started c. 1180, it remained unfinished due to the author's death c. 1183. Several CONTINUATIONS subsequently appeared, each attempting to finish what Chrétien de Troyes had started.

Percival

A variant of PERCEVAL[2].

Peredur

The Welsh name for Sir PERCEVAL[2], who appears in a work of the same name as the son of EFRAWG. He is also named as one of the cousins, the other being GWRGI, of the British prince GWEND-DOLEU, against whom they fought at the battle of ARTHURET.

Peredur

Welsh romance concerning the exploits and quests of Sir PERCEVAL[2] that has become included as a part of the MABINO-GION.

Perevida

One of the various names given as the mother of GALAHAD[1] by LANCELOT[2].

Perferren

Welsh tradition names Perferren as a niece of ARTHUR, the wife of BUGI and the mother of Saint BEUND.

Perilous Bridge

The bridge leading to the GRAIL CASTLE, according to PERLESVAUS.

Perimones

This knight, known as the RED KNIGHT[2], was defeated by GARETH.

Perlesvaus

A thirteenth-century French prose romance concerning the quest for the Holy GRAIL.

Pernam

The brother of King MARK[2] of CORNWALL and MELIODAS[1], according to the Italian romance TRISTANO RICCARDIANO.

Pernehan

According to the PROSE TRISTAN, the brother of King MARK[2] who was murdered by him.

Perse

Promised by her father to ZELOTES, she was rescued from him by ECTOR DE MARIS, who loved her.

Pertolepe

A knight who was defeated by GARETH, and was known as the GREEN KNIGHT[2].

Peter des Roches

The BISHOP OF THE BUTTERFLY, so called because this historical bishop of WINCHESTER (bishop 1204–38) was said to have been given by ARTHUR the power of closing his hand and opening it to reveal a butterfly. The *Lanercost Chronicle* re-counts how the bishop came across a house in which Arthur was still alive and banqueted him, his special gift being given to him to prove that his story was true.

Petit Brut

A French chronicle of the Arthurian period by Rauf de BOUN.

Petitcrieu

Owned by GILAN, Duke of SWALES, this fairy dog, wondrously coloured, tiny and having a sweet-sounding bell hanging from its neck, originally came from AVALON. Gilan gave it to TRISTAN.

Petroc, Saint

A well-known Cornish saint who may have originated in South WALES. The poet Dafydd Nanmor says that he was one of the seven survivors of the battle of CAMLANN, but it has been suggested that for this the poet used a local tradition.

Petrus

One of the companions of JOSEPH OF ARIMATHEA. He travelled to the ORKNEYS and converted the ruler, ORCANT, to Christianity, marrying the king's daughter, CAMILLE. According to the pedigree of JOHN OF GLASTONBURY, he was an ancestor of LOT.

Phagan

One of the two missionaries sent, c. AD 166, from Rome by Pope ELUTHERIUS at the request of the then king, LUCIUS, to invigorate the work at GLASTONBURY. He and his colleague DERUVIAN have subsequently come to be regarded as the founders of Glastonbury Abbey, though this is an anachronism as the abbey church dates from a later period.

Pharamond
Also FARAMOND

A legendary Frankish king who possibly has his origins in a similarly named historical ruler of the fifth century. In the Arthurian romances he appears as a freedman – that is, a slave who has been given his liberty – who seized the French throne, travelling in disguise to ARTHUR's court (Arthur was his enemy), but being discovered and expelled again. His daughter, BELIDE, fell in love with TRISTAN, but when he did not return her passion she died of a broken heart. This, however, did not prevent Pharamond from giving refuge to Tristan and GORVENAL after the death of MELIODAS[1]. The Italian romancer ARIOSTO says that Pharamond had a son, CLODION, who was defeated in combat by Tristan. Pharamond also appears in non-Arthurian romance, in particular one from the seventeenth century which says that he fell in love with the daughter of the king of Cimbri, ROSAMONDE.

Phariance

A knight who was a companion of BAN and BORS[2] when they came to the succour of ARTHUR, and took part in the battle of BEDEGRAINE. The elder BORS[1] eventually sent him into exile for murder and he became a follower of CLAUDAS.

Pharien

It is possible that this character is the same as PHARIANCE, probably a name adopted by him following his exile by BORS[1] and allegiance to CLAUDAS. His wife became the lover of King Claudas. Following the death of Bors, the latter's sons fell into his hands, but he soon passed them into the custody of Claudas.

Phelot

A treacherous knight who wanted to kill LANCELOT[2], so persuaded his wife to beseech Lancelot to climb a tree to retrieve her falcon. Ever chivalrous, Lancelot agreed, but had to remove his heavy armour to do so and, having done this, Phelot attacked the unarmed and unprotected knight. However, Lancelot took a sturdy branch and repelled the attack, striking Phelot on the side of the head, knocking him senseless. Lancelot then beheaded the unconscious knight with his own sword.

Philippon

King of England and father of MELIADICE. He was succeeded by his son-in-law, CLERIADUS.

Philosophine

According to the CONTINUATION of GERBERT, the wife of GALES LI CAUS and mother of PERCEVAL[2].

Pict(s)

The name applied to the inhabitants of northern BRITAIN during the Roman occupation, and also during the traditional Arthurian period. They are known to have been raiding in Britain at the time of the Roman withdrawal, and it has been suggested that VORTIGERN invited the SAXONS to Britain to oppose them. GEOFFREY OF MONMOUTH says that they would have been wiped out by ARTHUR had not the clergy interceded. BOECE stated that GUINEVERE died as their captive. Their forces made up a part of the army, along with Saxons and Scots, which was defeated by the young King Arthur at the battle of the River DOUGLAS. They were also put down again in Moray, along with Scots and Irish forces, by Arthur and HOEL[1].

Racially, the Picts were possibly a Celtic race, called Priteni in their own language, a name which is thought to have been one possible origin for Britain itself. The Irish referred to them as Cruthin, and applied this term to a similar race of people living in IRELAND. The Romans called them Picti (hence Picts), meaning 'painted folk'. Although they almost certainly preceded the Britons themselves, the Venerable BEDE states that they arrived after them, originating in Scythia, a region which lies in present-day Ukraine. Geoffrey of Monmouth seems to have picked up on this point and adds that their migration took place under the rule of King SODRIC, who suffered heavy losses at the hands of the British king MARIUS. However, Marius was said to have bestowed Caithness on them, possibly in order to suppress them. The medieval Irish poet Mael Mura of Othain maintained that they originated in Thrace.

Wherever or whatever their origins, the principal kings of the Pict kingdom during the traditional Arthurian period were said to have been Galem I (AD 495), Drust III and Drust IV (AD 510–25), Drust III alone (AD 525–30), Gartnait III (AD 530) and Cailtram (AD 537). This list should, however, be treated with extreme caution, as Pictish history is, to say the least, spartan.

Pinel

A cousin of LAMORAK who, following the latter's demise, attempted to poison GAWAIN[1] in revenge. Sir PINEL of IRELAND accidentally consumed the poison and GUINEVERE was at first accused of the murder. However, once the true facts were discovered, Pinel had to flee.

Plegrus

The lover of BLENZIBLY in Icelandic romance. He was killed by KALEGRAS, who subsequently became the father of TRISTAN by BLENZIBLY.

Poitiers

A duchy in western France that was given to BLEOBERIS, who had supported his father, LANCELOT[2], in his quarrel with ARTHUR.

Polidamas

The nephew of YDER and one of the KNIGHTS OF THE ROUND TABLE.

Pomparles Bridge

A bridge over the River Brue, also known as the Pons Perilis (cf. PERILOUS BRIDGE), on the main road from GLASTONBURY to Street. It is cited as one of the places from which EXCALIBUR was thrown when it was returned to the LADY OF THE LAKE.

Pope, The

The head of the Roman Catholic Church, the Pope, is mentioned in several of the Arthurian romances, whether fictional or actual. The fictitious Pope SULPICIUS – possibly cognate with Pope Simplicius (AD 468–83) – was said to have made GAWAIN[1] a knight. The pope was also said to have crowned ARTHUR as the emperor of Rome and to have sent the Bishop of ROCHESTER to mediate between Arthur and LANCELOT[2] in their war over GUINEVERE. The Salzburg Annals and Jean de Preis (1138–1400) claim that Pope Hilary (AD 461–68) was the contemporary of Arthur. Other popes in the traditional Arthurian period were Felix III, Gelasius I, Anastasius II, Symachus, Hormisdas, John I, Felix IV, Boniface II, John II, Agapitus I, Silverius and Vigilius.

Porrex

An early and legendary king of BRITAIN who, according to GEOFFREY OF MONMOUTH, was a successor of BRUTUS. After his death, so one tradition says, PRYDEIN came from CORNWALL and conquered Britain, thus leading to the association of Prydein as the eponym of Britain itself.

Powys

An early Welsh kingdom that was, in the Arthurian period, said to have been ruled by legendary kings such as CADELL I, CYNGEN I and BROCHMAEL I.

Preiddeu Annwfn

'Spoils of Annwfn'. Supposedly written by the great bard TALIESIN, this early Welsh poem, which dates from c. AD 900, describes an expedition ARTHUR makes to the OTHERWORLD to obtain an enchanted cauldron. It also describes various aspects of the supernatural realm. There is a glass fort (CAER WYDYR), and CAER SIDDI or CAER FEDDWIDD (the Fort of CAROUSAL), where a fountain runs with wine and no one ever knows illness or old age. It is thought that this story forms one of the sources for the later GRAIL legends.

Preseli Hills

A range of hills in DYFED, to the east of Fishguard, that can boast more Arthurian objects than any other region in BRITAIN for such a small area, among them BEDD ARTHUR and CARN ARTHUR.

Prester John

First mentioned by the chronicler Otto of Freising, this legendary monarch was thought to have ruled in either Asia or Africa. It was said that he attacked Ecbatana and defeated the Medes and the Persians, whose capital it was. A letter, claimed to have been written by Prester John, appeared in Europe during the twelfth century (perhaps c. 1185). It described the various wonders of his kingdom, and became vastly popular. Marco Polo identified him with an Asiatic ruler, but the fourteenth-century Jordanus de Sévérac placed his kingdom in Ethiopia.

Prester John appears in a number of the Arthurian legends. According to WOLFRAM VON ESCHENBACH, he was the son of FEIREFIZ and RAPANSE, which made him a cousin of ARTHUR and nephew of PERCEVAL[2]. In the Dutch romance *Lancelot*, he continues this association but is, this time, the son of Perceval. In *Tom a'Lincoln* he was the father of ANGLITORA, with whom TOM A'LINCOLN, Arthur's illegitimate son, eloped.

Priamus

A SARACEN knight whose wondrous line of descent was said to include the biblical Joshua, ALEXANDER THE GREAT, the Maccabees and Hector of Troy! He fought with GAWAIN[1] and then asked that knight to help in his conversion to Christianity, though the actual outcome of their combat is unknown. Priamus dabbed both sets of wounds with water from a vial that contained the Four Waters of Paradise, and they were both soon fully healed. Priamus, after his conversion, became a duke and one of the KNIGHTS OF THE ROUND TABLE.

Priory Oak

Another name for MERLIN'S TREE in CARMARTHEN.

Priure

According to DIU CRÔNE, the scaly envoy of this King of the Sea brought a cup to ARTHUR's court which would prove whether men or women were false. When tested, only Arthur was shown to be true.

Pro of Iernesetir

One of the aliases under which the wounded TRISTAN was said to have travelled to IRELAND to have his poisoned wounds healed by ISEULT[1]. Alternatively, he was said to have adopted a simple anagram of his name, TANTRIS.

Procides

The castellan (governor) of Limerick castle and gonfalonier (standard-bearer) of IRELAND, according to DURMART LE GALLOIS.

Prophécies de Merlin

A thirteenth-century French work detailing the prophecies made by MERLIN. It was allegedly written by Richard of IRELAND.

Prose Lancelot

A thirteenth-century French work that forms a part of the VULGATE VERSION.

Prose Merlin

The name given to two medieval romances about MERLIN, one English and one French.

Prose Tristan

A large thirteenth-century French work that describes the career of TRISTAN.

Prydein

Coming from CORNWALL following the death of PORREX, Prydein was said to have conquered the remainder of BRITAIN. It is this legend that has led to his being cited as a possible eponym for the country itself.

Pryderi

An important character from Celtic Welsh legend, Pryderi is mainly connected with the Arthurian legends through the story of BENDIGEID VRAN's expedition to IRELAND, and the fact that he was one of the seven British survivors who returned carrying the head of the fallen Bendigeid Vran. The others who returned with him were MANAWYDDAN FAB LLYR – to whom he gave his own mother RHIANNON as a wife, along with the seven cantrefs of DYFED – GLUNEU EIL TARAN (GLIFIEU), TALIESIN, YNAWC (YNAWAG), GRUDYEN (GRUDDIEU) and HEILYN.

Prydwen

According to Welsh tradition, *Prydwen* was the name of the ship in which ARTHUR made his expedition to the OTHERWORLD of ANNWFN. However, GEOFFREY OF MONMOUTH gives this name to Arthur's shield.

Pubidius

The ruler of Mathraval (WALES) who, in one version of the story of MERLIN, is named as the wizard's maternal grandfather.

Pucelle aux Blanche Mains

'Pucelle of the White Hands' or 'Maiden with the White Hands'. The fairy lover of GUINGLAIN who lived on the GOLDEN ISLAND.

Puck

A peculiarly British earth spirit who is a decided, if distant, relation of Pan of classical mythology. He had various names – Gruagach, Urisk, Boggart, Dobie and Hob – all of which reflect his earthy quality. He does not appear widely in the Arthurian tales, but is given as the impish servant to OBERON[1] in SHAKESPEARE'S A MIDSUMMER NIGHT'S DREAM.

Puck is described in a biography of him written in 1588 as the child of a young girl and a 'hee-fayrie'. He confines his mischief to the house, doing housework in exchange for cream or cake, and has the ability to change himself into any animal at will. One tale says that travellers, tempted to mount a strange horse on a wild moor, have often found themselves in the middle of a stream with nothing between their legs save a saddle!

Puffin

According to Cornish folklore, ARTHUR was reincarnated as a puffin after his death. Various other animal incarnations are also ascribed to Arthur, such as the CHOUGH or RAVEN.

Pulzella Gaia

The daughter of MORGAN[1] Le Fay by HEMISON, according to Italian romance. However, her name is in fact a title, simply signifying the Cheerful Damsel. Abducted by BURLETTA DELLA DISERTA, she was rescued by LANCELOT[2]. She became the lover of GAWAIN[1], but warned him to keep their affair a secret. He failed to keep his promise, and she no longer came when he summoned her. Gawain, however, who had rejected the advances of GUINEVERE, had to prove that Pulzella Gaia was his lover, or die. Pulzella Gaia arrived with her fairy army to rescue him, but warned that her mother would imprison her. This she did, making her stand in water up to her waist. Gawain then came to her aid, rescued her and imprisoned Morgan Le Fay.

Purgatory

The region of purification visited by GAWAIN[1] in the Middle Dutch romance WALEWIEN. It is described as being a boiling river into which the souls of the dead went, as black birds, to emerge again as white ones.

Purple Knight

A knight who was defeated, along with many others, by the GREAT FOOL, an unnamed nephew of ARTHUR and the hero of the Irish romance *Eachtra an Amadán Mor*.

Queen of Cyprus

An unnamed sister of ARTHUR, perhaps MORGAN[1] Le Fay. She sent Arthur an enchanted horn which was drunk from to test the fidelity of the drinker's wife. If the wife had been unfaithful, the contents would be spilled.

Queen of Eastland

According to Sir Thomas MALORY, one of the four enchantresses, associates of MORGAN[1] Le Fay, who captured LANCELOT[2]. Her accomplices were the QUEEN OF NORTHGALIS, the QUEEN OF SORESTAN and the QUEEN OF THE OUT ISLES.

Queen of Northgalis

An enchantress and an associate of MORGAN[1] Le Fay. She was one of the four sorceresses who imprisoned LANCELOT[2] until he chose which he loved. Her accomplices were the QUEEN OF EASTLAND, the QUEEN OF SORESTAN and the QUEEN OF THE OUT ISLES.

Queen of the Out Isles

According to Sir Thomas MALORY, one of the four enchantresses, associates of MORGAN[1] Le Fay, who captured LANCELOT[2]. Her accomplices were the QUEEN OF EASTLAND, the QUEEN OF NORTHGALIS and the QUEEN OF SORESTAN. The Out Isles are thought to be identifiable as the Hebrides.

Queen of Sorestan

A sorceress who fell in love with LANCELOT[2]. She, and three other enchantresses, imprisoned Lancelot in her castle, the CHATEAU DE LA CHARETTE, until he chose which one of them he loved. Her accomplices were the QUEEN OF EASTLAND, the QUEEN OF NORTHGALIS and the QUEEN OF THE OUT ISLES.

Queen of the Waste Lands

One of the queens aboard the barge that carried the dying ARTHUR to AVALON following the battle of CAMLANN. She is named as the enchantress who told PERCEVAL[2] of his mother's death.

Quest for the Holy Grail

See GRAIL

Queste del Sainte Graal

A thirteenth-century French romance that forms a part of the VULGATE VERSION, and which describes the Quest for the Holy GRAIL. It introduces GALAHAD[1] as the hero who achieved the object of the quest and is thought to have been written by a Cistercian.

Questing Beast

A curious beast, the offspring of a girl and the Devil, which was chased by PELLINORE and subsequently by PALAMEDES. It is described as having the head of a snake, the body of a leopard, the hindquarters of a lion and the feet of a hart. From its stomach came the noise of forty questing (baying) hounds, hence the name. This particular creature seems to have had its origin in an allegorical animal, variously described, with barking pups inside her. This creature was mentioned in PERLESVAUS and was reported to have been spotted by PERCEVAL[2].

Quintilian

The nephew of LUCIUS HIBERIUS, the Roman leader. While GAWAIN[1] was delivering a message to Lucius from ARTHUR, Quintilian made a derogatory comment regarding the Britons. In his anger, GAWAIN[1] beheaded him and had to flee Lucius's encampment.

R

Radigund

The queen of the AMAZONS who was killed by BRITOMART.

Ragnell

A loathsome-looking hag whom GAWAIN[1] married as the condition for ARTHUR being given the answer to a riddle posed to him and which none of his court could answer. Once married, she informed him that she could become beautiful either by day or by night, the former suiting her better, the latter suiting Gawain. Remembering the words of wisdom this lady had given Arthur as the response to the riddle 'What is it that a lady desires the most?', Gawain allowed the lady her own choice. As a result of his chivalrous and selfless choice, she became beautiful by both day and night.

Raguidel

A knight who was killed by GUENGA-SOAIN but whose dead body subsequently appeared near ARTHUR'S court on an apparently unmanned ship. With his body was a letter asking that his death be avenged and stating that the person who did this would be the only one able to draw rings from the fingers of the corpse. Sir GAWAIN[1] killed Guengasoain and returned to remove the rings from Raguidel's fingers.

Rathlean

The mother of the OTHERWORLD woman AILLEAN and thus, for a time, the mother-in-law of ARTHUR.

Raven

According to Cornish folklore, the soul of ARTHUR passed into a raven's body after his death, although it was also said to have become a CHOUGH or a PUFFIN. Some think that the raven was a later replacement for the chough when that species became extinct within the county.

Raynbrown

A knight and the son of Sir IRONSIDE.

Recesse

The kingdom of CARRAS, brother of King CLAUDAS.

Red Book of Hergest, The

A fourteenth-century manuscript that, along with THE WHITE BOOK OF RHYDDERCH, contains the MABINOGION cycle.

Red Knight

The title of at least five knights in the Arthurian legends.

1 The knight who stole a valuable cup from Arthur's court but was pursued, caught and killed by GAWAIN[1].
2 True name Sir PERIMONES, he was defeated by GARETH.
3 Sir IRONSIDE, the Red Knight of the Red Lands. He was besieging LYONESSE[1] when GARETH came to relieve that lady, and duly defeated him.
4 A title given to GAWAIN[1] in PERLESVAUS.
5 A knight who was defeated by the GREAT FOOL.

Red Rose Knight

The title given to TOM A'LINCOLN, the illegitimate son of ARTHUR and ANGELICA.

Remus

King of Rome, according to an unpublished Italian romance that tells how he, UTHER and TROIANO once again made the Trojans the rulers of Troy. In all probability he is the Remus who features in classical Roman mythology as the brother of Romulus, and the co-founder of Rome and the ROMAN EMPIRE.

Renoart

A warrior who appeared in the Guillaume d'Orange cycle of Arthurian stories. In the romance BATAILLE LOQUIFER, he was taken to AVALON by MORGAN[1] Le Fay and other fairies, and there he met ARTHUR. He became the lover of Morgan Le Fay, but soon left, though he was said to have fathered CORBON on Morgan Le Fay. The jilted sorceress persuaded KAPALU to sink Renoart's ship, but he was rescued by sirens (a siren being a sea nymph from classical mythology whose singing was thought capable of luring sailors to their deaths on the rocks).

Renwein

A variant of RONWEN, the daughter of HENGIST.

Repanse de Schoie

The GRAIL damsel with whom FEIREFIZ fell in love at ARTHUR's court. After Feirefiz's conversion to Christianity, the pair went to India, where they became the parents of PRESTER JOHN.

Restor de Tristram

'New Tristram', the name of the hero of a lost romance that was given to him by a disgruntled fairy who intended his life to be as miserable as his namesake. He was taken to the palace of MORGAN[1] Le Fay, but what happened to him once there remains unknown.

Rheged

A kingdom in the Cumbrian region of north-west BRITAIN which was ruled by URIEN during the traditional Arthurian period. It has been suggested that Urien was the historical original of ARTHUR, which would therefore mean that Rheged was Arthur's realm. This association seems to have sprung from Arthur's connections with CARLISLE, which lies within the kingdom.

Rhiannon

An important Celtic Welsh goddess, the horse goddess who is called Epona in GAUL, and Macha or Édain in IRELAND. The mother of PRYDERI, she was given by her son to the disinherited MANAWYDDAN FAB LLYR, following the expedition of BENDIGEID VRAN to Ireland.

R(h)ic(c)a

A variant of RHITTA CAWR.

Rhitta (Cawr)
Also RHICCA, RITHO

A giant who lived on YR WYDDFA FAWR (Mount SNOWDON) and had a cloak made of beards. He was killed by ARTHUR, whose beard he wanted for the collar to his cloak. He is, through the similarity of their stories, thought identifiable with RIENCE.

Rhiw Barfe

'The Way of the Bearded One' – a path that runs down the hill from BWLCH-Y-GROES, North WALES, so called for it is held that ARTHUR threw the slain RHITTA down this path to his grave at Tan-y-Bwlch.

Rhonabwy

The eponymous hero of the MABINOGION story of the DREAM OF RHONABWY. He fell asleep and dreamt that he accompanied IDDAWC and met KAY, one of ARTHUR's knights, as well as the king himself.

Rhongomyniad

The spear of ARTHUR, according to the MABINOGION story of CULHWCH AND OLWEN. It is thought that it equates with RON, the lance or spear mentioned by GEOFFREY OF MONMOUTH.

Rhydderch (Hael)

An historical king of STRATHCLYDE, SCOTLAND, who is usually referred to with his epithet 'Hael' (hael = 'generous'). He participated in the battle of ARTHURET,

Welsh tradition placing him on the side which opposed MERLIN. GEOFFREY OF MONMOUTH, however, in his VITA MERLINI, has Rhydderch fighting on the same side as the wizard, making him the husband of GANIEDA, Merlin's sister. His sword, DYRNWYN, is said to number among the THIRTEEN TREASURES of BRITAIN.

Rhygenydd

The owner of a crock that was considered one of the THIRTEEN TREASURES of BRITAIN.

Rhyverys

ARTHUR's master of hounds.

Rica

Named in the MABINOGION story of CULHWCH AND OLWEN as the chief elder of CORNWALL and father of GORMANT. Welsh tradition seems to equate Rica with GORLOIS, or at least with the latter's traditional role.

Riccarda

The wife of the KING WITH A HUNDRED KNIGHTS, according to the *Due Tristani*.

Rich Fisher

An alternative name sometimes used to refer to the FISHER KING.

Richard

The son of the king of Jerusalem who, according to the PROPHÉCIES DE MERLIN, was sent on a mission to ARTHUR's court by the POPE to obtain succour for Jerusalem, which was being besieged by the king of BAUDEC. Arthur responded by sending a force under the leadership of HENRY[1] the Courtly. When Richard himself became the king of Jerusalem, he attacked the pagan city of SARRAS but, as no one could defeat that city's giant ruler, a truce was called.

Richborough, Battle of

The battle which was fought as ARTHUR landed on his return from his Continental campaign at which AUGUSELUS was killed by MORDRED. It was the first of the three final battles fought by Arthur, on each occasion defeating his usurping nephew, Mordred.

Riculf

The chosen ruler of NORWAY following the death of King SICHELM. Though the dead king had bequeathed the kingdom to LOT, the people chose Riculf. ARTHUR, however, enforced Lot's rightful claim to the throne by invading Norway and killing Riculf.

Rieingulid

According to Welsh tradition, the sister of IGRAINE[1], thus ARTHUR's aunt. She was the mother of Saint ILLTYD.

Rience

A king who is variously made the ruler of NORTHGALIS, IRELAND, DENMARK or the LAND OF PASTURES AND GIANTS. The LIVRE D'ARTUS makes him a SAXON, while SPENSER makes him the father of BRITO-MART. When the young King ARTHUR was putting down the rebellion by the eleven rebel leaders at the very start of his reign, Rience was at war with LEODE-GRANCE. He is most famous for having a cloak made from the beards of eleven kings he had defeated. He thought that

ARTHUR's would make a fine collar to this cloak and demanded that he give it to him. War followed, during which BALIN and BALAN captured Rience and brought him to Arthur.

His story is remarkably similar to a story told in Welsh tradition about a giant, named RHITTA, RICCA or RITHO, associated with Mount SNOWDON, who also had a cloak made of beards and whom Arthur killed. He is presumably, therefore, the same character. More modern Welsh folklore makes him a robber whom Arthur slew and buried in the neighbourhood of Llanwchllyn.

Rigomer

The shortened, popularized version of MERVEILLES DE RIGOMER.

Riothamus

An historical British king who was been identified as the historical ARTHUR or UTHER, some claiming that the name is really a title meaning 'great king'. He brought a large army to the Continent to assist the emperor ANTHEMIUS against EURIC the Visigoth. He was subsequently defeated and disappeared in Burgundy.

Ritho

A variant of RHITTA.

Rivalin

1 According to GOTTFRIED VON STRASS-BURG, the ruler of PARMENIE and father of TRISTAN. He married BLANCHE-FLEUR[2], the sister of King MARK[2]. His name seems to originate in an historical Lord of Vitré, Rivalen, who was known to have flourished in the eleventh century.
2 A ruler of NANTES who attacked HOEL[1]

but was defeated in single combat by TRISTAN.

Riwallawn

A son of URIEN of RHEGED.

Roaz

An evil and villainous knight who laid siege to Queen AMENE, killing her husband and conquering most of her realm. WIGALOIS came to her aid and killed him.

Robert de Boron

The Burgundian author (*fl.* 1200) of two very important Arthurian romances, about whose life very little is known. His works were JOSEPH D'ARIMATHIA, which deals with the GRAIL legends, and MERLIN. It is thought that he may also have been responsible for the DIDOT PERCEVAL.

Robin Goodfellow

The son of OBERON[1] by a human girl.

Rochester

A town in KENT that has been suggested as the site of the battle of mount AGNED, as listed by NENNIUS.

Roges

Featuring in the Middle Dutch romance WALEWEIN, Roges was a prince who was turned into a fox by magic. He accompanied and helped GAWAIN[1] on one of his adventures and was eventually returned to his human form.

Roland

The hero of any number of Italian romances, in which he is known as ORLANDO. These romances concern the exploits of a legendary count of BRITTANY who was, according to legend, the nephew of the emperor Charlemagne. Legend says that in AD 778, as his army was returning from a Spanish expedition, it was attacked at Roncesvalles by the Basques or, more correctly, the SARACENS, who had been forewarned by the treachery of Ganelon (Roland's jealous stepfather). Roland refused to blow his horn to summon the emperor's aid until it was too late, and then died in the act of blowing it. The most famous romances concerning this character are ORLANDO INNAMORATOR by BOIARDO and ORLANDO FURIOSO by ARIOSTO, which was based on the earlier work and attempted to complete what Boiardo had left unfinished. It is through these and other Italian romances that the story of Roland has become inexorably intertwined with the Arthurian legends.

Roman de Brut

Written in French by the twelfth-century writer WACE, this work contains the first reference to the ROUND TABLE. It was quickly translated and expanded by LAYAMON in his BRUT, which was written between 1189 and 1199.

Roman des fils du roi Constant

Medieval French romance that names the wife of BAN of BRITTANY as SABE and gives him a daughter named LIBAN.

Roman Empire

Even though GEOFFREY OF MONMOUTH and Sir Thomas MALORY have the Roman Empire in full existence during the traditional Arthurian period, history tells us that, in the West, the Roman Empire ceased to exist in AD 476, though the Eastern or Byzantine Empire lasted for nearly 1,000 years longer. Sir Thomas Malory states that ARTHUR defeated the emperor LUCIUS HIBERIUS and was crowned emperor of Rome by the POPE. CLARIS ET LARIS also supports the idea of the Roman Empire existing during Arthur's time, stating that the emperor THEREUS invaded Britain but was defeated.

Ron

The lance or spear owned by ARTHUR. It is mentioned under this name by GEOFFREY OF MONMOUTH and would seem to equate with RHONGOMYNIAD, ARTHUR's spear, which appears in the MABINOGION story of CULHWCH AND OLWEN.

Ronwen

Also HROTHWINA, RENWEIN

Daughter of the SAXON leader HENGIST and sister to HARTWAKER, AESC, OCTA, EBISSA and SARDOINE. She married VORTIGERN, the county of KENT being given to her father as the bride price. Her name appears originally to have been HROTHWINA in ANGLO-SAXON, Ronwen being the Latinization of that name.

Rosamonde

The daughter of the king of the Cimbri who, in a non-Arthurian romance, was said to have been loved by PHARAMOND.

Rougemont

The castle of TALAC.

Rouland

The king of ERMINIA who, according to one of the medieval romances, was the father of TRISTAN by BLANCHEFLEUR[2], sister to King MARK[2].

Round Table

The most famous icon of the Arthurian sagas, the table in the great hall at ARTHUR's court at which Arthur seated his knights so that none had precedence over any other. Its origin seems a little confused, as does its actual size and shape. Commentators describe it variously as a complete disc, a ring, a semicircle or a broken ring having an opening for servants. Additionally, some say that Arthur sat at the table with his knights, while others say he sat alone at a smaller, separate table.

Originally, according to the majority view, the table belonged to UTHER. It then passed into the ownership of King LEODEGRANCE of CAMELIARD, and came to Arthur when he married Leodegrance's daughter, GUINEVERE, the Round Table, which could seat 150 knights, being a wedding gift.

It is first mentioned by the early twelfth-century writer WACE in his ROMAN DE BRUT, in which he says that the barons quarrelled over who had precedence, so Arthur had the table made. He is the only writer to have the curious position of the knights sitting within the circle formed by the table. When the work was translated and expanded by LAYAMON in BRUT (written 1189–99), the knights were found in their more normal position, around the outer edge of the table.

Layamon says that the quarrel arose during a Christmas feast and resulted in the death of several men. Shortly afterwards, while visiting CORNWALL, Arthur met a foreign carpenter who had heard of the fracas and offered to make a portable table at which 1,600 could sit without any having precedence over the others. Arthur commissioned the work and the table was completed within six weeks.

Other versions of the story credit the Round Table to MERLIN, and vary the number who could be seated at it. ROBERT DE BORON has the lowest number, with just fifty knights. The VULGATE VERSION makes this number 250, while Layamon's figure of 1,600 still remains the largest. The GRAIL legends further embroidered the stories surrounding the Round Table, saying that one seat at it, the SIEGE PERILOUS, remained unoccupied until GALAHAD[1] came to the court to take his rightful position, for that siege was reserved for the holiest of knights, he who would achieve the Quest for the Holy Grail.

The Round Table in WINCHESTER, which was for many years thought to have been the original – a view supported by Caxton when he wrote the preface for Sir Thomas MALORY'S MORTE D'ARTHUR – has since been proved (through the use of modern dating techniques) to be a replica. Dating from the fourteenth century, it still poses a very important question. If it is not the original, then is it an accurate copy?

Rowena

According to GEOFFREY OF MONMOUTH, Rowena was the daughter of HENGIST who married VORTIGERN. Her name does not appear in any works that pre-date Geoffrey of Monmouth, and it is thought that her name has Welsh origins rather than ANGLO-SAXON. She appears again in a much later work, *The Fairy of the Lake* (1801) by John Thelwall, in which she was in love with ARTHUR, though still married to Vortigern. More commonly it is RONWEN, the daughter of Hengist, who is married to Vortigern. It is possible that

Rowena is a simple transcriptive error, though when the Anglo-Saxon variant of HROTHWINA is considered this situation might be considered reversed, for Hrothwina to Rowena does need much imagination.

Rowland

The son of ARTHUR; according to the Scottish ballad CHILDE ROWLAND, *childe* signifying that Rowland was a young man of upper-class origins. His story seems to echo much earlier Celtic stories of journeys to the OTHERWORLD. His sister ELLEN disappeared, MERLIN claiming that she had been abducted by the fairies. The wizard gave him very precise instructions on how to rescue her, and her eldest brother set off. He too vanished, for he had not done all that Merlin instructed him. The next brother also vanished for the same reasons. However, Rowland followed Merlin's instructions implicitly, including killing everyone he came across after he had entered FAIRYLAND. He came to a hill, which he entered, and inside found a hall where his sister and his two brothers were in an enchanted state. He did battle with the king of ELFLAND and, by defeating him, secured the release of the prisoners.

Rummaret

First mentioned by WACE as the king of WENELAND who paid homage to ARTHUR while the latter was in ICELAND. LAYAMON, in his translation of Wace's work, referred to the kingdom of Rummaret as WINETLAND or WINET. Rummaret gave his son to Arthur as a hostage and was said to have helped to put down a fight in Arthur's hall. Various regions have been suggested for his realm, including Finland, GWYNEDD and the country of the Wends. However, the name Weneland may have a connection with Vinland, the Norse name for a part of North America which may, as is now thought, have been discovered in the Middle Ages.

Run

A son of URIEN of RHEGED.

Runalen

A son of king HOEL[1] of BRITTANY and brother of ISEULT[2] of the White Hands.

Russia

The realm of King BARATON, according to the Arthurian legends.

Rusticiano de Pisa

An Italian writer who was flourishing in 1298. Best known for having written down Marco Polo's *Travels* at the latter's dictation, he also produced a *Compilation* of Arthurian romances.

Sabe

The wife of BAN of BRITTANY, according to the medieval French romance ROMAN DES FILS DU ROI CONSTANT.

Sador

According to the PROSE TRISTAN, the son of BRONS, he married CHELINDE and became the father of APOLLO by her. They subsequently became separated and Chelinde, thinking Sador was dead, re-married. When he returned Apollo did not recognize his father and killed him.

Safere

The brother of PALAMEDES who was made the Duke of Languedoc and subsequently became a Christian.

Saga of Tristan and Isodd

An Icelandic version of the story of TRISTAN and ISEULT[1] which names BLENZIBLY as the mother of TRISTAN by KALEGRAS.

Saga of Tristram

The title of two renditions of the story of TRISTAN and ISEULT[1]. One is Norwegian in origin and dates from 1266, while the other, undated, has an Icelandic prov-enance. These two works are generally confused with each other and are com-monly simply referred to as TRISTRAM'S SAGA.

Sagremor

A descendant of the imperial family of CONSTANTINOPLE, the son of the king of HUNGARY and a KNIGHT OF THE ROUND TABLE. He had two brothers, both of whom became bishops, and a sister, CLAIRE, whom GUINGLAIN rescued from two giants who had taken her captive. He had a lover called NIOBE, but also fathered a child by the Irish princess ORAINGLAIS.

Saint Michel, Mont

A mount off the north coast of BRITTANY, where ARTHUR was said to have defeated and killed a giant.

Salisbury Plain

Sir Thomas MALORY makes this area in southern England the site of ARTHUR's final battle, the first reference to this siting appearing in the *Vulgate Morte Arthure*. The area is probably best known for STONEHENGE, which appears in the Arthurian legends as a memorial erected by MERLIN on the instructions of VORTIGERN.

Salmon of Llyn Llw

A gigantic fish on whose shoulders KAY and GWRHYR travelled to rescue MABON[2] from his place of imprisonment. The two heros were introduced to the Salmon of Llyn Llw by the oldest creature in all the world, the EAGLE OF GWERNABWY.

Samaliel

According to the PROSE TRISTAN, the son of FROLLO who went on to become a knight of great renown.

Samson, Saint

The patron saint of BRITTANY and one of the most important of the British missionary bishops of the sixth century, founding several churches in CORNWALL and IRELAND, before travelling across the Channel to continue his work in Brittany.

Born in Siluria, South WALES, c. AD 525, the son of Amwn, by Anna, daughter of MEURIG ap Tewdrig, Prince of Glamorgan. While being ordained as a deacon by DUBRICIUS, Bishop of CAERLEON-ON-USK, a white pigeon or dove flew in and came to rest on his shoulder, where it remained until the young deacon had been ordained and had received Holy Communion. Some time later, Samson asked ILLTYD to give him permission to live on a little island near Llantwit, where Piro, a holy priest, lived. Illtyd gave him permission, and Samson went there to study in a tiny cell.

In common with many of the Celtic saints, Samson had the ability to communicate with animals. When bishop at Dol, Brittany, his monks reported that they were disturbed in their devotions by the cries of wild birds. One night Samson gathered them to him in the courtyard and instructed them to remain silent. The following morning the birds were sent away, and no longer were the devotions of the monks disturbed by their wild cries. Samson died at Dol in AD 565.

His connection with the Arthurian legends exists solely because he has been suggested as the possible original for Sir GALAHAD[1].

Sandav

One of the few survivors of the battle of CAMLANN, his survival being attributed to his wondrous beauty, which meant that everyone mistook him for an angel and no one dared attack him.

Sanddef

Listed as one of the TWENTY-FOUR KNIGHTS of King ARTHUR's court.

Sangive

According to WOLFRAM VON ESCHENBACH, a sister of ARTHUR and the mother of CUNDRIE[1].

Saracen(s)

The ancient Greek and Roman term for an Arab. During the Middle Ages it was used by Europeans to refer to all Muslims, though Spaniards used the term Moor. Romancers connected the Saracens with the pagan city of SARRAS, even going so far as to say that they were a race of Jewish descent, ruled over by TOLLEME, that lived in CORNWALL.

Saraide

A servant of the LADY OF THE LAKE who saved BORS[2] and LIONEL from King CLAUDAS by means of her magical powers.

Sardoine

A daughter of HENGIST and sister to RONWEN, HARTWAKER, ASEC, OCTA and EBISSA.

Saris

The king of HUNGARY, according to CLARIS ET LARIS, which also says he captured Cologne but was subsequently killed by LARIS.

Sarmatian(s)

A barbarian people of RUSSIA from Roman times. One of their tribes was known as the ALANS, whose descendants, the OSSETES, still inhabit the Caucasus today. These people have a story that is very similar to that of the death of ARTHUR. This tells how their hero, BATRADZ, having received his mortal wound, instructed two of his companions to throw his sword into the water. Twice they pretended to have carried out the instruction, but the third time, when the sword was finally thrown, the water turned blood red and became stormy. It has been suggested that this is the origin of the EXCALIBUR story, as Sarmatian soldiers served in the Roman army in BRITAIN under Lucius Artorius Castus. Further, it has been suggested that this Artorius is the historical Arthur, and that this story was transferred from Batradz to him.

Sarras

A pagan city where Sir GALAHAD[1] was said to have perceived the GRAIL for the last time and then died. The location of the city is unknown, some sources saying it was to be found near Jerusalem and others placing it in BRITAIN. Little is known about the city other than its pagan status – the Roman god Mars was worshipped there – but the PROPHÉCIES DE MERLIN say that it was ruled by the pagan giant ALCHENDIC, though he eventually converted to Christianity. It is said that the SARACENS took their name from the city.

Savari

The king of SPAIN who abducted LIDOINE, the sister of LARIS. She was later rescued by ARTHUR.

Saxon(s)

The term generally applied within the Arthurian stories to the west Germanic invaders of BRITAIN who fought against ARTHUR. The invasions by these barbarian peoples, who had neither armour nor cavalry, began some time between AD 440 and 460. BEDE said that they originated in north GERMANY (Saxons), Schleswig (Angles) and Jutland (Jutes), though evidence also exists of FRISIAN involvement. Their languages coagulated into a single tongue, referred to as ANGLO-SAXON by Cambridge scholars and Old English by Oxford scholars. These invaders, whom Bede divided into three groupings (Figure 30) formed the ancestors of the modern English people.

Saynes

The kingdom conquered by ARTHUR and subsequently bestowed, along with the deposed king's daughter, on PARIS.

Scalliotta

An Italian variant for SHALOTT that appears in *Lancialotto Pancianti-chiano*.

```
                                    Saxons
         ┌────────────────────────────┬────────────────────────────┐
   East Saxons                  South Saxons                  West Saxons

                                    Angles
   ┌──────────────┬──────────────┐              ┌──────────────┬──────────────┐
East Angles   Middle Angles                          Mercians      Northumbrians
                                    Jutes
              ┌──────────────────────────────┬──────────────┐
          Kentishmen                                    Vectians*
```

*Inhabitants of the Isle of Wight.

Figure 30 *Bede's grouping of the three waves of barbarian invasions of Britain, and their descendant peoples*

Scalot

An Italian variant for SHALOTT that appears in *La damigiella Scalot*.

Schentefleurs

One of the three sons of GORNEMANT DE GOORT. Like his two brothers, he met with a violent end.

Schionatulander

The husband of SIGUNE, whose body she was carrying when she met PERCEVAL[2].

Scotland

During the traditional Arthurian period Scotland was divided between three peoples: the Britons, who occupied the Lowlands that had once been Roman territory (they never conquered the Highlands); and the PICTS and the Scots, occupying the land north of Hadrian's Wall, the latter having arrived from IRELAND and being the eponym of Scotland. GEOFFREY OF MONMOUTH asserts that AUGUSELUS ruled Scotland during ARTHUR's time, while BOECE avers in his SCOTORUM HISTORIAE that the king was EUGENIUS, an ally of MORDRED. The HISTORIA MERIADOCI says that URIEN was the king of Scots.

Historically, it is hard to say who ruled the Britons of STRATHCLYDE during this period, as reliable lists do not exist, but the Hiberno-Scottish kingdom of DALRIADA was ruled by Fergus More, Domangort, Comgall and AEDÁN MAC GABRAIN, though dates are unreliably recorded.

Scotorum Historiae

Written by the Scottish historian Hector BOECE (d. 1536), this work is interesting in that it contains Arthurian material from an anti-ARTHUR viewpoint.

Scottish Wilderness, Lord of the

See LORD OF THE SCOTTISH WILDERNESS

Seat of Danger, The

The literal translation of the SIEGE PERILOUS, the seat at the ROUND TABLE reserved for the knight who would succeed in the Quest for the Holy GRAIL.

Sebile

A sorceress and companion of MORGAN[1] Le Fay. Her name seems to originate in 'Sibyl' – a woman who, mostly in ancient Greece and Rome, was believed to be an oracle or prophetess.

Segurant the Brown

A knight of the OLD TABLE, the KNIGHT
OF THE DRAGON, and UTHER's mightiest
warrior.

Segwarides

A knight with whose wife TRISTAN had
an affair. The two knights fought and
Tristan won, but the two later became
reconciled. He became the ruler of
SERVAGE, which NABON gave to him.

Sennan Holy Well

A well in CORNWALL at which the SEVEN
KINGS OF CORNWALL were said to have
given praise following their victory at the
battle of VELLENDRUCHER.

Sentoge

The duchy created for GALIHODIN
because he supported LANCELOT[2] in his
quarrel with ARTHUR.

Sequence

The name of one of the swords owned by
ARTHUR.

Seraphe

The original, possibly pagan, name of
NASCIEN[1].

Servage

The island realm of NABON which he
gave to SEGWARIDES.

Sevain

The father of LIONORS and thus grandfather to LOHOLT, ARTHUR's son.

Seven Kings of Cornwall

An allegiance of seven kings who,
according to Cornish tradition, helped
ARTHUR to defeat the invading Danes at
the battle of VELLENDRUCHER. Afterwards
they were said to have given praise and
worshipped at the SENNAN HOLY WELL,
and then held a banquet at a rock called
the TABLE MAN. MERLIN subsequently
prophesied that the Danes would one day
return, a greater number of kings would
see this event, and that it would mark the
end of the world.

Seven-League Boots

Magical boots, invented by MERLIN, that
would enable the wearer to cover seven
leagues with each stride. A league is commonly measured at three miles (its actual
length varied from time to time), so these
boots could cover approximately twenty-
one miles per step.

Sewingshields

A place in NORTHUMBERLAND where
there used to stand a castle beneath
which ARTHUR, GUINEVERE and Arthur's
knights were allegedly asleep, awaiting
the call to return in the hour of BRITAIN's
greatest need. A bugle and a garter
were said to lie nearby, and it was necessary to blow the bugle and cut the garter
with a stone sword in order to raise the
sleepers.

Shakespeare, William

Born in Stratford-upon-Avon, Warwickshire, and living between 1564 and 1616,
Shakespeare is perhaps the best-known
playwright ever to have lived. He appears
to have drawn on Arthurian literature
and legend during the composition of
A MIDSUMMER NIGHT'S DREAM, for here

OBERON[1] has much the same role as he does in other Arthurian literature.

Shalott

Another name for ASTOLAT which has become widely known to English readers through Alfred, Lord Tennyson's *Lady of Shalott*. The name derives from the Italian variants of SCALOT, used in *La damigiella di Scalot*, and SCALLIOTTA, used in *Lancialotto Pancianti-chiano*.

Sherwood Forest

Though more normally associated with that other famous and well-loved legendary figure Robin Hood, Sir Thomas MALORY identifies the forest with that of BEDEGRAINE, a forest which saw a major battle between ARTHUR and the eleven rebellious leaders at the start of his reign.

Shoulsbarrow Castle

A fortress on Exmoor, lying just within Devon, that is said to have been used by King ARTHUR.

Sichelm

The king of NORWAY. The uncle of LOT, he bequeathed his realm to his nephew, but the throne was usurped and Lot's right of ascendancy had to be reinforced by ARTHUR.

Siege Perilous

The 'Perilous Seat' or 'Seat of Danger', a place at the ROUND TABLE, so named by MERLIN, who said it was reserved for the holiest of knights, the one who would achieve the GRAIL. When BRUMART, a nephew of King CLAUDAS, tried to sit on it, he was destroyed for his presumption. When GALAHAD[1], the destined knight, sat on it, his name appeared in gold letters either above the seat or on it.

Sigune

According to WOLFRAM VON ESCHEN-BACH, the cousin of PERCEVAL[2]. She also appears, though unnamed, in the works of CHRÉTIEN DE TROYES. The first meeting between PERCEVAL[2] and Sigune, in Wolfram von Eschenbach, occurs before he has visited the GRAIL CASTLE. When they meet she is carrying the body of her dead husband, SCHIONATULANDER. Chrétien de Troyes does not mention this encounter. The second time they meet, following Perceval's first and unrewarded visit to the Grail Castle, she chided him for his apparent lack of concern for AMFORTAS's suffering. Chrétien de Troyes, however, says she scolded him for not asking the GRAIL QUESTION. Later Sigune became a recluse and was eventually buried beside her husband.

Silva Caledoniae

'Wood of Scotland'. A wood located in the Lowlands of SCOTLAND that has been suggested as a possible site for one of ARTHUR'S BATTLES, that of CALEDON WOOD.

Silvius

The father of BRUTUS, he was accidentally killed by his son.

Sinadone

The Lady of Sinadone is said to have been rescued by LYBIUS DESCONUS, who was accompanied by the damsel ELLEN. The story appears in the appropriately titled romance *Lybius Desconus*.

Sir Gawain and the Carl of Carlisle

An unfinished English romance dating from c. 1400 which relates the tale of GAWAIN[1] and his dealings with the CARL OF CARLISLE. It was later followed in the sixteenth century by a new version, again incomplete, called the CARL OF CARLISLE.

Sir Gawain and the Green Knight

Also SIR GAWAYNE AND THE GREENE KNIGHT

A famous, but anonymous, English poem dating from c. 1346 that deals with the beheading contest undertaken by GAWAIN, and perhaps recalling memories of an ancient fertility ritual. It was followed approximately 100 years later by *The Green Knight*, though this is a much inferior telling of the story.

Sir Gawayne and the Greene Knight

The original spelling of SIR GAWAIN AND THE GREEN KNIGHT.

Sir Perceval of Galles

A fourteenth-century English romance that tells the story of PERCEVAL[2], but makes no mention of the GRAIL, or Perceval's part in the quest for that Holy vessel.

Slaughterbridge

The traditional Cornish location for the battle of CAMLANN, some six miles from DOZMARY POOL on Bodmin Moor, one of the many locations where EXCALIBUR was meant to have been returned to the LADY OF THE LAKE.

Snowdon, Mount

The highest mountain in North WALES (see YR WYDDFA FAWR).

Sodric

According to GEOFFREY OF MONMOUTH, he was the leader who brought the PICTS to BRITAIN. They were, however, soundly defeated by King MARIUS, but he still bestowed Caithness on them.

Soissons

The kingdom of CLOTHAIR before he became King of All the Franks.

Solomon

According to the pedigree of Gallet, the great-grandfather of ARTHUR and king of BRITTANY.

Sorcha

The realm of the father of RAGNELL, one of the various wives ascribed to GAWAIN[1].

Soredamor

The sister of GAWAIN[1] who married the Byzantine prince ALEXANDER[2], becoming the mother of CLIGÉS by him.

Sorelois

An Arthurian kingdom the ruler of which was called GLOIER and the capital SORHAUT. Many regions have been suggested for this kingdom, from Sutherland in the north to the Isles of Scilly in the south.

Sorestan

A kingdom in the vicinity of NORTH-GALIS, the ruler of which was said to be a witch.

Sorgales

An Arthurian kingdom that is said to be identical with South WALES.

Sorhaut

The name of the capital of the kingdoms of GORE and SORELOIS.

Sorlois

A kingdom that is now to be found in modern Iraq. The hand of FLORENCE, daughter of the king of Sorlois, was sought by ARTHUR of BRITTANY.

Souconna

The Celtic goddess of the River Saône.

Southampton

Port in Hampshire, southern England, where King HOEL[1] was said to have landed with a massive army when he came to the aid of his cousin, King ARTHUR.

Spain

During the traditional Arthurian period, this Iberian country was a Visigoth kingdom ruled by Alaric II (AD 484–507), Gesalaric (AD 507–11), Amalric (AD 511–31) and Theudis (AD 531–48). In the Arthurian stories ALIFATIMA, SAVARI, CLARIS and TRISTAN are all named as being rulers at various times.

Speckled Knight

One of the many knights said to have been defeated by the GREAT FOOL.

Spenser, Edmund

An English poet (c. 1552–99) who, though not much read in modern times, was esteemed as the Virgil of his day, enjoying great popularity among other poets. His most famous work, the epic, unfinished allegory THE FAERIE QUEENE, features the uncrowned King ARTHUR.

Spumador

According to SPENSER, ARTHUR's horse.

Stag of Rhedynfrc

Having been directed to this animal by the BLACKBIRD OF CILGWRI, the party helping CULHWCH in his search for OLWEN were passed on to the EAGLE OF GWERNABWY.

Stanzaic Morte Arthur

An English poem, possibly dating from the fourteenth century, that, in its 3,969 lines, deals with the latter part of ARTHUR's career.

Stater

The ruler of DEMETIA during the traditional Arthurian period, according to GEOFFREY OF MONMOUTH.

Stonehenge

The most famous of the large stone circles. Standing on SALISBURY PLAIN, Stonehenge was, according to Arthurian legend, erected as a memorial at the suggestion of MERLIN. It was allegedly brought over from IRELAND to be re-erected on its present site, this story perhaps containing some oral tradition that the ring was indeed transported over water. Also known as the GIANTS' RING, Stonehenge is not the original name and merely dates from medieval times. Archaeological evidence has shown that the ring was built in three stages. In c. 2800 BC a ditch and bank along with the heel stone were all that stood on the site. In c. 2000 BC blue-stone pillars, perhaps originating in the PRESELI HILLS, WALES, were brought to the site, transported up the Avon and erected. In c. 1500 BC the ring was completed when sarsen trilithons were erected.

Stradawl

The wife of COEL.

Stranggore

This Arthurian kingdom, perhaps to be identified with east WALES, was said to have been ruled by BRANDEGORIS.

Strathclyde

During the traditional Arthurian period this was a British kingdom lying in the Lowlands of SCOTLAND. The names and dates of the rulers are uncertain as no reliable lists or sources exist.

Suite du Merlin

A thirteenth-century French prose romance. One of the manuscripts that makes up this work is sometimes referred to as the HUTH-MERLIN.

Sulpicius

Said to have knighted GAWAIN[1], this fictitious POPE is perhaps to be identified with Pope Simplicius (pope 468–83).

Surluse

This kingdom, whose border with LOGRES was marked by the River ASSURNE, was perhaps identical with SORELOIS. GALE-HAUT made himself the ruler of Surluse and, while ARTHUR was living with the FALSE GUINEVERE, the kingdom was given to the genuine GUINEVERE by Galehaut.

Swales

The duchy of GILAN. Some commentators have made the simple assumption that Swales is cognate with South Wales ('S. Wales'), but this seems doubtful.

Swan Knight

A descendant of MEURVIN and ORIANT about whom nothing else is known. Later tradition equates the Swan Knight with LOHENGRIN because of his disguise as a swan when he came to the aid of ELSA, daughter of the DUKE OF BRABANT.

Sword in the Stone, The

The legendary method by which ARTHUR was identified as the true king. The invention of this test is attributed to MERLIN. As no king could be found, and following many years of feuding, Merlin went to the archbishop of CANTERBURY and counselled him that he would find the rightful king. All the lords of the realm and all the gentlemen of arms were called to London for a New Year's Day tournament, where the new ruler would be revealed.

Sir ECTOR, his son, KAY, and his adopted son, Arthur, were among those who rode to London for the jousting, Kay making much of the occasion, for he was to be made a knight. However, as they neared the tournament, Kay found that he was without his sword and sent Arthur back to their lodgings, for he had left it there. When Arthur arrived, he found that the innkeeper and all his family had already left for the tournament, and he could not gain entry. Turning back, he trudged dolefully through a churchyard, and there saw a sword embedded in a stone. He easily withdrew it and hastened back to his father and brother.

When Kay saw the sword, he read upon it the words Arthur had missed: 'Whosoever pulleth this sword from the stone is rightwise born King of All England.' Immediately Kay rejoiced and, showing the sword to his father, claimed that he had pulled the sword from the stone, and that he should be proclaimed king. Ector, however, made his son tell the truth and, taking both boys back to the churchyard, replaced the sword in the stone and bade Arthur withdraw it again. This he did with ease, but neither Ector nor Kay, who both attempted the feat, could move it.

Once more Arthur was asked to withdraw the sword, this time in public, and at the high feast of Pentecost he was crowned King of All England.

Sword of the Strange Hangings

A sword which had once belonged to the biblical King David of Israel. His son, Solomon, placed it aboard his ship, where it hung in hempen hangings made by Solomon's wife. This sword later appeared in the Arthurian legends, and had the hempen hangings replaced by some made from the hair of PERCEVAL[2]'s sister.

Syria

According to Sir Thomas MALORY, the sultan of Syria was a vassal lord of the Roman emperor LUCIUS HIBERIUS. However, elsewhere Syria was said to have been ruled by King NADUS, King NATALON and King EVANDER.

Table Man

A rock where the SEVEN KINGS OF CORNWALL, having given praise at SENNAN HOLY WELL, held a banquet following their victory at the battle of VELLENDRUCHER.

Table of the Wandering Companions

The table at ARTHUR's court where knights waiting to become KNIGHTS OF THE ROUND TABLE were seated.

Tacitus

Father of PATERNUS and greatgrandfather of CUNEDDA, according to the latter's traditional lineage.

Talac

According to the obscure Welsh text *Yder*, the castellan (governor) of the castle known as ROUGEMENT. At first he opposed ARTHUR, but the differences between them were eventually settled.

Taliesin

The radiant child of CERRIDWEN whose name has been applied as a title to the greatest Welsh poets. It is thought that an historical bard by the name of Taliesin lived a little later than the traditional Arthurian period, and that this reallife poet became entangled with an earlier Welsh tradition, giving rise to the composite character known today, and becoming incorporated into the later Arthurian stories. His story, which mirrors earlier customs and rites, is basically as follows.

In the middle of Lake Tegid there lived a man by the name of TEGID VOEL and his wife, Cerridwen, who is described as having the knowledge and powers of a witch. They had three children, a son whom they named MORFRAN AB TEGID, a daughter, CREIRWY, the fairest maiden in all the world (sometimes suggested as the prototype for GUINEVERE), and a second son, AFAGDDU, the most ill-favoured and hapless man in the whole world. Some sources say that Afagddu was simply a nickname applied to Morfran, but it does seem that they were actually separate characters.

As this was the beginning of the time of ARTHUR and the KNIGHTS OF THE ROUND TABLE, into whose company she desired Afagddu should one day be accepted, Cerridwen decided, according to the arts of the books of Fferyllt, to boil a cauldron of Inspiration and Science, which had to be boiled unceasingly for a year and a day, until three drops were obtained of the grace of Inspiration. These she intended for Afagddu, to instil in him all the graces he lacked.

Cerridwen placed GWION BACH, the son of GWREANG of Llanfair in Caereinion, POWYS, in charge of the cauldron, and a blind man named MORDA was to kindle the fire beneath it. She ordered them not to cease in their allotted tasks for a year and a day. Every day Cerridwen gathered the charm-bearing herbs required for the brew, but one day, nearing the end of the year, three drops of the red-hot fluid flew out of the cauldron and landed on the finger of Gwion Bach. Due to their great heat, he immediately sucked the finger, and upon doing so gained the full potency of the brew. Instantly becoming aware of the fact that Cerridwen was his greatest enemy, he fled. The cauldron burst into two and the remainder of the brew, poisonous now that it had rendered up the three divine drops, ran into a stream and poisoned the horses of GWYDDNO GARANHIR.

When Cerridwen returned and saw that her year's work was lost, she struck Morda over the head with a billet of wood intended for the fire until one of his eyes fell out on to his cheek. When he protested, Cerridwen realized that it was Gwion Bach who had robbed her, so she gave chase.

During this chase, which echoes the changing of the seasons, and totemic animals, there was a series of magical transmutations. Gwion Bach saw her chasing him and changed himself into a hare. Cerridwen countered by changing herself into a greyhound. Gwion Bach ran towards a river and, leaping in, changed himself into a fish. She in turn became an otter-bitch. Gwion Bach then transformed himself into a bird, so Cerridwen became a hawk. Then he saw a heap of winnowed wheat and, dropping on to it, turned himself into one of the grains, thinking that Cerridwen would never find him among the countless thousands of other grains. However, she followed and, changing herself into a hen, she swallowed Gwion Bach. Nine months later Cerridwen gave birth to a son which, by reason of his beauty, she could not kill. Instead she placed the baby in a leather bag and cast him into the sea.

This bag was found by ELPHIN, the son of Gwyddno Garanhir, and it was he who, on first seeing the head of the baby, named him Taliesin. Later Taliesin rescued Elphin when the latter had been imprisoned by MAELGWYN (MELKIN), an episode which forms the subject matter of Thomas Love Peacock's novel *The Misfortunes of Elphin* (1829).

Though the above is the normally accepted version of Taliesin's conception and birth, an alternative story says that he was magically created by GWYDION. Taliesin became famed for his poetry, being said to have addressed URIEN of RHEGED, but it seems that Taliesin was simply a visitor to Urien's realm, rather than a resident, his most likely provenance being South WALES. *The Book of Taliesin*, which was compiled during the fourteenth century, is thought to contain some authentic poems from this mythologized historical character. The manuscript for this work is now in the National Library of Wales in Aberystwyth.

His transition from Welsh tradition to Arthurian legend first appears in the Welsh poem PREIDDEU ANNWFN, where he is among the companions of Arthur during the latter's expedition to the OTHERWORLD. This story is itself derived from an earlier tradition that places Taliesin among the seven survivors of the expedition to IRELAND by BENDIGEID VRAN to rescue BRANWEN, returning with the head of the king for burial under the WHITE MOUNT in London. The others to survive this expedition, which exterminated the entire Irish race except for five pregnant women who hid in a cave, were PRYDERI, MANAWYDAN, GLUNNEU EIL TARAN (GLIFIEU). YNAWC (YNAWAG), GRUDYEN (GRUDDIEU) and HEILYN.

Both Welsh tradition and the VITA MERLINI make Taliesin a contemporary of

MERLIN, representing the two talking with each other. The verse ascribed to Taliesin is somewhat difficult to understand, being constructed in an obscure manner. This has led some commentators to ascribe the verse to Merlin, saying that it only later came to be attributed to Taliesin. Other sources add that Taliesin had a son named ADDAON, who was subsequently killed by LLONGAD GRWRM FARGOD EIDYN.

Tallas

According to CLARIS ET LARIS, the king of DENMARK who made LARIS a prisoner only for him to be rescued by CLARIS.

Tallwch

In Welsh tradition, the father of TRISTAN. His name appears to be a Welsh form of the Pictish name TALORC or TALORCAN, though this is by no means certain.

Talorc(an)

Pictish name that is thought to be the origin of TALLWCH, though this is open to speculation.

Tanaburs

A wizard who was said to be second in sorcery only to MERLIN, and to have lived in a time before UTHER became king. He cast a spell on Castle CARBONEK so that it would be found only by certain knights who chanced upon it.

Tancree

The niece of ARTHUR who married GUINGANBRESIL.

Taneborc

One of ARTHUR's residencies, which has been variously identified with EDINBURGH or Oswestry.

Tangled Wood

The realm of VALERIN.

Tantails

The wife of ALEXANDER[1], emperor of CONSTANTINOPLE, mother of ALEXANDER[2] and ALIS, and grandmother of CLIGÉS.

Tantris

The pseudonym used by TRISTAN when he visited IRELAND. It is a fairly simple anagram of TRISTAN.

Tarsan

The brother of King BAGDEMAGUS who was killed while in ARTHUR's service.

Tarsenesyde

The wife of LICONAUS and mother of ENIDE, according to EREC ET ENIDE.

Taulat

A villainous knight who came to ARTHUR's court and killed a knight in front of GUINEVERE, promising to return each year to do exactly the same. He was eventually defeated and killed by JAUFRÉ.

Taulurd

A giant who, according to GEOFFREY OF MONMOUTH, was killed by MARHAUS.

Tavola ritonda

A fourteenth-century Italian romance that dealt with a considerable number of Arthurian stories, thus making it an invaluable source of Italian romance.

Tawlbwrdd

A backgammon board, though sometimes said to be a chess board, which was counted among the THIRTEEN TREASURES of BRITAIN. It had a ground of gold and men of silver who would play themselves.

Tegau E(u)fron

In Welsh tradition, the wife of CARADOC BRIEFBRAS. She had three treasures; a mantle (cloak), a cup and a carving knife. She is identifiable with GUIGNIER, the wife of Caradoc Briefbras in Arthurian literature. Depending on which list is consulted, her treasures are sometimes included in the THIRTEEN TREASURES of BRITAIN.

Tegid Voel

A man, described as being of gentle lineage, who lived in the middle of Lake Tegid near Penllyn, WALES. He was the husband of CERRIDWEN, and father by her of MORFRAN AB TEGID, CREIRWY and AFAGDDU.

Telramund, Frederick de

The harasser of ELSA of BRABANT who was defeated in combat by LOHENGRIN.

Temper, River

The river that was said to separate the kingdom of GORE from SCOTLAND.

Templeise

According to WOLFRAM VON ESCHENBACH, the collective name for the knights who guarded the GRAIL.

Tenwi

A son of LOT and ANNA, according to Welsh tradition, and brother to MORDRED, PERFERREN and DENW.

Terdelaschoye

According to WOLFRAM VON ESCHENBACH, the fairy wife of MAZADAN, ARTHUR's great-grandfather, so presumably his great-grandmother. She is also described as an ancestress of PERCEVAL[2].

Terrabil, Castle

The castle in which GORLOIS was besieged by the forces of UTHER while the latter planned how he might lie with Gorlois's wife, IGRAINE[1]. Its location is not stated, and no reasonable site has yet been established or suggested with any authority.

Terre For(r)aine

Quite literally meaning 'Foreign Land', the realm of King KALAFES, who was converted from his pagan beliefs to Christianity by ALAN, and succeeded by JOSHUA[1], Alan's brother. The country has been possibly identified with LISTINOIS, the realm of King PELLEHAN in Arthurian times. The aunt of PERCEVAL[2] was once the queen of this country, and this has led to a further possible identification with the WASTE LAND of the GRAIL legends.

Terre Labur

The realm of KLINGSOR, according to WOLFRAM VON ESCHENBACH.

Terrestrial Paradise

The biblical Garden of Eden that, during the Middle Ages, was believed to still be in existence and able to be found. In the obscure medieval *Le Chanson d'Esclarmonde*, the heroine, ESCLARMONDE, is taken there by MORGAN[1] Le Fay and there bathes in the FOUNTAIN OF YOUTH.

Thaney

According to the LIFE OF SAINT KENTIGERN, the daughter of LOT and the mother of saint KENTIGERN.

Thanor

The king of CORNWALL who had help from the Irish against King PELIAS of LEONOIS. In repayment for this help, a yearly tribute had to be paid to IRELAND, a tribute over which TRISTAN had to fight MARHAUS.

Thereus

According to CLARIS ET LARIS, the emperor of Rome who invaded BRITAIN but was soundly defeated by ARTHUR.

Thirteen Treasures

The treasures or curiosities that MERLIN was said to have procured and then sailed away with, never to be seen again, in his glass boat. These mystical items alter from source to source, but most common among them are:

- DYRNWYN – the sword of RHYDDERCH HAEL, which would burst into flames from the cross to the point if any man apart from himself drew it.
- MWYS GWYDDNO – the hamper of GWYDDNO, which had the power to turn any meat placed on it, or in it, into sufficient to feed 100 people.
- CORN BRANGALED – the horn of BRANGALED, which could provide any drink desired.
- CADAIR, NEU CAR MORGAN MWYN-FAWR – the chair or car of MORGAN MWYNFAWR, which would carry a person seated in it wherever they wished to go. It is sometimes said that this was the transport of MORGAN[1] Le Fay, rather than Morgan Mwynfawr.
- HOGALEN TUDNO – the whetstone of TUDNO, which would sharpen only the weapon of a brave man.
- LLEN ARTHUR – the veil of ARTHUR, which made the wearer invisible.
- CYLLEL LLAWFRODEDD – a Druid sacrificial knife, said by some to have belonged to a character named LLAWFRODEDD.
- PAIS PADARN – the cloak of PADARN REDCOAT, which would make the wearer invisible.
- PAIR DRYNOG – the cauldron of DRYNOG, in which only the meat of a brave man would boil. Some sources name this as the cauldron that had once belonged to the giant DIWRNACH.
- DYSGYL A GREN RHYDDERCH – the platter of RHYDDERCH, upon which any meat desired would appear. Some sources name the owner of the magical dish as RHYGENYDD, and some include a crock that was also said to have belonged to Rhygenydd. This would, however, appear to be a confusion.
- TAWLBWRDD – a chess, or rather, backgammon board with a ground of gold and men of silver who would

play themselves. This is sometimes named as the GWYDDBWLL board belonging to GWENDDOLAU.

- MANTELL – a robe that would keep the wearer warm no matter how severe the weather. This is sometimes confused with Llen Arthur, and is then said to render the wearer invisible. Some say that it had once belonged to TEGAU EUFRON.
- MODRWY ELUNED – the ring of ELUNED, which conferred invisibility on the wearer. An unnamed stone also belonging to Eluned is sometimes mentioned in the list.
- The halter of CLYDNO EIDDYN.

Thitis

A sister of MORGAN[1] Le Fay.

Tholomer

The king of BABYLON who was at first friendly towards EVELAKE, giving him land, but when the latter ascended the throne of SARRAS the two were drawn into a war. Helped by JOSEPH OF ARIMATHEA, Evelake (apparently pagan at this time, so help from the saintly Joseph of Arimathea seems highly questionable) defeated Tholomer.

Thomas

An Anglo-Norman poet who flourished in the twelfth century and was the author of TRISTAN[1], the earliest extant text (c. 1155–70) of the legend of TRISTAN and ISEULT[1]. A fragment of 3,144 lines covering the final episodes, including the deaths of the lovers, still survives.

Thomas of the Mountain

The father of TOM THUMB who, unable to father any children, sent his wife to consult MERLIN. As a result Tom Thumb was born, growing to manhood within four minutes but never growing any taller.

Thompson

According to a Yorkshire legend, a potter who chanced on King ARTHUR and his knights asleep beneath Richmond Castle, thus adding this location in Yorkshire to the multitude of possible resting places for Arthur. On a table the potter saw a horn and a sword. Picking up the sword, he started to draw the blade from the scabbard, but dropped it when the sleeping knights began to stir.

Tigridia

The sister of DARERCA. She was said to have married GRALLO, the grandson of CONAN, thus becoming related by marriage to ARTHUR.

Timias

ARTHUR's squire in SPENSER's allegorical FAERIE QUEENE. It has been suggested that Timias is a characterization of Sir Walter Raleigh.

Tintagel

A village on the northern coast of CORNWALL and the site of the castle, home of Duke GORLOIS and his wife IGRAINE[1], where UTHER visited Igraine in the guise of her husband. The result of this union was ARTHUR, who was said to have been born there. The present castle is Norman, and shows no signs of any earlier structure, though this does not preclude the existence of a castle contemporary with King Arthur.

Tír inna mBan

The Irish OTHERWORLD 'Land of Women' that appears to have been the origin of MAIDENLAND.

Titania

The queen of the fairies and wife of OBERON[1]. She is perhaps best known from her appearance in SHAKESPEARE'S A MIDSUMMER NIGHT'S DREAM, where she quarrelled with her husband over a changeling boy.

Tolleme

Possibly identical with THOLOMER, Tolleme is described as the king of SARRAS who, having been converted to Christianity by JOSEPH OF ARIMATHEA, was defeated by EVELAKE. It has been suggested that Tolleme was the king of SYRIA, or alternatively that he ruled over a race of Jewish descent living in CORNWALL, these people being referred to as SARACENS.

Tollen, Saint

Saintly figure who was said to have defeated GWYNN AP NUDD, the Welsh Lord of the Dead and of the Underworld, on GLASTONBURY TOR.

Tolomeo

A chaplain to the POPE who, having served for a period as MERLIN'S scribe, became a cardinal.

Tom a'Lincoln

The RED ROSE KNIGHT, the illegitimate son of ARTHUR and ANGELICA. Raised by a shepherd, Arthur gave him the position of commander in the army, and in this capacity he successfully defeated the Portuguese. His son by CAELIA, the Fairy Queen, was known as the FAERIE KNIGHT. Having travelled to the realm of PRESTER JOHN, Tom a'Lincoln eloped with ANGLITORA, Prester John's daughter, and they had a son known as the BLACK KNIGHT[1]. However, Anglitora subsequently found out that Tom a'Lincoln was illegitimate and left him, becoming the mistress of the lord of an unnamed castle. When Tom a'Lincoln arrived at the castle in search of her, she murdered him. His ghost told his son by Anglitora, the Black Knight, what had happened, and he avenged his father's death. The Black Knight then met up with Tom a'Lincoln's other son, the Faerie Knight, and the two became travelling companions, eventually arriving in England. The story of Tom a'Lincoln is told in the romance *Tom a'Lincoln*, which was written by Richard Johnston (b. 1573). His family tree is as shown in Figure 31.

Tom Thumb

A well-known minuscule character whose connection to the Arthurian legends remains relatively limited. He is described as the son of THOMAS OF THE MOUNTAIN, who, having been unable to father any children, sent his wife to consult MERLIN. That great wizard told her that she would have a child, but that that child would be no bigger than her husband's thumb. She did indeed give birth to the minute Tom Thumb, who became a man within four minutes, but never grew any larger than he had been at first. His godmother was the Queen of the Fairies, and she gave him a hat of knowledge, a ring of invisibility, a girdle of transformation and shoes which could carry him over long distances with the greatest of ease. Tom Thumb was often present with King ARTHUR and the KNIGHTS OF THE

		Arthur	=	Angelica	Prester John
Caelia	=		Tom a'Lincoln	=	Anglitora
	The Faerie Knight			The Black Knight[1]	

Figure 31 *Family tree of Tom a'Lincoln*

ROUND TABLE, but died while engaged in a fight with an adder.

Tor

The son of PELLINORE or ARIES, though he is usually regarded as the illegitimate son of Pellinore and the wife of Aries. Tor killed ABELLEUS and was later made one of the KNIGHTS OF THE ROUND TABLE. He was killed on the occasion when LANCELOT[2] and his companions carried GUINEVERE off to safety.

Torc Triath

The king of boars in Irish mythology who corresponds to the giant boar TWRCH TRWYTH, which appears in the MABINO-GION, and against which Arthur and his men are sent by YSPADDADDEN in their quest to help CULHWCH win the hand of OLWEN.

Torec

The son of King YDOR who, when grown to manhood, attempted to recover the circlet that had belonged to his grandmother from MIRAUDE. She told him that she would marry him if he managed to overcome all the KNIGHTS OF THE ROUND TABLE. This he managed to do with the complicity of GAWAIN[1], who arranged matters with the other knights, and Miraude was therefore compelled to marry him.

Tortain

The result of the forced copulation of ELIAVRES and a sow.

Totnes

A town in south Devon, the older part of which occupies a steep hill overlooking the River Dart. It was here that BRUTUS and his Trojan refugees were said to have landed, their immigration being opposed by GOGMAGOG and the other giants who lived in BRITAIN. It is also the town where AMBROSIUS AURELIUS was said to have landed from BRITTANY and been proclaimed king.

Transeline

According to HUON DE BORDEAUX, a niece of ARTHUR and MORGAN[1] Le Fay.

Traprain Law

Located near EDINBURGH, this was the headquarters of a fifth-century king of the LOTHIAN region who has been thought of as cognate with LOT.

Trebes

The location of BAN's castle in BRITTANY. When CLAUDAS succeeded in destroying it, Ban was said to have died of a broken heart.

Trebuchet

Featuring in the GRAIL legends, Trebuchet was said to have made the GRAIL SWORD, and later to have repaired it. It has been suggested that his character owes its origins to TURBE, the father of the Irish smith god, GOIBHNIU.

Tregalen

According to Welsh tradition, the site of ARTHUR's final battle, in which he was victorious. He pursued the fleeing remnants of his enemies' army, but was killed at BWLCH-Y-SAETHU in Snowdonia by a flurry of arrows.

Tremeur

According to the legends surrounding CUNOMORUS, Tremeur was the son of either CUNOMORUS and TREPHINA or Trephina and JONAS. One tradition makes him the offspring of the first couple, also calling him GILDAS JUNIOR, while another makes his parents the second pair and gives him the alternative name of JUDWAL. While it would seem that the two are in fact the same, the various stories surrounding him are confused, so maybe there were two characters with this name.

Trenteny

The Lord of Trenteny was traditionally said to have killed a cow that belonged to Saint ENDELIENTA and then been killed, either by ARTHUR himself or at the king's order. No matter at whose hands he met his end, Endelienta restored him to life.

Trephina

The daughter of WAROK, chief of the VENETII, and a wife of CUNOMORUS. One tradition makes her the mother of

TREMEUR or GILDAS JUNIOR, after whose birth she was beheaded by Cunomorus. Gildas restored her to life and thereafter she was said to have carried her severed head around with her.

Tri-Novantum
Also TROIA NOVA, TROYNOVANT

A variant of Troynovant, 'New Troy', the name given by BRUTUS to his settlement on the River Thames that was later to become known as London.

Triad(s)

The name given to three collections of Welsh verse, listing items in groups of three and all containing a great deal of Arthurian material. While two sets are accepted as genuine, the third has been the subject of much controversy and is now considered a later emulation.

Tribuit

A river, the exact location of which remains a mystery, that was the site of one of ARTHUR's BATTLES.

Tristan

The most tragic of all the Arthurian heroes. A contemporary of ARTHUR, the nephew and champion of King MARK[2] of CORNWALL, he was also a KNIGHT OF THE ROUND TABLE. Most romancers give some account of his story, but there is a wide diversity in his lineage.

According to Sir Thomas MALORY, the most often quoted, he was the son of MELIODAS[1] and ELIZABETH, his relationship to Mark being as shown in Figure 32.

The Italian romance TRISTANO RICCARDIANO virtually echoes this, giving a very slightly different name to his mother, but naming his paternal grandfather as FELIX.

271

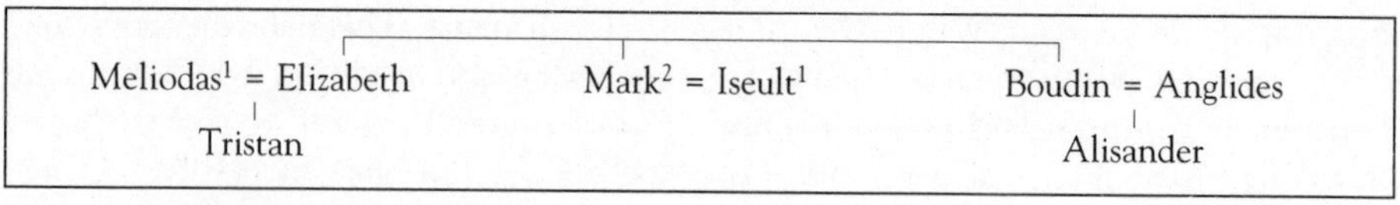

Meliodas[1] = Elizabeth	Mark[2] = Iseult[1]	Boudin = Anglides
Tristan		Alisander

Figure 32   *Relationship of Tristan to Mark according to Sir Thomas Malory*

In this case Tristan's family tree resembles the one shown in Figure 33.

GOTTFRIED VON STRASSBURG differs quite markedly in his TRISTAN AND ISOLDE (c. 1210), his courtly epic written in Middle High German and based on an earlier version by the Anglo-Norman poet THOMAS. He gives RIVALIN[1] and BLANCHE-FLEUR[2] as Tristan's parents, Blanchefleur being Mark's sister. Some sources replace Rivalin with King ROULAND of ERMINIA (Figure 34).

Tristan's story is basically as follows.

He was the son of King Meliodas, king of LIONES, and Elizabeth, sister of King Mark of Cornwall, and his mother died in childbirth. As a young man he entered the service of his uncle, King Mark, and when the latter refused to pay the customary tribute to IRELAND Tristan championed his uncle and killed MAR-HAUS, the Irish champion and brother of the Irish queen. However, during the combat Tristan received a poisoned wound and, being advised that he could be cured only in Ireland, he travelled there – quite wisely, considering the circumstances – under an assumed name, which was either TANTRIS (a simple anagram of Tristan) or PRO OF IERNSETIR. His wound was cured by Iseult, the daughter to King ANGUISH.

When Tristan returned to Cornwall, he told his uncle of the beauty of Iseult, and so taken was the king with his description that he sent Tristan back to Ireland to woo Iseult on his behalf. King Anguish agreed to the marriage and Tristan set off to bring Iseult back to his uncle. However, on the ship that carried them across the Irish Sea, he and Iseult mistakenly drank a love potion that was intended for Mark and his bride-to-be. Falling helplessly in love with each other, they embarked on their fated love affair. On Iseult's wedding night, she had her maid, BRANGIEN, take her place under cover of darkness, so that Mark would not know she had already laid with Tristan. Their affair continued undiscovered, but on one occasion Tristan's blood was spilt in Iseult's bed, and this gave rise to suspicion. Iseult was, however, very anxious to dispel this suspicion, and so undertook to swear on a hot iron that she

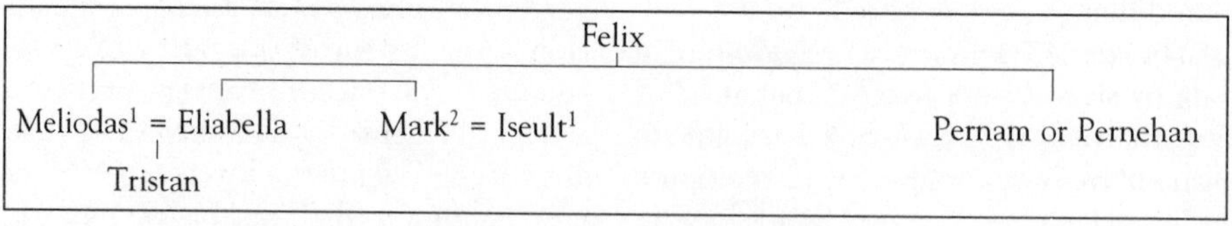

	Felix	
Meliodas[1] = Eliabella	Mark[2] = Iseult[1]	Pernam or Pernehan
Tristan		

Figure 33   *Relationship of Tristan to Mark according to* Tristano Riccardiano

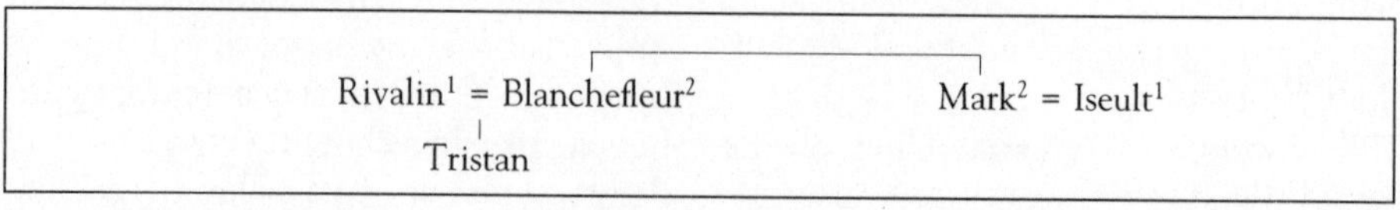

Rivalin[1] = Blanchefleur[2]	Mark[2] = Iseult[1]
Tristan	

Figure 34   *Relationship of Tristan to Mark according to Gottfried von Strassburg*

was not an adulteress. When the time came Iseult fell into the arms of a beggar (Tristan in disguise), and so was able to truthfully swear to Mark that none but the king and the beggar had held her.

Tristan now sensed that their love was doomed and hurried away from King Mark's court, crossing the channel and settling in BRITTANY. There he married the daughter of HOEL[1], king of Brittany, who was known as Iseult[2] of the White Hands. Various other names are given for Tristan's father-in-law: HAVELIN by EILHART, JOVELIN by GOTTFRIED VON STRASSBURG and GILIERCHINS in the Italian TAVOLA RITONDA. However, Tristan did not consummate his marriage with his wife, but did become the firm friend of her brother KAHEDRIN. Receiving yet another poisoned wound, Tristan believed that only Iseult, who had healed his earlier wound in Ireland, could again heal this wound, and so sent for her to come to his aid. Before the ship departed to fetch her, Tristan had obtained a promise from the captain that he would hoist white sails if she were on board when he returned, but black sails if she had declined to come. Jealous of her husband's undying love for Iseult, his wife lied to him on seeing the ship returning with white sails hoisted, saying instead that they were black. On hearing this, Tristan died, and when Iseult arrived and found that Tristan was dead, she too died, of a broken heart. King Mark buried them side by side, though Sir Thomas MALORY says that it was Mark who killed Tristan as he played the harp to Iseult by driving either a lance or a sword into his back. From Tristan's grave there grew a vine, while from Iseult's a rose sprang up. These two plants met and became inseparably entwined.

The origins of this famous love story are a little difficult to pin down. One suggestion is that it is Pictish, for Tristan is a Pictish name. This is further supported by the Welsh tradition which calls his father TALLWCH, which is itself perhaps a form of the Pictish name TALORC. Pictish king-lists say that King Talorc III, who was perhaps legendary, was succeeded by Drust V, leading to a possible identification between these two and the main characters of the legend. Obviously there have been many modifications to the story as it became more widely known, and it is now almost universally accepted that the final version is Breton. However, there is a great deal that is uniquely Cornish.

Near Fowey in Cornwall there is a stone (unremarkably known as the Fowey Stone) that bears the earliest-known inscription naming Tristan as the son of Cunomorus. Not far from Helston, Cornwall in Meneage, is a ford that was recorded as Hryt Eselt in the tenth century – the earliest known form of Iseult. These two simple facts would seem to suggest that as the story passed through Cornwall a local hero and heroine replaced those originally connected with the story. King Mark himself is called king of Cornwall, and is traditionally associated with Castle DORE near Galant. All these factors point directly to a Cornish origin, further supported in the earliest form of the romance itself, by the Norman-French poet BÉROUL. This firmly sets the story in south and mid-Cornwall, and mentions such places as Chapel Rock near Mevagissey (Tristan's Leap), and the Forest of Morrois (Moresk, near Truro), where the lovers once fled to hide from King Mark and his barons.

Other commentators have added other details to the story. Eilhart says that Tristan (called TRISTRAM by Sir Thomas Malory) was the first person to train dogs. Italian romance gave him and Iseult two children bearing their names, while the Icelandic SAGA OF TRISTRAM says Tristan had a son by Iseult of the White Hands who was named KALEGRAS. French romance gave Tristan and Iseult a single son, YSAIE THE SAD, and a grandson, MARC. Latterly the lovers became the subject of Richard Wagner's opera *Tristan and Isolde*.

Tristan

1 Twelfth-century text by the Anglo-Norman poet THOMAS that survives in a fragment of 3,144 lines and covers the later episodes in the story of TRISTAN and ISEULT[1], including the death of the lovers. This fragment is the earliest extant text covering the tragic love affair, and was written between c. 1155 and c. 1170.
2 Fragmentary twelfth-century text by the French writer BÉROUL. It is certainly later than that written by THOMAS, and was, in all probability, based on the earlier work, for it is remarkably similar in both content and style.

Tristan and Isolde

Early thirteenth-century (c. 1210) Middle High German courtly epic by GOTTFRIED VON STRASSBURG that was based on the earlier version by the Anglo-Norman poet THOMAS.

Tristan the Dwarf

Perversely this character from the Norwegian SAGA OF TRISTRAM was a large man who asked for TRISTAN's help against an evil man who had deprived him of both his wife and his castle.

Tristan the Stranger

Appearing in the Icelandic SAGA OF TRISTRAM, this character, with an over-inflated idea of his own prowess, asked TRISTAN to help him against seven brothers who had plundered his kingdom.

Tristan the Younger

According to Spanish and Italian romance, the son of TRISTAN and ISEULT[1], so called to distinguish him from his father. He succeeded MARK[2] as the king of CORNWALL and became a KNIGHT OF THE ROUND TABLE. While at CAMELOT, GUINEVERE became infatuated with him, but he did not return her feelings. He married the princess MARIA, daughter of King JUAN of Castile.

Tristano Panciatochiano

A fourteenth-century Italian romance concerning TRISTAN.

Tristano Riccardiano

A thirteenth-century Italian romance concerning TRISTAN.

Tristouse

The daughter of King BRIANT OF THE RED ISLE, who was born after her father's death and cast out to sea. She was rescued by an anonymous saviour, adopted and, when grown, married King YDOR. A sorrowful lady, she was said to have laughed for the very first time when she gave birth to her son, TOREC.

Tristram

The form of TRISTAN used by Sir Thomas MALORY, being the usual English form of the name, instances appearing in England since the twelfth century. A slightly less common version is TRISTREM.

Tristram's Saga

Form in which both the Norwegian and the Icelandic SAGA OF TRISTRAM are sometimes known.

Tristrem

A variant of TRISTAN.

Troas

The king of Thessaly who, as his name suggests, was of Trojan origin. He and his son, TROIANO, feature in an unpublished romance concerning the OLD TABLE.

Troia Nova
Also TRI-NOVANTUM, TROYNOVANT

A variant of Troynovant, 'New Troy', the name given to the settlement on the River Thames, founded by BRUTUS, that later became known as London.

Troiano

The son of King TROAS of Thessaly and a direct descendant of the Trojan hero Hector. He figures in an unpublished Italian romance concerning the OLD TABLE, which tells how he, UTHER and King REMUS of Rome (most probably the brother of Romulus in classical Roman mythology) joined forces to make the Trojan race the rulers of Troy once again.

Tronc

According to some sources, this was the name of an extremely ugly dwarf on whom the fairies took pity. Removing all traces of his ugliness, they gave him a kingdom, after which time he became known as OBERON[1].

Troynovant
Also TRI-NOVANTUM, TROIA NOVA

'New Troy', the name given by BRUTUS to the settlement he founded on the banks of the River Thames which subsequently became known as London.

Troynt

A little-used variant of TWRCH TRWYTH.

Tryamour

The lover of LANVAL who gave him the fairy horse BLANCHARD.

Tryffin

A king of DENMARK and father of DRUDWAS.

Trystan

A Welsh romance that names BACH BYCHAN as the page of TRISTAN.

Tudwal
Also TUTWAL

According to a number of Welsh pedigrees, a paternal ancestor of ARTHUR.

Tudwal Tudglyd

The owner of a whetstone that was counted among the THIRTEEN TREASURES of BRITAIN. It seems likely that he is the same as the character simply referred to as TUDWAL in the paternal ancestry of ARTHUR.

Tuis

The owner of a pig whose oil was sought by ARTHUR's warrior daughter MELORA. In Irish legend, Tuis was a king of Greece to whose realm the sons of Tuirenn went to obtain a pig skin which had healing properties. This, the older of the two legends, would seem to have been the origin of the Arthurian tale, or at least to have contributed to it in some part.

Turbe

The father of the Irish smith god GIOBHNIU. It has been suggested that he is the original of TREBUCHET, the smith who manufactured and subsequently repaired the GRAIL SWORD.

Turcans

According to the romance FLORIANT ET FLORETE, the king of ARMENIA.

Turinoro

The Count of Carthage and brother of the POPE, he came to the aid of LANCELOT[2] in his fight against ARTHUR, engaging the latter's forces while they were on their way back to BRITAIN. According to the TAVOLA RITONDA, GAWAIN[1] was killed in this encounter.

Turk and Gawain

An English poem thought to date from the very end of the fifteenth century (c. 1500). It tells the story of GROMER, who, through a magic spell, had been turned into a Turk, resuming his normal form again when the enchantment he was under was broken by GAWAIN[1], who, at Gromer's own request, cut off his head.

Turmwr Morvawr

A paternal ancestor of ARTHUR, according to Welsh genealogies, he is usually simply referred to as MORVAWR.

Turning Island

The island on to which NASCIEN[1] was put, having been rescued from prison. It was from here that he was alleged to have spotted the ship of SOLOMON.

Turquine

The brother of Sir CARADOS OF THE DOLOROUS TOWER, he had an immense hatred for LANCELOT[2]. In an attempt to lure Lancelot to him, he took ECTOR DE MARIS captive and threw him into his dungeons, along with several other prisoners he held at that time. Lancelot did indeed come to the rescue of Ector de Maris, and in the process killed Turquine and released all the captives.

Tutwal

A variant of TUDWAL that is found in the paternal lines of descent of ARTHUR from LLYR.

Twadell

The king of the Pygmies, a race described as being just two feet tall. During a jousting contest, he was overcome by TOM THUMB, and while the latter was ill Twadell provided the physician who treated him.

Twenty-Four Knights

The collective term for a list of knights resident at ARTHUR's court that is found in the Welsh work PEDWAR MARCHOG AR HUGAIN LLYS ARTHUR, which dates from some time around the fifteenth century or earlier. It has been suggested that this list forms a record of a company of knights that preceded the KNIGHTS OF THE ROUND TABLE. The knights recorded in this list were GWALCHMAI (GAWAIN[1]), DRUDWAS, ELIWLOD, BORS[2], PERCEVAL[2] (possibly PERCEVAL[1], his father), GALAHAD[1], LANCELOT[2] (possibly LANCELOT[1], the father of BAN), OWAIN, MENW, TRISTAN, EIDDILIG, NASIENS (possibly NASCIEN[1]), MORDRED, HOEL[1], BLAES, CADOG, PETROC, MORFRAN, SANDDEF, GLEWLWYD, CYON, ARON and LLYWARCH HEN.

Twrch Trwyth

A fierce boar which had originally been a king, transformed by God for his wickedness. Almost certainly a recollection of an earlier boar deity, the boar being a cult animal among the Celts, he corresponds directly to TORC TRIATH, the king of the boars in Irish mythology.

In the MABINOGION story of CULHWCH AND OLWEN, one of the tasks set CULHWCH by YSPADDADEN was to obtain the razor and comb (alternatively said to be a comb, razor and shears) from between the ears of this monstrous boar in order to barber Yspaddaden in preparation for Culhwch's marriage to OLWEN. The boar had already killed a great number of ARTHUR's men before the king and Culhwch caught up with it. Running it down, MABON[2] snatched the razor while CYLEDYR THE WILD obtained the shears. However, the boar then evaded them for a while, but, locating it again, they managed to procure the comb. They then forced the boar to jump off a cliff into the sea, at which point it swam away, never to be seen again.

Ty Gwydr

Quite literally a house of glass. MERLIN's home was thought to be one, being said to stand either on BARDSEY Island or on a boat in which he sailed away with the THIRTEEN TREASURES.

Ty-newydd Standing Stones

Also called CARRIG MEIBION ARTHUR, 'Stone's of Arthur's Sons', these stones in DYFED are traditionally a monument to ARTHUR's sons who were killed while hunting the boar TWRCH TRWYTH.

Tyolet

A knight who, in French romance, had been raised in the woods and had learned the language of the animals. He succeeded in rising to a challenge set by a lady who came to ARTHUR's court saying that she would marry whomsoever brought her the foot of a white stag, and give that successful knight her kingdom. Tyolet succeeded by killing the lions that guarded the stag but, being weary from the fight, he gave the foot to another knight to take back. This knight betrayed Tyolet, pretending that he had accomplished the task himself, but was later exposed and Tyolet justly rewarded.

Tyronoe

A sister of MORGAN[1] Le Fay.

Uallabh

The hero of a Scottish Gaelic folk-story who is probably to be identified with GAWAIN[1]. ARTHUR, who in this story is referred to as the king of IRELAND, married a mysterious woman who was brought to him on a bier, but had to fight a man whom the king took to be the woman's lover. This man defeated the king, but was in turn killed by Uallabh. It turned out that this man was the brother of the queen, and the son of the king, of Ineen, and he imprisoned Uallabh, who was freed by the younger sister of the queen. Uallabh eventually married the woman who had rescued him, and succeeded Arthur as the king of Ireland.

Uí Liatháin

An Irish dynasty that ruled the Welsh kingdom of DYFED and is believed to have been expelled by AGRICOLA during the traditional Arthurian period.

Ulfius

Sometimes called URFIN or URSIN in French romance. Ulfius was one of UTHER's knights, so presumably one of the knights of the OLD TABLE. It was he who persuaded MERLIN to help Uther sleep with IGRAINE[1], himself accompanying his king in the magical guise of Sir BRASTIAS, while Uther himself, under Merlin's enchantment, resembled GORLOIS. When the young ARTHUR was proclaimed king, Ulfius was made his chamberlain.

Ulrich von Zarzikhoven

The Swiss or German author (*fl.* 1200) of *Lanzelet*, which differs quite markedly from the story of LANCELOT[2] as told by CHRÉTIEN DE TROYES and other romancers.

Ur

According to an Irish romance, the father of ARTHUR. This is a misunderstanding on the part of the author of this romance, who did not understand that IUBHAR, the Irish name for Arthur's father, was actually a translation of UTHER. Instead he made Iubhar the grandfather and Ur the father.

Uranus

The guard who helped MELORA, ARTHUR's warrior daughter, to escape from the king of Asia.

Urbien

According to the pedigree of Gallet, the father of king SOLOMON of BRITTANY and grandfather of CONSTANTINE[1], who was in turn the grandfather of ARTHUR.

Urbs Legionis

The Latin name for CHESTER, which has led to its being identified with the CITY OF THE LEGIONS, though CAERLEON-ON-USK (Latin *Isca Legionis*) has also been identified as this site of one of ARTHUR'S BATTLES.

Urfin

Also URSIN

A variant of ULFIUS that is sometimes used in French romance.

Urgan

A giant who owned the magical fairy-dog PETITCRIEU. He was killed when TRISTAN fought him for the dog, which he intended to give as a present to ISEULT[1].

Urganda

According to the Spanish romance *Tirante lo blanco*, the sister of ARTHUR who went to CONSTANTINOPLE, where Arthur had become a prisoner of the emperor, who kept him in a cage. By some magical influence, possibly due to the cage he was held in, Arthur lacked intelligence until EXCALIBUR was placed in his hand, when he regained his senses. Urganda beseeched the emperor to release her brother, which he finally did.

Urian

The Lord of Moray and father of YWAIN. He is described as one of the three dispossessed Yorkist princes, along with LOT and ANGUSELUS, to whom ARTHUR restored their lands following the siege of YORK. It is quite likely that this name is simply a bad spelling of URIEN, though some sources do mention both characters quite independently.

Urien

An historical king, ruler of the Brythonic kingdom of RHEGED in north-west England c. AD 570, being assassinated c. AD 590 by an ally following his defeat of the Bernicians, inhabitants of a realm in the north-east of England. The father of OWAIN, RIWALLAWN, RUN and PASCEN, Urien was in later legend (though his actual rule was some time later than the traditional Arthurian period) made the contemporary of ARTHUR and the husband of MORGAN[1] Le Fay. The *Vulgate Merlin Continuation* calls his wife BRIMESENT. Welsh tradition made him the father of Owain by the daughter of the OTHERWORLD king of ANNWFN, while the TRIADS call him the son of CYNFARCH by NEFYN, the daughter of BRYCHAN, giving him a twin sister named ERFDDF. The actual location of Rheged, his kingdom, also seems to have caused considerable confusion among the various writers. Sir Thomas MALORY calls him the king of GORE, while GEOFFREY OF MONMOUTH makes him the king of MUREIF, which may be identical with Monreith, but is more generally thought to mean Moray. This latter choice is further supported by some sources naming URIAN as the king of Moray to whom Arthur restored the lands he had lost to the SAXONS. The medieval Latin romance HISTORIA MERIADOCI seems to complement this, calling Urien the king of the Scots.

Ursa Major

A constellation of the northern celestial hemisphere that is popularly referred to as the Great Bear. ARTHUR has become associated with it, some sources stating that this is because the Welsh word *arth* signifies a bear. Further association was made by the English astronomer William Smyth (1788–1869), who, in his

Speculum Hartwellianum, suggested that the circular motion of the constellation, which would have been well known even in Arthurian times, may have given rise to the original concept of the ROUND TABLE.

Ursin
Also URFIN

A variant of ULFIUS sometimes used in French romance.

Uther

Commonly referred to with the epithet PENDRAGON, Uther was the king of BRITAIN, the brother of AMBROSIUS AURELIUS, whom he succeeded, and father of ARTHUR. During his reign he fell in love with IGRAINE[1], the wife of GORLOIS, and therefore went to war with her husband. However, Uther was so sick with his love for Igraine that he was unable to participate in the war, and took to his pavilion. One of his knights, ULFIUS, went to visit the magician MERLIN, and persuaded him to alter Uther's appearance magically to that of Gorlois, on the condition that any child of the union be handed over to Merlin to be raised. This was agreed and the spell cast, Ulfius accompanying his master in the magical disguise of Sir BRASTIAS, and, on the very night that the disguised Uther laid with Igraine, her real husband died on the battle-field. Uther never revealed to Igraine the truth, and some time later he married her. When the child was born, Merlin arrived and took him away to be raised, that child, of course, being Arthur. Uther was said to have died within two years of his marriage to Igraine, some sources saying he died of a fever, others that he died in battle. He was buried at STONEHENGE.

According to the PROSE TRISTAN, Uther was once in love with the wife of ARGAN, but this jealous husband defeated Uther in combat and made him build a castle to make recompense. HENRY OF HUNTINGDON makes him the brother rather than the father of Arthur, while several legends associate him with Cumbria. The PETIT BRUT records his fight with a dragon-serpent in Westmorland, which is now a part of Cumbria, while local Cumbrian legend makes him a giant, saying that he founded the kingdom of MALLERSTANG, and attempted to divert the River EDEN to form the moat around his castle.

Some commentators have suggested that Uther came about as the result of a misunderstanding of the Welsh phrase *Arthur mab uther*, which was taken to mean 'Arthur, son of Uther', while it actually means 'Arthur, terrible son'. This theory has not found universal acceptance, for there is sufficient evidence to support an independent tradition regarding Uther.

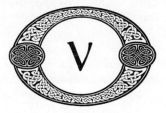

Vagor

The ruler of ILLE ESTRANGE or ESTRANGOT, father of MARABRON. He held LIONEL captive and arranged a fight between his son and his captive. However, as Lionel was injured, LANCELOT[2] took his place, defeated Marabron and so secured Lionel's release.

Valerin

The king of the TANGLED WOOD who lived in a castle on top of a high mountain that was both mist-bound and forest-bound, and which no one could enter unless Valerin instructed his monsters to allow them to pass. Claiming that GUINEVERE was betrothed to him before ARTHUR, Valerin claimed the queen, but was defeated in combat by her champion, LANCELOT[2]. None the less Valerin carried her off and, placing her in an enchanted sleep, imprisoned her in a castle surrounded by snakes. With the magical aid of the wizard MALDUC she was later freed.

Vallone

The domain of ESCORDUCARLA, who became enamoured of MERLIN and planned to take him prisoner. The plan backfired and she ended up as Merlin's prisoner instead.

Valyant

The king of WALES and a relation of LANCELOT[2].

Vannes and Nantes

The realm of CARADOC, who married YSAIVE.

Varlan

Also BRUTAN

A king of GALES who, in the Arthurian legends, is described as having been newly converted to Christianity. A mysterious ship arrived on the coast of BRITAIN carrying DAVID'S SWORD. Varlan used that sword to kill his enemy king LAMBOR and as a result of this ungodly act their kingdoms became the WASTE LAND of the GRAIL legends.

Vaux, Sir Roland de

The waker of GYNETH from the enchanted sleep MERLIN had caused her to fall into.

Vellendrucher

The site in CORNWALL of a legendary battle in which ARTHUR, assisted by the SEVEN KINGS OF CORNWALL, defeated the Danes. After their victory they gave thanks at SENNAN HOLY WELL and held a banquet at TABLE MAN.

Vendotia

The Latin name by which the North Welsh kingdom of GWYNEDD was known. It has its root in VENDOTII, the name of the people who inhabited the kingdom.

Vendoti(i)

Ancient British people who inhabited VENDOTIA, the North Welsh kingdom of GWYNEDD. GEOFFREY OF MONMOUTH names their king as CADWALLON.

Venetii

A Gaulish tribe, noted for the skill of its mariners, that was still considered to be in existence during the sixth century. Tradition states that TREPHINA, the daughter of their leader WAROK, married CUNOMORUS.

Vengeance Raguidel

A thirteenth-century French prose poem, usually attributed to Raoul, that covers GAWAIN[1]'s attempts to avenge the death of RAGUIDEL.

Vergulaht

The king of ASCALUN whom PERCEVAL[2] asked to find the GRAIL, but he passed this task on to GAWAIN[1], the lover of his sister ANTIKONIE.

Verona

The daughter of the king of NARSINGA whose carbuncle was required by ARTHUR's warrior daughter MELORA in order to set free her imprisoned lover, ORLANDO. She and her father were lured on to a ship by Melora and LEVANDER, the servant of the king of BABYLON who was accompanying Melora, but they became firm friends and Verona willingly gave up the jewel. She subsequently married Levander.

Veronica, Saint

Referred to as VERRINE in the GRAIL story.

Verrine

The name used within the GRAIL legends to refer to Saint VERONICA, who, so tradition claims, owned a cloth that had the image of Christ upon it. In the Grail story, Verrine uses the divine quality of this cloth to cure VESPASIAN of leprosy.

Verseria

The beautiful wife of FERRAGUNZE. To test her husband's claim that he never became jealous, it was arranged that Ferragunze should discover his wife in the embraces of GAWAIN[1]. However, true to his word, Ferragunze showed no signs of jealousy.

Vespasian

The Roman emperor between AD 69 and 79. He appears in the GRAIL legends as the liberator of JOSEPH OF ARIMATHEA from his imprisonment in Jerusalem. He was also said to have been cured of leprosy by VERRINE, who used a cloth she owned that had the image of Christ upon it.

Visit of Grey Ham

An Irish romance in which the OTHER-WORLD woman AILLEAN appears.

Vita Merlini

'Life of Merlin', an important Latin poetic description of the adventures of MERLIN, and his madness, that dates from the twelfth century and was written by GEOFFREY OF MONMOUTH some time after his *Historia Regum Britanniae*.

Viviane

A variant of VIVIENNE.

Vivien(ne)

The LADY OF THE LAKE, a later variant for the character who is named as NIMUE or NINIANE in early stories. Alfred, Lord Tennyson calls her Vivien, though the variant Vivienne is more common.

Vortigern

Following the assassination of King CONSTANTINE¹, which he had arranged, Vortigern first made CONSTANS, the dead king's son, a puppet king, but later also had him murdered and usurped the throne himself, with Pictish help. He then joined forces with the SAXONS HENGIST and HORSA, in order to repel the PICTS, who had previously helped him, abdicating in favour of his son VORTIMER. However, Vortimer was poisoned by his stepmother, so Vortigern once again became king. He fled to WALES after Hengist massacred the British princes on SALISBURY PLAIN, and there tried to build himself a tower on DINAS EMRYS (Mount Erith) in North WALES. However, every night the stones disappeared. MERLIN ascribed this to the presence of two dragons beneath the hill in a huge cavern within which there was also a subterranean lake. This was proved to be correct, confounding Vortigern's own seers, and Vortigern's tower was built. However, as the dragons were released,

Merlin prophesied Vortigern's death, and he was eventually burnt to death in the tower he had built by Constantine's son, AMBROSIUS AURELIUS. The story of Vortigern is first told by BEDE under his Latin name Uurtigernus, and later by GEOFFREY OF MONMOUTH.

Vortigern means 'overlord', so it seems likely, although not certain, that Vortigern was a title rather than a personal name. While Vortigern is generally believed to be an historical figure, there is no way of saying over how much of BRITAIN he had control, but NENNIUS gives us the date when he started his reign, AD 425. Geoffrey of Monmouth says that he married RONWEN, the daughter of Hengist, though another tradition says he may have married a daughter of MAXIMUS, the rebel Roman emperor who led an expedition to the Continent from Britain. He is credited with sons other than Vortimer, called CATIGERN, PASCHENT and FAUSTUS. Some commentators say he is to be considered identical to the unnamed proud tyrant mentioned in the works of GILDAS.

Vortimer

The son of VORTIGERN and brother, according to some sources, of CATIGERN, PASCHENT and FAUSTUS. He was king of BRITAIN for a short while when his father was either deposed or abdicated in his favour, but he was poisoned by his step-mother, after which his father regained the throne. Vortimer had said that after he died he should be buried in the place at which the SAXONS, whom he had opposed (though his father supported them), most commonly landed. A statue of him should also be erected there to frighten the invaders away. GEOFFREY OF MONMOUTH says that his wishes were not complied with, but the Welsh TRIADS say that his bones were buried in the chief

British ports. A similar tradition said that a statue of him was erected at Dover. While his father is almost universally regarded as historical, many commentators regard Vortimer as pure fiction.

Vran

The shortened and popularized version of BENDIGEID VRAN – BRÂN THE BLESSED.

Vulgate Version

A thirteenth-century collection of prose romances that consists of the PROSE LANCELOT; the QUESTE DEL SAINTE GRAAL and its prelude, ESTOIRE DEL SAINTE GRAAL; the MORT ARTU; the *Vulgate Merlin* and the *Vulgate Merlin Continuation*.

Wace, Robert

Twelfth-century author (*c.* 1115–83), born in Jersey, of the French ROMAN DE BRUT, which contains a substantial Arthurian section and is notable for making the first reference to the ROUND TABLE. It is a free Norman-French version of GEOFFREY OF MONMOUTH's fanciful early history of the kings of Britain, HISTORIA REGUM BRITANNIAE. Wace also wrote a number of other works, most notably the *Roman de Rou*, an epic of the exploits of the dukes of Normandy.

Wade

The father of the legendary smith WAYLAND who, with his son and grandson WIDIA, was said to have been brought to BRITAIN by the ANGLO-SAXONS.

Wales

Although nowadays a single country, as indeed it was sometimes portrayed in the Arthurian stories, it was, at that time, a patchwork of minor kingdoms that included GWYNEDD, DYFED and POWYS. The ESTOIRE DEL SAINTE GRAAL identifies Wales with the WASTE LAND of the GRAIL legends, but this is not a customary identification. The medieval Latin romance HISTORIA MERIADOCI says that the king of Wales was CARADOC, but ARTHUR and URIEN placed his son, MERIADOC, on the throne, but he resigned it to Urien. In other sources Wales is described as the kingdom of VALYANT, a relation of LANCELOT[2], or of HERZELOYDE, the mother of PERCEVAL[2].

Many of the most major Arthurian sources have a Welsh origin. Even the Continental romances owe much to Welsh tradition. There seems little doubt that Arthur and many of his knights have a Welsh provenance, which then progressed south into CORNWALL, which to this day has a very strong Welsh character.

Walewein

The Dutch name for GAWAIN[1].

Walewein

A Middle Dutch romance that is thought to date from the thirteenth century and concerns the exploits of GAWAIN[1]. Its authors are given as Penninc and Pieter Vostaert.

Walga(i)nus

The Latin version of GAWAIN[1]. GEOFFREY OF MONMOUTH is the only known source to use Walgainus, the normal being Walganus.

Walweitha

Possibly to be identified with Galloway, this was, according to WILLIAM OF MALMESBURY, the territory GAWAIN[1] was driven to, and subsequently ruled over, by the brother and nephew of HENGIST.

Warok

The chief of the VENETII whose daughter, TREPHINA, married CUNOMORUS.

Waste Land

The land laid waste in the GRAIL legends by the DOLOROUS STROKE which could be healed only by the asking of the GRAIL QUESTION. The LESTOIRE DE MERLIN says that it was ruled over by PELLINORE, while the ESTOIRE DEL SAINTE GRAAL identifies it with WALES. It is a far more extensive area in the DIDOT PERCEVAL, for in that work it is identified as comprising the whole of BRITAIN. Other sources identify the Waste Land with the GASTE FOREST.

Wayland

Legendary smith who was said to have been brought to BRITAIN, along with his father, WADE, and son, WIDIA, by the ANGLO-SAXONS. His name still exists in placenames, most famously near Uffington, Oxfordshire, where there is a long barrow known as Waylands Smithy.

Wecta

The son of WODEN and great-grandfather of HENGIST, according to the latter's claimed line of descent.

Weneland

The kingdom of RUMMARET, according to WACE. LAYAMON, in his translation of Wace's work, referred to the kingdom as WINETLAND, or simply WINET. Various regions have been suggested for this kingdom, including Finland, GWYNEDD and the country of the Wends. However, the name may have a connection with Vinland, the Norse name for a part of North America which may, as is now thought, have been discovered in the Middle Ages.

Westmer

The successor of ARVIRAGUS, according to the Lambeth Palace Library MS 84, during whose reign JOSEPH OF ARIMATHEA died.

Westwoods

A field near to the River CAM that has been suggested as the site of the battle of CAMLANN. Archaeological excavation has revealed a large number of skeletons on this site, bearing grim witness to the fact that a battle was once fought here, but whether or not that battle was Camlann is open to speculation.

White Book of Rhydderch, The

A fourteenth-century manuscript that, along with THE RED BOOK OF HERGEST, contains the MABINOGION cycle. It is today housed in the National Library of WALES, Aberystwyth, along with the BLACK BOOK OF CARMARTHEN and the *Book of Taliesin*.

White Knight

According to an Irish romance, the son of the king of FRANCE and one of ARTHUR's knights.

White Mount

The location within London to which PRYDERI, MANAWYDAN FAB LLYR, GLUNEU EIL TARAN (GLIFIEU), TALIESIN, YNAWC (YNAWAG), GRUDYEN (GRUDDIEU) and HEILYN took the severed head of BENDI-GEID VRAN. There they buried this head, with the face towards FRANCE, so that it might serve as a guardian for BRITAIN against all invaders. Later tradition says that ARTHUR subsequently dug it up, for he alone wished to be the British guardian.

White Stag

A white stag features in a number of the Arthurian stories, perhaps echoing some memory of a celtic pagan stag cult, as the Celts (along with many other cultures) held the white stag as an especially mystical animal. Arthurian tradition said that whoever hunted down a white stag could demand a kiss from the loveliest girl at ARTHUR's court. SAGREMOR was reported as having hunted one in RIGOMER, while in ERIC AT ENIDE one was hunted in the Forest of ADVENTURE. PERCEVAL[2] was said to have beheaded a white stag in the DIDOT PERCEVAL, while FLORIANT was said to have been brought by one to the castle of his foster mother, MORGAN[1] Le Fay.

Widia

The son of WAYLAND whose name, it is thought, was the origin of WITEGE.

Wigalois

The legitimate son of GAWAIN[1] by his wife, FLORIE[2], the niece of King JORAM. Having grown to manhood, Wigalois set out in search of his father, who, having left many years before, had not been able to find his way back home. Wigalois came to ARTHUR's court at CARDUEIL, into which he was admitted. When Queen AMENE's emissary, NEREJA, came to the court, Wigalois was sent to her succour. Guided by the ghost of Amene's slain husband, LAR, Wigalois accompanied Nereja back to her queen's realm. When he arrived he found that the entire kingdom, except for a single castle, had been overrun by the evil knight ROAZ. Wigalois fought Roaz in a night-long combat, eventually overcoming him. He then married LARIE, the daughter of Amene and Lar.

Wigalois

Thirteenth-century romance by WIRNT VON GRAFENBURG that tells the story of GAWAIN's legitimate son, WIGALOIS.

Wigan

This Lancashire town was locally thought to have been the site of one of ARTHUR's BATTLES, that of the River DOUGLAS.

Wihtgils

The great-great-grandson of WODEN and father of HENGIST, according to the line of descent claimed by the latter.

Wild Hunt

Common throughout European folklore, the Wild Hunt is a supernatural hunt in which the spectral hunters can be seen riding by, and the thundering of their horse's hoofs and baying of their hounds heard. In England this mystical spectacle was thought to have been seen in both Devon and Somerset and, sometimes, it was said to have been led by ARTHUR. Although most common on nights when there was a full moon, the Wild Hunt has also been reportedly heard at midday (cf. HUNTING CAUSEWAY).

Winchester

A city with many Arthurian associations. Early chroniclers identified it with CAMELOT, King ARTHUR's capital. The ROUND TABLE at Winchester dates from the fourteenth century (according to radiocarbon dating), and is thus not the original table, as was once thought. It is made of oak, measures eighteen feet in diameter and weighs 1.25 tons. The city, or at least somewhere in the area, is the site of the second battle Arthur fought against his usurping nephew, MORDRED. Once again Arthur defeated him, and then pursued him to the River CAMLANN, the site of Arthur's final battle, which marked the end of his reign.

Windfall Run

Local legend says that this place in America was where the wounded ARTHUR came to drink the healing waters of the GREAT SPIRITS SPRING.

Windsor

This town in Berkshire has present-day royal connections, but it was also said to have been the site of one of ARTHUR's residences. Before Arthur came to have a home there, the earl or count had rebelled against him, but was defeated and then executed.

Winet(land)

The kingdom of RUMMARET, according to LAYAMON, in his translation of WACE's work in which the earlier writer referred to WENELAND.

Winlogee

Appearing only on the Arthurian bas-relief in MODENA Cathedral, Winlogee is identified as a woman seated on the battlements with MARDOC. It has been suggested that she is identifiable with GUINEVERE.

Wirnt von Grafenberg

The thirteenth-century German, or Bavarian, author of WIGALOIS, a romance concerning the exploits of GAWAIN[1]'s son.

Witege

According to LAYAMON, the maker of ARTHUR's hauberk (a long coat of mail that is often sleeveless) that was called WYGAR or 'wizard'. If this is intended to be a personal name, it seems to be a form of WIDIA, the son of the legendary smith WAYLAND, who, together with his father, WADE, and son, had been brought to BRITAIN by the ANGLO-SAXONS. The name is also thought to appear in GEOFFREY OF MONMOUTH, but is susceptible to transcriptive errors.

Witta

The grandson of WODEN and grandfather of HENGIST, according to the latter's claimed line of descent.

Wlencing

The son of AELLE who accompanied his father when he defeated the Britons.

Wodan, -en

The chief god of the ANGLO-SAXONS, who invaded BRITAIN during the traditional Arthurian period. He is more commonly known by his Norse name of Odínn, but, as the Anglo-Saxon dynasties claimed their descent from him, it has been suggested that he was a deified leader. Most commentators think that he was always a mythical character. HENGIST claimed his descent from Woden was as shown in Figure 35.

```
Woden
  |
Wecta
  |
Witta
  |
Wihtgils
  |
Hengist
```

Figure 35 *Hengist's claimed descent from the god Woden*

Wolfram von Eschenbach

A German poet (*fl.* 1200) and author of *Parzival*, a work that dealt with the GRAIL Quest and PERCEVAL[2]'s part in it. He claimed his source was a writer named Kyot, but the existence of Kyot has been seriously questioned. He is also remembered as the author of several other works.

Wrnach

The giant owner of a sword that CULHWCH had to obtain as one of the tasks imposed by YSPADDADEN if he were to win the hand of OLWEN. KAY obtained it by trickery and killed Wrnach.

Wygar

'Wizard', the name of ARTHUR's hauberk (long, often sleeveless, coat of mail) that, according to LAYAMON, was made either by a wizard or by someone named WITEGE.

289

Y Saint Graal

The Welsh version of the GRAIL story.

Ydain

The mistress of GAWAIN[1] whom he had saved from being raped. When she tried to forsake him, he gave her to the dwarf DRUIDAN.

Yder

The son of NUC, a KNIGHT OF THE ROUND TABLE who fell in love with Queen GUENLOIE. She said she would marry Yder only on the condition that he brought her a knife that belonged to two giants. He succeeded in killing the giants and securing the knife, so the queen fulfilled her promise and married him. Other sources say that Yder married the daughter of GUENGASOAIN, whom he and GAWAIN[1] had slain to avenge the murder of RAGUIDEL. Yder was also said to have done battle against three giants who lived on BRENT KNOLL in Somerset. Accompanying ARTHUR to the hill, Yder went on ahead and fought the giants on his own. By the time Arthur and his retinue arrived, the battle was over and the three giants were dead, but Yder had also lost his life in the fray.

Ydor

Described as a king, Ydor was the father of TOREC.

Ygerna, -e

A variant of IGRAINE[1].

Yglais

According to PERLESVAUS, the niece of JOSEPH OF ARIMATHEA and the FISHER KING who became the mother of PERCEVAL[2].

Ymer Llydaw

According to the fourteenth-century Welsh BIRTH OF ARTHUR, the father of HOEL[1] by GWYAR, ARTHUR's sister.

Ynawag

A variant of YNAWC.

Ynawc
Also YNAWAG

One of the seven survivors who brought the severed head of BENDIGEID VRAN back from IRELAND, having totally annihilated the Irish race except for five pregnant women hiding in a cave. He and his companions, PRYDERI, MANAWYDDAN FAB LLYR, GLUNEU EIL TARAN (GLIFIEU), TALIESIN, GRUDYEN (GRUDDIEU) and HEILYN, took the head to London, where they buried it, the face turned forever towards France, on the WHITE MOUNT, as instructed by Bendigeid Vran.

Ynwyl

The father of ENID, according to the Welsh GEREINT AND ENID. His wife remains unnamed.

York, The siege of

A siege mounted by ARTHUR against the SAXON leader COLGRIN, who had sought refuge in the city following his defeat by Arthur at the battle of the River DOUGLAS. Arthur had, at one stage, to abandon the siege and go back to London, but later returned and this time relieved the siege with the help of King HOEL[1] of BRITTANY. Arthur restored the city to its former glory and returned to the lands of the three dispossessed Yorkist princes, LOT, URIAN and AUGUSELUS.

Yr Wyddfa (Fawr)

The original name for Mount SNOWDON that probably signified 'The Great Tomb', referring to a large cairn that once stood on its summit. This also gave rise to the name CLOGWYN CARNEDD YR WYDDFA – 'The Precipice of the Carn on Yr Wyddfa'. Another name is CARNEDD Y CAWR – 'The Giant's Carn' – and this poses the question, who was the giant buried atop the loftiest peak in WALES? The cairn itself was demolished in the nineteenth century and made into a kind of tower, which existed for some years before the present building was erected. According to Sir John Rhys in his *Celtic Folklore* (1901), this was the reputed grave of RHITTA CAWR, a giant sometimes known as RHICCA, who killed kings and clothed himself in a garment made from

their beards. His great enemy and ultimate conqueror was king ARTHUR, whose beard he desired for the collar of his cloak. GEOFFREY OF MONMOUTH refers to this giant as 'the giant RITHO whom Arthur slew on Mount ERYRI'.

Arthur himself is commemorated not far from the giant's cave at BWLCH-Y-SAETHU ('The Pass of the Arrows'). In the direction of Nanhwyen is the site of CARNEDD ARTHUR, where he is alleged to have been buried by his followers after a fierce battle which took place at the top of the pass. Having buried Arthur, his companions withdrew to the precipice of Lliwedd and took shelter in a cave called OGOF LANCIAU ERYRI – a vast cave in the precipitous cliff on the left-hand side, near the top of Llyn Llydaw. The cave entrance immediately closed behind them, and the young men fell asleep, resting on their shields. There they still await the day when Arthur will return in triumph to save BRITAIN from impending doom. It is alleged that they were once disturbed by a shepherd who, on seeing a light shining though the narrow entrance to the cave, started to crawl inside but hit his head against a large bell. Its loud clanging awakened the hundreds of sleeping knights, who were immediately on their feet and ready for battle. The shepherd left the cave at great speed and was never the same again.

Ys

A legendary city of BRITTANY that was supposed to have become submerged thanks to DAHUT or AHES, the daughter of the king. It has been suggested that this character, Dahut, may have, in some small way, contributed to the legend of MORGAN[1] Le Fay, for she was said to have been a fairy, referred to locally as a MARI-MORGAN. Gallet's pedigree says that GRALLO, the king of Ys, was related to CONSTANTINE[1], ARTHUR's grandfather.

Ysabele

The wife or lover of GAWAIN[1], according to the Middle Dutch romance WALEWEIN.

Ysaie the Sad

The son of TRISTAN and ISEULT[1] who was raised by a hermit. He was helped in his adventures by a dwarf, named TRONC, whom the fairies had given to him, this dwarf later being transformed into the fairy-king OBERON[1]. Ysaie married the daughter of King IRION, MARTHA, and they had a son named MARC.

Ysaive

A niece of ARTHUR, the wife of King CARADOC of VANNES AND NANTES. She became the lover of ELIAVRES, a knight with especially potent magical powers.

Ysbaddaden

A variant of YSPADDADEN, the giant father of OLWEN.

Ysgithyrwyn

According to Welsh tradition, a boar which was chased by ARTHUR and his faithful hound CABAL.

Yspaddadden

The *penkawr* or chief giant who appears in the MABINOGION story of CULHWCH AND OLWEN as the father of OLWEN who sets CULHWCH a series of seemingly impossibly tasks to complete if he is to be allowed to marry his daughter. Culhwch completes the tasks with the help of ARTHUR and marries Olwen. Yspaddaden was killed following the completion of the tasks by one of his enemies, GOREU.

Yvain

The French form of OWAIN, being used for both OWAIN and OWAIN THE BASTARD.

Ywerit

The father of BRÂN (BENDIGEID VRAN), according to Celtic sources. It is thought that he may be identifiable with IWERET, though IBERT has also been suggested in this role.

Zazamanc

The realm of BELCANE, the mother of FEIREFIZ by GAHMURET.

Zelotes

A youth who was promised he could have PERSE as a wife by her father. However, ECTOR DE MARIS already loved her and came to her rescue.

Zephyr

According to PERCEFOREST, a spirit who had a great love for BRITAIN. An ancestor of MERLIN, he gave PASSALEON to MORGAN[1] Le Fay.

Zitus

The name used in the Spanish romance ANNALES TOLEDANOS to refer to ARTHUR.

Bibliography

NB Works marked with an asterisk are to be regarded as essential core reference texts

Ackerman, R. W. *An Index of Arthurian Names in Middle English* (Stanford University Press, Stanford, 1952)

Alcock, L. *Arthur's Britain* (Allen Lane, London, 1971)

– *'By South Cadbury is that Camelot . . .'* (Thames & Hudson, London, 1972)

Alexander, Michael (trans.) *The Earliest English Poems* (Penguin Books, Harmondsworth, 1966)

Anderson, A. R. *Alexander's Gate, Gog and Magog and the Inclosed Nation* (Cambridge, Mass., 1932)

Anderson, F. *The Ancient Secret* (Aquarian Press, Orpington, 1987)

Anderson, J. *Royal Genealogies* (printed by James Bettenham for Charles Davis, London, 1736)

*Ariosto, Ludovico (trans. G. Waldman) *Orlando Furioso* (Oxford University Press, London, 1974)

Artos, A. *Arthur: The King of Light* (Lorien House, Black Mountain, 1986)

Ashe, G. *A Guidebook to Arthurian Britain* (Longmans, London, 1980)

– *Avalonian Quest* (Methuen, London, 1982)

– *The Discovery of King Arthur* (Guild, London, 1985)

– *From Caesar to Arthur* (Collins, London, 1960)

– *The Glastonbury Tor Maze* (Gothic Image, Glastonbury, 1979)

– *Kings and Queens of Early Britain* (Methuen, London, 1982)

Ashe, G. (ed.) *The Quest for Arthur's Britain* (Praeger, London, 1968)

Automobile Association/Ordnance Survey *Leisure Guide: Cornwall* (Automobile Association, Basingstoke, 1988)

– *Leisure Guide: Snowdonia and North Wales* (Automobile Association, Basingstoke, 1989)

– *Leisure Guide: Wessex* (Automobile Association, Basingstoke, 1988)

Baigent, M. *et al.* *The Holy Blood and the Grail* (Jonathan Cape, London, 1983)

Barber, Chris *Mysterious Wales* (David & Charles, Newton Abbot, 1982)

– *Ghosts of Wales* (John Jones, Cardiff, 1979)

Barber, R. *The Figure of Arthur* (London, 1972)

Barber, R. W. *Arthur of Albion* (Barrie & Rockliff with the Pall Mall Press, London, 1961)

Barber, W. T. *Exploring Wales* (David & Charles, Newton Abbot, 1982)

Baring-Gould, S. and J. Fisher *Lives of the British Saints* (Cymrroddorion Society, London, 1907–13)

*Bartrum, P. C. (ed.) *Early Welsh Genealogical Tracts* (University of Wales Press, Cardiff, 1966)

*Bede (trans. Leo Shirley-Price) *A History of the English Church and People* (Penguin Books, Harmondsworth, 1955)

– (trans. John Stevens) *The Ecclesiastical History of the English Nation* (J. M. Dent & Sons Ltd, Everyman's Library 479, undated)

Benjamin, R. *The Seed of Avalon* (Zodiac House, Westhay, 1986)

*Béroul (trans. A. S. Fredrick) *The Romance of Tristan* (Penguin Books, Harmondsworth, 1970)

Berry, Claude *Portrait of Cornwall* (Robert Hale, London, 1984)

Blackett, A. T. and A. Wilson *Arthur and the Charters of the Kings* (Byrd, Cardiff, 1981)

– *King Arthur King of Glamorgan and Gwent* Byrd, Cardiff, 1981)

Bogdanow, F. *The Romances of the Grail* (Manchester University Press, Manchester, 1966)

Borchardt, F. L. *German Antiquity in Renaissance Myth* (Johns Hopkins University Press, Baltimore, 1971)

Bradley, Marion *Holy Grail Across the Atlantic* (Hounslow Press, Willowdale, Ontario, 1988)

– *The Mists of Avalon* (Sphere, London, undated)

Branston, Brian *The Lost Gods of England* (Thames & Hudson, London, 1957)

Brengle, R. L. (ed.) *Arthur King of Britain* (Appleton-Century-Crofts, New York, 1964)

Brewer, E. C. *The Reader's Handbook* (Chatto & Windus, London, 1919)

Briel, H. and M. Herrmann *King Arthur's Knights and the Myths of the Round Table* (Klincksieck, Paris, 1972)

Briggs, K. M. *A Dictionary of Fairies* (Allen Lane, London, 1976)

Brinkley, R. F. *Arthurian Legend in the Seventeenth Century* (Johns Hopkins University Press, Baltimore, 1932)

Brodeur, A. G. *Arthur Dux Bellorum* (University of California Press, Berkeley, 1939)

*Bromwich, R. (ed. and trans.) *Trioedd Ynys Prydein* (University of Wales Press, Cardiff, 1966)

* – *The Welsh Triads* (University of Wales Press, Cardiff, 1961)

Brown, A. C. L. *The Origin of the Grail Legend* (Harvard University Press, Cambridge, Mass., 1943)

Bruce, J. D. *The Evolution of Arthurian Romance* (P. Smith, Gloucester, Mass., 1958)

*Bryant, N. (trans.) *Perlesvaus* (Boydell & Brewer, Cambridge, 1978)

Butler, H. *Ten Thousand Saints* (Westbrook Press, Kilkenny, 1972)

Caine, Mary *The Glastonbury Zodiac* (Grael Communications, Torquay, 1978)

Cary, G. A. *The Medieval Alexander* (Cambridge University Press, Cambridge, 1956)

Cavendish, R. *King Arthur and the Grail* Weidenfeld & Nicolson, London, 1978)

Chadwick, N. K. *The Age of Saints in the Early Celtic Church* (Oxford University Press, Oxford, 1961)

– *The Celts* (Penguin Books, Harmondsworth, 1970)

– *Early Brittany* (University of Wales Press, Cardiff, 1969)

Chambers, E. K. *Arthur of Britain* (Sidgwick and Jackson, London, 1927)

*Chrétien de Troyes *Arthurian Romances* (Dent, London, 1955)

* – (trans. N. Briant) *Perceval* (Boydell & Brewer, Cambridge 1982)

Clinch, R. and M. Williams *King Arthur in Somerset* (Bossiney Books, St Teath, 1987)

Coghlan, R. *The Encyclopaedia of Arthurian Legends* (Element Books, Shaftesbury, 1991)

– *Pocket Dictionary of Irish Myth and Legend* (Appletree Press, Belfast, 1985)

Cotterell, Arthur *A Dictionary of World Mythology* (Windward, Leicester, 1979)

Cunliffe, B. *The Celtic World* (The Bodley Head, London, 1979)

D'Arbois de Jubainville, H. (trans. R. I. Best) *The Irish Mythological Cycle* (Hodges & Figgis, Dublin, 1903)

Darrah, J. *The Real Camelot* (Thames & Hudson, London, 1981)

Davies, E. *Celtic Researches* (London, 1804)

Davies, T. R. *A Book of Welsh Names* (Sheppard Press, London, 1952)

*Day, M. L. (trans.) *De Ortu Waluuanii*, translated as *The Rise of Gawain* (Garland Press, New York, 1984)

Didot Perceval, translated as *The Romance of Perceval in Prose* (University of Washington Press, Seattle, 1966)

Dillon, M. and N. K. Chadwick *The Celtic Realms* (Weidenfeld & Nicolson, London, 1967)

– *The Celts*, (Weidenfeld & Nicolson, London, 1967)

Ditmas, E. M. R. *Tristan and Iseult in Cornwall* (Forrester Roberts, Gloucester, 1969)

Dunlop, J. C. *The History of Prose Fiction*, (Bell, London, 1888)

Ebbutt, M. J. *Hero-Myths and Legends of the British Race* (Harrap, London, 1910)

Edwards, G. *Hobgoblin and Sweet Puck* (BLES, London, 1974)

Egger, C. *Lexicon Nominum Virorum et Mulierum* (Studuèm, Rome, 1963)

Eisner, S. *The Tristan Legend* (Northwestern University Press, Evanston, 1969)

Entwhistle, W. J. *The Arthurian Legend in the Literature of the Spanish Peninsula* (Dent, London, 1925)

Farmer, D. H. *The Oxford Dictionary of Saints* (Clarendon Press, Oxford, 1978)

Fedrick, Alan S. (trans.) *'The Romance of Tristan' by Béroul and 'The Tale of Tristan's Madness'* (Penguin Books, Harmondsworth, 1970)

Ferrante, J. M. *The Conflict of Love and Honor* (Mouton, The Hague, 1973)

Field, J. *Place Names of Great Britain and Ireland* (David & Charles, Newton Abbot, 1980)

Fletcher, R. H. *Arthurian Material in the Chronicles* (Ginn, Boston, 1906)

Flutre, L.-F. *Tables des noms propres* (Poitiers, 1962)

*Gantz, J. (trans.) *The Mabinogion* (Penguin Books, Harmondsworth, 1976)

Gardner, E. G. *The Arthurian Legend in Italian Literature* (Dent, London, 1930)

Garmonsway, G. J. (trans.) *Anglo-Saxon Chronicle* (J. M. Dent & Sons Ltd, Everyman's Library 624, London, undated)

*Geoffrey of Monmouth (trans. L. Thorpe) *History of the Kings of Britain* (Penguin Books, Harmondsworth, 1966)

* – (trans. J. J. Parry) *Vita Merlini* (University of Illinois Press, Urbana, 1925)

Gibbs, R. *The Legendary XII Hides of Glastonbury* (Llanerch, Lampeter, 1988)

Gold, Nicholas *The Queen and the Cauldron* (Old Byland Books, Helmsley, undated)

Goodrich, N. L. *King Arthur* (Watts, Danbury, 1986)

*Gottfried von Strassburg (trans. A. T. Hatto) *Tristan* (Penguin Books, Harmondsworth, 1960)

*Graves, R. *The White Goddess* (Faber & Faber, London, 1961)

Greed, J. A. *Glastonbury Tales* (St Trillo, Bristol, 1975)

Grimm, J. *Teutonic Mythology* (Dover, New York, 1966)

*Guest, Lady Charlotte (trans.) *The Mabinogion* (J. Jones, Cardiff, 1977)

Heline, C. *Mysteries of the Holy Grail* (New Age, Los Angeles, 1963)

Hewins, W. A. S. *The Royal Saints of Britain* (London, 1929)

Hole, C. *English Folklore* (New York, 1940)

Holmes, U. T. and M. A. Klenke *Chrétien de Troyes and the Grail* (University of North Carolina Press, Chapel Hill, 1959)

Holweck, F. G. *A Biographical Dictionary of Saints* (Herder, St Louis, 1924)

Hunt, Irvine (ed.) *Norman Nicholson's Lakeland – A Prose Anthology* (Robert Hale, London, 1991)

Jackson, Kenneth Hurlstone (trans.) *A Celtic Miscellany* (Penguin Books, Harmondsworth, 1971)

Jarman, A. O. H. *The Legend of Merlin* (University of Wales Press, Cardiff, 1960)

*John of Glastonbury *The Chronicle of Glastonbury Abbey* (Boydell & Brewer, Woodbridge, 1984)

*Jones, G and T. (trans.) *The Mabinogion*, (Dent, London, 1949)

Jones, Lewis W. *King Arthur in History and Legend* (Cambridge University Press, Cambridge, 1911)

Jowett, G. *Drama of the Lost Disciples* (Covenant, London, 1961)

Jung, E. and M.-L. von Franz *The Grail Legend* (Hodder & Stoughton, London, 1972)

Kalinke, M. E. *King Arthur North by Northwest* Reitzel, Copenhagen, 1982)

Kendrick, T. D. *British Antiquity* (London, 1950)

Knight, G. *The Secret Tradition in the Arthurian Legend* (Aquarian Press, Wellingborough, 1984)

Lacy, N. J. (ed.) *The Arthurian Encyclopedia* (Garland Press, New York, 1986)

Lawhead, Stephen *Taliesin – Book I of the Pendragon Cycle* (Lion Publishing, Oxford, 1988)

– *Merlin – Book II of the Pendragon Cycle* (Lion Publishing, Oxford, 1988)

– *Arthur – Book III of the Pendragon Cycle* (Lion Publishing, Oxford, 1989)

(NB The three books listed by Stephen Lawhead are *fiction*, but they are worthy of attention as they draw heavily on the Arthurian legends and give a modern interpretation of them.)

Lewis, L. S. *St Joseph of Arimathea at Glastonbury* (Clarke, Cambridge, 1982)

Lloyd, J. E. *A History of Wales* (Longmans, London, 1939)

Loomis, R. S. *Arthurian Tradition and Chrétien de Troyes* (Columbia University Press, New York, 1949)

– *Celtic Myth and Arthurian Romance* (Columbia University Press, New York, 1927)

– *The Grail: From Celtic Myth to Christian Symbol* (University of Wales Press, Cardiff, 1963)

– *'The Romance of Tristram and Ysolt' by Thomas of Britain* (Columbia University Press, New York, 1951)

– *Wales and the Arthurian Legend* (University of Wales Press, Cardiff, 1956)

Loomis, R. S. (ed.) *Arthurian Literature in the Middle Ages* (Clarendon Press, Oxford, 1959)

Luttrell, C. *The Creation of the First Arthurian Romance* (London, 1974)

*Mac an tSaoi, M. (ed.) *Dhá Scéal Artúraíochta (Visit of Grey Ham)* (Dublin Institute for Advanced Studies, Dublin, 1946)

Mac Biocaill, G. *Ireland Before the Vikings* (Gill & Macmillan, Dublin, 1972)

*Malory, Sir Thomas *Le Morte d'Arthur* (Penguin Books, Harmondsworth, 1969)

Mann, Nick *The Cauldron and the Grail*, (Annenterprise of Glastonbury, undated)

*Marie de France (trans. E. Mason) *Lays* (Dent, London, 1955)

Markale, J. *King Arthur: King of Kings* (Gordon & Cremonesi, London, 1977)

Mathias, M. *Glastonbury* (David & Charles, Newton Abbot, 1979)

Mattarasso, P. M. *The Redemption of Chivalry* (Droz, Geneva, 1979)

*Mattarasso, P. M. (trans.) *The Quest of the Holy Grail (Quest Saint Graal)* (Penguin Books, Harmondsworth, 1969)

Matthews, C. *Arthur and the Sovereignty of Britain* (Arkana, London, 1989)

– *Mabon and the Mysteries of Britain* (Arkana, London, 1987)

Matthews, J. *The Elements of the Arthurian Tradition* (Element, Shaftesbury, 1989)

– *The Elements of the Grail Tradition* (Element, Shaftesbury, 1990)

– *Gawain: Knight of the Goddess* (Aquarian Press,

Wellingborough, 1990)

– The Grail (Thames & Hudson, London, 1981)

Matthews, J. and C. The Arthurian Guide to British and Irish Mythology (Aquarian Press, Wellingborough, 1988)

Matthews J. and M. Green The Grail Seeker's Companion (Aquarian Press, Wellingborough, 1986)

Matthews, J. and R. J. Steward Legendary Britain (Blandford Press, London, 1989)

– Warriors of Arthur (Blandford Press, London, 1987)

Michell, John The Traveller's Key to Sacred England: A Guide to the Legends, Lore and Landscape of England's Sacred Places (Harrap Columbus, London, 1989)

Miller, R. Will the Real King Arthur Please Stand Up? (Cassell, London, 1978)

Millican, C. B. Spenser and the Table Round (Harvard University Press, Cambridge, Mass., 1932)

Moorman, C. and R. An Arthurian Dictionary (University of Mississippi Press, Jackson, 1978)

Morris, J. The Age of Arthur (Weidenfeld & Nicolson, London, 1973)

*Morris, J. (ed. and trans.) British History and the Welsh Annals (Phillimore, Chichester, 1980)

Newsted, H. Bran the Blessed in Arthurian Romance (Columbia University Press, New York, 1939)

Opie, I. and P. The Classic Fairy Tales (London, 1973)

O'Rahilly, Cecile (ed.) 'Tain Bo Cuailnge' from the 'Book of Leinster' (Institute of Advanced Studies, Dublin, 1967)

O'Rahilly, T. F. Early Irish History and Mythology (Institute of Advanced Studies, Dublin, 1946)

O'Sullivan T. D. The 'De excidio' of Gildas (Brill, Leiden, 1978)

Owen, D. D. R. The Evolution of the Grail Legend (Oliver & Boyd, Edinburgh, 1968)

Palmer, Kingsley The Folklore of Somerset (B. T. Batsford, London, 1976)

Paton, L. Studies in the Fairy Mythology of Arthurian Romance (Boston, 1903)

Paton, Lucy Allen (ed.) Arthurian Chronicles Represented by Wace and Layamon (J. M. Dent, London, 1912)

– Morte Arthur: Two Early English Romances Morte Arthur and Le Morte Arthur (J. M. Dent, London, 1912/36)

Pears Encyclopedia of Myths and Legends (4 vols.; general eds. Mary Barker and Christopher Cook) Vol. 2: Western & Northern Europe; Central & Southern Africa (ed. Sheila Savill, Pelham Books, London, 1978)

Radford and Swanton Arthurian Sites in the West (Exeter University, Exeter, undated)

Ratcliffe, E. The Great Arthurian Timeslip (ORE, Stevenage, 1978)

Reid, M. J. C. The Arthurian Legend (Edinburgh, 1938)

Reiser, O. L. This Holyest Erthe (Perennial, London, 1974)

Rhys, J. Celtic Folklore (Clarendon Press, Oxford, 1901)

– Studies in the Arthurian Legend (Clarendon Press, Oxford, 1891)

*Robert de Boron History of the Holy Grail (London, 1861)

Roberts, A. (ed.) Glastonbury: Ancient Avalon, New Jerusalem (Rider, London, 1978)

Robinson, J. A. Two Glastonbury Legends (Cambridge University Press, Cambridge, 1926)

Rolleston, T. W. Celtic Myths and Legends (Studio Editions, London, 1986)

Ross, A. Pagan Celtic Britain (Routledge & Kegan Paul, London, 1967)

Rowling, Marjorie The Folklore of the Lake District (B. T. Batsford, London, 1976)

Ruoff, J. E. Macmillan's Handbook of Elizabethan and Stuart Literature (Macmillan, London, 1975)

Rutherford, W. The Druids (Aquarian Press, Wellingborough, 1983)

Saklatvala, B. Arthur: Roman Britain's Last Champion (David & Charles, Newton Abbot, 1967)

Senior, M. Myths of Britain (Orbis, London, 1979)

*Sommer, H. O. (ed.) Vulgate Version (Carnegie Institution, Washington, 1908–16)

Spence, L. The Minor Traditions of British Mythology (London, 1948)

*Spenser, Edmund The Faerie Queene (various editions/compilations/anthologies)

Stewart, R. J. Celtic Gods, Celtic Goddesses (Blandford, London, 1990)

– The Mystic Life of Merlin (Arkana, London, 1986)

– The Prophetic Vision of Merlin (Arkana, London, 1985)

Stewart, R. J. (ed.) The Book of Merlin (Blandford, Poole, 1987)

– Merlin and Women (Blandford, London, 1988)

Stone, B. (trans.) Sir Gawain and the Green Knight (Penguin Books, Harmondsworth, 1959)

Stuart-Knill, Sir Ian The Pedigree of Arthur (Kingdom Revival Crusade, Sidmouth, 1977)

Tatlock, J. S. P. The Legendary History of Britain (University of California Press, Berkeley, 1950)

*Thoms, W. J. (ed.) *A Collection of Early English Prose Romances* (Pickering, London, 1858)

*Tolkien, J. R. R. and E. V. Gordon (eds.) *Sir Gawain and the Green Knight* (2nd edition revised by N. Davis; Clarendon Press, Oxford, 1967)

Tolstoy, N. *The Quest for Merlin* (Hamish Hamilton, London, 1985)

Treharne, R. F. *The Glastonbury Legends* (Cresset, London, 1967)

*Ulrich von Zatzikhoven (trans. K. G. T. Webster) *Lancelot* (Columbia University Press, New York, 1951)

*Vance, T. E. (trans.) *Knight of the Parrot* (Garland Press, New York, 1986)

Vendryes, J. *et al. Lexique étymologique de l'irlandais ancien* (Paris, 1959)

Vickery, A. R. *The Holy Thorn of Glastonbury* (Toucan Press, Guernsey, 1979)

Vinaver, E. (ed.) *The Works of Sir Thomas Malory* (3 vols.; Clarendon Press, Oxford, 1947)

*Wace and Layamon *Arthurian Chronicles* (Dent, London, 1962)

Waddell, L. A. *The British Edda* (Chapman & Hall, London, 1930)

Webster, R. G. *Guinevere: A Study in Her Abductions* (Milton, Mass., 1951)

Wentz, E. *The Fairy Faith in Celtic Countries* (C. Smythe, Gerrards Cross, 1977)

West, G. D. *An Index of Proper Names in French Arthurian Prose Romances* (University of Toronto Press, Toronto, 1978)

– *An Index of Proper Names in French Arthurian Verse Romances* (University of Toronto Press, Toronto, 1969)

Weston, Jessie L. *From Ritual to Romance* (Doubleday, Garden City, 1957)

– *The Legend of Sir Gawain* (David Nutt, London, 1897)

Weston, Jessie L. (trans.) *'Parzival', A Knightly Epic by Wolfram von Eschenbach* (Daivd Nutt, London, 1894)

Westwood J. *Albion: A Guide to Legendary Britain* (Granada, London, 1985)

Whitehead, J. *Guardian of the Grail* (Jarrolds, London, 1959)

Whitlock, Ralph *The Folklore of Devon* (B. T. Batsford, London, 1977)

– *The Folklore of Wiltshire* (B. T. Batsford, London, 1976)

Wildman, S. G. *The Black Horsemen* (John Baker, London, 1971)

*Williams, R. (trans.) *Y Saint Greal* (London, 1876)

*Wirnt von Grafenberg (trans. J. W. Thomas) *Wigalois* (University of Nebraska Press, Lincoln, Nebraska, 1977)

*Wolfram von Eschenbach (trans. A. T. Hatto) *Parzival* (Penguin Books, Harmondsworth, 1980)

Wright, Esmond (ed.) *AA Visitor's Guide to Britain* (Webb & Bower/Automobile Association, 1987)

Also worthy of attention is the film *Excalibur*, directed by John Boorman. This gives a good visual account of the main Arthurian legend, though it has obviously been doctored to appear to a cinema audience and as such mixes some of the legends to give better continuity to the finished film.

Many films have been made concerning Arthurian legends over the years. They range in quality from the charming *Sword in the Stone* cartoon from Disney, telling their version of the early life of Arthur, through the truly outrageous telling of the Quest for the Holy Grail in *Monty Python and the Holy Grail*, to the blood and guts rendition of *Excalibur*. Each is worthy of at least one viewing, but they should all be taken lightly, as they are subject to the director's artistic licence.